THE WORKS
AND CORRESPONDENCE OF
DAVID RICARDO

VOLUME II

PLAN OF THE EDITION

THE WORKS
AND CORRESPONDENCE OF
DAVID RICARDO

EDITED BY
PIERO SRAFFA
WITH THE COLLABORATION OF
M. H. DOBB

VOLUME II
NOTES ON MALTHUS'S PRINCIPLES
OF POLITICAL ECONOMY

PUBLISHED FOR THE ROYAL ECONOMIC SOCIETY

CAMBRIDGE UNIVERSITY PRESS
CAMBRIDGE
LONDON · NEW YORK · MELBOURNE

3 - 3 - 87

Published by the Syndics of the Cambridge University Press
The Pitt Building, Trumpington Street, Cambridge CB2 1RP
Bentley House, 200 Euston Road, London NW1 2DB
32 East 57th Street, New York, NY 10022, USA
296 Beaconsfield Parade, Middle Park, Melbourne 3206, Australia

ISBN 0 521 06067 2

First published 1951
Reprinted 1957 1966 1976

Printed in Great Britain
at the
University Printing House, Cambridge
(Euan Phillips, University Printer)

CONTENTS OF VOLUME II

INTRODUCTION

I

MALTHUS'S *Principles of Political Economy* appeared early in
April 1820.[1] While at various times, whether in the form of a new
edition of his pamphlet on Rent of 1815 or of a supplementary
volume to the *Essay on Population* which should deal with his views
on Agriculture and Manufactures,[2] he had been thinking of a more
general work on Political Economy, it was only after the publication of Ricardo's *Principles* that the project of a separate treatise
crystallised. From the first this was intended as an answer to
Ricardo; and late in 1817 Malthus was writing to him: 'I am
meditating a volume as I believe I have told you, and I want to
answer you, without giving my work a controversial air.'[3] In
the spring of 1818 he writes to Professor Prévost of Geneva: 'I am
at present engaged in a volume on those subjects in Political
Econy. the principles of which do not yet. appear to be quite
settled and in this I shall advert frequently to Mr Ricardo's work.
I shall not however be ready for the press till next Spring.'[4] By
August 1818 Malthus had read part of his manuscript to Ricardo;[5]
and again when he visited Gatcomb Park in December he read to
Ricardo 'some more of his intended publication'.[6] The book was
actually advertised as being 'in the Press' in November 1818.[7]
But publication was delayed, as Ricardo told Mill in a letter of
28 Dec. 1818, partly because Murray thought the end of the
following year would be the most favourable time, 'and partly,

---

[1] It was advertised in the *Monthly
Literary Advertiser* of 10 April 1820
as 'just published', price 15*s*.
[2] Below, VII, 26–7.
[3] Letter from Malthus 3 Dec. 1817,
ib. 215; and cp. letter of 12 Oct. 1817,
ib. 194.
[4] Letter of 30 March 1818, published
by G. W. Zinke in *Journal of
Economic History*, May 1942, vol. II,
p. 178.

[5] Ricardo to Malthus, 20 Aug. 1818,
below, VII, 284.
[6] Ricardo to Mill, 22 Dec. 1818,
ib. 372. Another chapter was shown
to Ricardo while the book was in
the press (below, VIII, 173).
[7] In the *Monthly Literary Advertiser*
of 10 Nov. 1818; see below, VII,
329.

I think, from doubts which he [Malthus] cannot help entertaining of the correctness of his opinions'.[1] As the time now fixed for publication approached, Malthus wrote to Ricardo on 10 Sept. 1819: 'I have been delayed and led away as usual by thoughts relating to the subjects of some of our discussions.... I think I have a fourth or a fifth to write yet; and having composed the different parts at different times and not in their natural order, I have still much to put out and put in, before it will be fit to send to the press.'[2]

A few months before the book came out, McCulloch, presuming that it would be a defence of Malthus's views on the Corn Laws, had written to Ricardo: 'I think that justice will not be shown either to the science or the country, if it be not handled pretty roughly';[3] and a little later he asked Ricardo to send him notes on the book when it was published.[4] This Ricardo agreed to do: 'When I have read Mr. Malthus book I will make known to you my opinion on the passages which will be found in it in opposition to our theory.'[5]

When in April 1820 the book appeared, Ricardo gave it a first reading—'rather in haste and after different intervals of time.'[6] He explains to McCulloch: 'I thought of noticing the particular points on which Mr. M and I differ, and to have offered some defence of my opinions, but I should have little else to do but to restate the arguments in my book, for I do not think he has touched them'.[7] He expresses disagreement particularly with Malthus's measure of value (he 'adopts a measure of value very different from mine, but he no where adheres to it'), and with his doctrine of rent; he considers 'the most objectionable chapter in Mr. Malthus' book' to be 'that perhaps on the bad effects from too great accumulation of capital'; and accuses Malthus of having misunderstood him regarding improvements on the land ('he has not acted quite fairly by me in his remarks on that passage in my

---

[1] Below, VII, 379–80 and cp. 376.
[2] Below, VIII, 64, 66.
[3] Letter of 5 Dec. 1819, *ib*. 138–9; cp. also 167.
[4] Letter of 2 April 1820, *ib*. 176.
[5] Letter to McCulloch, 8 April 1820, *ib*. 177–8.

[6] Letter to McCulloch, 2 May 1820, *ib*. 183. Curiously, two days later he writes to Malthus that he has read his book, 'with great attention' (*ib*. 183).
[7] *ib*. 180.

book which says that the interest of the landlord is opposed to that of the rest of the community'). He adds: 'At present I feel a real difficulty, for I confess I do not very clearly perceive what Mr. Malthus system is.'[1]

About three months later (during a stay at Brighton in the second half of July) Ricardo read Malthus's book a second time, and expressed himself 'even less pleased with it than I was at first'.[2] He writes to Mill from Brighton on 27 July 1820: 'I have had no books here but Malthus's and my own. I am reading the former with great attention, and noting the passages which I think deserving of comment. They are more numerous than I expected. If I were to answer every paragraph, containing what I think an erroneous view of the subject on which the book treats, I should write a thicker volume than his own.'[3]

For a time after he had retired to Gatcomb on 9 August,[4] Ricardo was largely occupied in revising his own *Principles* for edition 3. Two months later, in a letter of 14 Oct. 1820 to Mill (who in the interval had been staying with him at Gatcomb 'for more than three weeks'),[5] he said: 'I take advantage of every leisure hour to work on my reply to Malthus—I consider it as an agreeable amusement, and say every thing that offers. It will not probably be desirable to publish it—if I do send it forth it will want a great deal of lopping'.[6] On 16 November he announces: 'My notes on Malthus (such as they are) are finished';[7] and a week later he tells McCulloch: 'I have been employed for some little time in writing notes on Mr Malthus' last work, which as yet I have shown to no one.... I have, wherever I met with a passage on which I wished to animadvert, quoted the page, and the first few words of the passage, and then have written my short comment.'[8] On the next day he informs Malthus: 'I have made notes on every passage in your book which I dispute, and have supposed myself about publishing a new edition of your work,

[1] *ib.* 180–2. Cp. also letter to Malthus, 4 May 1820, *ib.* 183–6.
[2] Letter to McCulloch, 2 Aug. 1820, *ib.* 215.
[3] *ib.* 212.
[4] *ib.* 230.
[5] *ib.* 231.
[6] *ib.* 283.
[7] Letter to Mill, *ib.* 296.
[8] *ib.* 297–8.

and at liberty to mark the passage with a reference to a note at the bottom of the page. I have in fact quoted 3 or 4 words of a sentence, noting the page, and then added my comment.'[1] (The idea of putting his criticisms in the form of notes to a special edition of Malthus's work may have been suggested by Say's treatment of Ricardo's own *Principles* in the French edition which had recently been published.)

These letters indicate that the possibility of publishing the Notes had not been entirely ruled out by Ricardo while he was writing them. Just before their completion Mill had offered to advise him about publication ('I shall be glad, when you have finished your notes...if you will transmit them to me, and give me an opportunity of advising with you; because, the time about which you will most probably come to town, will be the time best for publication').[2] At first Ricardo had entertained the alternative idea of 'publishing them as an appendix' to the third edition of his own *Principles*; but had been 'strongly dissuaded from it by Mill'.[3]

However, in asking McCulloch to read the Notes, he disclaims any intention of publication: 'If the criticism were just, and the principles I advocate correct, still it would not I think be desirable to publish it—first, because Mr. Malthus book, I am told, has not excited much interest, and these dry, and perhaps not very clearly expressed comments upon it, will excite still less.'[4] And in a letter to Trower of 26 Nov. 1820 he writes: 'The whole might occupy about 150 pages if printed. It is not however probable that I shall publish them, because they are not in an inviting form, and would consequently have few readers.'[5] McCulloch, after reading the Notes, advised against publication, on the ground that they were 'by far too controversial' and in their present shape involved 'a good deal of tedious and unnecessary repetition';[6] and Ricardo

[1] Below, VIII, 301.
[2] Letter to Ricardo, 13 Nov. 1820, *ib*. 292–3.
[3] Ricardo to Trower, 14 Jan. 1821, *ib*. 333. Mill's dissuasion no doubt

had been during his visit to Gatcomb in August–September 1820.
[4] *ib*. 298.
[5] *ib*. 305.
[6] Letter from McCulloch, 22 Jan. 1821, *ib*. 340.

decided 'for the present' to 'do nothing with them'.[1] Trower
also, some months later, declared them unsuitable for publication
'in their present shape'.[2] Meanwhile Malthus, far from encouraging Ricardo's idea of an annotated edition, had at once intimated
his intention of himself preparing a new edition, and had followed
this with an announcement in the press of its impending publication.[3] However, a number of changes in edition 3 of Ricardo's
Principles embody material from these Notes.[4]

Malthus had intended to visit Gatcomb in December 1820 and
to see Ricardo's Notes before revising his own book;[5] and in
view of this Ricardo refrained from sending the Notes immediately
to McCulloch, in order that Malthus should have a chance of
seeing them.[6] On hearing from Malthus, however, that the visit
had to be postponed, Ricardo dispatched them to McCulloch in
Edinburgh; and when Malthus a week later (in the middle of
December) came to Gatcomb at short notice, the Notes were no
longer there for him to see.[7] According to Ricardo's account of
the visit: 'Mr. Malthus and I had a great deal of discussion, and on
some points understood each other's objections better than before,
but yet there remains the greatest difference between us.'[8]
McCulloch kept the Notes several weeks, after which they were
seen by Malthus,[9] and later by Trower.[10] At the end of 1821, they
were once more sent to McCulloch at his request.[11] There is no
record of when they were actually seen by Mill. To Mill's offer of
13 Nov. 1820 to advise about the best mode of publication
Ricardo had replied: 'I cannot think of imposing on you the task
of reading them, particularly as it would be necessary for you to
read also the passages in Malthus on which I comment.'[12] That at

[1] Letter to McCulloch, 25 Jan. 1821,
ib. 342.
[2] *ib.* 395.
[3] Letter from Malthus, 27 Nov.
1820 (*ib.* 308) and Murray's advertisement in the *Monthly Literary
Advertiser*, 10 Jan. 1821 (*ib.* 341).
[4] See above, I, Introduction, section
VII.
[5] Below, VIII, 308.
[6] *ib.* 314–5.

[7] *ib.* 318, 324, 334.
[8] Letter to McCulloch, 17 Jan. 1821,
ib. 336.
[9] Ricardo writes on 2 March 1821:
'Mr. Malthus has now had my notes
for 5 weeks' (*ib.* 349); and Malthus
still had them on 25 April (*ib.* 373).
[10] *ib.* 393.
[11] Below, IX, 135, 138.
[12] Below, VIII, 296.

some stage they were read by Mill is shown by the jottings in his handwriting on the MS, quoted below; but these may have been made after Ricardo's death.

II

The discussion between Ricardo and Malthus on the Notes, as we have seen, was chiefly carried out in conversation, except for Ricardo's comments on the possibility of a general glut, which were taken up by Malthus in a letter of 7 July 1821[1]—a letter which initiated a brief correspondence between them in the course of that month. Meanwhile Malthus proceeded with his plans for a second edition. After his first move in this direction at the end of 1820, which has been mentioned above, he returned to the task two years later, in December 1822, when he wrote to his friend Prévost: 'I am very anxious to get out as soon as I possibly can another edition of my last work, in which there will be some new views on *a standard of value* which require a good deal of care and consideration.'[2] This however bore fruit, not in a new edition of that work, but in *The Measure of Value Stated and Illustrated* which he published as a separate pamphlet in 1823. Its publication gave rise to further correspondence with Ricardo which extended over the last months of Ricardo's life.

It was not till 1836 that a second edition of Malthus's *Principles of Political Economy* appeared; it was published posthumously by his friend Bishop Otter,[3] Malthus having died in 1834. It is not quite clear what exactly the editor's part was in preparing the work for publication. He says in the 'Advertisement' prefixed to the volume (p. xi) that Malthus had died 'before he had completed the whole of the alterations which he had in contemplation, and while he was yet occupied in correcting and improving the latter parts of the work'. He acknowledges that he has 'slightly varied' the text in some places, and omitted 'some passages'.

---

[1] Below, IX, 9 ff.
[2] Letter of 23 Dec. 1822, in *Journal of Economic History*, vol. II, p. 188.

[3] 'Second Edition with Considerable Additions from the Author's Own Manuscript and an Original Memoir', London, Pickering, 1836.

The changes in this edition are extensive, but in general they do not appear to be carried out with a view to meeting Ricardo's criticisms. Indeed, they seem rather to be on the defensive against a new generation of critics who linked Malthus in their attacks with Ricardo.

There is thus some indication, firstly that Malthus was engaged on revisions for a second edition in the years 1820 to 1822, and secondly that he carried out another revision in the closing years of his life. We are able to find confirmation of this from Malthus's working copy of his *Principles of Political Economy*, 1820, with numerous alterations mostly in his own handwriting which has been preserved.[1] These alterations fall into two clearly distinct parts: (*a*) corrections extending over the first two-thirds of the book and written in the margin or on slips inserted, and (*b*) a set of 17 pages of MS, consisting of a revision of parts of Chapter II, mainly of Section vi, 'Of the Labour which a Commodity will command, considered as a Measure of real Value in Exchange'.

As compared with the published second edition, the changes in (*a*) appear to be much more connected with the controversy with Ricardo in the early '20's. Thus it is significant that the most extensive revisions in (*a*) are in Section v of Chapter II ('Of Money, when uniform in its cost, considered as a Measure of Value'), which is the second of the sections devoted to a discussion of the measure of value proposed by Ricardo; whereas the second edition omits this section altogether. There are other indications of the period to which (*a*) belongs. In particular, a footnote to a passage inserted at page 261 refers to the date of publication of 'the quarto edition of the Essay on Population' (which was 1803) as 'nearly twenty years ago'. This footnote occurs in the second edition, p. 235, altered to 'above thirty years ago'. Also, such inserted slips of paper in (*a*) as have dated watermarks bear the dates 1819, 1820 and 1822. Thus it would appear that (*a*) belongs

[1] This copy has recently (1949) been presented to the Marshall Library of Economics at Cambridge by Mr R. A. Bray, of Shere, a descendant of Malthus' sister. The Marshall Library has also the original MS of a large part of the first edition (acquired in 1944).

to the period of the abortive preparations for a new edition between 1820 and 1822.

As regards (b), however, such of its pages as have dated water-marks belong to 1828; while in one place on the MS a reference to 'the time of George IV' is changed to 'William IV'.[1] Thus these pages must have been written between 1828 and 1830.

While some of the corrections in (a) have found their way into the second edition, the differences are very considerable. It is, therefore, clear that the revision mentioned by Otter, and em-bodied in the published second edition, cannot be (a) unless Otter himself carried out a more extensive work of revision than he acknowledged. On the other hand (b), most of which is embodied in the second edition with comparatively slight changes,[2] evidently belongs to Malthus's final revision.

III

For almost a century the Notes disappeared from sight. McCulloch, in the early versions of his *Life and Writings of Mr. Ricardo*,[3] had said: 'He also left very full "Notes" on Mr. Malthus's Principles of Political Economy, which we trust will be published. They contain a most able vindication of his own doctrines from the objections of Mr. Malthus, and an exposition of the mistakes into which he conceives Mr. Malthus has fallen.' But in the later versions of the *Life* (such as that prefixed to his own edition of Ricardo's *Works*, 1846) he replaced the phrase, 'which we trust will be published' with the sentence: 'But we doubt whether they have sufficient interest to warrant their publication'.[4]

[1] This significant correction was pointed out by Dr Bonar, who first studied this copy of Malthus's book and called the editor's attention to its existence.
[2] These passages are on p. 87, p. 93 and pp. 95–109 of the second edition.
[3] *Edinburgh Annual Register for 1823* and the pamphlet *Memoir of the Life and Writings of David Ricardo*, London, 1825.

[4] In his *Literature of Political Economy*, 1845, McCulloch in a note on Malthus's *Principles* also referred to Ricardo's Notes: 'Mr. Ricardo left a manuscript volume of obser-vations on this work, principally in reply to the interminable criticism of Mr. Malthus on his peculiar doctrines.' (p. 18.)

It was only in 1919 that the MS came to light. The discovery was made by Mr Frank Ricardo, a great-grandson of the economist, at Bromesberrow Place, Ledbury (formerly the residence of Ricardo's eldest son Osman), who describes it as follows in a letter of 28 Oct. 1925 to Professor J. H. Hollander: 'It was, I think, in the autumn of 1919—or may be the spring—that I was going through some furniture stored in the lumber room at Bromesberrow, and I came upon this MS. wrapped in brown paper and casually put away in a box together with some old ornaments. I recognized it as an original MS. of David Ricardo but whether it had been published I did not then know.'[1] The find was reported by Mr Frank Ricardo to the British Museum, which communicated with Professor T. E. Gregory; and the Notes were published in 1928, with a lengthy introduction by Professor Hollander and short summaries of the relevant parts of Malthus's text prefixed to each Note and prepared by Professor Gregory.[2] Acknowledgement is due to the editors and to the publishers, The Johns Hopkins Press, for permission to use their edition.

IV

The MS consists of a title-page and 222 loose sheets (as counted by Hollander) cut to a size of about $4\frac{3}{4} \times 7\frac{3}{4}$ inches. They are written by Ricardo on both sides, and were numbered first in pencil on one side only from 1 to 199. These numbers were superseded by a final pagination in ink on both sides of the paper from 1 to 412. Pages were added or taken out at various stages of composition, resulting in duplications and omissions in both paginations. Thus in the ink pagination there are intermediate pages numbered $147\frac{1}{2}$, $148\frac{1}{2}$, $167\frac{1}{4}$, $167\frac{1}{2}$, etc. and in some cases there are pages without a number. There are also frequent insertions on smaller slips, some of them loose and some stuck on to the page with wafers.

---

[1] Quoted in Hollander's Introduction to Notes on Malthus, 1928, p. xi.

[2] Baltimore, The Johns Hopkins Press, 1928, pp. cviii, 246.

The MS is cased in two cardboard book-covers which from their size and colour (blue and buff) may have been taken from a copy of Malthus's book. On the inside of one of the covers there are some pencil notes in James Mill's handwriting.[1]

V

The method adopted in the present edition follows Ricardo's hint (when he 'supposed' himself 'about publishing a new edition' of Malthus's work):[2] namely, of giving Malthus's text at the top and Ricardo's Notes at the bottom. This also conforms to Professor Cannan's idea, when he criticised the Hollander-Gregory edition: 'What was really wanted was a reprint of Malthus's book with Ricardo's notes added, each in its proper place at the foot of the page'.[3]

Larger type has been used for Ricardo's Notes than for Malthus's text. Consecutive numbers have been given to the Notes; and these have been inserted in bold type at the end of each passage commented upon. In the first three of the Notes Ricardo gives an indication of the end as well as the beginning of the passage in question. But in subsequent Notes only the beginning is quoted in the MS, so that the correct position of the reference number in the text is in some cases uncertain and has had to be guessed.

In distributing Ricardo's commentary under Malthus's text, an 'opening' (*i.e.* two pages facing one another) has been treated as a single page, and as a result a Note may sometimes be found on the opposite page to its reference in the text.

The page-numbers of the original edition of Malthus have been reproduced in the margin. This has made it possible for

---

[1] They are as follows:
'p. 349 On subdivision of property among children.
372 Foreign trade does not augment value.
137 Rent comes all out of profits.
154 Reduction in cost of production never goes to rent.'
The references are to the ink pagination of the MS and correspond to pp. 386, 402, 157, 187 below.
[2] Above, p. ix–x.
[3] *Economica*, Nov. 1929, p. 358.

Ricardo's references to those pages to be retained unchanged. On the other hand, Malthus's page-references to Ricardo's *Principles* (which in the original are to Ricardo's edition 2) have been adjusted to the pagination of Volume I of the present edition and enclosed in square brackets.

As a rule the text of Malthus has been given in full. Only such portions of the text as are not relevant, even indirectly, to Ricardo's commentary have been cut[1] and replaced by the corresponding parts of the very extensive 'Summary of the Contents' given by Malthus at the end of his book (where it occupies 70 pages). These parts have been enclosed in square brackets, and can be recognised at a glance by the quick succession of page-numbers in the margin. (It is to be noted that the position of these in such cases can only be approximately correct.)

Malthus's original Index has been included, with its page-references adapted to the present edition.

The editor's footnotes to Ricardo's commentary are distinguished by numbers and by generally being arranged in double column (while Malthus's footnotes to his own text are marked by asterisks and extend across the page). They give all the corrections in the MS which seemed to be of any possible interest, however remote. The various changes made by Ricardo are indicated by the use of the formulas 'replaces', 'del.' (for deleted) and 'ins.' (for inserted). These terms describe successive stages in the expression of Ricardo's thought as can be inferred from study of the MS. They do not, however, describe the *form* in which the alterations were carried out. Thus 'replaces' may alternatively indicate: (1) the crossing out of a passage and the rewriting of it between the lines; (2) the recasting of it by adding and removing words here and there; and (3) the copying out of a long passage (sometimes of more than one page) in the course of which alterations were made in the expression. The fact of the sheets being written on both sides involved, whenever a passage had to be added, recopying of all the matter that followed on the same sheet.

[1] The omitted portions amount to rather less than a third of the original.

The spelling, punctuation and abbreviations of Ricardo's MS have been retained, except for '&' which has been spelt 'and', and M^r, M^{rs} and D^r, which have been printed in the more usual form of Mr., Mrs. and Dr. The opening quotations of each Note, which in the MS are in quotes, have been given instead in italics.

The present volume has been printed, for Malthus's text, from the first edition of 1820 and, for Ricardo's Notes, from a copy of the Hollander-Gregory edition which was corrected by collation with the original MS a number of times both by editor and printer. Consequently, although attention has not been drawn specifically to the errors which abound in that edition and often distort the sense, the reader can be assured that, where a different reading is given in the present volume, this has not been done without consideration of the alternative version.

This volume, with its special typographical difficulties, has been dependent even more than the others upon the skill and ingenuity of the printers of the Cambridge University Press.

NOTES ON MALTHUS

PRINCIPLES

OF

POLITICAL ECONOMY

CONSIDERED

WITH A VIEW TO THEIR PRACTICAL

APPLICATION.

———◆———

By the Rev. T. R. MALTHUS, M.A. F.R.S.

PROFESSOR OF HISTORY AND POLITICAL ECONOMY IN THE
EAST INDIA COLLEGE, HERTFORDSHIRE.

═══════

LONDON:

JOHN MURRAY, ALBEMARLE-STREET.

————

1820.

Notes on
Mr. Malthus work "Principles
of Political Economy, considered
with a view to their practical
application"

By

David Ricardo

CONTENTS

Chapter III.   Of the Rent of Land

Chapter IV.   Of the Wages of Labour

4

PRINCIPLES
OF
POLITICAL ECONOMY

INTRODUCTION

[The science of political economy resembles more the sciences 1
of morals and politics than the science of mathematics.

This conclusion, founded on a view of the subjects about 2
which political economy is conversant, is further strengthened by
the differences of opinion which have prevailed among those who
have directed a great portion of their attention to this study.

The Economists and Adam Smith differed on some important
questions in political economy, though they agreed on others still
more important.

Among the most distinguished modern writers, differences of 3
opinion continue to prevail on questions of great importance.

The correct determination of these questions is of great 4
practical consequence.

An agreement among the principal writers in Political Economy
is very desirable with a view to the authority of the science in its
practical application.

In the present state of the science, an endeavour to settle some 5
important yet controverted points may be more useful than an
attempt to frame a new and complete treatise.]

The principal cause of error, and of the differences which prevail
at present among the scientific writers on political economy,
appears to me to be | a precipitate attempt to simplify and gene- 6
ralize; and while their more practical opponents draw too hasty
inferences from a frequent appeal to partial facts, these writers
run into a contrary extreme, and do not sufficiently try their
theories by a reference to that enlarged and comprehensive experience which, on so complicated a subject, can alone establish their
truth and utility.

To minds of a certain cast there is nothing so captivating as
simplification and generalization. It is indeed the desirable and
legitimate object of genuine philosophy, whenever it can be

effected consistently with truth; and for this very reason, the natural tendency towards it has, in almost every science with which we are acquainted, led to crude and premature theories.

In political economy the desire to simplify has occasioned an unwillingness to acknowledge the operation of more causes than one in the production of particular effects; and if one cause would account for a considerable portion of a certain class of phenomena, the whole has been ascribed to it without sufficient attention to the facts, which would not admit of being so solved. I have always thought that the late controversy on the bullion question presented a signal instance of this kind of error. Each party being possessed of a theory which would account for an unfavourable exchange, and an excess of the market price above the mint price of bullion, adhered to that single view of the question, which it had been accustomed to consider as correct; and scarcely one writer seemed willing | to admit of the operation of both theories, the combination of which, sometimes acting in conjunction and sometimes in opposition, could alone adequately account for the variable and complicated phenomena observable.* (1)

It is certain that we cannot too highly respect and venerate that admirable rule of Newton, not to admit more causes than are necessary to the solution of the phenomena we are considering, but the rule itself implies, that those which really are necessary must be admitted. Before the shrine of truth, as discovered by facts and experience, the fairest theories and the most beautiful classifications must fall. The chemist of thirty years ago may be allowed to regret, that new discoveries in the science should dis-

---

* It must be allowed, however, that the theory of the Bullionists, though too exclusive, accounted for much the largest proportion of the phenomena in question; and perhaps it may be said with truth that the Bullion Report itself was more free from the error I have adverted to than any other work that appeared.

---

(1) Page 6. *Each party being possessed of a theory which &c. &c.—observable.*

Mr. Malthus must here allude to the dispute whether the alteration in the relative value of bullion, and paper, was owing to a rise of bullion or to a fall of paper.

The settling of this dispute was of no importance to the

turb and confound his previous systems and arrangements; but he is not entitled to the name of philosopher, if he does not give them up without a struggle, as soon as the experiments which refute them are fully established.

The same tendency to simplify and generalize, produces a still greater disinclination to allow of modifications, limitations, and exceptions to any rule or proposition, than to admit the operation of more causes than one. Nothing indeed is so unsatisfactory, and gives so unscientific and unmas-|terly an air to a proposition 8 as to be obliged to make admissions of this kind; yet there is no truth of which I feel a stronger conviction than that there are many important propositions in political economy which absolutely require limitations and exceptions; and it may be confidently stated that the frequent combination of complicated causes, the action and reaction of cause and effect on each other, and the necessity of limitations and exceptions in a considerable number of important propositions, form the main difficulties of the science, and occasion those frequent mistakes which it must be allowed are made in the prediction of results.

To explain myself by an instance. Adam Smith has stated, that capitals are increased by parsimony, that every frugal man is a public benefactor,† and that the increase of wealth depends upon the balance of produce above consumption.‡ That these propositions are true to a great extent is perfectly unquestionable. No considerable and continued increase of wealth could possibly take place without that degree of frugality which occasions, annually, the conversion of some revenue into capital, and creates a balance of produce above consumption; but it is quite obvious that they are not true to an indefinite extent, and that the principle

† Wealth of Nations, Book II. c. iii. pp. 15–18. 6th edit.
‡ Book IV. c. iii. p. 250.

---

real question, for whichever party was right, it did not alter the fact, nor vary the degree, of the depreciation. It was rather a dispute about the causes of the depreciation, and could not be settled satisfactorily, because there was no standard to which reference could be made to ascertain whether gold had risen or paper had fallen in value.

of saving, pushed to excess, would destroy the motive to production.(2) If every person were satisfied with the simplest food,
the poorest clothing, and the meanest houses, it is certain that no
9 other sort | of food, clothing, and lodging would be in existence;
and as there would be no adequate motive to the proprietors of
land to cultivate well, not only the wealth derived from conveniences and luxuries would be quite at an end, but if the same

---

(2) p. 8. *Adam Smith has stated &c.—production.*

Mr. Malthus says these propositions are true to a great
extent, but it is quite obvious he adds that they are not true
to an indefinite extent. But why? because the principle of
saving pushed to excess, would destroy the motive to production.

But the argument is not about the motive to production,
in that every body is agreed—the accumulation of capital
may go on so much faster, than labourers can be increased,
that productions must cease increasing in the same proportion as capital[1], from want of hands; and when they do[2]
increase, the labourers by their comparative scarcity to
capital, can command so large a portion of the produce as
to afford no adequate motive to the capitalist to continue to
save.

All men will allow then that savings may be so rapid and
profits so low in consequence[3] as to diminish the motive for
accumulation, and finally to destroy it altogether. But the
question yet remains, Does not the increase of wealth
depend upon the balance of produce above consumption?
Can this question be answered otherwise than in the
affirmative?

It is true, says Mr. Malthus, but of this increased produce

[1] 'in the same proportion as capital' is inserted.
[2] Replaces 'or if it does'.

[3] 'and profits so low in consequence' is ins.

divisions of land continued, the production of food would be prematurely checked, and population would come to a stand long before the soil had been well cultivated. If consumption exceed production, the capital of the country must be diminished, and its wealth must be gradually destroyed from its want of power to produce; if production be in a great excess above consumption, the motive to accumulate and produce must cease from the want

the capitalist will get so small a proportion, that he will have no motive to assist in increasing the quantity of produce. I agree with Mr. Malthus; in the distribution of the actual produce the capitalist may get so little for profit, and the labourer so much for wages, that no motive may exist for the capitalist[4] continuing to be parsimonious. Now a dispute about the effects of parsimony is one thing, and about the *motives* for being parsimonious another.[5]

I should not have noticed this passage here if I did not know that it forms the most important subject for discussion in Mr. Malthus' work, and is frequently brought forward under different points of view. Mr. Malthus will be found to maintain not only the opinion, which is just, that the profits of the capitalist will be diminished by an increase of productions under the circumstances supposed; but also the opinion which is wholly inconsistent with it that the wages of the labourer will be likewise reduced.[6] Productions altogether are increased, a selection may be freely made what those productions shall be, and yet neither the capitalist nor the labourer shall be benefited by them, altho they must be awarded to one or other of them[7].

[4] 'the capitalist' is ins.
[5] Replaces 'Now a dispute about increasing productions by saving is one thing, and about the *motives* for increasing them another.'

[6] First written simply '; but also the wages of the labourer.'
[7] 'in certain proportions to be agreed upon' is deleted here.

of will to consume. The two extremes are obvious; and it follows that there must be some intermediate point, though the resources of political economy may not be able to ascertain it, where, taking into consideration both the power to produce and the will to consume, the encouragement to the increase of wealth is the greatest.

[The necessity of limitations and exceptions illustrated in the rules which relate to the division of land.

10   The tendency to premature generalization among political economists occasions also an unwillingness to bring their theories to the test of experience.

11   The first business of philosophy is to account for things as they are.

A comprehensive attention to facts is necessary, both to prevent the multiplication of theories, and to confirm those which are just.

12   The science of political economy is essentially practical, and applicable to the common business of human life.

13   Some eminent political economists think that, though exceptions may exist to the general rules of political economy, they need not be noticed.

14   But the most perfect sincerity, together with the greatest degree of accuracy attainable, are necessary to give that credit and circulation to general principles, which is so desirable.

15   Another class of persons seem to be satisfied with what has been already done in political economy, and shrink from further inquiries, if they do not immediately see the practical results to which they lead.

Such a tendency, if indulged too far, strikes at the root of all improvement in science.

16   More of the propositions in political economy will bear the test of *cui bono* than those of any other department of human knowledge.

Further inquiries, however difficult, should be pursued, both with. a view to the improvement and completion of the science, and the practical advantages likely to result from them.

17   It is of great importance to draw a line, with tolerable precision, between those cases where the expected results are certain, and those where they are uncertain.

Practical statesmen, who have not leisure for the necessary

inquiries, should not object, under the guidance of a sound discretion, to make use of the leisure of others.

The principle of non-interference, necessarily limited in practice—1st, By some duties connected with political economy, which it is universally acknowledged belong to the sovereign. 18

2dly, By the prevalence, in almost every country, of bad regulations, which require to be amended or removed. 19

3dly, By the necessity of taxation.

The propriety of interfering but little, does not supersede, in any degree, the use of the most extensive professional knowledge either in a statesman or a physician. 20

One of the specific objects of the present work is to fit the general rules of political economy for practice, by endeavouring to consider all the causes which concur in the production of particular phenomena. 21

This mode of proceeding is exposed to a danger of an opposite kind to that which arises from a tendency to simplification, a danger which Adam Smith has not always avoided.

A just mean between the two extremes is the point aimed at with a view of arriving at the truth.] 22

Many of the doctrines of Adam Smith, which had been considered as settled, have lately been called in question by writers entitled to great attention; but they have often failed, as it appears to me, to make good their objections; and in all such cases I have thought it desirable to examine anew, with reference to such objections, the grounds on which his doctrines are founded.

It has been my wish to avoid giving to my work a controversial air. Yet to free it entirely from controversy, while one of my professed objects is to discuss controverted opinions, and to try their truth by a reference to an enlarged experience, is obviously not possible. There is one modern work, in particular, of very high reputation, some of the fundamental principles of which have appeared to me, after the most mature deliberation, to be erroneous; and I should not have done jus-|tice to the ability with which it is written, to the high authority of the writer, and the interests of the science of which it treats, if it had not specifically engaged a considerable portion of my attention. I allude to Mr. Ricardo's work, "*On the Principles of Political Economy and Taxation.*" 23

I have so very high an opinion of Mr. Ricardo's talents as a political economist, and so entire a conviction of his perfect sincerity and love of truth, that I frankly own I have sometimes felt almost staggered by his authority, while I have remained unconvinced by his reasonings. I have thought that I must unaccountably have overlooked some essential points, either in my own view of the subject, or in his; and this kind of doubt has been the principal reason of my delay in publishing the present volume. But I shall hardly be suspected of not thinking for myself on these subjects, or of not feeling such a degree of confidence in my own conclusions, after having taken full time to form them, as to be afraid of submitting them to the decision of the public.

To those who are not acquainted with Mr. Ricardo's work, and do not properly appreciate the ingenuity and consistency of the system which it maintains and developes with so much ability, I am apprehensive that I shall appear to have dwelt too long upon some of the points on which we differ. But as they are, for the most part, of great importance both theoretically and practically, and as it appeared to me extremely desirable, with a view to the

24 interests of the science, that they│should, if possible, be settled, I did not feel myself justified in giving less time to the consideration of them.

I am far from saying that I may not be wrong in the conclusions at which I have arrived, in opposition to those of Mr. Ricardo. But I am conscious that I have taken all the means to be right, which patient investigation and a sincere desire to get at the truth can give to the actual powers of my understanding. And with this consciousness, both with respect to the opinions I have opposed, and those which I have attempted to establish, I feel no reluctance in committing the results to the decision of the public.

T. R. MALTHUS.

East India College,⎫
   Dec. 1, 1819. ⎰

CHAPTER I

ON THE DEFINITIONS OF WEALTH
AND PRODUCTIVE LABOUR

SECTION I

On the Definitions of Wealth

[A definition of wealth is desirable, though it may not be easy 25 to give one not liable to some objection.

The liberty of a writer to define his terms as he pleases, pro- 26 vided he always uses them in the sense proposed, may be doubted, as an inquiry may be rendered futile by an inadequate or unusual definition.

The comparative merits of the systems of the Economists, and of Adam Smith, depend mainly upon their different definitions of wealth.

The Economists have confined the term wealth within too 27 narrow limits.

Lord Lauderdale and other writers have given definitions which extend it too far.]

If we wish to attain any thing like precision in our inquiries, when we treat of wealth, | we must narrow the field of inquiry, and 28 draw some line, which will leave us only those objects, the increase or decrease of which is capable of being estimated with more accuracy.

The line, which it seems most natural to draw, is that which separates material from immaterial objects, or those which are capable of accumulation and definite valuation, from those which rarely admit of these processes, and never in such a degree as to afford useful practical conclusions.

Adam Smith has no where given a very regular and formal definition of wealth; but that the meaning which he attaches to the term is confined to material objects, is, throughout his work, sufficiently manifest. His prevailing description of wealth may be said to be, "the annual produce of land and labour." The objections to it, as a definition, are, that it refers to the sources of wealth before we are told what wealth is, and that it is besides not sufficiently discriminate, as it would include all the useless products of the earth, as well as those which are appropriated and enjoyed by man. (3)

To avoid these objections, and to keep at an equal distance from a too confined or too indiscriminate sense of the term, I should define wealth to be, those *material* objects which are necessary, useful, or agreeable to mankind. And I am inclined to believe, that the definition, thus limited, includes nearly all the objects which usually enter into our conceptions when we speak

29 of wealth or riches; an advantage of considerable importance, | so long as we retain these terms both in common use, and in the vocabulary of political economy.

It is obviously, indeed, rather a metaphorical than a strict use of the word wealth, to apply it to *every* benefit or gratification of which man is susceptible; and we should hardly be prepared to acknowledge the truth of the proposition which affirmed, that riches were the sole source of human happiness.

It may fairly, therefore, I think, be said, that the wealth spoken of, in the science of political economy, is confined to material objects.

A country will therefore be rich or poor according to the abundance or scarcity with which these material objects are supplied, compared with the extent of territory; and the people will be rich or poor according to the abundance with which they are supplied, compared with the population.

---

(3) p. 28. *The line—man.*

M. Say objects to this division,[1] but I think there is real use in dividing our enquiries about[2] those material objects which are capable of accumulation, and definite valuation, from those which rarely admit of such processes. Mr. Malthus'

[1] *Traité d'Économie politique*, 4th ed., 1819, p. 122.   [2] Replaces 'in confining our enquiries to'.

SECTION II

On Productive and Unproductive Labour

[The question of productive labour is dependent upon the definition of wealth, both in the system of the Economists, and in that of Adam Smith.

The application of the term *productive* to the labour which is productive of wealth, however defined, is obviously useful. 30

Adam Smith's definition of productive labour has been thought by some to be too extended, and by others too confined.

It would be difficult to proceed in our inquiries into the nature and causes of the wealth of nations, without some classification of the different kinds of labour.

Such a classification is necessary—1st. To explain the nature of capital, and its effect in increasing national wealth.] 31

Secondly, it is stated by Adam Smith, and it must be allowed to be stated justly, that the produce which is annually saved is as regularly consumed as that which is annually spent, but that it is consumed by a different set of people. (4) If this be the case, and if saving be allowed to be the immediate cause of the increase of capital, it must | be absolutely necessary, in all discussions relating to the progress of wealth, to distinguish by some particular title a set of people who appear to act so important a part in accelerating this progress. Almost all the lower classes of people of every society are employed in some way or other, and if there were no grounds of distinction in their employments, with reference to their effects on the national wealth, it is difficult to conceive what would be the use of saving from revenue to add to capital, as it would be merely employing one set of people in preference to another, when, according to the hypothesis, there 32

---

definition of wealth has in it nothing objectionable; he states it to be those material objects, which are necessary, useful, or agreeable, to mankind.

(4) p. 31. *Secondly it is stated by A. Smith &c. &c.*

This is an important admission from Mr. Malthus, and will be found to be at variance with some of the doctrines which he afterwards maintains.

is no essential difference between them. How then are we to explain the nature of saving, and the different effects of parsimony and extravagance upon the national capital? No political economist of the present day can by saving mean mere hoarding; and beyond this contracted and inefficient proceeding, no use of the term, in reference to national wealth, can well be imagined, but that which must arise from a different application of what is saved, founded upon a real distinction between the different kinds of labour which may be maintained by it.

If the labour of menial servants be as productive of wealth as the labour of manufacturers, why should not savings be employed in their maintenance, not only without being dissipated, but with a constant increase of value? But menial servants, lawyers, or physicians, who save from their salaries, are fully aware that their savings would be immediately dissipated again if they were 33 advanced to | themselves instead of being employed in the maintenance of persons of a different description. To consider the expenditure of the unproductive labourers of Adam Smith, as advances made to themselves, and of the same nature as the advances of the master-manufacturer to his workmen, would be at once to confound the very useful and just distinction between those who live upon wages and those who live upon profits, and would render it quite impossible to explain the frequent and important operations of saving from revenue to add to capital, so absolutely necessary to the continued increase of wealth.*

It is not the question at present whether saving may or may not be carried too far (a point which will be considered in its proper place); but whether we can talk intelligibly of saving and accumulation, and discuss their effects on national wealth without allowing some distinction in the different kinds of labour.

Thirdly, it has been stated by Adam Smith, and stated truly, that there is a balance very different from the balance of trade, which, according as it happens to be favourable or unfavourable, 34 occasions the prosperity or decay of every nation: this | is the balance of the annual produce and consumption. If in given

---

* One of the most able impugners of the doctrine of Adam Smith respecting productive labour is Mr. Ganilh, in his valuable Work on the various Systems of Political Economy; but he appears to me to fail entirely, when he attempts to shew that savings are preserved instead of being destroyed, when consumed by the idle classes. I cannot understand in what sense it can be said that menial servants annually reproduce the capital by which they are fed. Book III. c. ii.

periods the produce of a country exceeds its consumption, the means of increasing its capital will be provided, its population will soon increase, or the actual numbers will be better accommodated, and probably both. (5) If the consumption in such periods fully equals the produce, no means of increasing the capital will be afforded, and the society will be nearly at a stand. If the consumption exceeds the produce, every succeeding period will see the society worse supplied, and its prosperity and population will be evidently on the decline.

But if this balance be so important, if upon it depends the progressive, stationary, or declining state of a society, surely it must be of importance to distinguish those who mainly contribute to render this balance favourable from those who chiefly contribute to make the other scale preponderate. Without some such distinction we shall not be able to trace the causes why one nation is thriving and another is declining; and the superior riches of those countries where merchants and manufacturers abound, compared with those in which the retainers of a court and an overgrown aristocracy predominate, will not admit of an intelligible explanation.

[The increasing riches and prosperity of Europe since the feudal times could hardly be explained, if mere personal services were considered as equally productive of wealth with the labours of merchants and manufacturers.

If some distinction be necessary between the different kinds of labour, the next inquiry is, what this distinction should be? 35

The distinction adopted by the Economists would not enable us to explain those appearances in different countries, which, in common language, are allowed to proceed from different degrees of wealth. 36

The opposite opinion to that of the Economists has been already discussed, in the endeavour to shew that some distinction in the different kinds of labour is necessary. 37

A distinction between the different kinds of labour is the corner-stone of Adam Smith's work.

Another sort of distinction, however, might be made, different 38

---

(5) p. 34. *If in given periods &c. &c.*

This also is most true and very important to be remembered.

from that of Adam Smith, which would not invalidate his reasonings.]

If we do not confine wealth to tangible and material objects, we might call all labour productive, but productive in different degrees; and the only change that would be required in Adam Smith's work, on account of this mode of considering the subject, would be, the substitution of the terms more productive and less productive, for those of productive and unproductive.

All labour, for instance, might be stated to be productive of value to the amount of the value paid for it, and in proportion to the degree in which the produce of the different kinds of labour, when sold at the price of free competition, exceeds in value the price of the labour employed upon them.

---

(6) p. 38. *Upon this principle the labours of agriculture &c.*

It is not true of any disposeable labour, that it would be most productive of value in agriculture; because it would be employed on land for which no rent would be paid; and consequently it would only return a value equal to the value of the labour employed, and of the profits of the capital [1] engaged; and this is what any other capital however employed would do.

The produce before obtained from the land might be of greater value in consequence of any new difficulty in the production of corn, and the consequence of this rise of value would be a different distribution of the produce, a larger portion going to rent a smaller portion going to profit. But this value would not add to the greatness or power of the country—for the country would have been richer and greater if the new difficulty in producing corn had not occurred, and consequently if the price had not risen.

It is not true that those labourers would produce most value "whose operations were most assisted by capital or the results of previous labours." I agree with Mr. Malthus that

---

[1] The remainder of the paragraph replaces 'employed.'

Upon this principle the labours of agriculture would, generally speaking, be the most productive; because the produce of nearly all the land actually in use is not only of sufficient exchangeable value to pay the labourers employed upon it, but the profits of the stock advanced by the farmers, and the rents of the land let by the proprietors. Next to the labours of agriculture, those labours would in general be most productive the operations of which were most assisted by capital or the results of previous labour, as in all those cases the exchangeable value produced would most exceed the value of the labour employed in the production, and would support, in the shape of profits, the greatest number of additional persons, and tend most to the accumulation of capital. (6) |

---

they must [2] return a commodity not only of the value of the [3] capital, with its profits, that employs them, but of the value also of the profits of the fixed capital by which their labour has been assisted. But I do not see why this circumstance should "tend most to the accumulation of capital."

Capital is saved from profits. Now whether a man has £10,000 in machinery, and employs only £1,000 in supporting labour; or whether he has £11,000 which he employs all [4] in the support of labour, his profits will be the same; for with equal capitals equal profits will be made; and I can not comprehend why the income of one should be more easily accumulated as [5] Capital, than the income of the other.

[2] 'in such case' is del. here.
[3] The preceding paragraph and the first part of this paragraph replace: 'It is not true that those labourers would be most productive, the operations of whom were most assisted by capital, or the results of previous labour; because if I employ 100 men and £10,000 capital I must have returned to me all that the 100 men destroy, and the profits on the £10,000 capital in the value of the commodities produced. If I employ 2,000 men and £10,000 capital I must have what the 2,000 men consume and the profits on £10,000 capital. Mr. Malthus appears to think that the value of the return will be in proportion to the capital employed—the labourers must return a commodity not only of the value of the' etc.
[4] 'all' replaces 'directly'.
[5] 'as' replaces 'into'.

39 The labour least productive of wealth would be that, the results of which were only equal in exchangeable value to the value paid for such labour, which would support therefore no other classes of society but the labourers actually employed, would replace little or no capital, and tend the least directly and effectively towards that kind of accumulation which facilitates future production. In this last division of productive labour would, of course, be found all the unproductive labourers of Adam Smith.

This mode of considering the subject has, perhaps, some advantages in particular points over that of Adam Smith. It would establish a useful and tolerably accurate scale of productiveness, instead of dividing labour only into two kinds, and drawing a hard line of distinction between them. It would determine, in the very definition, the natural pre-eminence of agriculture, which Adam Smith is obliged to explain afterwards, and, at the same time, shew the numerous cases where an increase of manufacturing and mercantile labour would be more productive, both to the state and to individuals, than an increase of agriculture; as in all those where, from a greater demand for manufactured and mercantile products, compared with the produce of the land, the profits of manufacturing and mercantile capital were greater than both the rent and profits combined of labour employed upon new and less fertile land. (7)

It would answer sufficiently to all the reasonings of Adam
40 Smith on the accumulation of capi-|tal, the distinction between capital and revenue, the nature and effects of saving, and the balance of produce and consumption, merely by using the terms more and less productive, for productive and unproductive; and

---

(7) p. 39. *This mode of &c.*

The premises being unfounded, with regard to agriculture, so is the conclusion. Neither Mr. Malthus, nor Adam Smith, have yet shown "the natural pre-eminence of Agriculture", "in the scale of productiveness."

(8) p. 40. *Agricultural labour would stand in the first rank &c.*

I shall have other opportunities of examining the soundness of this classification. At present, I shall only say, that

would have the additional advantage of keeping more constantly in view the necessary union of capital and skill with the more productive kinds of labour; and thus shew the reason why all the labourers of a savage nation might, according to Adam Smith, be productive, and yet the nation increase very slowly in wealth and population, while a rapid increase of both might be taking place in an improved country under a proportion of productive labourers very much inferior.

With regard to the kinds of labour which Adam Smith has called unproductive, and for which classification his theory has been most objected to, their productiveness to the amount of their worth in the estimation of the society, varying, of course, according to the different degrees of skill acquired, and the different degrees of plenty or scarcity in which they are found, would be fully allowed, though they would still always be distinguished from those more productive kinds of labour which support other classes of the society besides the labourers themselves.

Agricultural labour would stand in the first rank, for this simple reason, that its gross produce is sufficient to maintain a portion of all the three great classes of society; those who live upon rent, those who live upon profits, and those who live | upon 41 wages. Manufacturing and mercantile labour would stand in the next rank; because the value of its produce will support a portion of two of these orders of society. And the unproductive labourers of Adam Smith would stand in the third rank of productiveness; because their labours directly support no other classes but themselves. (8)

This seems to be a simple and obvious classification, and

---

men are happy in proportion as they have an abundance of the commodities they want. If it were the abundance of corn, and the facility with which it was obtained, which gave it the pre-eminence contended for, I should agree to Mr. M.'s conclusion, but the contrary is the fact. Why does the value of corn afford a rent? and why does that rent rise from time to time? because corn rises as it becomes more difficult to produce it. Increase the difficulty, and the value of corn, as well

places the different kinds of labour in a natural order with regard to productiveness, without interfering in any respect with their mutual dependence on each other as stimulants to each other's increase.

[The great objection to this system is, that it makes the *payment* for labour, instead of the quantities of the product, the criterion of productiveness.

42   Yet if we once desert matter, we must adopt this criterion, or every human exertion to avoid pain and obtain pleasure is productive labour.

And if we *do* adopt this criterion, the very same kind of labour will be productive, or not, according as it is paid for, or not.

43   Unproductive labourers are of great importance in the production of wealth indirectly, as demanders, but they cannot, with propriety, be said to create the wealth which pays them.

44   Adam Smith's distinction, which draws the line between what is matter and what is not matter, is probably the most useful and the least objectionable.

---

as of rent, rise still higher. Now unless this peculiar difficulty of obtaining, in the required abundance, a commodity we want, be an advantage, I can see no just reason for the classification adopted. If our supply of coal to accommodate an increasing demand were obtained with more and more labour, coal would rise in value, and many mines would afford a great increase of rent, as well as the usual profits of stock. Would this entitle coal, and the employments connected with it, to any particular pre-eminence? Coals would have a greater value, but it would be from scarcity:—would it not be better to have coals of less value, and in greater plenty? I ask then whether it would not also be very desirable to have corn of less value, and in greater abundance? If Mr. Malthus answers, yes, rent is gone, and the pre-eminence he contends for is gone. If he answer, no, I should like to have some better proofs of the pre-eminence he contends for.[1]

[1] Replaces 'If he answer, no, I trust he will find few to agree with him.'

Susceptibility of accumulation is essential to our usual conceptions of wealth.

Capability of definite valuation is necessary to enable us to 45 estimate the amount of wealth obtained by any kind of labour.

The labour realized upon material products is the only labour 46 which is at once susceptible of accumulation and definite valuation.

The objection of M. Garnier, respecting musical instruments, and the tunes played upon them, answered.

Objections of M. Garnier, respecting the servants of govern- 47 ment, answered.

Some unproductive labour is of much more use and importance 48 than productive labour, but is incapable of being the subject of the gross calculations which relate to national wealth.

Having confined the definition of wealth to material objects, 49 productive labour is that labour which is productive of wealth, that is, so directly productive of it, as to be estimated in the value of the objects produced.

The object of this discussion is not to make subtle distinctions, 50 but to bespeak assent to a useful classification.]

CHAPTER II

ON THE NATURE AND MEASURES
OF VALUE

SECTION I

Of the different Sorts of Value

51   [Two sorts of value are generally admitted—value in use, and value in exchange.

52   The term value is so rarely understood as meaning the mere utility of an object, that if this interpretation of it be retained, it should never be applied without the addition—*in use*.

Value in exchange is founded upon the will and power to exchange one commodity for another.

If nature had, in the first instance, made such a distribution of commodities as now takes place previous to consumption, their exchangeable values could not have been known.

53   An exchange implies not only the power and will to give one article for another more wanted, but a reciprocal demand in the owner of the article wanted for the one proposed to be exchanged for it.

When this reciprocal demand exists, the quantity of one commodity which is given for another, depends upon the relative estimation in which each is held, founded upon the

---

(9) p. 54. *Each commodity &c.*

In all that Mr. M. has yet said about exchangeable value, it appears to depend a great deal on the wants of mankind, and the relative estimation in which they hold commodities. This would be true if men from various countries were to meet in a fair, with a variety of productions, and each with a separate commodity, undisturbed by the competition of any other seller. Commodities, under such circumstances, would be bought and sold according to the relative wants of those attending the fair—but when the wants of society are well

desire to possess, and the difficulty or facility of procuring possession.

Owing to the difference of desires and powers, the bargains thus made were, in the first instance, very different from each other.

By degrees], as is very happily described by Turgot, a current 54 value of all commodities in frequent use would be established.*

It would be known, not only that a pound of venison was worth four pounds of bread, but that it was also worth perhaps a pound of cheese, a quarter of a peck of wheat, a quart of wine, a certain portion of leather, &c. &c. each of an average quality.

Each commodity would in this way measure the exchangeable value of all others, and would, in its turn, be measured by any one of them. Each commodity would also be a representative of value. The possessor of a quart of wine might consider himself in possession of a value equal to four pounds of bread, a pound of cheese, a certain portion of leather, &c. &c. and thus each commodity would, with more or less accuracy and convenience, possess two essential properties of money, that of being both a representative and measure of value.† (9)

[But the frequent want of reciprocal demand, except in large fairs, would throw great obstacles in the way of an average valuation of commodities.

To secure this reciprocal demand, every man would endeavour 55 to keep by him some commodity so generally in request that it would rarely be refused in exchange for what he might want.

* Formation et Distribution des Richesses, § xxxv.   † *Id.* § xli.

---

known, when there are hundreds of competitors who are willing to satisfy those wants, on the condition only that they shall have the known and usual profits, there can be no such rule for regulating the value of commodities.

In such a fair as I have supposed, a man might be willing to give a pound of gold, for a pound of iron, knowing the uses of the latter metal; but when competition freely operated, he could not give that value for iron, and why? because iron would infallibly sink to its cost of production—cost of production being the pivot about which all market price moves.

Cattle were used for this purpose among pastoral nations, on account of the facility of keeping them, and of the frequent exchanges of which they must have been the subject.

56   It is necessary that the commodity adopted for the medium of exchange and measure of value should be in frequent use, and its value well known.

Notwithstanding the peculiar aptitude of the precious metals for a medium of exchange and measure of value, they had not been used for that purpose in Mexico when first discovered.

57   In the old world, where the arts of smelting and refining ores seem to have been known at a very remote period, the appropriate qualities of the precious metals pointed them out in the earliest times as the commodity best fitted for a medium of exchange and measure of value.

When they had been adopted as a general measure of value, they would almost always be the article named, and the quantity of the precious metals for which commodities would exchange, might properly be called their nominal value.

58   This nominal value has been sometimes designated by the term price, which thus represents a more confined sense of the term value.

The introduction of a measure of nominal and relative value, was a step of the highest importance in the progress of society.]

It is very justly observed by Adam Smith, that it is the nominal value of goods, or their prices only, which enter into the consideration of the merchant. It matters very little to him, whether a hundred pounds, or the goods which he purchases with this sum, will command more or less of the necessaries and conveniences of life in Bengal than in London. What he wants is an instrument by

59   which he can obtain the commodities in which he | deals and estimate the relative values of his sales and purchases. His returns

---

(10) p. 58. *It is very justly observed &c. &c.*

I cannot agree with Adam Smith, or with Mr. Malthus, that it is the nominal value of goods, or their prices only, which enter into the consideration of the merchant. He has clearly nothing to do with the value of the necessaries and conveniences of life in Bengal, when he purchases Muslin there,

come to him wherever he lives; and whether it be in London or Calcutta, his gains will be in proportion to the excess of the amount at which he sells his goods compared with the amount which they cost him to bring to market, estimated in the precious metals. (10)

But though the precious metals answer very effectually the most important purposes of a measure of value, in the encouragement they give to the distribution and production of wealth; yet it is quite obvious that they fail as a measure of the exchangeable value of objects in different countries, or at different periods in the same country.

If we are told that the wages of day-labour in a particular country are, at the present time, fourpence a day; or that the revenue of a particular sovereign, 700 or 800 years ago, was 400,000*l.* a year; these statements of nominal value convey no sort of information respecting the condition of the lower classes of people, in the one case, or the resources of the sovereign, in the other. Without further knowledge on the subject, we should be quite at a loss to say, whether the labourers in the country mentioned were starving, or living in great plenty; whether the king in question might be considered as having a very inadequate revenue, or whether the sum mentioned was so great as to be incredible.* |

It is quite obvious that in cases of this kind, and they are of 60 constant recurrence, the value of wages, incomes, or commodities estimated in the precious metals, will be of little use to us alone. What we want further is some estimate of a kind which may be denominated real value in exchange, implying the quantity of the necessaries and conveniences of life which those wages, incomes,

---

* Hume very reasonably doubts the possibility of William the Conqueror's revenue being £400,000 a year, as represented by an ancient historian, and adopted by subsequent writers.

---

with a view to sell them in England; but as he must pay for his goods, either in money, or in goods, and expects to sell them with a profit in money, or in goods, he can not be indifferent to the real value of the medium in which his profits, as well as the value of the goods, are to be realised.[1]

[1] Replaces 'his profit, as the value of the goods, is to be realized.'

or commodities will enable the possessor of them to command. Without this knowledge, the nominal values above mentioned may lead us to the most erroneous conclusions; and in contra-distinction to such values, which often imply an increase or decrease of wealth merely in name, the term real value in exchange seems to be just and appropriate, as implying an increase or decrease in the power of commanding real wealth, or the most substantial goods of life. (11)

---

(11) p. 60. *It is quite obvious &c. &c.*

It is undoubtedly true that by hearing simply that a king possessed at some former time £400,000 a year, we should be quite at a loss to know whether the labourers in the country were starving or living in great plenty. It might be very proper in order to ascertain the real power of this monarch, to inquire what the price of corn and labour was in the country at such time. But having done this, it would be quite wrong to say we had found out what the real value of that king's revenue was. We are told by Humbold, and the fact is a good deal insisted on by Mr. Malthus, that in South America, on a given portion of land with a given[1] quantity of labour   [2] times the quantity of human sustenance can be obtained than from the same quantity of land and with the same quantity of labour[3] in Europe.

A king then in that country might probably with the labour of one thousand men, employed in Agriculture, support an army there 10 times greater than could be supported[4] by a king here having the same number of men at his disposal to provide necessaries. Would he therefore be said to have a revenue of 10 times the value[5]? Mr. Malthus would

---

[1] 'given' replaces 'very small'.
[2] Blank in MS: according to Humboldt, as quoted by Malthus, p. 382, *twenty five.* Humboldt, however, says nothing about the quantity of labour.

[3] 'and with the same quantity of labour' is ins.
[4] The remainder of this sentence replaces 'by the same number of men in England'.
[5] Replaces 'of equal value'.

That a correct measure of real value in exchange would be very desirable cannot be doubted, as it would at once enable us to form a just estimate and comparison of wages, incomes, and commodities, in all countries and at all periods; but when we consider what a measure of real value in exchange implies, we shall feel doubtful whether any one commodity exists, or can easily be supposed to exist, with such properties, as would qualify it to become a standard measure of this kind. Whatever article, or even

---

answer, yes; because he estimates the real value of a revenue by the number of men's labour you are enabled to command with it.

In money value their revenues might be nearly equal,— they might be nearly equal if estimated in iron, cloth, tea, sugar and any other commodity, but in the power of commanding labour the American Monarch might have a very decided superiority. Now to what would this be owing? to the very low value of labour in America—the revenue of the two kings would in my opinion be nearly equal, but in the expenditure of these equal revenues, a great deal of labour, which was cheap, could be obtained by one, a small quantity of labour, which was dear, could be got by the other.

Mr. Malthus justly complains of gold and silver as being variable commodities, and therefore not fit for a measure of real value, for times distant from each other. What we want is a standard measure of value which shall be itself invariable, and therefore shall accurately measure the variations[6] of other things.

And on what does Mr. Malthus fix as an approximation to this standard?

The value of labour. A commodity shall be said to rise or fall accordingly as it can command more or less labour. Mr. Malthus then claims for his standard[7] measure invaria-

---

[6] 'variations' replaces 'value'.   [7] 'standard' is ins.

mass of articles, we refer to, must itself be subject to change; and all that we can hope for is an approximation to the measure which is the object of our search. |

61   We are not however justified, on this account, in giving a different definition of real value in exchange. if the definition already adopted be at once the most usual and the most useful. We have the power indeed arbitrarily to call the labour which has been employed upon a commodity its real value; but in so doing

---

bility! No such thing; he acknowledges that it is subject to the same contingencies and variations as all other things. Why then fix on it? It may be very useful to ascertain from time to time the power of any given revenue to command labour, but why select a commodity that is confessedly variable for a standard measure of value? I can see no reason given but this because "it has been already adopted as the most usual and the most useful." If this be true we have still a right to reject it if it answer not the end for which it was proposed.

Whatever commodity any man selects as a measure of real value, has no other title for adoption, but its being a less variable commodity than any other, and therefore if after a time another commodity possessing this quality in a superior degree be discovered, that ought to be the standard adopted.[1]

Whoever then proposes a measure of real value is bound to shew that the commodity he selects is the least variable of any known.

Does Mr. Malthus comply with this condition?

In no respect whatever. He does not even acknowledge that invariability is the essential quality of a measure of real value, for he says a measure of real value implies a certain[2] quantity of the necessaries and conveniences of life, acknow-

---

[1] The last three paragraphs, be-   [2] 'a certain' replaces 'the'.
ginning 'And on what', are ins.

we use words in a different sense from that in which they are customarily used; we confound at once the very important distinction between *cost* and *value*; and render it almost impossible to explain, with clearness, the main stimulus to the production of wealth, which, in fact, depends upon this distinction.

The right of making definitions must evidently be limited by their propriety, and their use in the science to which they are applied. After we have made a full allowance for the value of

---

ledging that these necessaries and conveniences of life are as variable as any of the commodities whose value they are selected to measure. A piece of silk is worth a quarter of corn, and it becomes worth two quarters of corn—it has doubled in real value says Mr. Malthus—but may not corn have fallen to half its former value, or is it invariable?

It is not invariable answers Mr. Malthus and may have fallen to half its former value. But if that has been the case in the instance mentioned silk has not risen in value—why then should you say it has? the two opinions are not consistent, you must claim invariability for your standard, or abandon it as a measure of real value.

Two commodities are exchangeable for each other—one commands in the market a certain quantity of the other. All at once they both vary in value as compared with all other things, and with each other. With one I can obtain a less quantity than before of iron, tea, sugar, ³ with the other I can obtain a greater quantity of these commodities. Estimated in one of these commodities therefore all other things will appear to have fallen, estimated in the other they will appear to have risen.

If we were sure that nothing had varied except the two commodities, if we knew that precisely the same quantity of labour was required for their production either of the com-

³ Blank in MS: 'cloth' is mentioned below.

commodities in use, or their intrinsic capacities for satisfying the wants of mankind, every other interpretation of the term value seems to refer to some power in exchange; and if it do not refer to the power of an article in exchange for some one commodity named, such as money, it must refer to its power in exchange for 3 or 4, 5 or 6, 8 or 10 together, to the mass of commodities com-

---

modities I have mentioned, tea, sugar, iron, cloth would be an accurate measure of the variations of the other two. I do not think that Mr. Malthus would deny this. Suppose one exchanged for 20 p.c. more cloth than before I should be nearly certain that it would also exchange for 20 p.c. more of iron, or of tea; and if labour had not varied, for 20 p.c. more of labour also, and I should be justified in saying that it had risen 20 p.c. in real value. Suppose the other, on the contrary, would purchase 20 p.c. less of each of these commodities than before. I should be equally justified in saying that it had fallen 20 p.c., in real value. Estimated in each other, one would appear to have risen 40 p.c., and the other to have fallen in a proportionate degree. Now this is the arbitrary definition which I am accused of making—I endeavor to measure the variations in the real value of commodities by comparing their value at different times with another commodity which I have every reason to believe has not varied, and Mr. Malthus does not object to it while I confine it to a large class of commodities. If gold varied compared with all other things, by exchanging for a greater quantity of them, he would call it a rise in the value of gold. If iron, sugar, lead &c. &c. did the same he would still use the same language, but if corn rose, or labour rose, compared with all other commodities, he would say it is not corn or labour which have risen—they are my standard—you must say that corn and labour have remained stationary and all other commodities have fallen. It would be in vain to urge

bined, or to its power of commanding labour which most nearly represents this mass.

There can be no question of the propriety and usefulness of a distinction between the power of a commodity in commanding the precious metals, and its power of commanding the necessaries and conveniences of life, including labour. It is a | distinction 62

---

that new difficulties had occurred in the production of corn —that it was brought from a greater distance, or from employing poorer land more labour was bestowed in order to procure a given quantity, he would acknowledge the fact— he would acknowledge this would be a just cause for saying that any other commodity similarly circumstanced had risen in value, but it would not be allowed for corn, because he had notwithstanding its acknowledged variability chosen that for his standard. We may well apply to him his own observation "We have the power indeed arbitrarily to call corn a measure of real value, but in doing so we use words in a different sense from that in which they are customarily used." "The right of making definitions must evidently be limited by their propriety, and their use in the science to which they are applied."[1]

Length can only be measured by length, capacity by capacity, and value by value. Mr. Malthus thinks that "the term real value in exchange seems to be just and appropriate as implying an increase or decrease in the power of commanding real wealth, or the most substantial goods of life." He does not say the power of commanding real value, but real wealth, he measures value by its power of commanding wealth. But perhaps Mr. Malthus considers wealth as synonymous with value! no, he does no such thing he sees a manifest distinction between them. See page 339 where he says "Wealth, however, it will be allowed, does not always in-

[1] Malthus's p. 61; above, pp. 30-31.

absolutely called for, whenever we are comparing the wealth of
two nations together, or whenever we are estimating the value of
the precious metals in different states and at different periods of
time. (12) And till it has been shewn that some other interpretation of the term real value in exchange, either agrees better with

---

crease in proportion to the increase of value; because an
increase of value may sometimes take place under an actual
diminution of the necessaries, conveniences and luxuries of
life." A given quantity of wealth cannot be a measure of real
value unless it have itself always the same value. There is no
wealth which may not vary in value. Machinery may make
2 pair of stockings of the value of one. Improvements in
Agriculture may make 2 quarters of corn of the value of one,
yet a quarter of corn and a pair of stockings will always constitute the same portion of wealth. Wealth is estimated by
its utility to afford enjoyment to man; value is determined by
facility or difficulty of production. The distinction is marked,
and the greatest confusion arises from speaking of them as
the same.[1]

Mr. Malthus accuses me of confounding the very important
distinction between cost and value. If by cost, Mr. Malthus
means the wages paid for labour, I do not confound cost and
value, because I do not say that a commodity the labour on
which cost a £1,000, will therefore sell for £1,000; it may
sell for £1,100, £1,200, or £1,500,—but I say it will sell for
the same as another commodity the labour on which also
cost £1,000; that is to say, that commodities will be valuable
in proportion to the quantity of labour expended on them[2].
If by cost Mr. Malthus means cost of production, he must
include profits, as well as labour; he must mean what Adam

[1] The Note originally ended here;
the remainder is ins.
[2] 'and the respective quantities
will be represented by their cost,
at the same time and place' is
deleted here.

the sense in which the words are generally applied, or is decidedly more useful in an inquiry into the nature and causes of the wealth of nations, I shall continue to think, that the most proper definition of real value in exchange, in contradistinction to nominal value in exchange, is, the power of commanding the necessaries

---

Smith calls natural price, which is synonymous with value.[3]

A commodity is at its natural[4] value, when it repays by its price,[5] all the expences that have been bestowed, from first to last to produce it and[6] bring it to market. If then my expression conveys the same meaning as cost of production, it is nearly what I wish it to do.

The real[7] value of a commodity I think means the same thing as its cost of production, and the relative[8] cost of production of two commodities is nearly in proportion to the quantity of labour from first to last respectively bestowed upon them. There is nothing arbitrary in this language; I may be wrong in seeing a connection where there is none, and that is a good argument against the adoption of my measure of value, but then the objection rests on an error in principle, and not on an error in nomenclature.

(12) p. 61. *There can be no question &c., &c.*

I agree with Mr. Malthus, but we have the power to do this by ascertaining the value of money, in the command of labour, for any time that we may wish to make the comparison.

It is not necessary for this purpose to constitute necessaries, conveniences or labour the measure of real value.

---

[3] A remark pencilled by Ricardo on the margin, and then rubbed out, is faintly legible: 'I do not say a commodity will be worth its cost in labour, but in proportion to its cost in labour.' Cp. *Principles*, ed. 3, above, I, 47, n.

[4] 'natural' is written above 'just', which however is not deleted.
[5] 'at the usual rate,' is del. here.
[6] 'produce it and' is ins.
[7] 'real' is ins.
[8] 'relative' is ins.

and conveniences of life, including labour, as distinguished from the power of commanding the precious metals.

[There are then three sorts of value;—1. Value in use, or the utility of an object. 2. Nominal value in exchange, or value in money. 3. Real value in exchange, or value in necessaries, conveniences and labour.

63   These distinctions are in the main those of Adam Smith, and belong to his system.]

SECTION II

Of Demand and Supply as they affect Exchangeable Value

The terms Demand and Supply are so familiar to the ear of
64 every reader, and their application in | single instances so fully understood, that in the slight use which has hitherto been made of them, it has not been thought necessary to interrupt the course of the reasoning by explanations and definitions. These terms, however, though in constant use, are by no means applied with precision. And before we proceed farther, it may be advisable to clear this part of the ground as much as possible, that we may be certain of the footing on which we stand. This will appear to be the more necessary, as it must be allowed, that of all the principles in political economy, there is none which bears so large a share in the phenomena which come under its consideration as the principle of supply and demand.

It has been already stated, that all value in exchange depends upon the power and will to exchange one commodity for another; and when, by the introduction of a general measure of value and medium of exchange, society has been divided, in common language, into buyers and sellers, demand may be defined to be,

---

(13) p. 64. *Demand may be defined to be the will combined with the power to purchase.*

This definition of demand must be remembered, because in the subsequent part of his work Mr. M. appears to forget it. In the last chapter, where he speaks of the pernicious consequences arising from a want of demand, he appears to me

the will combined with the power to purchase, (13) and supply, the production of commodities combined with the intention to sell them. In this state of things, the relative values of commodities in money, or their prices, are determined by the relative demand for them, compared with the supply of them; and this law appears to be so general, that probably not a single instance of a change of price can be found which may not be satisfactorily traced to some previous change in the causes which affect the demand or supply. |

In examining the truth of this position we must constantly bear 65 in mind the terms in which it is expressed; and recollect that, when prices are said to be determined by demand and supply, it is not meant that they are determined either by the demand alone or the supply alone, but by their relation to each other.

But how is this relation to be ascertained? It has been sometimes said that supply is always equal to demand, because no permanent supply of any commodity can take place for which there is not a demand so effective as to take off all that is offered. In one sense of the terms in which demand and supply have occasionally been used, this position may be granted. The actual *extent* of the demand, compared with the actual *extent* of the supply, are always on an average proportioned to each other. If the supply be ever so small, the extent of the effective demand cannot be greater; and if the supply be ever so great, the extent of the demand, or the consumption, will either increase in proportion, or a part of it will become useless and cease to be produced. It cannot, therefore, be in this sense that a change in the proportion of demand to supply affects prices; because in this sense demand and supply always bear the same relation to each other. And this uncertainty in the use of these terms renders it an absolutely necessary preliminary in the present inquiry clearly to ascertain what is the nature of that change in the mutual relation

---

to forget that the power as well as the will to purchase is required. He says, that men will not demand because they prefer indolence to work; but they cannot produce if they will not work; and if they do not produce, they may have the will, but they want the other essential quality of demand; they want the power.

of demand and supply, on which the prices of commodities so
entirely depend. |

66   The demand for a commodity has been defined to be, the will
combined with the power to purchase it.

The greater is the degree of this will and power with regard to
any particular commodity, the greater or the more intense may
be fairly said to be the demand for it. But however great this will
and power may be among the purchasers of a commodity, none
of them will be disposed to give a high price for it, if they can
obtain it at a low one; and as long as the abilities and competition
of the sellers induce them to bring the quantity wanted to market
at a low price, the real intensity of the demand will not shew
itself. (14)

If a given number of commodities, attainable by labour alone,
were to become more difficult of acquisition, as they would
evidently not be obtained unless by means of increased exertion,
we might surely consider such increased exertion, if applied, as
an evidence of a greater intensity of demand, or of a power and
will to make a greater sacrifice in order to obtain them.

In fact it may be said, that the giving a greater price for a commodity absolutely and necessarily implies a greater intensity of
demand; and that the real question is, what are the causes which
either call forth or render unnecessary the expression of this
intensity of demand?

It has been justly stated, that the causes which tend to raise the
price of any article estimated in some commodity named, and
supposed for short periods not essentially to vary, are an increase
67   in | the number or wants of its purchasers, or a deficiency in its

---

(14) p. 66. *The greater is the degree &c.*

I agree with Mr. Malthus (see 54)[1]; however great the
demand for a commodity may be, its price will be finally
regulated by the competition of the sellers,—it will settle at
or about its natural price; that price, which, as Adam Smith
observes,[2] is necessary to give the current rate of wages to the
workmen, and the current rate of profits to the capitalist. On

[1] *i.e.* Note (9) above.   [2] *Wealth of Nations*, Bk. I, ch.
vii; Cannan's ed., vol. I, p. 57.

supply; and the causes which lower the price are a diminution in the number or wants of its purchasers, or an increased abundance in its supply.

The first class of these causes is obviously calculated to call forth the expression of a greater intensity of demand, and the other of a less.

If, for instance, a commodity which had been habitually demanded and consumed by a thousand purchasers were suddenly to be wanted by two thousand, it is clear that before this increased extent of demand could be supplied, some must go without what they wanted; and it is scarcely possible to suppose that the intensity of individual demand would not increase among a sufficient number of these two thousand purchasers, to take off all the commodity produced at an increased price. At the same time, if we could suppose it possible that the wills and powers of the purchasers, or the intensity of their demand, would not admit of increase, it is quite certain that, however the matter might be settled among the contending competitors, no rise of price could take place.

In the same manner, if a commodity were to be diminished one half in quantity, it is scarcely possible to suppose that a sufficient number of the former purchasers would not be both willing and able to take off the whole of the diminished quantity at a higher price; but if they really would not or could not do this, the price could not rise.

On the other hand, if the permanent cost of producing the commodity were doubled, it is evident | that only such a quantity 68 could be permanently produced as would supply the wants of

---

a comparison of the uses of iron, and gold, the demanders might be both able and willing to give more for iron, than for gold; but they cannot; the competition of the sellers prevents it and sinks the value of both metals to their cost of production, to their natural price.—The market price of a commodity may from an unusual demand, or from a deficiency of supply, rise above its natural price, but this does not overturn the doctrine that the great regulator of price is cost of production.

those who were able and willing to make a sacrifice for the attain-
ment of their wishes equal to double the amount of what they did
before. The quantity of the commodity which would be brought
to market under these circumstances might be extremely different.
It might be reduced to the supply of a single individual, or might
remain precisely the same as before. If it were reduced to the
supply of a single individual, it would be a proof that only one of
all the former purchasers was both able and willing to make an
effective demand for it at the advanced price. If the supply
remained the same, it would be a proof that all the purchasers
were in this state, but that the expression of this intensity of
demand had not before been rendered necessary. In the latter
case, there would be the same quantity supplied and the same
quantity demanded; but there would be a much greater intensity
of demand called forth; and this may be fairly said to be a most
important change in the relation between the supply and the
demand of these commodities; because, without the increased
intensity of demand, which in this case takes place, the commodity
would cease to be produced; that is, the failure of the supply
would be contingent upon the failure of the power or will to
make a greater sacrifice for the object sought.

Upon the same principles, if a commodity were to become
much more abundant, compared with the former number of
69 purchasers, this in-|creased supply could not be all sold, unless the
price were lowered. Each seller wishing to dispose of that part
of the commodity which he possessed would go on lowering it
till he had effected his object; and though the wills and powers of
the old purchasers might remain undiminished, yet as the commodity could be obtained without the expression of the same
intensity of demand as before, this demand would of course not
then shew itself.

A similar effect would obviously take place from the consumers of a commodity requiring a less quantity of it.

If, instead of a temporary abundance of supply compared with

---

(15) p. 69. *If instead &c.*

Mr. Malthus here substantially admits, that it is not the
relation of demand to supply, which finally and permanently
regulates the price of commodities, but the cost of their pro-

the demand, the cost of producing any particular commodity were greatly diminished, the fall of price would in the same manner be occasioned by an increased abundance of supply, either actual or contingent. (15) In almost all practical cases it would be an actual and permanent increase, because the competition of sellers would lower the price; and it very rarely happens that a fall of price does not occasion an increased consumption. On the supposition, however, of the very rare case that a definite quantity only of the commodity was required, whatever might be its price, it is obvious that from the competition of the producers a greater quantity would be brought to market than could be consumed, till the price was reduced in proportion to the increased facility of production; and this excess of supply would be always contingent on the circumstance of the price being at any time higher than the price which returns average profits. | In this case of a fall of 70 prices, as in the other of a rise of prices, the actual quantity of the commodity supplied and consumed may possibly, after a short struggle, be the same as before; yet it cannot be said that the demand is the same. It may indeed exist precisely in the same degree, and the actual consumers of the commodity might be perfectly ready to give what they gave before rather than go without it; but such has been the alteration in the means of supply compared with the demand, that the competition of the producers renders the same intensity of demand no longer necessary to effect the supply required; and not being necessary, it is of course not called forth, and the price falls.

It is evidently, therefore, not merely *extent* of actual demand, nor even the extent of actual demand compared with the extent of actual supply, which raises prices, but such a change in the relation between supply and demand as renders necessary the expression of a greater intensity of demand, in order either peaceably to divide any actual produce, or prevent the future produce of the same kind from failing.

And, in the same manner, it is not merely *extent* of actual

---

duction. On the other hand I do not deny, that in the progress of the rise or fall of commodities, there may be, what is usually termed, an increased demand, or an increased supply.

supply, nor the extent of the actual supply compared with the actual demand, that lowers prices, but such a change in the relation of the supply, compared with the demand, as renders a fall of price necessary, in order to take off a temporary abundance, or to prevent a constant excess of supply contingent upon a diminu- |
71 tion in the cost of production, without a proportionate diminution in the price of the produce.

If the terms demand and supply be understood and used in the way here described, there is no case of price, whether temporary or permanent, which they will not determine; and in every instance of bargain and sale it will be perfectly correct to say that the price will depend upon the relation of the demand to the supply.

I wish it particularly to be observed that in this discussion I have not given any new meaning to the terms, demand and supply. In the use which I have occasionally made of the words *intense* and *intensity* as applied to demand, my sole purpose has been to explain the meaning which has hitherto always been attached to the term demand when it is said to raise prices. Mr. Ricardo in his chapter *On the influence of demand and supply on prices**, observes, that "the demand for a commodity cannot be said to increase, if no additional quantity of it be purchased or consumed." But it is obvious, as I have before remarked, that it is not in the sense of mere extent of consumption that demand raises prices, because it is almost always when the prices are the lowest that the *extent* of consumption is the greatest. This, therefore, cannot be the meaning hitherto attached to the term, demand, when it is said to raise prices. Mr. Ricardo, however, subsequently quotes Lord Lauderdale's statements respecting
72 value†, and allows them to be true, | as applied to monopolized commodities, and the market prices of all other commodities for

* Principles of Polit. Econ. chap. xxx. p. [382]. 2d edit.
† Id. p. [384].

---

(16) p. 72. *This is true if we include all the component parts of price stated by Adam Smith, though not if we consider only those stated by Mr. Ricardo.*

By cost of production I invariably mean wages and profits, Adam Smith includes rent. I may have two loaves on my

MEASURES OF VALUE

43

a limited period. He would allow, therefore, that the deficiency
of any article in a market would occasion a great demand for it,
compared with the supply, and raise its price, although in this
case less than usual of the article must be purchased by the consumers. Demand, in this sense, is obviously quite different from
the sense in which Mr. Ricardo had before used the term. The one
implies extent of consumption, the other intensity of demand, or
the will and power to make a greater sacrifice in order to obtain
the object wanted. It is in this latter sense alone that demand
raises prices; and my sole object in this section is to shew that,
whenever we talk of demand and supply as influencing prices,
whether market or natural, the terms should always be understood
in the sense in which Mr. Ricardo and every other person has
hitherto understood them, when speaking of commodities bought
and sold in a market.

SECTION III

Of the Cost of Production as it affects Exchangeable Value

It may be said, perhaps, that even according to the view given
of demand and supply in the preceding section, the permanent
prices of a great mass of commodities will be determined by the
cost of their production. This is true, if we in-|clude all the com- 73
ponent parts of price stated by Adam Smith, though not if we
consider only those stated by Mr. Ricardo. (16) But, in reality,
the two systems, one of which accounts for the prices of the great
mass of commodities by the cost of their production, and the
other accounts for the prices of all commodities, under all circumstances, permanent as well as temporary, by the relation of
the demand to the supply, though they touch each other neces-

---

table one obtained from very fertile land, the other from the
very worst in cultivation; in the latter there will not be any
rent, the whole of its value will be only sufficient to pay
wages and profit. It is this loaf which will regulate the value
of all loaves, and although it will be true that the rent which

sarily at a greater number of points, have an essentially different origin, and require, therefore, to be very carefully distinguished.

In all the transactions of bargain and sale there is evidently a principle in constant operation, which can determine, and does actually determine, the prices of commodities, quite independently of any considerations of cost, or of the quantity of labour and capital employed upon their production. And this is found to operate, not only permanently upon that class of commodities which may be considered as monopolies, but temporarily and immediately upon all commodities, and strikingly and preeminently so upon all sorts of raw produce.

It has never been a matter of doubt that the principle of supply and demand determines exclusively, and very regularly and accurately, the prices of monopolized commodities, without any reference to the cost of their production; and our daily and uniform experience shews us that the prices of raw products, particularly of those which are most affected by the seasons, are at the moment of their sale determined always by the higgling of | the market, and differ widely in different years and at different times, while the labour and capital employed upon them may have been very nearly the same. This is so obvious, that probably very few would hesitate to believe what is certainly true, that, if in the next year we could by any process exempt the farmers from

74

---

the other loaf will afford will be equal to all the difference in the expence of growing the corn of which it is made [1] and the corn of which the standard loaf is made, yet it is only in consequence of this difference that rent is paid. Twenty different loaves all selling for the same price may yield different portions of rent, but it is one only, that which yields no rent, which regulates the value of the rest, and which must be considered as the standard. In truth then in the cost of production of all agricultural produce there is no rent, for

[1] The remainder of the sentence replaces 'yet it is in consequence of this difference in the fertility of the land on which this corn is grown and the fertility of that on which the corn is grown from which the other loaf is made, and which regulates the value of all corn that rent is paid.'

all cost in the production of their corn and cattle, provided no change were made in the quantity brought to market, and the society had the same wants and the same powers of purchasing, the prices of raw products would be the same as if they had cost the usual labour and expense to procure them.

With regard, therefore, to a class of commodities of the greatest extent, it is acknowledged that the existing market prices are, at the moment they are fixed, determined upon a principle quite distinct from the cost of production, and that these prices are in reality almost always different from what they would have been, if this cost had regulated them. (17)

There is indeed another class of commodities, such as manufactures, particularly those in which the raw material is cheap, where the existing market prices much more frequently coincide with the cost of production, and may appear, therefore, to be exclusively determined by it. Even here, however, our familiar experience shews us that any alteration in the demand and supply quite overcomes for a time the influence of this cost; and further, when we come to examine the subject more closely, we find that the cost of production | itself only influences the prices of these 75 commodities as the payment of this cost is the necessary condition of their continued supply.

But if this be true, it follows that the great principle of demand

---

the value of that produced from the capital last employed yields a compensation for wages, and a compensation for profits of capital, but no compensation for[2] rent. In this sense only do I differ from Adam Smith.

(17) p. 74. *With regard &c.*

It is admitted by every body that demand and supply govern market price, but what is it determines supply at a particular price? cost of production. Why is corn almost invariably higher here than in France? not on account of the greater demand for it, but on account of its superior cost of production in this country.

[2] 'compensation for' is ins.

and supply is called into action to determine what Adam Smith calls natural prices as well as market prices. (18)

It will be allowed without hesitation that no change can take place in the market prices of commodities without some previous change in the relation of demand and supply. And the question is, whether the same position is true in reference to natural prices? This question must of course be determined by attending carefully to the nature of the change which an alteration in the cost of production occasions in the state of the demand and supply, and particularly to the specific and immediate cause by which the change of price that takes place is effected.

We all allow, that when the cost of production diminishes, a fall of price is generally the consequence; but what is it, specifically, which forces down the price of the commodity? It has been shewn in the preceding section that it is an actual or contingent excess of supply.

We all allow that, when the cost of production increases, the prices of commodities generally rise. But what is it which specifically forces up the price? It has been shewn that it is a contingent failure of supply. Remove these contingencies, that is, let the extent of the supply remain exactly the same, without contingent failure or excess, whether the price of production
76 rises or falls, and | there is not the slightest ground for supposing that any variation of price would take place.

If, for instance, all the commodities that are consumed in this

_____

(18) p. 75. *But if this be true*

The author forgets Adam Smith's definition of natural price, or he would not say that demand and supply could determine natural price. Natural price is only another name for cost of production. When any commodity sells for that price which will repay the wages for labour expended on it, will also afford rent, and profit at their then current rate, Adam Smith would say that commodity was at its natural price. Now these charges would remain the same, whether commodities were much or little demanded, whether they sold at a high or low market price. A hatter can produce

country, whether agricultural or manufactured, could be produced, during the next ten years, without labour, and yet could
only be supplied exactly in the same quantities as they would be
in a natural state of things; then, supposing the wills and the
powers of the purchasers to remain the same, there cannot be a
doubt that all prices would also remain the same. But, if this be
allowed, it follows, that the relation of the supply to the demand,
either actual or contingent, is the dominant principle in the determination of prices whether market or natural, and that the cost
of production can do nothing but in subordination to it, that is,
merely as this cost affects actually or contingently the relation
which the supply bears to the demand. (19)

It is not however necessary to resort to imaginary cases in order
to fortify this conclusion. Actual experience shews the principle
in the clearest light.

In the well known instance, noticed by Adam Smith, of the
insufficient pay of curates, notwithstanding all the efforts of the
legislature to raise it,* a striking proof is afforded that the *permanent* price of an article is determined by the demand and supply,
and not by the cost of production. The real cost of production
would, in this case, be more likely to be increased than diminished
by the | subscriptions of benefactors; but being paid by others 7
and not by the individuals themselves, it does not regulate and
limit the supply; and this supply, on account of such encourage-

* Wealth of Nations, Book I. c. x. p. 202. 6th edit.

10,000 hats at the same rate of charge that he can produce
1000,—their natural price whether he produces the one
quantity or the other¹ is therefore the same, but their market
price will depend on supply and demand—the supply will be
finally determined by the natural price—that is to say by the
cost of production.

(19) p. 76. *If for instance*

These positions those which have preceded them and
those which follow² are not that I know of disputed by any
body.

¹ Last nine words are ins.   ² Last nine words are ins.

ment, becoming and continuing abundant, the price is and must always be low, whatever may be the real cost of the education given.

The effects of the poor-rates in lowering the wages of labour present another practical instance of the same kind. It is not probable that public money should be more economically managed than the income of individuals. Consequently the cost of rearing a family cannot be supposed to be diminished by parish assistance; but, a part of the expense being borne by the public, a price of labour adequate to the maintenance of a certain family is no longer a necessary condition of its supply; and as, by means of parish rates, this supply can be obtained without such wages, the real costs of supplying labour no longer regulate its price.

In fact, in every kind of bounty upon production, the same effects must necessarily take place; and just in proportion as such bounties tend to lower prices, they shew that prices depend upon the supply compared with the demand, and not upon the costs of production.

But the most striking instance which can well be conceived to shew that the cost of production only influences the prices of commodities as it regulates their supply, is continually before our eyes, in the artificial value which is given to Bank notes, by |
78 limiting their amount. Mr. Ricardo's admirable and efficient plan for this purpose proceeds upon the just principle, that, if you can

---

(20) p. 77. *But the most striking*

I quite agree with Mr. Malthus observations in this paragraph,[1] but he forgets that the issuers of paper money which has no value are in possession of a peculiar privilege. If every man might issue paper money in what quantity he pleased and which he was under no obligation to redeem [2] how long would it have any value above its cost of production.

Mr. Malthus mistakes the question—I do not say that the value of a commodity will always conform to its natural

[1] The following passage is del. here: 'but they are not applicable to any other commodity but paper money. Money is not consumed.'
[2] Last nine words are ins.

limit the supply of notes, so that they shall not exceed the quantity of gold which would have circulated, if the currency had been metallic, you will keep the notes always of the same value as gold. And I am confident he would allow that if this limitation could be completely effected without the paper being exchangeable for gold, the value of the notes would not be altered. But, if an article which costs comparatively nothing in making, though it performs one of the most important functions of gold, can be kept to the value of gold by being supplied in the same quantity, it is the clearest of all possible proofs that the value of gold itself no further depends upon the cost of its production, than as this cost influences its supply, and that if the cost were to cease, provided the supply were not increased, the value of gold in this country would still remain the same. (20)

It does not, however, in any degree follow from what has been said, that labour and the costs of production have not a most powerful effect upon prices. But the true way of considering these costs is, as the necessary condition of the supply of the objects wanted.

Although, at the time of the actual exchange of two commodities, no circumstance affects it but the relation of the supply to the demand; yet, as almost all the objects of human desire are obtained by the instrumentality of human exertion, it is | clear 79 that the supply of these objects must be regulated—first, by the

---

price without an additional supply, but I say that the cost of production regulates the supply, and therefore regulates the price.

And let me further observe that I say this is true only in cases where there is no monopoly, and every one is free to supply the commodities in such quantity as he chuses. All the instances brought forward by Mr. Malthus are either cases of close monopoly or cases where a part of the natural price is paid by other people, as in the instance of poor rates sinking the price of labour; or bounties on production sinking the value of the commodity raised, the producer being entitled to the bounty.

quantity and direction of this exertion; secondly, by the assistance which it may receive from the results of previous labour; and thirdly, by the abundance or scarcity of the materials on which it has to work, and of the food of the labourer. It is of importance, therefore, to consider the different conditions which must be fulfilled, in order that any commodity should continue to be brought to market.

The first condition is, that the labour which has been expended on it should be so remunerated in the value of the objects given in exchange, as to encourage the exertion of a sufficient quantity of industry in the direction required, as without such adequate remuneration the supply of the commodity must necessarily fail. If this labour should be of a very severe kind, few comparatively would be able or willing to engage in it; and, upon the common principles of exchangeable value before explained, it would rise in price. If the work were of a nature to require an uncommon degree of dexterity and ingenuity, a rise of price would take place in a greater degree; but not certainly, as stated by Adam Smith, on account of the esteem which men have for such talents,* but on account of their rarity, and the consequent rarity of the effects produced by them. In all these cases the remuneration will be regulated, not by the intrinsic qualities of the commodities produced, but by the state of the demand for them compared with 80 the supply, and of course by the demand and supply | of the sort of labour which produced them. If the commodities have been obtained by the exertion of manual labour exclusively, aided at least only by the unappropriated bounties of nature, the whole remuneration will, of course, belong to the labourer, and the usual value of this remuneration, in the existing state of the society, would be the usual price of the commodity.

The second condition to be fulfilled is, that the assistance which may have been given to the labourer, from the previous accumulation of objects which facilitate future production, should be so remunerated as to continue the application of this assistance to the production of the commodities required. If by means of certain advances to the labourer of machinery, food, and materials previously collected, he can execute eight or ten times as much work as he could without such assistance, the person furnishing them might appear, at first, to be entitled to the difference between

* Wealth of Nations, Book I. c. vi. p. 71. 6th edit.

the powers of unassisted labour and the powers of labour so
assisted. But the prices of commodities do not depend upon their
intrınsic utility, but upon the supply and the demand. The increased powers of labour would naturally produce an increased
supply of commodities; their prices would consequently fall; and
the remuneration for the capital advanced would soon be reduced
to what was necessary, in the existing state of the society, to bring
the articles to the production of which they were applied to
market. With regard to the labourers employed, as neither their
exertions nor their skill would | necessarily be much greater than 81
if they had worked unassisted, their remuneration would be
nearly the same as before, and would depend entirely upon the
exchangeable value of the kind of labour they had contributed,
estimated in the usual way by the demand and the supply. It is
not, therefore, quite correct to represent, as Adam Smith does,
the profits of capital as a deduction from the produce of labour.
They are only a fair remuneration for that part of the production
contributed by the capitalist, estimated exactly in the same way
as the contribution of the labourer.

The third condition to be fulfilled is, that the price of commodities should be such as to effect the continued supply of the food
and raw materials used by the labourers and capitalists; and we
know that this price cannot be paid without yielding a rent to the
landlord on almost all the land actually in use. In speaking of the
landlords, Adam Smith's language is again exceptionable. He
represents them, rather invidiously, as loving to reap where they
have never sown, and as obliging the labourer to pay for a licence
to obtain those natural products, which, when land was in common, cost only the trouble of collecting.† But he would himself
be the first to acknowledge that, if land were not appropriated, its
produce would be, beyond comparison, less abundant, and consequently dearer; and, if it be appropriated, some persons or
other must necessarily be the proprietors. It matters not to the
society whether these | persons are the same or different from the 82
actual labourers of the land. The price of the produce will be
determined by the general supply compared with the general
demand, and will be precisely the same, whether the labourer pays
a rent, or uses the land without rent. The only difference is that,
in the latter case, what remains of this price, after paying the

† Wealth of Nations, Book I. ch. vi. p. 74. 6th edit.

labour and capital, will go to the same person that contributed the labour, which is almost equivalent to saying, that the labourer would be better off, if he were a possessor of land as well as labour —a fact not to be disputed, but which by no means implies that the labourer, who in the lottery of human life has not drawn a prize of land, suffers any hardship or injustice in being obliged to give something in exchange for the use of what belongs to another. The possessors of land, whoever they may be, conduct themselves, with regard to their possessions, exactly in the same way as the possessors of labour and of capital, and exchange what they have, for as many other commodities as the society is willing to give them for it.

The three conditions therefore above specified must, in every society, be necessarily fulfilled, in order to obtain the supply of by far the greater part of the commodities which it wants; and the compensation which fulfils these conditions, or the price of any exchangeable commodity, may be considered as consisting of three parts—that which pays the wages of the labourer employed 83 in its production; that which pays the profits of capital | by which such production has been facilitated; and that which pays the

---

(21) p. 83. *The price which fulfils &c.*

In this account of necessary or natural price Mr. Malthus has in substance said the same as Adam Smith has done, in all which I fully agree, but[1] is he not inconsistent in maintaining that natural price is regulated by supply and demand. Indeed in the latter part of Page 84 he says that the value of the[2] component parts of natural price or cost of production is itself determined by the relation of the demand to the supply[3] of those component parts. Now here Mr. Malthus entirely changes his original proposition. He began by saying that the natural price of a commodity depended upon the relation of the demand to the supply of[4] that commodity,

[1] 'I think it is not regulated by supply and demand.' is del. here.
[2] 'value of the' is ins.
[3] Replaces 'by the demand and supply'.
[4] Replaces 'upon the demand for or supply of'.

rent of land, or the remuneration for the raw materials and food furnished by the landlord;—the price of each of these component parts being determined exactly by the same causes as those which determine the price of the whole.

The price which fulfils these conditions is precisely what Adam Smith calls the natural price. I should be rather more disposed to call it the necessary price, because the term necessary better expresses a reference to the conditions of supply, and is, on that account, susceptible of a more simple definition. (21) To explain natural price, Adam Smith is obliged to use a good deal of circumlocution; and though he makes it on the whole sufficiently clear, yet, as he calls to his assistance two other terms, each of which might almost as well have been used as the one adopted, the definition is not quite satisfactory.* If, however, we use the term suggested, the definition of necessary price will be very easy and simple. It will be, the price necessary, in the actual circumstances of the society, to bring the commodity regularly to the market. This is only a shorter description of what Adam Smith means by natural price, as contradistinguished from market price,

* Book I. chap. vii.

—a proposition which I dispute; he now says that the natural price of a commodity depends upon the demand for and supply of the instruments necessary for its production, that is to say that its cost depends on the varying value of the labour, of the profits, and of the rent of which such cost is made up. On this subject I shall have some remarks to make in another part of this work:—I content myself with pointing out here the essential difference between the two propositions —the latter in fact is this "The natural price of a commodity may rise or fall because its cost of production may rise or fall." No one would dispute this. This is only saying that cost of production is regulated by [5] the laws which determine rent, profits and wages. We shall see how far these are influenced by supply and demand.[6]

5 Replaces 'depends on'.   6 Last two sentences are ins.

or the price at which commodities actually sell in the market, which, from the variations of the seasons or the accidental mis-calculations of the suppliers, are sometimes sold higher and 84 sometimes lower than | the price which is necessary to fulfil the conditions of a regular supply.

When a commodity is sold at this its natural price, Adam Smith says, it is sold for precisely what it is worth. But here, I think, he has used the term worth in an unusual sense. Commodities are continually said to be worth more than they have cost, ordinary profits included; and according to the customary and proper use of the term *worth*, we could never say, that a certain quantity of corn, or any other article, was not worth more when it was scarce, although no more labour and capital might have been employed about it. The *worth* of a commodity is its market price, not its natural or necessary price; it is its value in exchange, not its cost; and this is one of the instances in which Adam Smith has not been sufficiently careful to keep them separate.*

But if it appear generally that the cost of production only determines the prices of commodities, as the payment of it is the necessary condition of their supply, and that the component parts of this cost are themselves determined by the same causes which determine the whole, it is obvious that we cannot get rid of the principle of demand and supply by referring to the cost of pro-duction. Natural and necessary prices appear to be regulated by this principle, as well as market prices; and the only difference is, that the former are regulated by the ordinary and average relation of the demand to the supply, and the latter, when they differ from 85 the | former, depend upon the extraordinary and accidental rela-tions of the demand to the supply.

* Book I. chap. vii.

SECTION IV

Of the Labour which a Commodity has Cost considered as a Measure of Exchangeable Value

Adam Smith, in his chapter on the real and nominal price of commodities,† in which he considers labour as an universal and accurate measure of value, has introduced some confusion into his inquiry by not adhering strictly to the same mode of applying the labour which he proposes for a measure.

Sometimes he speaks of the value of a commodity as being determined by the quantity of labour which its production has cost, and sometimes by the quantity of labour which it will command in exchange.

These two measures are essentially different; and, though certainly neither of them can come under the description of a standard, one of them is a very much more useful and accurate measure of value than the other.

When we consider the degree in which labour is fitted to be a measure of value in the first sense used by Adam Smith, that is, in reference to the quantity of labour which a commodity has cost in its production, we shall find it radically defective. |

In the first place, a moment's consideration will shew us that it cannot be applied in a positive sense. It is indeed almost a contradiction in terms to say that the exchangeable value of a commodity is proportioned to the quantity of labour employed upon it. Exchangeable value, as the term implies, evidently means value in exchange for some other commodities; but if, when more labour is employed upon one commodity, more labour is also employed on the others for which it is exchanged, it is quite obvious that the exchangeable value of the first commodity cannot be proportioned to the labour employed upon it. If, for instance, at the same time that the labour of producing corn increases, the labour of producing money and many other commodities increases, there is at once an end of our being able to say with truth that all things become more or less valuable in proportion as more or less labour is employed in their production. In this case it is obvious that more labour has been employed upon corn, although a bushel of corn may still exchange for no more money nor labour

† Book I. chap. v.

than before. The exchangeable value of corn, therefore, has certainly not altered in proportion to the additional quantity of labour which it has cost in its production. (22)

But, even if we take this measure always in a relative sense, that is, if we say that the exchangeable value of commodities is determined by the *comparative* quantity of labour expended upon each, there is no stage of society in which it will be found correct.|

In the very earliest periods, when not only land was in common, but scarcely any capital was used to assist manual exertions, exchanges would be constantly made with but little reference to the quantity of labour which each commodity might have cost. The greatest part of the objects exchanged would be raw products of various kinds, such as game, fish, fruits, &c. with regard to which, the effects of labour are always uncertain. One man might have employed five days' labour in procuring an object which he would subsequently be very happy to exchange for some other object that might have cost a more fortunate labourer only two, or perhaps one day's exertion. And this disproportion between the exchangeable value of objects and the labour which they had cost in production would be of perpetual recurrence.

I cannot, therefore, agree either with Adam Smith or Mr. Ricardo in thinking that, "in that rude state of society which precedes both the accumulation of stock and the appropriation of land, the

---

(22) p. 86. *If for instance*

I see no inconsistency, in such case, in saying that corn, labour, and money have all altered in exchangeable [1] value. I compare them with the value of sugar, iron, shoes, cloth, copper &c. &c., and I find that they will exchange for more of all these things than before; where then can be the impropriety of saying that these three commodities have risen in value, altho they exchange for precisely the same quantity of each other as before? I am under an absolute necessity of saying this, or of saying that sugar, iron, shoes, cloth, copper and a thousand other commodities have fallen in value, and

[1] 'exchangeable' is ins.

proportion between the quantities of labour necessary for ac-
quiring different objects seems to be the only circumstance which
can afford any rule for exchanging them for one another."* The
rule, which would be acted upon in the exchange of commodities,
is unquestionably that which has been so happily described by
Turgot, and which I have stated in the first section of this chapter.
The results of this rule might or might not agree, on an average,
with those of the rule | founded on the quantity of labour which   88
each article had cost; but if they did not, or if commodities were
found by accident, or the labour employed upon them was utterly
unknown when they were brought to market, the society would
never be at a loss for a rule to determine their exchangeable value;
and it is probable that the exchanges actually made in this stage
of society would be less frequently proportioned to the labour
which each object had cost than in any other.

But in fact there is scarcely any stage of society, however
barbarous, where the cost of production is confined exclusively
to labour. At a very early period, profits will be found to form
an important part of this cost, and consequently to enter largely
into the question of exchangeable value as a necessary condition of
supply. To make even a bow and arrow, it is obviously necessary
that the wood and reed should be properly dried and seasoned;

* Principles of Polit. Econ. c. i. p. [13]. 2d edit.

---

if I adopt this latter term does not Mr. Malthus's objection
offer itself in full force, that while all these commodities will
exchange for each other in the same proportions as before,
we affirm that their value has fallen? Suppose the mines were
not to afford the same quantity of silver that they usually
have done with the same quantity of labour, and that in
consequence silver doubled in value. If tea sold for 8/- p.r
lb. before, it would then sell for 4/-. If corn had sold for
80/- p.r quarter, it would then sell for 40/-. But suppose tea
to become scarce, and to rise in this valuable medium to 8/-,
and corn to be obtained with more labour, and to rise to
80/-, would it not still be true that corn, tea, and money had
all doubled in value?

and the time that these materials must necessarily be kept by the workman before his work is completed, introduces at once a new element into the computation of cost. We may estimate the labour employed in any sort of capital just upon the same principle as the labour employed in the immediate production of the commodity. But the varying quickness of the returns is an entirely new element, which has nothing to do with the quantity of labour employed upon the capital, and yet, in every period of society, the earliest as well as the latest, is of the utmost importance in the determination of prices. (23) |

89   The fixed capital necessary to hollow out a canoe, may consist of little more than a few stone hatchets and shell chisels; and the labour necessary to make them might not add much to the labour subsequently employed in the work to which they were applied; but it is likewise necessary that the workman should previously cut down the timber, and employ a great quantity of labour in various parts of the process very long before there is a possibility of his receiving the returns for his exertions, either in the use of the canoe, or in the commodities which he might obtain in exchange for it; and during this time he must of course advance the whole of his subsistence. But the providence, foresight, and postponement of present enjoyment for the sake of future benefit and profit, which are necessary for this purpose, have always been considered as rare qualities in the savage; and it can scarcely admit of a doubt that the articles which were of a nature to require this long preparation would be comparatively very scarce, and would have a great exchangeable value in proportion to the quantity of labour which had been actually employed upon them, and on the capital necessary to their production. On this account, I should think it not improbable, that a canoe might, in such a

---

(23) p. 87. *In the very earliest &c.*

In all the observations of Mr. Malthus on this subject I most fully concur. I have myself stated that in proportion as fixed capital was used; as that fixed capital was of a durable character; and in proportion to the time which must elapse before commodities can be brought to market, the general principle of the value of commodities being regulated by the

state of society, possess double the exchangeable value of a number of deer, to produce which successively in the market might have cost precisely the same number of days' labour, including the necessary fixed capital of the bows and arrows, &c. used for killing them; and | the great difference of price in this case would   90 arise from the circumstance that the returns for the labour of killing each successive deer always came in within a few days after it was employed, while the returns for the labour expended on the canoe were delayed perhaps beyond a year. Whatever might be the rate of profits, the comparative slowness of these returns must tell proportionally on the price of the article; and, as there is reason to think that among savages the advances necessary for a work of slow returns would be comparatively seldom made, the profits of capital would be extremely high, and the difference of exchangeable value in different commodities which had cost in their production, and in the production of the necessary capital, the same quantity of labour, would be very great.

If to this cause of variation we add the exception noticed by Mr. Ricardo, arising from the greater or less proportion of fixed capital employed in different commodities, the effects of which would shew themselves in a very early period of savage life; it must be allowed that the rule which declares "that commodities never vary in value unless a greater or less quantity of labour be bestowed on their production," cannot possibly, as stated by Mr. Ricardo, be "of universal application in the early stages of society."*

In countries advanced in civilization, it is obvious that the same causes of variation in the ex-|changeable value of commo-   91 dities, independently of the labour which they may have cost,

* Principles of Polit. Econ. p. [58, n. 1]. 2d edit.

---

quantity of labour necessary to their production, was modified; but I was of opinion, and still am of opinion, that in the relative variation of commodities, any other cause, but that of the quantity of labour required for production, was comparatively [1] of very slight effect. Mr. Malthus remark that this cause operates in every stage of society is most just.

[1] 'comparatively' is ins.

must prevail, as in the early periods of society, and as might be expected some others. Probably indeed the profits of stock will not be so high, and consequently neither the varying proportions of the fixed capitals, nor the slowness or quickness of the returns will produce the same proportionate difference on prices; but to make up for this, the difference in the quantity of fixed capital employed is prodigious, and scarcely the same in any two commodities; and the difference in the returns of capital varies sometimes from two or three days to two or three years.

The proposition of Mr. Ricardo, which shews that a rise in the price of labour lowers the price of a large class of commodities,* has undoubtedly a very paradoxical air; but it is nevertheless true; and the appearance of paradox would vanish if it were stated more naturally. (24)

Mr. Ricardo would certainly allow that the effect he contemplates is produced by a fall of profits, which he thinks is synonymous with a rise of wages. It is not necessary here to enter into the question how far he is right in this respect; but undoubtedly

* Principles of Polit. Econ. pp. [60] and [63]. 2d edit.

---

(24) p. 91. *The proposition of Mr. Ricardo &c.*

I am glad to have Mr. Malthus assent to the truth of my proposition. He says "no one could have thought the proposition paradoxical, or even in the slightest degree improbable, if he had stated that a fall of profits would occasion a fall of price in those commodities, where from the quantity of fixed capital employed, the profits of that capital had before formed the principal ingredient in the cost of production." Now I confess that I feared Mr. Malthus himself would have found the proposition paradoxical, because in some of his works he has maintained that a rise in the price of corn will be followed by an equal rise in the price of labour, and by an equal rise in the price of *all* commodities; and it was only after further consideration that he thought it fit to reduce the proportion in which commodities would vary when corn varied, and to fix it at 25 or 20 p.c., when corn varied $33\frac{1}{3}$—that is to say no one could have thought the proposition paradoxical, or even in the slightest degree improbable, if he had stated that a fall of profits would occasion a fall of price in those commodities, where from the quantity of fixed capital employed, the profits of that capital had before formed the principal ingredient in the cost of production. But this is what he has in | substance said. In the 92 particular case which he has taken to illustrate his proposition, he supposes no other labour employed than that which has been applied in the construction of the machine, or fixed capital used; and consequently the price of the yearly produce of this machine would be formed merely of the ordinary profits of the £20,000 which it is supposed to have cost, together with a slight addition to replace its wear and tear. Now it is quite certain that if, from any cause whatever, the ordinary profits of stock should fall, the price of the commodity so produced would fall. This is sufficiently obvious. But the effects arising from an opposite supposition, equally consistent with facts, have not been sufficiently considered by Mr. Ricardo, and the general result has been totally overlooked.

The state of the case, in a general view of it, seems to be this.

---

when corn varies 100 p.c. commodities are to vary 75 to 60 p.c.[1]—Mr. Malthus made no exceptions.[2] Mr. Malthus may say that a rise in the price of corn and labour is a very different thing from a fall of profits—so it is, if the rise is owing only to a fall in the value of the medium in which price is estimated; in which case there is no real rise in the value of corn and labour, and therefore no fall of profits. Mr. Malthus I believe would find it difficult to shew that there can be any fall in the rate of profits unless there be a real rise in the value of labour. That only is a real rise in the value of labour when a larger proportion of the whole produce, or the value of a larger proportion,[3] is devoted to the payment of wages—not

[1] Malthus's *Grounds of an Opinion*, 1815, pp. 38–9 and 41. Ricardo had criticized these opinions of Malthus in his *Principles*, above, I, 419–420.

[2] This sentence is ins.
[3] 'or the value of a larger proportion,' is ins.

There is a very large class of commodities, in the production of which, owing to the quantity of fixed capital used and the long time that elapses before the returns of the capital, whether fixed or circulating, come in, the proportion which the value of the capital bears to the value of the labour which it yearly employs is, in various degrees, very considerable. In all these cases it is natural to suppose, that the fall of price arising from a fall of profits should, in various degrees, more than counterbalance the rise of price which would naturally be occasioned by a rise in the price of labour; and consequently on the supposition of a rise in the money price of labour and a fall in the rate of profits, all these commodities will, in various degrees, naturally fall in price.|

93   On the other hand, there is a large class of commodities, where, from the absence of fixed capital and the rapidity of the returns of the circulating capital from a day to a year, the proportion which the value of the capital bears to the quantity of labour which it employs is very small. A capital of a hundred pounds, which was

---

the proportion of the produce of one manufacture only but of all.

If the clothier is obliged from a general rise of wages to devote a larger portion of his cloth to the payment of wages, we may be quite sure that the hatter will devote a larger proportion of his hats, the shoemaker a larger proportion of his shoes and the iron founder a larger proportion of his iron to the same purpose. Every [1] other capitalist will be obliged to do the same, and even the farmer, though the price of his commodity rises, will after paying rent [2] have less of it, and of that less quantity he must pay away a larger proportion than before [3] to his labourers. [4] Mr. Malthus I now understand would agree to the following proposition. In all cases where the rise in the price of corn, is followed by a rise in the

[1] Last three lines replace 'that the hatter, the shoemaker, the ironmaster, and every'.
[2] 'after paying rent' is ins.
[3] 'than before' replaces 'of the whole', which had been ins.
[4] The Note originally ended here; the remainder is ins.

returned every week, could employ as much labour annually as 2,600*l*. the returns of which came in only at the end of the year; and if the capital were returned nearly every day, as it is practically, in some few cases, the advance of little more than the wages of a man for a single day might pay above 300 days' labour in the course of a year. Now it is quite evident, that out of the profits of these trifling capitals it would not only be absolutely impossible to take a rise in the price of labour of seven per cent., but it would be as impossible to take a rise of ½ per cent. On the first supposition, a rise of only ½ per cent. would, if the price of the produce continued the same, absorb more than all the profits of the 100*l*.; and in the other case much more than all the capital advanced. If, therefore, the prices of commodities, where the proportion of labour is very great compared with the capital which employs it, do not rise upon an advance in the price of labour, the production of such commodities must at once be given up. But they certainly will not be given up. Consequently upon a rise in the price of

---

money price of wages[5], and a fall of profits, so far from its being true that all other commodities would also rise in price, there will be a large class which will absolutely fall[6]—some which will not vary at all, and another large class which will rise[7]. This I believe to be a correct opinion. The last class will rise only in a trifling degree, because though they will rise on account of the rise of the price of labour, they will fall on account of the fall of profits. The[8] fall from the latter cause, will, in a great measure, balance the rise from the former.

See Mr. Malthus opinion Page 95 "What then becomes of the doctrine that the exchangeable valué of commodities is proportional to the labour which has been employed on them? &c. &c."

[5] Replaces 'by a rise of wages'.
[6] Replaces 'so far from its being true, that a large class of commodities will rise in price, they will do the contrary they will absolutely fall'.

[7] 'in a small proportion' was first ins. here, and then del.
[8] 'little' is del. here.

labour and fall of profits, there will be a large class of commodities
94 which will rise in price; and it cannot be correct | to say, "that no
commodities whatever are raised in exchangeable value merely
because wages rise; they are only so raised when more labour is
bestowed on their production, when wages fall, or when the
medium in which they are estimated falls in value"*. (25) It is
quite certain that merely because wages rise and profits fall, all
that class of commodities (and it will be a large class) will rise in
price, where, from the smallness of the capital employed, the fall
of profits is in various degrees more than overbalanced by the rise
of wages. (26)

There will, however, undoubtedly be a class of commodities
which, from the effects of these opposite causes, will remain
stationary in price. But from the very nature of the proposition,
this class must theoretically form little more than a line; and
where, I would ask, is this line to be placed? Mr. Ricardo, in order
to illustrate his proposition, has placed it, at a venture, among
those commodities where the advances consist solely in the pay-

* Ricardo's Political Economy, p. [63, n. 3]. 2d edit.

---

(25) p. 93. *Consequently upon a rise in the price of labour*

I inadvertently omitted to consider the converse of my
first proposition. Mr. Malthus is quite right in asserting that
many commodities in which labour chiefly enters, and which
can be quickly brought to market will rise, with a rise in the
value of labour.[1] See last remark.

(26) p. 94. *It is quite certain that merely because wages rise &c.*

It is curious to observe how Mr. Malthus here adopts the
language he condemns, he talks of a rise of wages, of a rise
of the price of commodities &c. &c., always supposing that
money is stationary in value, and therefore a measure of the

[1] McCulloch criticizes this Note in letter 417 of 22 Jan. 1821; see Ricardo's reply, letter 418 of 25 Jan., and cp. letter 421. Ricardo considers the converse case in ed. 3 of *Principles*, above, I, 35 and 43.

ment of labour, and the returns come in exactly in the year.† But
the cases are extremely rare where the returns of a capital are
delayed for a year, and yet no part of this capital is employed
either in the purchase of materials or machinery; and in fact there
seems to be no justifiable ground for pitching upon this peculiar
case as precisely the one where, under any variation in the price
of labour, the price of the commodity remains the | same, and a 95
rise or fall of wages is exactly compensated by a fall or rise of
profits. At all events it must be allowed, that wherever the line
may be placed, it can embrace but a very small class of objects;
and upon a rise in the price of labour, all the rest will either fall or
rise in price, although exactly the same quantity of labour continues to be employed upon them.

What then becomes of the doctrine, that the exchangeable value
of commodities is proportioned to the labour which has been
employed upon them? Instead of their remaining of the same
value while the same quantity of labour is employed upon them,
it appears that, from well known causes of constant and universal

† Polit. Econ. p. [59]. 2d edit.

---

real value of other things; for if money was not stationary in
value;—if wages rose in money value, merely because money
fell; it would not be true that profits would fall;—it would
not be true that some commodities would rise some would
fall, and a few remain stationary—for they would all rise.
That definition which he calls arbitrary he nevertheless
adopts.[2] If he says that the medium I have chosen is variable,
then none of his conclusions are just:—if he[3] admits its
invariability, then there is an end of his objection against the
medium under the conditions I have supposed[4] as a measure
of real value.

[2] The following is del. here:
'Supposing he had used his own
measure of value could he have
explained the effects of a rise
of wages on relative value—on
profits &c.? Would he have
come to the same conclusions?
Certainly not for if'.
[3] 'denies' is del. here.
[4] 'under the conditions I have
supposed' is ins.

operation, the prices of all commodities vary when the *price* of labour varies, with very few exceptions; and of what description of commodities these few exceptions consist, it is scarcely possible to say beforehand. (27)

But the different proportions of fixed capital, and the varying quickness of the returns of circulating capital, are not the only causes which, in improved countries, prevent the exchangeable value of commodities from being proportioned to the quantity of labour which has been employed upon them. Where commerce prevails to any extent, foreign commodities, not regulated, it is acknowledged, by the quantity of labour and capital employed upon them, form the materials of many manufactures. In civilized states taxation is every where making considerable changes in 96 prices with-|out any reference to labour. And further, where all the land is appropriated, the payment of rent is another condition of the supply of most of the commodities of home growth and manufacture.

It is unquestionably true, and it is a truth which involves very important consequences, that the cost of the main vegetable food of civilized and improved countries, which requires in its production a considerable quantity of labour and capital, is resolvable almost entirely into wages and profits, as will be more fully explained in the next chapter. But though it follows that the price of corn is thus nearly independent of rent, yet as this price, so

---

(27) p. 95. *What then becomes of the doctrine &c.*

Mr. Malthus shews that in fact the exchangeable value of commodities is not *exactly* proportioned to the labour which has been employed on them, which I not only admit now, but have never denied.

He proves then that quantity of labour is not a perfect measure of value; but what are its deviations from a perfect measure on account of the circumstances which he mentions? —if they are slight, as I contend they are, then we are still in possession of a measure tolerably accurate, and in my opinion more nearly approximating to truth, than any that has been yet proposed. Mr. Malthus's proposed measure has

determined, does actually pay rent on the great mass of the lands of the country, it is evident that the payment of rent, or, what comes to the same thing, of such a price as will pay rent, is a necessary condition of the supply of the great mass of commodities.

Adam Smith himself states, that rent "enters into the composition of the price of commodities in a different way from wages and profit." "High or low wages or profit (he says) are the causes of high or low price; high or low rent is the effect of it. It is because high or low wages and profit must be paid, in order to bring a particular commodity to market, that its price is high or low. But it is because its price is high or low, a great deal more, or very little more, or no more, than what is sufficient to pay those wages and profits, that if affords a high rent, or a low rent, or no rent at all."* In this passage Adam Smith distinctly | allows that 97 rent is a consequence, not a cause of price; but he evidently does not consider this admission as invalidating his general doctrine respecting the component parts of price. Nor in reality is it invalidated by this admission. It is still true that the cost of the great mass of commodities is resolvable into wages, profits, and rent. Some of them may cost a considerable quantity of rent, and a small quantity of labour and capital; others a great quantity of labour and capital, and a small quantity of rent; and a very few may be nearly resolvable into wages and profits, or even wages

* Wealth of Nations, Book I. c. xi. p. 226. 6th edit.

---

none of the qualities of a measure of value, the imperfections on the score of variability which he himself attributes to it, are greater than any which he imputes to the one which I propose. Money price Mr. M. justly[1] calls nominal price. The principles of political Economy cannot be explained by the changes which take place in nominal[2] price. Every one who attempts to explain those principles should adopt the best measure of real value that he can obtain, for that purpose.

Mr. M. has adopted one which he thinks the best, and to the use of that he should have confined himself.

[1] 'justly' is ins.   [2] 'nominal' replaces 'real'.

alone. But, as it is known that the latter class is confined to a very small proportion of a country's products, it follows that the payment of rent is an absolutely necessary condition of the supply of the great mass of commodities, and may properly be considered as a component part of price. (28)

Allowing then that the price of the main vegetable food of an improving country is determined by the quantity of labour and capital employed to produce it under the most unfavourable circumstances, yet if we allow, at the same time, that an equal value of produce is raised on rich land with little labour and capital, we can hardly maintain, with any propriety of language, the general proposition that the quantity of labour realized in different commodities regulates their exchangeable value.* On account of the varieties of soil alone constant exchanges are taking place, which 98 directly | contradict the terms in which the proposition is expressed; and in whatever way rent may be regulated, it is obviously necessary to retain it as an ingredient in the costs of production in reference to the great mass of commodities; nor will the propriety of thus retaining it be affected by the circumstance, that the rent paid on commodities of the same description is variable, and in some few cases little or none.

Under the full admission, therefore, just made, that the price of the main vegetable food of an improving agricultural country is, in reference to the whole quantity produced, a necessary price, and coincides with what is required to repay the labour and capital which is employed under the most unfavourable circumstances, and pays little or no rent, we still do not seem justified in altering the old language respecting the component parts of price, or what I should be more disposed to call the necessary conditions of supply.

But there are some parts of the land and of its products which

* Ricardo's Polit. Econ. c. i. p. [13].

---

(28) p. 97. *But as it is known &c. &c.*

See Remark [(16), on p. 72.][1]

[1] MS reads 'See Remark 72—Page 16½ 17', referring to the earlier agination of MS.

have much more the character of a monopoly than the main food of an improving country; and it is universally acknowledged that the exchangeable value of commodities which are subjected either to strict or partial monopolies cannot be determined by the labour employed upon them. The exchangeable value of that vast mass of property in this country which consists of the houses in all its towns, is greatly affected by the strict monopoly of ground rents; and the necessity of paying these rents must affect the prices of al-|most all the goods fabricated in towns. (29) And though with 99 regard to the main food of the people it is true that, if rents were given up, an equal quantity of corn could not be produced at a less price; yet the same cannot be said of the cattle of the country. Of no portion of this species of food is the price resolvable into labour and capital alone.

All cattle pay rent, and in proportion to their value not very far from an equal rent. In this respect they are essentially different from corn. By means of labour and dressing, a good crop of corn may be obtained from a poor soil, and the rent paid may be quite trifling compared with the value of the crop; but in uncultivated land the rent must be proportioned to the value of the crop, and, whether great or small per acre, must be a main ingredient in the price of the commodity produced. It may require more than an hundred acres in the highlands of Scotland to rear the same weight of mutton as might have been reared on five acres of good pasture; and something no doubt must be allowed for the greater labour of attendance and the greater risk on a poor soil and in an exposed situation; but independently of this deduction, which would probably be inconsiderable, the rent paid for the same quantity of mutton would be nearly the same. If this rent were greatly diminished, there cannot be a doubt that the same quantity of cattle might be produced in the market at much lower prices without any diminution of the profits or wages of any of the

---

(29) p. 98. *And the necessity of paying these rents must affect the prices of almost all the goods fabricated in towns.*

If the goods were not superior in quality, one does not see what inducement a buyer should have to purchase them in the dearer market.

100 persons concerned; and consequently it is impossible to esti-|mate
the value of cattle by the quantity of labour and capital, and still
less by the mere quantity of labour which has been expended
upon them. (30)

It may possibly be said that although rent is unquestionably
paid on all and every part of the cattle produced in this country;
yet that the rent of uncultivated land is determined by the price
of cattle; that the price of cattle is determined by the cost of production on such good natural pastures or improved land as would
yield a considerable rent if employed in raising corn, because the
poor uncultivated lands of a populous country are never sufficient
to produce all the animal food required; that the rents of the
different qualities of land which must thus be devoted to the
rearing of cattle depend upon the price of the main food of the
country; and that the price of the main food of the country depends
upon the labour and capital necessary to produce it on the worst

---

(30) p. 99. *All cattle pay rent &c.*

The value of cattle is regulated by the value of corn, if
therefore it be shewn that the corn which regulates the
general[1] value of that commodity, only affords wages and
profits, cattle, obtained under the same circumstances, will
yield no rent. I do not mean to say that corn raised or cattle
fed on fertile land, pay no rent, only that some corn and
some cattle yield no rent, and that this corn and cattle regulate the value of all other corn and cattle. If I manure a field,
at some expence, and make it yield more grass, and fat an
additional ox upon it, what portion of the price of that ox
affords a rent? the value of the ox only replaces capital and
its profits. Mr. Malthus says "if rent were greatly diminished,
there cannot be a doubt that the same quantity of cattle
might be produced in the market at much lower prices,
without any diminution of the profits or wages of any of the
persons concerned"—true it might be produced, but the

[1] 'general' is ins.

land actually so employed. This is to be sure rather a circuitous method of proving the intimate connection between cattle and labour, and certainly will not justify us in saying that the relative value of sheep and shirts is proportioned to the comparative quantity of labour expended upon each.

But in fact one of the links in this chain of dependence will not hold, and the connexion between cattle and labour is thus at once broken off. Though the price of the main food of a country depends upon the labour and capital necessary to produce it on the worst land in use; yet the rent of land, as will be shewn more fully in the next | chapter, is not regulated by the price of produce. 101 Among the events of the most common occurrence in all nations, is an improvement in agriculture which leads to increased produce and increased population, and after a time to the cultivation of naturally poorer land, with the same price of produce, the same price of labour, and the same rate of profits. (31) But in this case

---

question is, would it? If as Mr. Malthus allows rent is the effect and not the cause of high price—if it be true that "there is no just reason to believe that if the landlords were to give the whole of their rents to their tenants, corn would be more plentiful and cheaper;"*—if "the effect of transferring all rents to tenants would be merely the turning them into gentlemen"* then neither corn nor cattle could be produced at lower prices on the lands actually in cultivation, because "the last additions made to our home produce are sold at the cost of production."*

(31) p. 101. *Among the events &c.*

I can understand, that in consequence of improvements in agriculture, land of a worse quality may be cultivated, with a lower² price of produce, than would have been cultivated if no such improvement had taken place; because a large

* *Inquiry into the Nature and Progress of Rent* Page 57.

² 'a lower' replaces 'the same'.

the rents of all the old lands in tillage must rise, and with them of course the rents of natural pastures and the price of cattle, without any change in the price of labour or any increased difficulty in producing the means of subsistence.

The statement just made applies to many other important com-

---

quantity, at a low price, may be of greater value, than a smaller quantity, at a higher price; but with a lower price of corn—wages will be low[1], and profits will be high, and it is only because profits are higher that the worse land can be cultivated. Suppose a nation had cultivated its lands as highly as was practicable, and profits were so low that no inducement existed[2] to push its cultivation any further—that the labour of ten men on the lands not yet cultivated could not return a[3] produce of a value sufficient to clothe as well as feed the cultivators—such land would not be cultivated—suppose now improvements in agriculture to take place, and consequently the ten men on this bad land could raise 30 p.c. more produce than[4] they could raise before; this land would then be cultivated, if the population increased;—but under these circumstances corn would be at a lower price,—labour at a lower price, and profits higher than before; and on no other conditions could this poorer land afford any profits to the cultivator. How great an error then must it be for Mr. Malthus to say, that with the same price of produce, the same price of labour, and *the same rate of profits*, naturally poorer land would be taken into cultivation.

In the whole of this discussion Mr. Malthus forgets that the fact of rent not being a component part of price[5], does

[1] 'low' replaces 'lower', and five words below 'high' replaces 'higher'.
[2] 'existed' is written in pencil above 'was offered', which however is not del.
[3] 'surplus' is del. here.
[4] Replaces 'raise double the produce'.
[5] Replaces 'forgets that the proof of no rent being paid

modities, besides animal food. In the first place, it includes wool and raw hides, the materials of two most important manufactures; and applies directly to timber and copse wood, both articles of great consequence. And secondly, there are some products, such as hops, for instance, which cannot be grown upon poor soils.

---

not depend on his proving that all lands actually taken into cultivation do pay rent.[6] If he could make out to every body's satisfaction, that there was no land in cultivation, for which a rent was not paid, he would be as far as before from settling the question that rent formed a component part of price. If I can employ more capital on my land, without paying any additional rent for so doing, I can raise some[7] corn, some cattle, some hops and some of every other agricultural produce, into the value of which no rent will enter as a component part. It is the quantity so raised, and the price at which I can afford to sell it, which regulates the value of all other corn, cattle and hops, and till this is denied, and can be refuted, the proposition is in my opinion established, that rent is not a necessary constituent of price.—I hope what I have said may be considered as a sufficient refutation of Mr. Malthus's assertion that "there is no portion of wool, leather, flax, and timber produced in this country which comes from land that can be so described" that is to say for which rent is not paid. In his *Inquiry into the nature of rent* he has justly observed "It will always answer to any farmer who can command capital, to lay it out on his land, if the additional produce resulting from it will fully repay the profits of his stock, *although it yields nothing to his landlord*" [p.] 36. This is unanswerable. Into the price of such additional produce no rent enters.

[6] Replaces 'does not depend ['only' is ins. here] on worse lands being taken into cultivation.'

[7] 'some' here and below, and 'some of' further down in this sentence are ins.

Such products it is impossible to obtain without paying a rent; and if this rent varies, while the quantity of labour employed in the production of a given quantity of corn remains the same, there can be no ground whatever for asserting that the value of such products is regulated by labour.

If it be said that the doctrine which entirely rejects rent, and resolves the prices of all commodities into wages and profits, never refers to articles which have any connexion with monopoly, 102 it may be answered, that this exception includes the great | mass of the articles with which we are acquainted. The lands which afford the main supply of corn are evidently a species of monopoly, though subject to different laws and limits from common monopolies; and even the last land taken into cultivation for corn, if it has an owner, must pay the small rent which it would yield in natural pasture. It has just been shewn that monopoly must in the most direct manner affect the price of cattle, the other great branch of human food; and with regard to the materials of clothing and lodging, there are very few that do not actually pay a rent, not only on the great mass of each kind, but on those which are grown on the poorest land actually employed for their production. To say that the prices of wool, leather, flax, and timber are determined by the cost of their production on the land which pays no rent, is to refer to a criterion which it is impossible to find. I believe it may be safely asserted that there is no portion of wool, leather, flax, and timber produced in this country which comes from land that can be so described.

We cannot, therefore, get rid of rent in reference to the great mass of commodities. In the case where we come the nearest to it, namely, in the production of the main food of the country, the

---

(32) p. 103. *If we were determined &c.*

If equal capitals yielded commodities of nearly equal value, there might be some grounds for this argument; but as from a capital employed in valuable machinery, and[1] steam engines[2], a commodity of a very different value is obtained than from a capital, of the same value, employed

[1] 'and' is replaced by 'such as' in the copy sent to Trower on 26 Nov. 1820, letter 403.

[2] 'altho of the same value as a capital which employs labour only,' is del. here.

attempt to resolve the exchangeable value of all the different portions of this food into labour and profits alone, involves a contradiction in terms; and as no error seems to arise from considering rent as a component part of price, after we have properly explained its origin and progress, it appears | to me essential, both   103 to correctness of language and correctness of meaning, to say that the cost of producing any commodity is made up of all the wages, all the profits, and all the rent which in the actual circumstances of the society are necessary to bring that particular commodity to market in the quantity required; or, in other words, that the payment of these expenses is the necessary condition of its supply.

If we were determined to use only one term, it would certainly be more correct to refer to capital rather than to labour; because the advances which are called capital generally include the other two. (32) The natural or necessary prices of commodities depend upon the amount of capital which has been employed upon them, together with the profits of such capital at the ordinary rate during the time that it has been employed. But as the amount of capital advanced consists of the amount of wages paid from the first to the last, together with the amount of rent paid either directly to the landlord or in the price of raw materials, the use of the three terms seems to be decidedly preferable, both as more correct, (rent being, in many cases, not an advance of capital,) and also as conveying more of the information that is wanted.

But if rent enters into the raw materials of almost all manufactures, and of almost all capital, both fixed and circulating, the advance necessary to pay it will greatly affect the amount of capital employed, (33) and combined with the almost infinite variety that must take place in the duration of | these advances,   104

---

chiefly in the support of labour, it is at once obvious that the one term, thought to be the more correct by Mr. Malthus, would be the most incorrect that could be imagined.

(33) p. 103. *But if rent*

A farmer who pays a high rent, requires no greater capital than one who pays a low rent. He pays a high rent not because he employs a more valuable capital, but because the same capital yields him a more valuable return. He pays it too, after he has sold the produce.

will most essentially affect that part of price which resolves itself into profits.

Supposing, what is probably not true, that there is land in an improved and populous country which pays no rent whatever directly; yet rent will be paid even by the cultivator of such land in the timber which he uses for his ploughs, carts, and buldings, in the leather which he requires for harness, in the meat which he consumes in his own family, and in the horses which he purchases for tillage. These advances, as far as rent alone is concerned, would at once prevent the price of the produce from being proportioned to the quantity of labour employed upon it; and when we add the profits of these advances according to their amount and the periods of their return, we must acknowledge that even in the production of corn, where no direct rent is paid, its price must be affected by the rent involved in the fixed and circulating capital employed in cultivation.

Under all the variations, therefore, which arise from the different proportions of fixed capital employed, the different quickness of the returns of the circulating capital, the quantity of foreign commodities used in manufactures, the acknowledged effects of taxation, and the almost universal prevalence of rent in the actual state of all improved countries, we must I think allow that, however curious and desirable it may be to know the exact quantity of labour which has been employed in the production of each particular commodity, it is certainly not this labour which determines | their relative values in exchange, at the same time and at the same place.

But if, at the same place and at the same time, the relative values of commodities are not determined by the labour which they have cost in production, it is clear that this measure cannot determine their relative values at different places and at different times. If, in London and at the present moment, other causes besides labour concur in regulating the average prices of the articles bought and sold, it is quite obvious, that because a commodity in India now, or in England 500 years ago, cost in its production double the quantity of labour which it does in London at present, we could not infer that it was doubly valuable in exchange; nor, if we found from a comparison of money prices, that its value in exchange were double compared with the mass of commodities, could we with any degree of safety infer that it had cost, in its production, just double the quantity of labour.

If, for instance, it were to appear that a yard of fine broad cloth in the time of Edward the Third cost in its fabrication twenty days' common labour, and in modern times only ten, it would follow of course that by improvements of different kinds, the facility of fabricating broad cloth had been doubled; but to what extent this circumstance would have affected its relative value in exchange, it would not be possible to determine without an appeal to facts. The alteration in its exchangeable value generally, or in reference to the mass of com-|modities, would of course depend   106 upon the proportionate facility or difficulty with which other commodities were fabricated, and in reference to particular articles, the labour of fabricating which had remained the same, or was accurately known, it would still depend upon all those circumstances which have already been stated, as preventing the labour which a commodity has cost in its production, from being a correct measure of relative value, even at the same place and at the same time.

In order to shew that the quantity of labour which a commodity has cost is a better measure of value than the quantity which it will command, Mr. Ricardo makes the supposition, that a given quantity of corn might require only half the quantity of labour in its production at one time which it might require at another and subsequent period, and yet that the labourer might be paid in both periods with the same quantity of corn;* in which case, he says, we should have an instance of a commodity which had risen to double its former exchangeable value, according to what he conceives to be the just definition of value, although it would command no more labour in exchange than before.

This supposition, it must be allowed, is a most improbable one. But, supposing such an event to take place, it would strikingly exemplify the incorrectness of his definition, and shew at once the marked distinction which must always exist between cost and value. We have here a clear case | of increased cost in the quantity   107 of labour to a double amount; yet it is a part of the supposition that the commodity, which has been thus greatly increased in the cost of its production, will not purchase more of that article,

* Principles of Political Economy, chap. i. p. [15]. 2d edit.

which is, beyond comparison, the most extensive and the most important of all the objects which are offered in exchange, namely, labour. This instance shews at once that the quantity of labour which a commodity has cost in its production, is not a measure of its value in exchange. (34)

It will be most readily allowed that the labour employed in the production of a commodity, including the labour employed in the production of the necessary capital, is the principal ingredient among the component parts of price, and, *other things being equal*, will determine the relative value of all the commodities in the same country, or, more correctly speaking, in the same place. But, in looking back to any past period, we should ascertain the relative values of commodities at once, and with much more accuracy, by collecting their prices in the money of the time. For this purpose, therefore, an inquiry into the quantity of labour which each commodity had cost, would be of no use. And if we were to infer that, because a particular commodity 300 years ago had cost ten days' labour and now costs twenty, its exchangeable

---

(34) p. 106. *We have here a clear case of increased cost &c.*

I confess I do not understand this passage. Is cost estimated by quantity of labour? I understand Mr. Malthus to say it is; then the cost of corn is doubled, because it requires twice the quantity of labour and he says its value is not doubled because it will exchange for no greater quantity of labour. But how will it exchange for linen, hats, shoes, iron and every other commodity? it will command double the quantity [1] of them; then, according to my view, it has doubled in value. But it will not exchange for double the quantity of labour? certainly not, and why? because the value of labour rises with the value of corn, not indeed in the same proportion, because corn is not the only thing consumed by the labourer; but the value of labour rises, and will therefore also command more linen, shoes, hats, iron and every other commodity.

[1] 'the quantity' is ins.

value had doubled, we should certainly run the risk of drawing a conclusion most extremely wide of the truth.

It appears then, that the quantity of labour | which a commodity 108 has cost in its production, is neither a correct measure of relative value at the same time and at the same place, nor a measure of real value in exchange, as before defined, in different countries and at different periods.

SECTION V

Of Money, when uniform in its cost, considered as a Measure of Value

Upon the principle, that the labour which a commodity has cost in its production, is at once a measure of real and relative value, it has been thought, that if there were any article to be found which would at all times cost the same quantity of labour

---

The proof that Mr. Malthus offers, that corn has not doubled in value, is, that it will not command so much of a thing, which has at the same time risen in value.

But what is meant by a quantity of labour, being the cost of a commodity?—by cost, is always meant the expence of production[2] estimated in some commodity, which has value, and it always includes profits of stock. The cost of production of two commodities, as I before observed,[3] may be in proportion to the quantity of labour employed on them, but it is essentially different from the labour itself. "This instance," Mr. Malthus adds, "shews at once that the quantity of labour which a commodity has cost in its production is not a measure of its value in exchange"—certainly not, in Mr. Malthus measure of value in exchange[4].

---

[2] 'the expence of production' replaces 'value'.
[3] Above, Note (11), p. 34.

[4] The words that follow the quotation are ins.

in its production, it might be used as an accurate and standard measure of value.* It is acknowledged that the precious metals do not possess this quality. The world has been at different periods supplied from mines of different degrees of fertility. This difference of fertility necessarily implies that different quantities of labour are at different times required in the production of the same quantity of metal; and the different degrees of skill applied at different periods in the working of mines, must be an additional source of variableness in the quantity | of labour which a given weight of coin has cost to bring it to market.

109

It may be curious however to consider how far the precious metals would be an accurate measure of the quantities of labour employed upon each commodity, even if these sources of variableness were removed, and if it were really true that given quantities of the metals always required in their production the same quantity of labour.

It is an acknowledged truth that the precious metals, as they are at present procured and distributed, are an accurate measure of exchangeable value, at the same time and in the same place; and it is certain that the supposition here made would not destroy, or in any respect impair, this quality which they now possess. But it was shewn in the last section that the exchangeable value of commodities is scarcely ever proportioned to the quantity of labour employed upon them. It follows therefore necessarily that the money prices of commodities could not, even on the supposition here made, represent the quantity of labour employed upon them.

There is indeed no supposition which we can make respecting the mode of procuring the precious metals, which can ever render the prices of commodities a correct measure of the quantity of labour which they have severally cost. These prices will always be found to differ at least as much from the quantity of labour employed upon each commodity, as the quantity of labour does from their exchangeable values. To shew this, let | us suppose; first, that the precious metals require for their production at the mines which yield no rent, a certain quantity of fixed and circulating capital employed for a certain time. In this case, it follows

110

* Ricardo on the Principles of Political Economy and Taxation, ch. i. p. [54]. 2d edit.

from the reasonings of the preceding section and even from the admissions of Mr. Ricardo, that none of the commodities which would exchange for a given quantity of silver, would contain the same quantity of labour as that silver, except those which had been produced, not only by the same quantity of labour, but by the same quantities of the two kinds of capital employed for the same time and in the same proportions: and, in the case of a rise in the price of labour, all commodities which still contained the same quantity of labour would alter in price, except those very few which were circumstanced exactly in the same manner with regard to the capitals by which they were produced as the precious metals.

Let us suppose, secondly, that the production of the precious metals required no fixed capital, but merely advances in the payment of manual labour for a year. This case is so very unusual, that I should almost doubt whether any commodities could be found which would at once be of the same exchangeable value, and contain the same quantity of labour as a given portion of the precious metals; and of course upon a rise in the price of labour, almost all commodities would rise or fall in price.

Let us suppose, thirdly, that labour alone, without any advances above the food of a day, were suf-|ficient to obtain the precious metals, that is, that half an ounce of silver and $\frac{1}{15}$ of an ounce of gold could always, on an average, be found by a day's search on the sea-shore. In this case it is obvious that every commodity, which had required in its production any sort or quantity of capital beyond the advance of necessaries for a day, would differ in price from any portion of gold or silver which had cost the same quantity of labour. With regard to the effects of a rise in the price of labour, they cannot be the subject of our consideration, as it is evident that no rise in the price of labour could take place on the present supposition. A day's labour must always remain of the same money price, and corn could only rise as far as the diminution in the necessaries of the labourer would allow. Still, however, though the money price of the labourer could not rise, the rate of profits might fall; and on a fall in the rate of profits, every commodity would fall compared with money.

On either of the above suppositions, the operation of the causes mentioned in the last section would so modify the prices of commodities, that we should be as little able as we are at present, to infer from these relative prices the relative proportions of labour employed upon each commodity. (35)

But independently of the causes here adverted to, the precious metals have other sources of variation peculiar to them. On account of their durability, they conform themselves slowly and

112 with difficulty to the varieties in the qualities of other | commodities, and the varying facilities which attend their production.

The market prices of gold and silver depend upon the quantity of them in the market compared with the demand; and this quantity has been in part produced by the accumulation of hundreds of years, and is but slowly affected by the annual supply from the mines.

It is justly stated by Mr. Ricardo* that the agreement of the market and natural prices of all commodities, depends at all times upon the facility with which the supply can be increased or diminished, and he particularly notices gold, or the precious metals, as among the commodities where this effect cannot be speedily

* Principles of Political Economy and Taxation, ch. xiii. p. [191].

---

(35) p. 110. *Let us suppose &c.*

The objections made here to gold as a measure of value on the supposition that it always required the same quantity of labour to produce it are in substance the very same that were made in the last section to labour itself as a regulator of value. It was there shewn that commodities did not vary exactly in proportion to the quantity of labour which they required for their production:—it is now shown that they do not vary relatively to one particular commodity [1] *exactly* in proportion to the quantity of labour required [2] for the production of them, and the particular commodity.

(36) p. 112. *The market prices of gold*

It was never contended that gold under the present circumstances was a good measure of value, it was only hypothetically, and for the purpose of illustrating a principle,

[1] 'relatively to one particular commodity' is ins.   [2] The remainder of the sentence replaces 'for each.'

produced. Consequently if by great and sudden improvements in machinery, both in manufactures and agriculture, the facility of production were generally increased, and the wants of the population were supplied with much less labour, the value of the precious metals compared with commodities ought greatly to rise; but, as they could not in a short time be adequately diminished in quantity, the prices of commodities would cease to represent the quantity of labour employed upon them. (36)

Another source of variation peculiar to the precious metals would be the use that is made of them in foreign commerce; and unless this use were given up, and the exportation and importation of them were prohibited, it would unquestionably | answer to some countries possessing peculiar advantages in their exportable commodities, to buy their gold and silver abroad rather than procure them at home. At this present moment, I believe it is unquestionably true that England purchases the precious metals with less labour than is applied to obtain them directly from the mines of Mexico. But if they could be imported by some countries   113

---

supposed that all the known causes of the variability of gold, were removed. In the case supposed by Mr. Malthus, gold would not be brought to market in the same quantity as before, unless its market price was equal to, or exceeded, its natural price; the reduction of the quantity would slowly elevate its price.

I said[3] "suppose all variations in the value of gold to cease, it would then be a good measure of value. I know they cannot cease—I know it is a metal liable to the same variations as other things and therefore not a good measure of value, but I beg you to suppose all causes of variation removed, that we may speak about the variations of other things in an unvarying measure without confusion." Am I answered by being told that gold is variable, and that I have omitted to mention some of the causes of its variation?[4]

[3] In substance, *Principles*, above,   [4] This paragraph is ins.
I, 87, n. 1.

from abroad with less labour than they could be obtained at home, it would answer to other countries to export them in exchange for commodities, which they either could not produce on their own soil, or could obtain cheaper elsewhere. And thus, in reference to the relative value of commodities both in different countries at the same period, and in the same country at different periods, it is obvious that the prices in money might be subject to considerable variations, without being accompanied by any proportionate variations in the quantities of labour which they had cost.

The objections hitherto considered in this and the preceding sections are some of those which present themselves upon the supposition that each nation possessed mines, or even could procure at home the precious metals at all times with the same quantity of labour without capital; but these, it must be allowed, are extravagant hypotheses. If however we were to assume the more natural one, of the mines, wherever they are, and in all ages, costing always the same quantity of labour and capital in the working, we should see immediately from the present distribution
114 of the precious me-|tals, how little comparatively they could be depended upon as measuring, in different countries and at different times, the quantities of labour which commodities have cost.

If indeed the fertility of the mines were always the same, we should certainly get rid of that source of variation which arises from the existing contrary quality, and of the effects of such a discovery as that of the American mines. But other great and obvious sources of variation would remain. The uniform fertility of the mines would not essentially alter the proportions in which the precious metals would be distributed to different countries; and the great differences, which are now known to take place in their value in different places, when compared with corn and labour, would probably continue nearly the same.

According to all the accounts we have received of prices in Bengal, a given quantity of silver will there represent or command six or eight times more labour and provisions than in England. In all parts of the world articles of equal money prices exchange for each other. It will consequently happen that, in the commerce carried on between the two countries, the product of a day's English labour must exchange for the product of five or six days of Indian labour, after making a sufficient allowance for the difference of profits.

Perhaps it will be said that the high comparative value of silver in India arises mainly from the effects of the discovery of the American mines not having yet been adequately communicated to this part of the world: but it must be recollected that the | discovery is now of long standing; and that the difference in the relative value of gold and silver, compared with their values in Europe, which most clearly indicated an incomplete communication, is now at an end. I am disposed to think therefore, that the high value of silver in India arises mainly from other causes. But at all events the difference is now so enormous as to allow of a great abatement, and yet to leave it very considerable.

It is not however necessary to go to India in order to find similar differences in the value of the precious metals, though not perhaps so great. Russia, Poland, Germany, France, Flanders, and indeed almost all the countries in Europe, present instances of great variations in the quantity of labour and provisions which can be purchased by a given quantity of silver. Yet the relative values of the precious metals in these countries must be very nearly the same as they would be, if the American mines had been at all times of a uniform fertility: and consequently, by their present relative values, we may judge how little dependence could be placed on a coincidence in different countries between the money prices of commodities and the quantities of labour which they had cost, even on the supposition that money was always obtained from the mines in America by the same quantity of labour and capital.

But if we are not fully satisfied with this kind of reference to experience, it is obvious that the same conclusion follows inevitably from theory. In those countries where the precious metals are | necessarily purchased, no plausible reason can be assigned why the quantity of them should be in proportion to the difficulty of producing the articles with which they are purchased.

When the English and Indian muslins appear in the German markets, their relative prices will be determined solely by their relative qualities, without the slightest reference to the very different quantities of human labour which they may have cost; and the circumstance that in the fabrication of the Indian muslins five or six times more labour has been employed than in the

English, will not enable them to command greater returns of money to India. (37)

In the ports of Europe no merchants are to be found who would be disposed to give more money for Swedish wheat, than Russian, Polish, or American, of the same quality, merely because more labour had been employed in the cultivation of it, on account of

---

(37) p. 114. *According to all accounts &c. &c.*

I most distinctly admit that gold and silver may be of very different values in different countries[1], particularly if their value be measured by the quantity of[2] corn and labour which they will command. I have indeed endeavored to shew[3] that this difference[4] is owing to three causes; first, the expence attending the purchase of gold and silver, with bulky commodities, on account of the expence attending their conveyance to the markets where gold and silver are sold. Secondly, on account of the distance of the voyage which will still further enhance these expence. Thirdly the different rates of profit in different countries, owing to the unequal accumulations of capitals in proportion to the fertility of the land. If labour were much higher in Yorkshire, than in Gloucestershire, profits would be lower, and capital would

[1] The sentence originally ended here; 'particularly if measured by corn and labour' was then ins., and finally it was expanded as above.

[2] 'the quantity of' replaces 'the value of', which had been ins.

[3] Above, I, 145.

[4] The six lines that follow in the Note replace an earlier version, in which the causes enumerated were only two—what is now the second being then merely a clause of the first: 'is owing to two causes, one, the expences attending the purchase of gold and silver with bulky commodities, if the purchasers possess no others, particularly if the commodities with which the purchase is made must be conveyed to a great distance. In the country importing gold, all that expence, [ins. here: 'the value of'] all that quantity of labour in fact, must be realized in the gold. [This sentence is replaced by 'The expences of importing gold must be increased and must therefore raise its value.'] Secondly, the different rate of profits in different countries' etc.

its being grown on a more barren soil. If India and Sweden
therefore had no other means of buying silver in Europe than by
the export of muslins and corn, it would be absolutely impossible
for them to circulate their commodities at a money price, compared with other countries, proportioned to the relative difficulty
with which they were produced, or the quantity of labour which

---

by degrees be removed from the former to the latter place;
so that each district would have that portion of the general
capital which it could most beneficially employ;—not so
between independent countries. Capital does not move from
England to Poland, merely because labour is cheaper there;
and for this reason, gold will be low in value compared with
labour in one place, high in another.

I do not however agree with Mr. Malthus' calculation. In
comparing a day's labour of one country, with a day's labour
of another, we must take into our consideration [5] the different
quantities of labour, which may be comprised under the
general term of a day's labour. Mr. Malthus has dwelt much
on the disinclination to work, and on the indolence of
labourers, in countries where food is obtained with the
utmost facility, he surely then will not compare a day's work
of a South American or of a Hindoo, with the day's work of
an Englishman, or a Frenchman. Does Mr. Malthus really
believe that there is five or six times *more labour* employed
on Indian Muslins than on English?—Besides omitting the
consideration which I have just mentioned,[6] he surely does
not reckon the labour bestowed on machines, such as steam
Engines etc., on coals &c. &c.: Does not the labour on these
constitute [7] a part of the labour bestowed on the muslins?

---

[5] The remainder of the sentence
replaces 'the intensity of labour.'
[6] Last nine words are ins.
[7] ': Does not the labour on these
constitute' replaces 'as not constituting'; and the question-mark
at the end replaces a full stop.

had been employed upon them. It is indeed universally allowed, that the power of purchasing foreign commodities of all kinds depends upon the relative cheapness, not the relative dearness, of the articles that can be exported; and therefore, although the 117 actual currency of an individual country, other cir-|cumstances being nearly equal, may be distributed among the different commodities bought and sold, according to the quantity of labour which they have severally cost, the supposition that the same sort of distribution would take place in different countries, involves a contradiction of the first principles of commercial intercourse.*

It appears then that no sort of regularity in the production of the precious metals, not even if all countries possessed mines of their own, and still less if the great majority were obliged to purchase their money from others, can possibly render the money prices of commodities a correct measure of the quantity of labour which has been employed upon them, either in the same or different countries, or at the same or different periods.

How far the precious metals so circumstanced, may be a good measure of the *exchangeable* value of commodities, though not of the labour which has been employed upon them, is quite another question. It has been repeatedly stated that the precious metals, in whatever way they may be obtained, are a correct measure of exchangeable value at the same time and place. And certainly the less subject to variation are the modes of procuring them, the more they will approach to a measure of exchangeable value at different times and in different places. |

118   If, indeed, they were procured according to one of the suppositions made in this section, that is, if each nation could at all times obtain them by the same quantity of labour without any advances of capital, then, with the exception of the temporary disturbances occasioned by foreign commerce and the sudden invention of machinery, the exchangeable value in money in reference to the labour which it would command, would be the same in all countries and at all times; and the specific reason why the precious metals would in this case approach near to a correct measure of real value in exchange is, that it is the only

---

* Mr. Ricardo very justly states that, even on the supposition which he has made respecting the precious metals, the foreign interchange of commodities is not determined by the quantity of labour which they have relatively cost.

supposition in which their cost in labour can ever be the same as their exchangeable value in labour. In the case supposed, money would certainly be of a uniform value. It would at all times both cost the same quantity of labour and command the same quantity; but we have seen that, in reference to those commodities where any sort of capital was used, their values, compared either with the precious metals or each other, could never be proportioned to the labour which they had cost.

SECTION VI

Of the Labour which a Commodity will command, considered as a Measure of real Value in Exchange

When we consider labour as a measure of value in the sense in which it is most frequently applied | by Adam Smith, that is, 119 when the value of an object is estimated by the quantity of labour of a given description (common day-labour, for instance) which it can command, it will appear to be unquestionably the best of any one commodity, and to unite, more nearly than any other, the qualities of a real and nominal measure of exchangeable value.

In the first place, in looking for any one object as a measure of exchangeable value, our attention would naturally be directed to that which was most extensively the subject of exchange. Now of all objects it cannot be disputed, that by far the greatest mass of value is given in exchange for labour either productive or unproductive.

Secondly, the value of commodities, in exchange for labour, can alone express the degree in which they are suited to the wants and tastes of society, and the degree of abundance in which they are supplied, compared with the desires and numbers of those who are to consume them. By improvements in machinery, cloth, silks, cottons, hats, shoes, money, and even corn, for some years might all be very greatly increased in quantity at the same time. Yet while this remarkable alteration had taken place in these commodities, the value of any one of them in exchange for any other, or even compared with the mass of the others collectively, might remain exactly the same. It is obvious therefore that, in order to express the important effects arising from facility of

production, we must take into our consideration either the quan-|
120 tity of labour which commodities have cost, or the quantities of
labour which they will command. But it was shewn in the last
two sections, that the quantity of labour, which commodities
have cost, never approaches to a correct measure of exchangeable
value, even at the same time and place. Consequently, our attention is naturally directed to the labour which commodities will
command.

Thirdly, the accumulation of capital, and its efficiency in the
increase of wealth and population, depends almost entirely upon
its power of setting labour to work; or, in other words, upon its
power of commanding labour. (38) No plenty of commodities
can occasion a real and permanent increase of capital if they are
of such a nature, or have fallen so much in value that they will not
command more labour than they have cost. (39) When this

---

(38) p. 119. *In the first place &c.*

The reader will observe that the quality which appears to
be most sought after by Mr. Malthus in a measure of real
value is not invariability, but one "which is most extensively
the subject of exchange." "Secondly, the value of commodities, in exchange for labour, can alone express the degree
of abundance in which they are supplied, compared with the
desires and number of those who are to consume them.
Thirdly, the accumulation of capital depends upon its power
of setting labour to work." Now these are important enquiries with reference to other questions but I ask, what can
they have to do with a measure of real value? "I object to
your measure of value says Mr. Malthus because it is not so
invariable as you represent it,—there are causes of variation
which affect it for which you have not made due allowance."
Who would not suppose then that when he proposed a
measure of value he would propose one free from these
objections? He does quite the contrary, he proposes a
measure which is not only variable in itself, but is particularly

happens from permanent causes, a final stop is put to accumulation; when it happens for a time only, a temporary stop to accumulation takes place, and population is in both cases affected accordingly. As it appears then that the great stimulus to production depends mainly upon the power of commodities to command labour, and especially to command a greater quantity of labour than they have cost, we are naturally led to consider this power of commanding labour as of the utmost importance in an estimate of the exchangeable value of commodities.

These are some of the general considerations which, in a search for a measure of value, would direct our first attention to the labour which commodities will command; and a more particular con-|sideration of the qualities of this measure will convince us   121 that no one other object is equally adapted to the purpose.

It is universally allowed that, in the same place, and within

---

variable, on account of its connection with other variable commodities, and in his reasons for chusing it gives several which have no reference to the subject, for nothing is to be considered in a measure of value but its invariability or its near approach to that character.

(39) p. 120. *No plenty of commodities &c.*

This is true in whatever medium you chuse to measure exchangeable value.

Estimated in iron, sugar, coffee, a commodity has cost me a certain quantity of one of these articles—I will not produce it, unless it will exchange for more of that particular article. Estimated in labour, it has cost me a certain value, I will not produce it if it will not exchange for more. Estimated in quantity of labour, I will not produce it, if it will not command a greater quantity than has been employed in its production.[1] Mr. Malthus makes nearly the same observation in the next two pages.

[1] This sentence (where the medium is the quantity of labour, as opposed to the value of labour of the preceding sentence) is inserted.

moderately short periods of time, the precious metals are an unexceptionable measure of value; but whatever is true of the precious metals with respect to nominal prices, is true of labour applied in the way proposed.

It is obvious, for instance, that, in the same place and at the same time, the different quantities of day-labour which different commodities can command, will be exactly in proportion to their relative values in exchange; and, if any two of them will purchase the same quantity of labour of the same description, they will invariably exchange for each other.

The merchant might safely regulate his dealings, and estimate his commercial profits by the excess of the quantity of labour which his imports would command, compared with his exports. Whether the value of a commodity had arisen from a strict or partial monopoly; whether it was occasioned principally by the scarcity of the raw material, the peculiar sort of labour required in its construction, or unusually high profits; whether its value had been increased by an increased cost of production, or diminished by the application of machinery; whether its value at the moment depended chiefly upon permanent, or upon temporary causes;—in all cases, and under all circumstances, the
122 quantity of labour which it will command, or, what comes | to the same thing, the quantity of labour or labour's worth, which people will give to obtain it, will be a very exact measure of its exchangeable value. In short, this measure will, in the same place, and at the same time, exactly accord with the nominal prices of commodities, with this great advantage in its favour, that it will serve to explain very accurately and usefully all variations of value, without reference to a circulating medium.

It may be said, perhaps, that in the same place and at the same time exactly, almost every commodity may be considered as an accurate measure of the relative value of others, and that what has just been said of labour may be said of cloth, cotton, iron, or any other article. Any two commodities which at the same time and in the same place would purchase or command the same quantity of cloth, cotton or iron, of a given quality, would have the same relative value, or would exchange for each other. This is no doubt true, if we take the same time precisely; but not, if a moderate latitude be allowed, such as may be allowed in the case of labour or of the precious metals. Cloth, cotton, iron and similar commodities, are much more exposed to sudden changes of value, both from the variations of demand, and the influence of machinery and other causes, than labour. Day-labour, taking the average of summer and winter, is the most steady of all exchangeable articles; and the merchant who, in a foreign venture, the returns of which were slow, was sure of gaining fifteen per cent. estimated in labour, would be much more secure | of finally 123 gaining fifteen per cent. of real profits, than he, who could only be sure of gaining fifteen per cent. estimated in cloth, cotton, iron, or even money.

While labour thus constitutes an accurate measure of value in the same place, and within short periods of time, it approaches the nearest of any one commodity to such a measure, when applied to different places and distant periods of time.

Adam Smith has considered labour in the sense here understood as so good a measure of corn, or, what comes to the same thing, he has considered corn as so good a measure of labour, that in his Digression on the value of silver during the four last centuries, he has actually substituted corn for labour, and drawn the same conclusions from his inquiry as if the one were always an accurate measure of the other.

In doing this I think he has fallen into an important error, and drawn inferences inconsistent with his own general principles. At the same time, we must allow that, from century to century, and in different and distant countries where the precious metals greatly vary in value, corn, as being the principal necessary of life, may fairly be considered as the best measure of the real exchangeable value of labour; and consequently the power of a commodity to command labour will, at distant times and in different countries, be the best criterion of its power of commanding the first necessary of life—corn.

With regard to the other necessaries and conve-|niences of life, 124 they must in general be allowed to depend still more upon labour than corn, because in general more labour is employed upon them after they come from the soil. And as, *all other things being equal*, the quantity of labour which a commodity will command will be in proportion to the quantity which it has cost; we may fairly presume that the influence of the different quantities of labour which a commodity may have cost in its production, will be sufficiently taken into consideration in this estimate of value, together with the further consideration of all those circumstances, besides the labour actually employed on them in which they are not equal. The great pre-eminence of that measure of value, which consists in the quantity of labour which a commodity will command, over that which consists in the quantity of labour which has been actually employed about it, is, that while the latter involves merely one cause of exchangeable value, though in general the most considerable one; the former, in addition to this cause, involves all the different circumstances which influence the rates at which commodities are actually exchanged for each other.

It is evident that no commodity can be a good measure of real value in exchange in different places and at distant periods, which is not at the same time a good measure of nominal value in these places and at these distant periods; and in this respect it must be allowed, that the quantity of common labour that an article will command, which necessarily takes into account every cause that 125 in-|fluences exchangeable value, is an unexceptionable measure.

It should be further remarked, that although in different countries and at distant periods, the same quantity of labour will command very different quantities of corn—the first necessary of life; yet in the progress of improvement and civilization it generally happens, that when labour commands the smallest quantity of food, it commands the greatest quantity of other commodities, and when it commands the greatest quantity of food, it commands the smallest quantity of other necessaries and conveniences; so that when, in two countries, or in two periods differently advanced in improvement, two objects command the same quantity of labour, they will often command nearly the same quantity of the necessaries and conveniences of life, although they may command different quantities of corn.

It must be allowed then that, of any one commodity, the quantity of common day-labour which any article will command, appears to approach the nearest to a measure of real value in exchange.

---

(40) p. 125. *But still labour &c.*

The reader is particularly requested to remark the character for invariability, which Mr. Malthus gives to the measure of real value, proposed by himself.

But still, labour, like all other commodities, varies from its plenty or scarcity compared with the demand for it, and, at different times and in different countries, commands very different quantities of the first necessary of life; and further, from the different degrees of skill and of assistance from machinery with which labour is applied, the products of labour are not in proportion to the quantity exerted. Consequently, labour, in any sense in | which the term can be applied, cannot be considered as an   126
accurate and standard measure of real value in exchange. And if the labour which a commodity will command cannot be considered in this light, there is certainly no other quarter in which we can seek for such a measure with any prospect of success. (40)

SECTION VII

Of a Mean between Corn and Labour considered as a Measure of Real Value in Exchange

No one commodity then, it appears, can justly be considered as a standard measure of real value in exchange; and such an estimate of the comparative prices of all commodities as would determine the command of any one in particular over the necessaries, conveniences, and amusements of life, including labour, would not only be too difficult and laborious for use, but generally quite impracticable. Two objects, however, might, in some cases, be a better measure of real value in exchange than one alone, and yet be sufficiently manageable for practical application.

A certain quantity of corn of a given quality, on account of its capacity of supporting a certain number of human beings, has always a definite and invariable value in use; but both its real and | nominal value in exchange is subject to considerable variations,   127
not only from year to year, but from century to century. (41) It

---

(41) p. 126. *A certain quantity of corn &c. &c.*

This is also a measure proposed by Mr. Malthus, and the same account of its invariability is given, as he before gave of the invariability of labour.

is found by experience that population and cultivation, notwithstanding their mutual dependence on each other, do not always
proceed with equal steps, but are subject to marked alternations
in the velocity of their movements. Exclusive of annual variations,
it appears that corn sometimes remains dear, compared with
labour and other commodities, for many years together, and at
other times remains cheap, compared with the same objects, for
similar periods. At these different periods, a bushel of corn will
command very different quantities of labour and other commodities. In the reign of Henry VII., at the end of the 15th and
beginning of the 16th centuries, it appears, from the statute price
of labour and the average price of wheat, that half a bushel of this
grain would purchase but little more than a day's common labour;
and, of course, but a small quantity of those commodities in the
production of which much labour is necessary. A century afterwards, in the latter part of the reign of Elizabeth, half a bushel of
wheat would purchase three days' common labour, and, of course,
a considerable quantity comparatively of those commodities on
which labour is employed. Consequently, from century to century as well as from year to year, a given quantity of corn appears
to measure very imperfectly the quantity of the necessaries, con-
128 veniences, and amusements of | life, which any particular com-
modity will command in exchange.

The same observation will hold good if we take day-labour,
the measure proposed by Adam Smith; and the same period in
our history will illustrate the variation from century to century of
this measure. In the reign of Henry VII. a day's labour, according
to the former statement, would purchase nearly half a bushel of

---

(42)¹ p. 128. *Though neither of these two objects*

A complete fallacy seems to me to be involved in the whole
of this argument. Corn is a variable commodity says
Mr. Malthus, and so is labour variable, but they always vary
in different directions; if therefore I take a mean between the
two, I shall probably obtain a measure approaching to the
character of invariability.

¹ A copy of this Note, with a   to Trower on 26 Nov. 1820,
few variants, was sent by Ricardo   letter 403.

wheat, the chief necessary of life, and consequently the chief article in the general estimate of real value in exchange. A century afterwards, a day's labour would only purchase one-sixth of a bushel,—a most prodigious difference in this main article. And though it may be presumed that a day's labour in both periods would purchase much more nearly the same quantity of those articles where labour enters as a principal ingredient, than of corn, yet the variations in its command over the first necessary of life, at different periods, must alone disqualify it from being an accurate measure of real value in exchange from century to century.

Though neither of these two objects, however, taken singly, can be considered as a satisfactory measure of value, yet by combining the two, we may perhaps approach to greater accuracy.

When corn compared with labour is dear, labour compared with corn must necessarily be cheap. At the period that a given quantity of corn will command the greatest quantity of the necessaries, conveniences, and amusements of life, | a given quantity of 129 labour will always command the smallest quantity of such objects; and at the period when corn commands the smallest, labour will command the greatest quantity of them.

If, then, we take a mean between the two, we shall evidently have a measure corrected by the contemporary variations of each in opposite directions, and likely to represent more nearly than either the same quantity of the necessaries, conveniences, and amusements of life, at the most distant periods, and under all the varying circumstances to which the progress of population and cultivation is subject. (42)

For this purpose, however, it is necessary that we should fix

---

Now *do* corn and labour vary in different directions? When corn rises in relative value to labour, labour falls in relative value to corn, and this is called varying in different directions. When cloth rises in price, it rises as compared with gold, and gold falls as compared with cloth, but this does not prove that they vary in different directions, for at the same time gold may have risen as compared with iron, hats, leather, and every commodity except cloth. What then would be the fact? that they had varied in the same direction

upon some measure of corn which may be considered, in respect
of quantity, as an equivalent to a day's labour; and perhaps in
this country, a peck of wheat, which is about the average daily
earnings of a good labourer in good times, may be sufficiently
accurate for the object proposed. Any commodity therefore
which, at different periods, will purchase the same number of
days' labour and of pecks of wheat, or parts of them, each taken
in equal proportions, may be considered, upon this principle, as
commanding pretty nearly the same quantity of the necessaries,
conveniences, and amusements of life; and, consequently, as
preserving pretty nearly its real value in exchange at different
periods. And any commodity which at different periods is found
to purchase different quantities of corn and labour thus taken,
130 will evidently have varied compared with a | measure subject to

---

—gold may have risen 10 p.c. in value compared with all
things but cloth; and cloth may have risen compared with all
things 25 p.c., excepting with gold, relatively to which it
would have risen only 15 p.c. We should think it strange in
these circumstances to say that in chusing a measure of value
we would take a mean between cloth and gold, because they
varied different ways, when it is absolutely demonstrable
that they have varied the same way. Now this is what
Mr. Malthus has done in respect to corn and labour. A country
finds increasing difficulties in supplying the corn necessary
for a continually augmenting population, and in consequence
corn rises as compared with all other commodities. As corn
rises, which forms so material an article of consumption to
the labourer, though not the only one, labour also rises, but
not so much as corn:—if corn rises 20 p.c., labour may
possibly[1] rise 10 p.c. In these circumstances, estimated in
corn, labour appears to have fallen—estimated in labour corn
appears to have risen—but it is evident that they have both
risen, though in different degrees, for they will both be more

[1] Copy to Trower 'probably'.

but little variation, and consequently may be presumed to have varied proportionably in its real value in exchange.

In estimating the real value in exchange of commodities in different countries, regard should be had to the kind of food consumed by the labouring classes; and the general rule should be to compare them in each country with a day's labour, and a quantity of the prevailing sort of grain, equal to the average daily earnings of a good labourer. Thus, if the money price of a commodity in England would purchase five days' labour and five pecks of corn, and the money price of a commodity in Bengal would purchase five days' labour, and five times the quantity of rice usually earned in a day by a good labourer, according to an average of a very considerable period, these commodities might be considered in each country as of equal real value in exchange;

---

valuable estimated in all other commodities. A mean then is taken between two commodities which are confessedly variable, and it is taken on the principle that the variation of one corrects the effects of the variation of the other;—as however I have proved that they vary in the same direction, I hope Mr. Malthus will see the expediency of relinquishing so imperfect, and so variable a standard.

From Mr. Malthus argument in this place one would suppose that labour fell when corn rose, and consequently that with a given quantity of iron, leather, cloth &c. more labour could be obtained [2], the contrary is the fact, labour, as well as corn, rises as compared with these commodities. Mr. Malthus says so himself in page 125 "In the progress of improvement and civilization it generally happens, that when labour commands the smallest quantity of food, it commands the greatest quantity of other commodities"—what is this but saying that when a great quantity of other commodities is given for food, a greater [3] quantity of other things is also given for labour, or in other words that when food rises, labour rises?

[2] 'obtained' replaces 'bestowed'.   [3] Copy to Trower 'a great'.

and the difference in their money values would express pretty
nearly the different values of silver in England and Bengal.

The principal defect of the measure here proposed arises from
the effect of capital, machinery and the division of labour in
varying, in different countries and at different periods, the results
of day-labour and the prices of manufactured commodities: but
these varying results no approximation hitherto suggested has
ever pretended to estimate; and, in fact, they relate rather to
riches than to exchangeable value, which, though nearly connected, are not always the same; and on this account, in an esti-
131 mate of value, the cheapness arising from | skill and machinery
may without much error be neglected. (43)

Mr. Ricardo asks "why should gold, or corn, or labour be the
standard measure of value, more than coals or iron, more than
cloth, soap, candles, and the other necessaries of the labourer?
Why, in short, should any commodity, or all commodities together, be the standard, when such a standard is itself subject to
fluctuations in value*?" I trust that the question here put has
been satisfactorily answered in the course of this inquiry into the
nature and measures of value. And I will only add here that some
one, or more, or all commodities together, must of necessity be
taken to express exchangeable value, because they include every

* Princ. of Polit. Econ. c. xx. p. [275]. 2d edit.

---

(43) p. 130. *In an estimate of value, the cheapness arising from
skill and machinery may without much error be neglected.*

What is this but saying that in an estimate of value it is of
no importance what quantity of labour may be applied to the
production of commodities? This I think must be an oversight for Mr. Malthus uniformly allows that the quantity of
labour employed on commodities is the main cause of their
value. How can it indeed be denied?

(44) p. 131. *The sacrifice of toil and labour made in the production of a commodity; that is its cost, or more properly
speaking a portion of its cost.*

Mr. M. as I have said before[1] misunderstands me—I do not

[1] Above, p. 34.

thing that can be given in exchange. Yet a measure of exchangeable value thus formed, it is acknowledged, is imperfect; and we
should certainly have been obliged to Mr. Ricardo if he had substituted a better. But what measure has he proposed to substitute?
The sacrifice of toil and labour made in the production of a commodity; that is, its *cost*, or, more properly speaking, a portion of
its cost, from which its value in exchange is practically found,
under different circumstances, to vary in almost every degree.
Cost and value are always essentially different. A commodity,
the cost of which has doubled, may be worth in exchangeable
value no more than before, if other commodities have likewise
doubled. When the cost of commodities however is esti-|mated   132
upon the principles of Adam Smith, their money cost and average
money value will generally meet. But when cost is estimated
upon the principles of Mr. Ricardo, by the quantity of labour
applied, the labour cost and labour value scarcely ever agree.
Wherever there are profits, (and the cases are very rare indeed in
which there are none,) the value of a commodity in exchange for
labour is uniformly greater than the labour which has been employed upon it.

We have therefore to choose between an imperfect measure of
exchangeable value, and one that is necessarily and fundamentally
erroneous. (44)

---

say a portion of its cost measures its exchangeable value—but
I say its whole value will be *in proportion* to a portion of its
cost, and I do not say this without allowing for modifications
and exceptions—though I consider them of no great magnitude. Without misunderstanding me Mr. Malthus could never
apply the following observation to my doctrine "Wherever
there are profits, (and the cases are very rare indeed in which
there are none) the value of a commodity in exchange for
labour is uniformly greater than the labour which has been
employed upon it." If I had said that the value of commodities was the same thing as the value of the labour
expended on them, the remark would have been well
founded, but I have said that the relative value of com-

If Mr. Ricardo says that by value, when he uses it alone, he does not mean exchangeable value, then he has certainly led us into a great error in many parts of his work; and has finally left us without substituting any measure of exchangeable value for the one to which he objects. There never was any difficulty in finding a measure of cost, or indeed of value, if we define it to be cost. The difficulty is, to find a measure of real value in exchange, in contradistinction to nominal value or price. There is no question as to an accurate standard, which is justly considered as unattainable. But, of all the articles given in exchange, labour is, beyond comparison, the largest and most important; and next to it stands corn. The reason, why corn should be preferred to coals or iron, is surely very intelligible. The same reason combined with others holds for preferring labour to corn. And the reasons 133 given in this section are, I trust, suffi-|cient for preferring, in some cases, a mean between corn and labour to either of them taken separately. Where corn is not one of the articles to be measured, as in the case of an estimate of the value of the precious metals, or any particular commodity, a mean between corn and labour is certainly to be preferred to labour alone; but where corn is one of the main articles to be measured, as in an estimate of the exchangeable value of the whole produce of a country, the command of such produce over domestic and foreign labour is still the best criterion to which we can refer. |

---

modities is [1] in proportion to the quantity of labour bestowed on them. That value may be double what the labour cost. The comparison between Mr. Malthus's proposed measure and the one which I have proposed is thus summed up "We have therefore to choose between an imperfect measure of exchangeable value, and one that is necessarily and fundamentally erroneous."

[1] 'at all times' is del. here.

CHAPTER III

OF THE RENT OF LAND

SECTION I

Of the Nature and Causes of Rent

The rent of land may be defined to be that portion of the value 134
of the whole produce which remains to the owner of the land,
after all the outgoings belonging to its cultivation, of whatever
kind, have been paid, including the profits of the capital employed,
estimated according to the usual and ordinary rate of the profits
of agricultural stock at the time being.

It sometimes happens that, from accidental and temporary
circumstances, the farmer pays more, or less, than this; but this
is the point towards which the actual rents paid are constantly
gravitating, and which is therefore always referred to when the
term is used in a general sense.

Rent then being the excess of price above what is necessary to
pay the wages of the labour and the profits of the capital employed
in cultivation, the first object which presents itself for inquiry, is,
the cause or causes of this excess of price.

After very careful and repeated revisions of the subject, I do
not find myself able to agree entirely | in the view taken of it, 135
either by Adam Smith, or the Economists; and still less, by some
more modern writers.

Almost all these writers appear to me to consider rent as too
nearly resembling, in its nature, and the laws by which it is
governed, that excess of price above the cost of production, which
is the characteristic of a common monopoly.

Adam Smith, though in some parts of the eleventh chapter of
his first book he contemplates rent quite in its true light,* and has

---

* I cannot, however, agree with him in thinking that all land which
yields food must *necessarily* yield rent. The land which is successively taken
into cultivation in improving countries, may only pay profits and labour.
A fair profit on the stock employed, including, of course, the payment of
labour, will always be a sufficient inducement to cultivate. But, practically,
the cases are very rare, where land is to be had by any body who chooses
to take it: and probably it is true, almost universally, that all appropriated
land which yields food in its natural state, always yields a rent, whether
cultivated or uncultivated.

interspersed through his work more just observations on the subject than any other writer, has not explained the most essential cause of the high price of raw produce with sufficient distinctness, though he often touches on it; and by applying occasionally the term monopoly to the rent of land, without stopping to mark its more radical peculiarities, he leaves the reader without a definite impression of the real difference between the cause of the high price of the necessaries of life, and of monopolized commodities. |

136   Some of the views which the Economists have taken of the nature of rent appear to me also, to be quite just; but they have mixed them with so much error, and have drawn such unwarranted inferences from them, that what is true in their doctrines has produced little effect. Their great practical conclusion, namely, the propriety of taxing exclusively the neat rents of the landlords, evidently depends upon their considering these rents as completely disposeable, like that excess of price above the cost of production, which distinguishes a common monopoly.

M. Say, in his valuable Treatise on Political Economy, in which he has explained with great clearness many points not sufficiently developed by Adam Smith, has not treated the subject of rent in a manner entirely satisfactory. In speaking of the different natural agents which, as well as the land, co-operate with the labours of man, he observes: "Heureusement personne n'a pu dire, le vent et le soleil m'appartiennent, et le service qu'ils rendent doit m'être payé." * And, though he acknowledges that, for obvious reasons, property in land is necessary, yet he evidently considers rent as almost exclusively owing to such appropriation, and to external demand. (45)

* Vol. II. p. 124. Of this work a new and much improved edition has lately been published, which is highly worthy the attention of all those who take an interest in these subjects.

_____

(45) p. 136. *Mr. Say in his valuable Treatise &c.*

Can any one doubt that if a person could appropriate to himself the wind and the sun, he would be able to command a rent for the uses to be derived from them?

(46) p. 137. *The prevailing opinions*

As I have dedicated a chapter in my Political Economy

In the excellent work of M. de Sismondi, *De la Richesse Commerciale*, he says, in a note on the | subject of rent: "Cette partie 137 de la rente foncière est celle que les Economistes ont décorée du nom du *produit net*, comme étant le seul fruit du travail qui ajoutât quelque chose à la richesse nationale. On pourroit, au contraire, soutenir contre eux, que c'est la seule partie du produit du travail, dont la valeur soit purement nominale, et n'ait rien de réelle: c'est en effet le résultat de l'augmentation de prix qu'obtient un vendeur en vertu de son privilège, sans que la chose vendue en vaille réellement davantage."†

The prevailing opinions among the more modern writers in our own country have appeared to me to incline towards a similar view of the subject; and, not to multiply citations, I shall only add, that in a very respectable edition of the *Wealth of Nations*, lately published by Mr. Buchanan, of Edinburgh, the idea of monopoly is pushed still farther. And, while former writers, though they considered rent as governed by the laws of monopoly, were still of opinion that this monopoly in the case of land was necessary and useful, Mr. Buchanan sometimes speaks of it even as prejudicial, and as depriving the consumer of what it gives to the landlord. (46)

In treating of productive and unproductive labour in the last volume, he observes, that,‡ "The neat surplus by which the Economists estimate the utility of agriculture, plainly arises from the high price of its produce, which, however advantageous | to 138 the landlord who receives it, is surely no advantage to the consumer who pays it. Were the produce of agriculture to be sold for a lower price, the same neat surplus would not remain, after defraying the expenses of cultivation; but agriculture would be still equally productive to the general stock; and the only difference

† Vol. I. p. 49.   ‡ Vol. IV. p. 134.

---

to the consideration of this subject,[1] I shall not go over the whole again but shall content myself at the present moment with saying that it appears to me that M. Sismondi, and Mr. Buchanan are substantially right in the opinions which Mr. Malthus has quoted from their works.

[1] Ch. xxxii, 'Mr. Malthus's Opinions on Rent.'

would be, that, as the landlord was formerly enriched by the high price, at the expense of the community, the community will now profit by the low price, at the expense of the landlord. The high price in which the rent or neat surplus originates, while it enriches the landlord who has the produce of agriculture to sell, diminishes, in the same proportion, the wealth of those who are its purchasers; and on this account it is quite inaccurate to consider the landlord's rent as a clear addition to the national wealth."

In other parts of this work he uses the same, or even stronger language, and in a note on the subject of taxes, he speaks of the high price of the produce of land as advantageous to those who receive it, but proportionably *injurious* to those who pay it. "In this view," he adds, "it can form no general addition to the stock of the community, as the neat surplus in question is nothing more than a revenue transferred from one class to another, and, from the mere circumstance of its thus changing hands, it is clear that no fund can arise out of which to pay taxes. The revenue which pays for the produce of land exists already in the hands of those 139 who purchase that produce; | and, if the price of subsistence were lower, it would still remain in their hands, where it would be just as available for taxation, as when by a higher price it is transferred to the landed proprietor."*

That there are some circumstances connected with rent, which have a strong affinity to a natural monopoly, will be readily allowed. The extent of the earth itself is limited, and cannot be enlarged by human demand. The inequality of soils occasions, even at an early period of society, a comparative scarcity of the best lands; and this scarcity is undoubtedly one of the causes of rent properly so called. On this account, perhaps the term *partial monopoly* may be fairly applicable to it. But the scarcity of land,

* Vol. III. p. 212.

---

(47) p. 139. *That quality of the earth &c.*

That is to say it yields a greater value in return than the value of the labour expended on it. In this it agrees with every occupation in which man engages. If produce of all kinds did not fulfil those conditions it would not be produced.

thus implied, is by no means alone sufficient to produce the effects observed. And a more accurate investigation of the subject will shew us how different the high price of raw produce is, both in its nature and origin, and the laws by which it is governed, from the high price of a common monopoly.

The causes of the excess of the price of raw produce above the costs of production, may be stated to be three.

First, and mainly, That quality of the earth, by which it can be made to yield a greater portion of the necessaries of life than is required for the maintenance of the persons employed on the land. (47)

2dly, That quality peculiar to the necessaries of life of being able, when properly distributed, to | create their own demand, or to raise up a number of demanders in proportion to the quantity of necessaries produced. (48)   **140**

And, 3dly, The comparative scarcity of fertile land, either natural or artificial.

The quality of the soil here noticed as the primary cause of the high price of raw produce, is the gift of nature to man. It is quite unconnected with monopoly, and yet is so absolutely essential to the existence of rent, that without it no degree of scarcity or monopoly could have occasioned an excess of the price of raw produce above what was necessary for the payment of wages and profits.

If, for instance, the soil of the earth had been such, that, however well directed might have been the industry of man, he could not have produced from it more than was barely sufficient to maintain those whose labour and attention were necessary to its products; though, in this case, food and raw materials would have been evidently scarcer than at present, and the land might have been in the same manner monopolized by particular owners;

---

(48) p. 139. *That quality peculiar*

This appears to me quite fallacious. I have given my reasons for thinking so in my work on Polit. Econ.[1] See also remark on Page 142[2].

[1] Above, I, 404-9.   [2] Note (51) below.

yet it is quite clear, that neither rent nor any essential surplus produce of the land in the form of high profits and high wages could have existed. (49)

On the other hand, it will be allowed, that in whatever way the produce of a given portion of land may be actually divided, whether the whole is distributed to the labourers and capitalists, or a part is awarded to a landlord, the *power* of such land to yield rent is exactly proportioned to its fertility, or to the general

141 surplus which it can be | made to produce beyond what is strictly necessary to support the labour and keep up the capital employed upon it. If this surplus be as 1, 2, 3, 4, or 5, then its *power* of yielding a rent will be as 1, 2, 3, 4, or 5; and no degree of monopoly—no possible increase of external demand can essentially alter their different *powers*.

But if no rent can exist without this surplus, and if the power of particular soils to pay rent be proportioned to this surplus, it follows that this surplus from the land, arising from its fertility, must evidently be considered as the foundation or main cause of all rent.

Still however, this surplus, necessary and important as it is, would not be sure of possessing a value which would enable it to command a proportionate quantity of labour and other commodities, if it had not a power of raising up a population to consume it, and, by the articles produced in return, of creating an effective demand for it. (50)

It has been sometimes argued, that it is mistaking the principle of population to imagine, that the increase of food or of raw produce alone can occasion a proportionate increase of population. This is no doubt true; but it must be allowed, as has been justly observed by Adam Smith, that "when food is provided, it is

---

(49) p. 140.

"If there had been no surplus produce there could not have been any rent." In this all men are agreed.

(50) p. 141.

"Or if this surplus produce were not in demand it could have no value, and then rent could not be paid for it." If there be an increase of people we have the means of providing

comparatively easy to find the necessary clothing and lodging."
And it should always be recollected, that land does not produce
one commodity alone, but, in addition to that most indispensable
of all commodities—food, | it produces the materials for clothing,   142
lodging, and firing.*

It is therefore strictly true, that land produces the necessaries
of life—produces the means by which, and by which alone, an
increase of people may be brought into being and supported. In
this respect it is fundamentally different from every other kind
of machine known to man; and it is natural to suppose that the
use of it should be attended with some peculiar effects.

If an active and industrious family were possessed of a certain
portion of land, which they could cultivate so as to make it yield
food, and the materials of clothing, lodging, and firing, not only
for themselves but for five other families, it follows, from the
principle of population, that, if they properly distributed their
surplus produce, they would soon be able to command the labour
of five other families, and the value of their landed produce would
soon be worth five times as much as the value of the labour which
had been employed in raising it. But if, instead of a portion of
land | which would yield all the necessaries of life, they possessed   143
only, in addition to the means of their own support, a machine
which would produce hats or coats for fifty people besides them-

* It is however certain that, if either these materials be wanting, or the
skill and capital necessary to work them up be prevented from forming,
owing to the insecurity of property or any other cause, the cultivators will
soon slacken in their exertions, and the motives to accumulate and to increase their produce will greatly diminish. But in this case there will be
a very slack demand for labour: and, whatever may be the nominal cheapness of provisions, the labourer will not really be able to command such
a portion of the necessaries of life, including, of course, clothing, lodging,
&c. as will occasion an increase of population.

for them—this is an essential condition to the maintenance
of an increased population—but it leaves undecided the
question whether the people are produced because you have
raised the corn, or whether the corn is produced because you
have increased the people, and have also all the means of providing[1] for their sustenance as well as for their other wants.

[1] The remainder of the sentence replaces 'for them.'

selves, no efforts which they could make would enable them to
ensure a demand for these hats or coats, and give them in return
a command over a quantity of labour considerably greater than
their fabrication had cost. For a long time, and by possibility for
ever, the machine might be of no more value than that which
would result from its making hats or coats for the family. Its
further powers might be absolutely thrown away from the want
of demand; and even when, from external causes totally independent of any efforts of their own, a population had risen to
demand the fifty hats, the value of them in the command of labour
and other commodities might permanently exceed but very little
the value of the labour employed in making them. (51)

After the new cotton machinery had been introduced into this
country, a hundred yards of muslin of a certain quality would not
probably command more labour than twenty-five yards would
before; because the supply had increased faster than the demand,
and there was no longer a demand for the whole quantity produced at the same price. But after great improvements in agriculture have been adopted upon a limited tract of land, a quarter of
wheat will in a short time command just as much labour as before;
because the increased produce, occasioned by the improvements
144 in cultiva-|tion, is found to create a demand proportioned to the
supply, which must still be limited; and the value of corn is thus
prevented from falling like the value of muslins.

---

(51) p. 142. *If an active and industrious*

The value of their landed property would not be increased
till there was a demand for the additional produce. If they
were tenants and had a money rent to pay they would ruin
themselves by increasing the supply of produce before a
demand existed for it. The money value of the whole produce
would be less than when the quantity was less, and they
would have the same money rent to pay. This was the
peculiar evil under which the farmers suffered at the termination of the war, when the ports were opened. No producer
can have any interest in supplying his commodity in a greater
abundance than it is demanded at its natural price. As soon

Thus the fertility of the land gives the power of yielding a rent, by yielding a surplus quantity of necessaries beyond the wants of the cultivators; and the peculiar quality belonging to the necessaries of life, when properly distributed, tends strongly and constantly to give a value to this surplus by raising up a population to demand it.

These qualities of the soil and of its products have been, as might be expected, strongly insisted upon by the Economists in different parts of their works; and they are evidently admitted as truths by Adam Smith, in those passages of the *Wealth of Nations*, in which he approaches the nearest to the doctrines of the Economists. But modern writers have in general been disposed to overlook them, and to consider rent as regulated upon the principles of a common monopoly, although the distinction is of great importance, and appears obvious and striking in almost any instance that we can assume.

If the fertility of the mines of the precious metals all over the world were diminished one half, it will be allowed that, as population and wealth do not necessarily depend upon gold and silver, such an event might not only be consistent with an undiminished amount of population and wealth, but even with a considerable increase of both. In this case however it is quite certain | that the rents, profits, and wages paid at the different mines in the world might not only not be diminished, but might be considerably   145

---

as it sinks in the market below its natural price, that is to say as soon as the wants of the *existing* population are satisfied, there can be no motive for producing it, but every motive to cease to produce it.

If Mr. Malthus had merely said that with the facility of providing food, population will rapidly increase, because food is one of the most important objects of consumption, it would be impossible to differ with him; but he invariably insists that the increase of population, does not depend on the means which we possess of providing for it, or rather which the people themselves have of providing for their offspring, but on the previous provision of food, which is laid up for them.

increased. But if the fertility of all the lands in the world were to be diminished one half;* inasmuch as population and wealth strictly depend upon the quantity of the necessaries of life which the soil affords, it is quite obvious that a great part of the population and wealth of the world would be destroyed, and with it a great part of the effective demand for necessaries. (52) The largest portion of the lands in most countries would be thrown completely out of cultivation, and wages, profits, and rents, particularly the latter, would be greatly diminished on all the rest. I believe there is hardly any land in this country employed in producing corn, which yields a rent equal in value to the wages of the labour and the profits of the stock necessary to its cultivation. If this be 146 so, then, in the case supposed, | the quantity of produce being

* Mr. Ricardo has supposed a case (p. [403].) of a diminution of fertility of one-tenth, and he thinks that it would increase rents by pushing capital upon less fertile land. I think, on the contrary, that in any well cultivated country it could not fail to lower rents, by occasioning the withdrawing of capital from the poorest soils. If the last land before in use would do but little more than pay the necessary labour and a profit of 10 per cent. upon the capital employed, a diminution of a tenth part of the gross produce would certainly render many poor soils no longer worth cultivating. And, on Mr. Ricardo's supposition, where, I would ask, is the increased demand and increased price to come from, when, from the greater quantity of labour and capital necessary for the land, the means of obtaining the precious metals, or any other commodities, to exchange for corn, would be greatly reduced?

---

(52) p. 145. *But if the fertility &c.*

I acknowledge that a great part of the population and wealth of the world would be destroyed, but the question is concerning the rents of the landlords and not concerning the wealth of the world [1]—one third of 100 millions is more than one fourth of 120 millions. To suppose the fertility of the land diminished one half, is a most extravagant supposition —I made it only to illustrate a principle. Mr. Malthus has misunderstood me—I fully acknowledge the interest which landlords have in the increased fertility of their land, and in improvements in agriculture, for they cannot fail ultimately to reap the benefit,[2] all I contend for, is, that the immediate

[1] Last eight words are ins.   [2] Last nine words are ins.

only half of what was before obtained by the same labour and capital, it may be doubted whether any land in England could be kept in tillage. All effective demand for corn of home growth would be at an end; and if a supply could not be obtained from abroad, the population of the country must be diminished to perhaps one-fifth of its former amount.

The produce of certain vineyards in France, which, from the peculiarity of their soil and situation, exclusively yield wine of a certain flavour, is sold, of course, at a price very far exceeding the cost of production. And this is owing to the greatness of the competition for such wine, compared with the scantiness of its supply, which confines the use of it to so small a number of persons that they are able, and, rather than go without it, willing to give an excessively high price. But, if the fertility of these lands were increased so as very considerably to increase the produce, this produce might so fall in value as to diminish most essentially the excess of its price above the cost of production. While, on the other hand, if the vineyards were to become less productive, this excess might increase to almost any extent.*|

* Mr. Ricardo says, (p. [405].) in answer to this passage, that, "*given the high price*, rent must be high in proportion to abundance and not scarcity," whether in peculiar vineyards or on common corn lands. But this is begging the whole of the question. (53) The price cannot be given. By the force of external demand and diminished supply the produce of an acre of Cham-

---

effects are injurious to them, and if the principle of population were not strong might be permanently[3] injurious to them.

(53) p. 146. *But this is begging the whole of the question*

What does Mr. Malthus say in this passage but that the rent of corn land is limited by its limited[4] power of feeding people—that these vineyards are not limited within so narrow a range. I admit his argument, but it does not change the principle.

---

[3] First written 'were not so strong would be permanently', then revised 'were not strong would be   more or less permanently', and finally corrected as above.
[4] 'limited' is here ins.

147   The obvious cause of these effects is, that, in all common monopolies, the demand is exterior to, and independent of, the production itself. The number of persons, who might have a taste for scarce wines, and would be desirous of entering into a competition for the purchase of them, might increase almost indefinitely, while the produce itself was decreasing; and its price, therefore, would have no other limit than the numbers, powers, and caprices of the competitors for it.

In the production of the necessaries of life, on the contrary, the demand is dependent on the produce itself, and the effects are therefore widely different. In this case it is physically impossible that the number of demanders should increase, while the quantity of produce diminishes, since the demanders can only exist by means of the produce. (54)

In all common monopolies, an excess of the value of the produce above the value of the labour employed in obtaining it, may be

paigne grapes might permanently command fifty times the labour that had been employed in cultivating it; but no possible increase of | external demand or diminution of supply could ever permanently enable the produce of an acre of corn to command more labour than it would support.

---

(54) p. 147. *In this case it is physically impossible*

The question is not about the number of the demanders, but of the sacrifices which they will be willing to make to obtain the commodity demanded. On that must its value depend.

(55) p. 147. *In all common monopolies*

Here is an unfounded distinction. In the partial monopoly of the land, which produces necessaries, (says Mr. M.) such an excess of the value of the produce above the value of the labour, employed in obtaining it, can only be created by the qualities of the soil,—in the other case they are ["]created by external demand." The qualities of the soil can do nothing in either case without external demand. The rent of our most fertile lands is greater now than it was 100 years ago: Why? Because of the increase of external demand, compared with

created by external demand. In the partial monopoly of the land which produces necessaries, such an excess can only be created by the qualities of the soil. (55)

In common monopolies, and all productions except necessaries, the laws of nature do very little towards proportioning their value in exchange to their value in use. The same quantity of grapes or cottons might, under different circumstances, be worth permanently three or three hundred days la-|bour. In the production of necessaries alone, the laws of nature are constantly at work to regulate their exchangeable value according to their value in use; and though from the great difference of external circumstances, and particularly the greater plenty or scarcity of land, this is seldom or ever fully effected; yet the exchangeable value of a given quantity of necessaries in commanding labour always tends to approximate towards the value of the quantity of labour which it can maintain, or in other words, to its value in use. (56)

In all common monopolies, the price of the produce, and consequently the excess of price above the cost of production, may increase without any definite bounds. In the partial monopoly of the land which produces necessaries, the price of the produce

(margin: 148)

---

the facility[1] of supplying it. The qualities of the soil were the same then as now, yet rent did not increase, till external demand increased.

(56) p. 148. *In the production of necessaries &c.*

Why is this? because population is found to increase invariably with the means of providing for it, and therefore its value in corn does not rise—but population and necessaries are not necessarily linked together so intimately—it is not difficult to conceive that with better education and improved habits, a day's labour may become[2] much more valuable estimated even in what are now called[3] the necessaries of the labourer.

---

[1] 'facility' replaces 'means'.   [3] 'what are now called' is ins.
[2] 'doubly' is del. here.

cannot by any possibility exceed the value of the labour which it can maintain; and the excess of its price above the cost of its production is subjected to a limit as impassable. This limit is the surplus of necessaries which the land can be made to yield beyond the lowest wants of the cultivators, and is strictly dependent upon the natural or acquired fertility of the soil. Increase this fertility, the limit will be enlarged, and the land may yield a high rent; diminish it, the limit will be contracted, and a high rent will become impossible; diminish it still further, the limit will coincide with the cost of production, and all rent will disappear. (57)

In short, in the one case, the power of the produce to exceed in price the cost of the production depends mainly upon the 149 degree of the monopoly; | in the other, it depends entirely upon the degree of fertility. This is surely a broad and striking distinction.*

* Yet this distinction does not appear to Mr. Ricardo to be well founded! c. xxxi. p. [405]. 2d edit.

---

(57) p. 148. *In all common monopolies*
In the whole of this paragraph I most fully concur.

(58) p. 149. *It is extraordinary that Mr. Ricardo*
The two opinions appear to me to be quite consistent with each other. It is the expence of producing the last portions of corn which regulate its value, and the value of all other corn that comes to market. Corn raised under more favorable circumstances, and on more fertile land, will afford a rent in proportion to the difference of expence in raising it. This rent then is the condition on which you obtain the whole quantity of corn required—for you could not obtain the additional quantity but on worse land;—to encourage its production its price must rise, and the consequence of a rise of price is rent on[1] the more fertile land. Now this rent is not a clear gain—if landlords receive more the buyers of bread pay more, and therefore I may without meaning the slightest reflection on landlords, which in this case could

[1] 'on' replaces 'to'.

Is it, then, possible to consider the price of the necessaries of life as regulated upon the principle of a common monopoly? Is it possible, with M. de Sismondi, to regard rent as the sole produce of labour, which has a value purely nominal, and the mere result of that augmentation of price which a seller obtains in consequence of a peculiar privilege: or, with Mr. Buchanan, to consider it as no addition to the national wealth, but merely as a transfer of value, advantageous only to the landlords, and proportionably *injurious* to the consumers?†

Is it not, on the contrary, a clear indication of a most inestimable quality in the soil, which God has bestowed on man—the quality

† It is extraordinary that Mr. Ricardo (p. [400].) should have sanctioned these statements of M. Sismondi and Mr. Buchanan. Strictly, according to his own theory, the price of corn is always a natural or necessary price. In what sense then can he agree with these writers in saying, that it is like that of a common monopoly, or advantageous only to the landlords, and proportionably *injurious* to the consumers? (58)

---

only proceed from the grossest ignorance, say that this is a transfer of wealth, advantageous to the landlords and proportionably *injurious* to the consumers. ·

Perhaps in no part of his book has Mr. Malthus so much mistaken me as on this subject—he represents me as supporting the doctrine that the interests of landlords are constantly opposed to those of every other class of the community, and one would suppose from his language that I considered them as enemies to the state. From what I have just said it will be seen, that I think rent, and the increase of rent, the necessary and unavoidable condition of an increased supply of corn for an increasing population. The whole tenor of my work on Polit. Econ. shews the same thing, and it was hardly fair to select a particular passage, which appeared to have a different meaning, and which was applicable only to particular circumstances. In my work,² I have spoken with great approbation of that passage in Mr. Malthus's

² *Principles*, above I, 74–75.

of being able to maintain more persons than are necessary to work
it? Is it not a part, and we shall see farther on that it is an absolutely necessary part, of that surplus produce from the land,
which has been justly stated to be the source of all power and
150 enjoyment; and without which, in fact, there would | be no cities,

---

former work[1], where he says, that the effect of landlords
giving up their whole rent would not make corn cheaper—
this I think was not placing the landlord in an invidious light
in regard to the consumer. All I meant to say of the landlords
interest, was, that it would be for his advantage that the
machine which he had for producing corn should be in
demand—that in fact his rent depended on it;—that on the
contrary it was the interest of the consumer to use the foreign
machine, if that would do the work cheaper. It is only in this
case, that the interests of the landlord and consumer really,
if well understood,[2] come in contact,—in this case I am sure
they do come in contact, and there is nothing which I have
said that I wish to recall on that subject.

I have indeed observed that improvements in agriculture
were in their immediate effects injurious to the landlord, and
beneficial to consumers, but that ultimately when population
increased, the advantage of the improvement was transferred
to the landlord.[3] To this opinion I also adhere, but in saying
so I cast no reproach on landlords—they have not the power
to arrest improvements, nor would it be their interest to do
so if they could. Great improvements in any branch of production are in their first effects injurious to the class who are
engaged in that branch, but this is the statement of a fact or
of an opinion[4], and cannot be supposed to cast any injurious

---

[1] *Inquiry into...Rent*, p. 57.

[2] 'really, if well understood,' is ins.

[3] Above, I, 79–80 and 412; and
cp. 81, n. 1.

[4] The phrase is not a slip for 'of a
fact *not* of an opinion', as the Johns
Hopkins ed. suggests, mistaking
Ricardo's modesty for arrogance.

no military or naval force, no arts, no learning, none of the finer manufactures, none of the conveniences and luxuries of foreign countries, and none of that cultivated and polished society, which not only elevates and dignifies individuals, but which extends its beneficial influence through the whole mass of the people?

---

reflections. Mr. Malthus is not justified by any thing I have said in pointing me out as the enemy of landlords, or as holding any less favorable opinion[5] of them, than of any other class of the community.

Indeed, I do not see that Mr. Malthus's language is very different from my own; in page 152 he says "The fall of profits and wages which practically takes place, undoubtedly transfers a portion of the produce to the landlord" "The transfer from profits and wages, and such a price of produce as yields rent which have been objected to as injurious, and as depriving the consumer of what it gives to the landlord, are absolutely necessary in order to obtain any considerable addition to the wealth and revenue of the first settlers in a new country" Here the transfer is admitted, but it is said to be necessary—I say exactly the same thing, and in page 138 Mr. Malthus quotes a passage from Mr. Buchanan for the purpose of condemning it, which appears to me to express only the same opinion. "The high price in which the rent or neat surplus originates, while it enriches the landlord who has the produce of agriculture to sell, diminishes, in the same proportion the wealth of those who are its purchasers; and on this account it is quite inaccurate to consider the landlord's rent as a clear addition to the national wealth.["]

---

[5] The first part of this sentence replaces 'I know full well that I am not deserving of half the kind things which Mr. Malthus says of me, but I know also that I do not merit being held up as the enemy of landlords, or of holding any worse opinion'.

SECTION II

On the necessary Separation of the Rent of Land from the
Profits of the Cultivator and the Wages of the Labourer

In the early periods of society, or more remarkably perhaps, when the knowledge and capital of an old society are employed upon fresh and fertile land, the surplus produce of the soil shews itself chiefly in extraordinary high profits, and extraordinary high wages, and appears but little in the shape of rent. While fertile land is in abundance, and may be had by whoever asks for it, nobody of course will pay a rent to a landlord. But it is not consistent with the laws of nature, and the limits and quality of the earth, that this state of things should continue. Diversities of soil and situation must necessarily exist in all countries. All land cannot be the most fertile: all situations cannot be the nearest to navigable rivers and markets. But the accumulation of capital beyond the means of employing it on land of the greatest natural fertility, and the most advanta-|geously situated, must necessarily lower profits; while the tendency of population to increase beyond the means of subsistence must, after a certain time, lower the wages of labour.

The expense of production will thus be diminished; but the value of the produce, that is, the quantity of labour, and of the other products of labour (besides corn) which it can command, instead of diminishing, will be increased. There will be an increasing number of people demanding subsistence, and ready to offer their services in any way in which they can be useful. The

---

(59)[1] p. 152. *Mr. Ricardo has quite misunderstood me &c. &c.*

I certainly did misunderstand Mr. Malthus. He says he stated "three causes as necessary to the production of rent and he could not possibly have meant to say that rent should vary always and exactly in proportion to one of them." I should think that my inference that he did was the natural

[1] The whole of this Note is ins. Cp. the footnote added in ed. 3 of Ricardo's *Principles*, above, I, 404.

exchangeable value of food will therefore be in excess above the cost of production, on all the more fertile lands; and this excess is that portion of the general surplus derived from land which has been peculiarly denominated rent.

The quality of the earth first mentioned, or its power to yield a greater portion of the necessaries of life than is required for the maintenance of the persons employed in cultivation, is obviously the foundation of this rent, and the limit to its possible increase. The second quality noticed, or the tendency of an abundance of food to increase population, is necessary both to give a value to the surplus of necessaries which the cultivators can obtain on the first land cultivated; and also to create a demand for more food than can be procured from the richest lands. And the third cause, or the comparative scarcity of fertile land, which is clearly the natural consequence of the second, is finally necessary to separate a portion of the ge-|neral surplus from the land, into the specific 152 form of rent to a landlord.*

* Mr. Ricardo has quite misunderstood me, when he represents me as saying that rent immediately and necessarily rises or falls with the increased or diminished fertility of the land. (p. [404].) How far my former words would bear this interpretation the reader must judge; but I was not aware that they could be so construed; and having stated three causes as necessary to the production of rent, I could not possibly have meant to say that rent would vary always and exactly in proportion to one of them. I distinctly stated, indeed, that in the early periods of society, the surplus produce from the land, or its fertility, appears but little in the shape of rent. (59) Surely he has expressed himself most inadvertently while correcting me, by referring to the comparative scarcity of the most fertile land as the only cause of rent, (p. [403].) although he has himself acknowledged, that without positive fertility, no rent can exist. (p. [404].) If the *most* fertile land of any country were still very poor, such country could yield but very little rent.

---

one if the other causes were at the time inoperative. One of the causes stated by Mr. Malthus as necessary to the production of rent is the comparative scarcity of the most fertile land. If he had said increase this comparative scarcity and rent will rise—I should have agreed with him, and here would have been one cause influencing rent without any interference from the other two [2]. So when talking of what

[2] The last two lines, beginning 'and here', are ins.

Nor is it possible that rents should permanently remain as parts of the profits of stock, or of the wages of labour. (60) If profits and wages were not to fall, then, without particular improvements in cultivation, none but the very richest lands could be brought into use. The fall of profits and wages which practically takes place, undoubtedly transfers a portion of produce to the landlord, and forms a part, though, as we shall see farther on, only a part of his rent. But if this transfer can be considered as injurious to the consumers, then every increase of capital and population must be considered as injurious; and a country which might maintain well ten millions of inhabitants ought to be kept down to a million. The transfer from profits and wages, and such a price of
153   produce as yields | rent, which have been objected to as injurious, and as depriving the consumer of what it gives to the landlord, are absolutely necessary in order to obtain any considerable addition to the wealth and revenue of the first settlers in a new country; and are the natural and unavoidable consequences of that increase of capital and population for which nature has provided in the propensities of the human race.

When such an accumulation of capital takes place on the lands

---

he calls another cause of rent, the fertility of the land, and the excess of its produce beyond what is necessary to support the labourers, employed on it, he said, "Diminish this plenty, diminish the fertility of the soil and the excess will disappear["],—he did appear to me to identify the excess or surplus produce with rent, and he appeared to me to lead his readers to infer that rent rose and fell with the quantity of this surplus produce. And after reading Mr. Malthus's work which is now before me he appears to me by his language frequently to convey an impression to the mind of his reader that rent rises and falls with the rise and fall of the quantity of surplus produce beyond what is bestowed on the actual labourers. In page 228 Mr. Malthus says, "But if it be granted as it must be that a limitation in the power of pro-

first chosen, as to render the returns of the additional stock employed less than could be obtained from inferior land,* it must evidently answer to cultivate such inferior land. But the cultivators of the richer land, after profits had fallen, if they paid no rent, would cease to be mere farmers, or persons living upon the profits of agricultural stock; they would evidently unite the characters of landlords and farmers—a union by no means uncommon, but which does not alter in any degree the nature of rent, or its essential separation from profits and wages.

If the profits of stock on the inferior land taken into cultivation were thirty per cent. and portions of the old land would yield forty per cent., ten per cent. of the forty would obviously be rent by whomsoever received. When capital had further accumulated, | and labour fallen† on the more eligible lands of a country, other　154 lands, less favourably circumstanced with respect to fertility or

---

* The immediate motive for the cultivation of fresh land can only be the prospect of employing an increasing capital to greater advantage than on the old land. A rise in the market-price of corn could not alone furnish such a motive.

† When a given portion of labour and capital yields smaller returns, whether on new land or old, the loss is generally divided between the

---

ducing food is obviously necessary to man confined to a limited space, then the value of the actual quantity of land which he has received depends upon the small quantity of labour necessary to work it compared with the number of persons which it will support or in other words, *upon that specific surplus so much underrated by Mr. Ricardo, which by the laws of nature terminates in rent.*"

(60) p. 152. *Nor is it possible &c.*

A part of what in future will be rent forms now the profits of stock. It is incorrect I think to talk of rent forming at any[1] time the profits of stock, rent is formed from profits of stock, it was not rent when it was profits.

[1] 'past' is del. here.

situation, might be occupied with advantage. The expenses of cultivation, including profits, having fallen, (62) poorer land, or labourers and capitalists, and wages and profits fall at the same time. This is quite contrary to Mr. Ricardo's language. But the wages we refer to are totally different. He speaks of the cost of producing the necessaries of the labourer; I speak of the necessaries themselves. In the same language Mr. Ricardo says, (p. [114].) that the rise of rent never falls upon the farmer. Yet does not the fall of profits go to rent? It is of very little consequence to the farmer and labourer, even on Mr. Ricardo's theory, that they continue to receive between them the same nominal sum of money, if that sum in exchange for necessaries is not worth half what it was before. (61)

---

(61) p. 154. *When a given portion &c., &c.*

True the loss of *quantity* is generally divided between the labourers and capitalists, but we are not talking of quantity, we are talking of value. Will the labourer have less value? if quantity and value be the same thing, and in raw produce they are, according to Mr. Malthus, he will;—but if with the reduction of quantity the value rises, it is certain that the labourer will have a smaller quantity, and a greater value— the farmer will have both a smaller quantity, and a smaller value.

(62) p. 154. *The expences of cultivation having fallen &c. &c.*

In what medium fallen? Not in money—not in Mr. Malthus' measure of value, wages. Except in corn the commodity which requires more labour and rises in value, the expences of cultivation would have risen in value.[1]

(63) p. 154. *And at every step it is clear that if the price of produce do not fall the rent of land must rise.*

It is curious to observe how Mr. Malthus explains the laws of rent, of profits, etc. without having recourse to his own measure of real value;—he contents himself with a medium

[1] An earlier version of this Note read: 'In what medium fallen? Except in corn, and only in that, because corn would rise, the ex- pences of cultivation, including even the fall in profits, would not have fallen.'

land more distant from rivers and markets, though yielding at
first no rents, might fully repay these expenses, and fully answer
to the cultivator. And again, when either the profits of stock, or
the wages of labour, or both, have still further fallen, land still
poorer or still less favourably situated, might be taken into cultivation. And at every step it is clear, that if the price of produce
do not fall, the rent of land must rise. (63) And the price of
produce will not fall so long as the industry and ingenuity of the
labouring classes, assisted by the capitals of those not employed

---

which he condemns, and deems variable. If he says that
during the changes he explains, the medium is varying, then
the alteration in price may be owing to the variation in the
medium, and his account of a rise of rent, and a fall of wages,
is quite unsatisfactory. If he says that to illustrate his argument, he supposes the medium invariable, then he has done
what he condemns in me, for I have only supposed that all
the causes of variation in gold were removed, and that it was
itself invariable.

But Mr. Malthus has another better measure of real value,
why then does he not uniformly use it? there is no information given by telling us of alteration in nominal value. If
Mr. Malthus supposes gold in the case he now mentions
invariable, it ought to agree with his better standard. If
Mr. Malthus chuses the medium which I use, he ought to
argue fairly with² it, he ought to say, not that the price of
produce would not fall, but that it would absolutely rise, for
it is the demand for corn which is the original cause of the
cultivation of new land. It is the high price of corn, which
finally lowers profits, because the smaller quantity obtained
on new land at a high price, will not compensate for the
higher wages, which are consequent on the higher price of
corn. To be consistent then if Mr. Malthus talks of money

² 'with' is written above 'from', which however is not del.

upon the land, can find something to give in exchange to the cultivators and landlords, which will stimulate them to continue undiminished their agricultural exertions, and maintain their excess of produce. |

155   It may be laid down, therefore, as an incontrovertible truth, that as a nation reaches any considerable degree of wealth, and any considerable fullness of population, the separation of rents,

---

prices he must say that corn, rent, and wages would rise, but profits would fall. But with these higher wages the labourer will get less necessaries and[1] enjoyments than before; and therefore in Mr. Malthus's medium[2] they should be called lower wages. I acknowledge that the labourer will get less of these enjoyments, but that does not prove his wages of less value. If I gave a man a shilling a week for the purpose only of buying sugar, and from the effects of a hurricane, sugar should rise to double its former value, no one would, I think, deny that I should give a greater value to the man if I gave him eighteen pence a week, altho' it would purchase him less sugar than one shilling purchased him before. But my complaint against Mr. Malthus now is that he neither uses my language consistently, nor his own. In his own he would have been obliged to say "Population increasing, and there being a demand for a great quantity of corn, all other commodities would have fallen in value, that is to say they would have fallen in the standard which I have chosen, corn, which is of course invariable. The consequence of this fall of value of all commodities would be also a fall of wages, but not in the same proportion as the fall of commodities, consequently if the standard be corn goods will have probably fallen 20 p.c., if it be labour they will have fallen 10 p.c. But as my standard is itself a commodity, and may be increased in

---

[1] 'necessaries and' is ins.

[2] 'in Mr. Malthus's medium' is ins.

as a kind of fixture upon lands of a certain quality, is a law as invariable as the action of the principle of gravity; (64) and that rents are neither a mere nominal value, nor a value unnecessarily and injuriously transferred from one set of people to another; but a most real and essential part of the whole value of the national property, and placed by the laws of nature where they are, on the land, by whomsoever possessed, whether by few or

---

quantity, there is much greater temptation to increase it, than to increase any other commodity, for as compared with labour this commodity has increased in value,[3] all others compared with labour have fallen in value, and consequently greater profits will be obtained by the production of corn: —this however is a wrong conclusion,—it would be true if land of equal fertility could be taken into cultivation, but recourse must be had to poorer land. The smaller quantity obtained on this land, will bear the same relation to the quantity of labour employed[4] as the quantity of corn obtained in exchange for any manufactured goods, will bear to the labour that obtained them; consequently the final result of the increase of population, and the greater demand for corn, will be, a fall in the value of all commodities, lower profits, lower corn wages, and a transfer of a part of the produce, of the better lands, from profits to rent. Landlords will benefit in two ways, first in getting more corn for rent, secondly in getting all goods for a less quantity of corn." This is the way I should explain the laws of rent, and profit, if I adopted Mr. Malthus's language, it differs not in principle from my own, every thing is the same except the medium in which value is estimated.

(64) p. 155. *It may be laid down &c., &c.*

Who denies this? I have expressly affirmed it.[5]

---

[3] 'as compared with' is del. here. [5] Above, I, 77.
[4] 'employed' is ins.

many, whether by the landlord, the crown, or the actual cultivator.

This then is the mode in which rent would separate itself from
profits and wages, in a natural state of things, the least interrupted
by bad government, or any kind of unnecessary monopoly; but
in the different states in which mankind have lived, it is but too
well known that bad government and unnecessary monopolies
have been frequent; and it is certain that they will essentially
modify this natural progress, and often occasion a premature
formation of rent.

In most of the great eastern monarchies, the sovereign has
been considered in the light of the owner of the soil. This premature monopoly of the land joined with the two properties of
the soil, and of its products first noticed, has enabled the government to claim, at a very early period, a certain portion of the
produce of all cultivated land; and under whatever name this
156 may be taken, it is | essentially rent. It is an excess both of the
quantity, and of the exchangeable value of what is produced
above the actual costs of cultivation. (65)

But in most of these monarchies there was a great extent of
fertile territory; the natural surplus of the soil was very considerable; and while the claims upon it were moderate, the remainder was sufficient to afford such ample profits and wages as
could not be obtained in any other employment, (66) and would
allow of a rapid increase of population.

It is obvious, however, that it is in the power of a sovereign

---

(65) pp. 155–156. *And under whatever name this may be taken
it is essentially rent.*

Profits come out of the surplus produce; if profits were
taxed, the tax would come out of the surplus produce, but it
would not therefore come out of rent. Here Mr. Malthus iden-
tifies surplus produce with rent. See remark [(59) on p.] 152.

(66) p. 156. *Such ample profits and wages as could not be
obtained &c.*

Why should profits and wages, in agriculture, at any period
of society, be greater than in any other employment?

who is owner of the soil in a very rich territory to obtain, at an early stage of improvement, an excessive rent. (67) He might, almost from the first, demand all that was not necessary to allow of a moderate increase of the cultivators, which, if their skill was not deficient, would afford him a larger *proportion* of the whole produce in the shape of a tax or rent, than could probably be obtained at any more advanced period of society; but then of course only the most fertile lands of the country could be culti- vated; and profits, wages and population would come to a premature stop.

It is not to be expected that sovereigns should push their rights over the soil to such an extreme extent, as it would be equally contrary to their own interest, and to that of their subjects; but there is reason to believe that in parts of India, and many other eastern countries, and probably even in China, the progress of taxation on the land, founded upon the sovereign's right to the soil, together with other customary payments out of the raw produce, have | forcibly and prematurely lowered the profits of 157 stock, and the wages of labour on the land, and have thrown great obstacles in the way of progressive cultivation and population in latter times, while much good land has remained waste. This will always be the case, when, owing to an unnecessary monopoly, a greater portion of the surplus produce is taken in the shape of rent or taxes, than would be separated by the natural fall of profits and wages. But whatever may be the nature of the monopoly of land, whether necessary or artificial, it will be observed that the

---

(67) p. 156. *It is obvious &c.*

An excessive rent could only be obtained by these means, at such a time.[1] The rent would be created by raising pre- maturely the value of corn as compared with all other things. Would Mr. Malthus deny that this rent, though[2] profitable to the government, would be proportionably injurious to consumers?

[1] 'To tax the produce of the land is the same thing as to diminish its fertility. Mr. Malthus allows here then that to diminish' is del. here.

[2] 'though' replaces 'however'.

power of paying a rent or taxes on the land, is completely limited by its fertility; and those who are disposed to underrate the importance of the two first causes of rent which I have stated, should look at the various distributions of the produce in kind which take place in many parts of India, where, when once the monopoly has enabled the sovereign to claim the principal part of the rent of the soil, every thing else obviously depends upon the surplus of necessaries which the land yields, and the power of these necessaries to command labour (68).

It may be thought, perhaps, that rent could not be forcibly and prematurely separated from profits and wages so as unnaturally to reduce the latter, because capital and labour would quit the land if more could be made of them elsewhere; but it should be recollected, that the actual cultivators of the soil in these countries are generally in a very low and degraded condition; that very little capital is employed by them, and scarcely any which they |
158 can remove and employ in another business; that the surplus produce possessed by the government soon raises up a population to be employed by it, so as to keep down the price of labour in other departments to the level of the price in agriculture; and that the small demand for the products of manufacturing and commercial industry, owing to the poverty of the great mass of society, affords no room for the employment of a large capital, with high profits in manufactures and commerce. (69) On account of these causes which tend to lower profits, and the difficulty of collecting money, and the risk of lending it which tend to raise interest, I have long been of opinion, that though the rate of interest in different countries is almost the only criterion from which a judgment can be formed of the rate of profits; yet that in such countries as India and China, and indeed in most of the eastern and southern regions of the globe, it is a criterion subject

---

(68) p. 157. *But whatever may be the nature &c.*

Who is disposed to underrate the importance of fertility in the land? The surplus produce is necessarily limited by the fertility of the land.

(69) p. 157. *It may be thought*

Capital and labour would get no greater advantage in

to the greatest uncertainty. In China, the legal interest of money is three per cent. per month.* But it is impossible to suppose, when we consider the state of China, so far as it is known to us, that capital employed on land can yield profits to this amount; or, indeed, that capital can be employed in any steady and well-known trade with such a return.

In the same way extraordinary accounts have been given of the high rate of interest in India; | but the state of the actual 159 cultivators completely contradicts the supposition, that, independently of their labour, the profits upon their stock is so considerable; and the late reduction of the government paper to six per cent. fully proves that, in common and peaceable times, the returns of capital, which can be depended upon in other sorts of business, are by no means so great as to warrant the borrowing at a very high rate of interest.

It is probable that, with the exception of occasional speculations, the money that is borrowed at the high rates of interest noticed in China and India, is borrowed in both countries, rather with a view to expenditure or the payment of debts, than with a view to profit.

Some of the causes, which have been noticed as tending prematurely and irregularly to raise rents and lower profits in the countries of the east, operated without doubt to a certain extent in the early stages of society in Europe. At one period most of the land was cultivated by slaves, and in the *metayer* systems which succeeded, the division of the crop was so arranged as to allow the cultivator but little more than a scanty subsistence. In this state of things the rate of profits on the land could have

---

* Penal Code, Staunton, p. 158. The market-rate of interest at Canton is said, however, to be only from twelve to eighteen per cent. Id. note XVII.

---

other employments, not for the reasons stated by Mr Malthus, but because as soon as the tax affected profits, by first absorbing the rent, it would raise the price of raw produce. The rise in the price of raw produce would raise wages and affect the profits equally in all employments, so that there would be no temptation to remove capital from the land.

but little to do with the general rate of profits. The peasant could not, without the greatest difficulty, realize money and change his profession; and it is quite certain that no one who had accumulated a capital in manufactures and commerce, would employ it in cultivating the lands of others as a *metayer*. There would thus be 160 little or no | interchange of capital between trade and agriculture, and their profits might in consequence be very unequal.

It is probable however, as in the case of China and India above mentioned, that profits would not be excessively high. This would depend indeed mainly upon the supply of capital in manufactures and commerce; if capital were scarce, compared with the demand for the products of these kinds of industry, profits would certainly be high; (70) and all that can be said safely is, that we cannot infer that they were very high, from the very high rates of interest occasionally mentioned.

Rent then has been traced to the same common nature with that general surplus from the land, which is the result of certain qualities of the soil and its produce; and it has been found to commence its separation from profits and wages, as soon as they

---

(70) p. 160. *This would depend &c.*

What have profits to do with the supply of[1] capital employed in manufactures and commerce?

Profits in agriculture would be high, if the return to the farmer, after paying his rent, was great, in quantity, compared to the quantity which he must expend for the support of his labourers and other necessary outgoings. Profits mainly depend on the fertility of that land, for which little or no rent is paid.

(71) p. 161. *Such an accumulation of capital as will lower the profits of stock.*

It is here inferred that a fall of profits is a necessary consequence of an accumulation of capital. No mistake can be greater.

(72) p. 161. *Such an increase of population*

It is here also inferred that a fall of wages would neces-

[1] 'the supply of' is ins.

begin to fall from the scarcity of fertile land whether occasioned by the natural progress of a country towards wealth and population, or by any premature and unnecessary monopoly of the soil.

SECTION III

Of the Causes which tend to raise Rents in the ordinary Progress of Society

In tracing more particularly the laws which govern the rise and fall of rents, the main causes | which diminish the expenses of 161 cultivation, or reduce the costs of the instruments of production, compared with the price of produce, require to be more specifically enumerated. The principal of these seem to be four:—1st, Such an accumulation of capital as will lower the profits of stock; (71) 2dly, such an increase of population as will lower the wages of labour; (72) 3dly, such agricultural improvements, or such in-

---

sarily follow an increase of population; it is evident that this must depend on the demand for people. It is also asserted that a rise of rent will necessarily follow a fall of[2] wages. By wages, here, Mr. Malthus means corn, not money wages. Now suppose the corn wages of labourers to fall throughout the country, what temptation would that offer to cultivate fresh land? In the first instance none—the sole effect would be to raise profits.

The rise of profits might lead to fresh accumulations—to an increased demand for labour—to an increase of people— to a higher price of produce, and to an increase of cultivation. Low wages then only operate as they may lead to the accumulation of capital, the first cause of the rise of rent mentioned by Mr. Malthus, and would only produce that effect, if the land to be taken into cultivation were less fertile than that already cultivated.

[2] 'corn' was ins. here, and then del.

crease of exertions as will diminish the number of labourers necessary to produce a given effect; (73) and 4thly, such an increase in the price of agricultural produce, from increased demand, as, without nominally lowering the expense of production, will increase the difference between this expense and the price of produce.

If capital increases so as to become redundant in those depart-

---

(73) p. 161. *3dly Such agricultural improvements*

This is precisely the same as the last cause, and would lead probably to the accumulation of capital by increasing the rate of profits. Mr. Malthus' great mistake seems to be this He first lays down, what is certainly true, that rent is derived from the surplus produce of the land; he then argues that every thing which will augment this surplus produce will raise rent.* But he forgets that profits are also paid out of the surplus produce, and therefore although I agree with him, that a fall of wages,[1] will increase the surplus produce, I do not agree with him that this increase will go to rent—it will infallibly go to profit. I do not say that it will always remain a part of profit, for with the increase of population, and the employment of additional capital on the land, it is highly probable that a part if not the whole and more than the whole[2] of these profits may be transferred to rent.

Mr. Malthus knows, and admits, that rent is the difference between the produce of two equal capitals employed on[3] the cultivation of the land. I ask him then confidently if that difference is increased by a fall of wages?[4] Mr. Malthus may say that improvements on the land, if they increase the

* See 152.[5]

---

[1] 'and improvements in agriculture' is del. here.
[2] Last nine words are ins.
[3] 'different' is del. here.

[4] The Note originally ended here; the remainder is ins.
[5] Note (59) above.

ments where it has been usually employed with a certain rate of profits, it will not remain idle, but will seek employment either in the same or other departments of industry, although with inferior returns, and this will tend to push it upon less fertile soils.

In the same manner, if population increases faster than the demand for it, the labourers must content themselves with a smaller quantity of necessaries; and, the expense of labour in kind

---

produce on all land in equal proportions, will increase the difference, in corn produce [6] between equal capitals employed on the land. True, but will this difference be of greater value, and if it be not will it lead to increased cultivation? [7] will it command more shoes, clothes, furniture, &c. &c.? No,—it may possibly command more labour, that is to say, as labour falls, an equal value of rent will command more. But so will every other equal income in the country and therefore the cultivation of land will not be preferred to any other employment of capital [8]. The capitalist will not only obtain an income of greater value, and therefore obtain more of all commodities that he is desirous of consuming, but with an equal quantity of money, he can command an increased quantity of labour. In this last particular he will be on a par with the landlord. The stockholder will participate in this common advantage, he will receive the same money dividend, but nothing will be lowered in price except labour.

This is on the supposition that the landlord receives an increased corn rent, but he will receive for a considerable time a less corn rent. The improvements in agriculture will increase faster than the population [9] can be increased, consequently capital will be withdrawn from the land, for though

---

[6] 'in corn produce' is ins.
[7] Last eleven words, beginning 'and if', are ins.
[8] Last sixteen words, beginning 'and therefore', are ins.
[9] 'than the population' replaces 'than people'.

being thus diminished, land may be cultivated which could not have been cultivated before. (74)

The two first causes, however, here mentioned sometimes act so as to counterbalance one another. An increase of capital raises the wages of labour, and a fall of wages raises the profits of stock; but | these are only temporary effects. In the natural and regular progress of a country towards the accumulation of stock and the increase of population, the rate of profits and the real wages of

162

---

there would not be an increased demand for corn, there would be an increased demand for other things.

To withdraw capital from the land must be accompanied with a fall of rent. If the corn rent did not fall, the money rent would, and if the prices of all the commodities on which rent was expended, did not fall, which they would not, Mr. Malthus would probably allow that this was a real fall of rent.

I think I see a tenant going to his landlord with £90 instead of a hundred, the prices of all commodities, except corn, being nearly the same as before, and telling him that he had brought him an increase of rent. He would say I have had it proved to me that corn and labour are the only measures of real value—with 90£ you can obtain more corn, and more labour, than you could before with £100[1], you have therefore an increase of rent, the apparent[2] fall is merely nominal. The landlord in all probability would say that it was sufficiently real, since notwithstanding the increase of his rent in this real standard, he was less able to command most of the necessaries and all the luxuries[3] of life.

I know this argument may be retaliated on myself, it may be said you on many occasions say that wages are increased because they rise in your standard of value, the unfortunate labourer however finds when he goes to market with his

[1] 'with £100' is ins.
[2] 'apparent' is ins.
[3] Replaces 'command all the necessaries and enjoyments'.

labour permanently fall together. This may be effected by a permanent rise in the money price of corn, accompanied by a rise, but not a proportionate rise, in the money wages of labour. The rise in the money price of corn is counterbalanced to the cultivator by the diminished quantity of produce obtained by the same capital; and his profits, as well as those of all other capitalists, are diminished, by having to pay out of the same money returns higher money wages; while the command of the labourer over

increased wages he can obtain a less quantity of one of the chief necessaries[4] of life—he then would as you before represented respecting the landlord be content to receive lower wages, if he could get increased comforts. To this I answer that the grievance of the labourer is that the one commodity which he most wants is risen in value, all except corn have remained at the same price, and therefore he can with his wages command more of them all; except this one commodity[5] estimated in the mass of commodities, his wages are really increased.

In the former case, estimated in the mass of commodities the landlord's rent was lowered,—it was increased only if estimated in one single commodity.

(74) p. 161. *In the same manner if population &c.*

If labourers required less corn wages one can easily understand why their employers should be willing to employ the additional corn capital, which wd. revert to them, in manufactures[6]; but one can see no reason why they should be induced to cultivate more, and poorer[7] land. Why produce more of a commodity, if the consumption of it be not increased?

[4] Replaces 'of all the necessaries and conveniences'.
[5] 'except this one commodity' is ins.

[6] Replaces 'to employ an additional capital in manufactures'.
[7] ', and poorer' is ins.

the necessaries of life is of course contracted by the inadequate rise of the price of labour compared with the price of corn.

But this exact and regular rise in the money price of corn and labour is not necessary to the fall of profits; indeed it will only take place in the regular way here described, when money, under all the changes to which a country is subjected, remains of the same value, according to the supposition of Mr. Ricardo,* a case which may be said never to happen. Profits may undoubtedly fall, and rent be separated, under any variations of the value of money. All that is necessary to the most regular and permanent fall of profits (and in this Mr. Ricardo would agree with me) is, that an increased proportion of the value of the whole produce obtained by a given quantity of capital, should be absorbed by

163 labour. On the land, this | is effected by a diminution of the produce, obtained by the same capital without a proportionate diminution of the part absorbed by labour, which leaves less for profits, at the same time that the real wages of the labourer are diminished. (75) But it is obvious that if a smaller quantity of the

* Princ. of Polit. Econ. ch. i. p. [54]. 2d ed.

---

(75) p. 162. *All that is necessary &c.*

I quite agree with Mr. Malthus in the principle here laid down, but I should think it a great error to say that wages had fallen, when it was agreed that the labourer "had an increased proportion of the value of the whole produce obtained by a given quantity of capital.["] Value is I think measured by[1] proportions.

(76) p. 163. *Mr. Ricardo has observed*

Mr. Malthus asks me where the high real wages of America will finally go? I answer they will go with almost the whole of the rest of the surplus produce to rent. But the question is what are the successive steps by which they will arrive at rent. First, they will, when they fall, raise profits.—High profits lead to new accumulations—new accumulations to an increased demand for labour, to an increase of people—to

[1] 'the' is del. here.

necessaries of life derived from a given capital employed on the land, be sufficient to supply both the capitalist and the labourer,† the expenses of cultivation will be diminished, poorer land may be cultivated under the new rates of wages and profits, and rent will rise on that which was before in cultivation. (77)

The third cause enumerated as tending to raise rents by lowering the expenses of cultivation compared with the price of the produce is, such agricultural improvements or such increase of exertions, as will diminish the number of labourers necessary to produce a given effect. (78)

† Mr. Ricardo has observed (p. [411].) in reference to the second cause which I have here stated, as tending to raise rents, "that no fall of wages can raise rents; for it will neither diminish the portion, nor the value of the portion of the produce which will be allotted to the farmer and labourer together." But where, I would ask, will the high real wages of America finally go? to profits? or to rent? If labourers were permanently to receive the value of a bushel of wheat a day, none but the richest lands could pay the expense of working them. An increase of population and a fall of such wages would be absolutely necessary to the cultivation of poor land. How then can it be said that a fall of wages is not one of the causes of a rise of rents? (76)

---

the cultivation of poorer land and finally to an increase of rent.

Mr. Malthus is for jumping over these intermediate steps, and leads his reader to conclude, that every fall of wages, and the effects of² every improvement on the land, are immediately transferred to rent. In this instance, I represent the landlords in a more favorable point of view than he does.

(77) p. 163. *But it is obvious &c. &c.*

This is correct provided there be a demand for the produce—that is absolutely essential to increased cultivation. Mere quantity of produce will not compensate the producer.

(78) p. 163. *The third cause*

Here expences of producing are compared with the price of produce—this supposes an adequate demand for the produce. The question in dispute is taken for granted.

² 'the effects of' is ins.

In improving and industrious countries, not deficient in stimulants, this is a cause of great efficacy. If the improvements
introduced were of such a nature as considerably to diminish
164 the costs of | production, without increasing in any degree the
quantity of produce, then, as it is quite certain that no alteration
would take place in the price of corn, the extravagant profits of
the farmers would soon be reduced by the competition of capitals
from manufactures and commerce; and as the whole *arena* for the
employment of capital would rather have been diminished than
increased, profits on land as well as elsewhere would soon be at
their former level, and the increased surplus from the diminished
expenses of cultivation would go to increase the rents of the
landlords. (79)

But if these improvements, as must always be the case, would
facilitate the cultivation of new land, and the better cultivation
of the old with the same capital, more corn would certainly be

---

(79) p. 163. *If the improvements were of such a nature &c.*

How can the cost of production be reduced without
increasing the quantity of produce, or[1] without lowering
price? The supposition involves a contradiction.

The manufacturers are making low profits, and the farmers
high ones, what is to make their profits meet? The reduction
of the price of corn which would infallibly be effected without
any more capital being employed on the land. What is meant
by an improvement? I do not understand the meaning of
the word if it be not that with the same quantity of labour
a greater quantity of produce[2] can be obtained: although
then the price of produce should fall, profits would rise,
because the whole produce, at a low price, would be worth
more than the former whole produce at a higher price.

But the cost of labour would fall with the fall of corn,
consequently profits would finally settle at the proportion
between the corn expended and the corn obtained. How

[1] Last seven words are ins.   [2] Replaces 'with the same capital
a greater produce'.

brought to market. This would lower its price; but the fall would be of short duration. The operation of that important cause noticed in the early part of this chapter, which distinguishes the surplus produce of the land from all others, namely, the power of the necessaries of life, when properly distributed, to create their own demand, or in other words the tendency of population to press against the means of subsistence, would soon raise the prices of corn and labour, and reduce the profits of stock to their former level, while in the mean time every step in the cultivation of poorer lands facilitated by these improvements, and their application to all the lands of a better quality before cultivated, would universally have raised rents: and thus, under an improving system of cultivation, rents might continue rising without any rise in the exchangeable | value of corn, or any fall in the real 165 wages of labour, or the general rate of profits. (80)

The very great improvements in agriculture which have taken

---

could rent rise? Would any thing raise rent but taking poorer land in cultivation? But you might take poorer land into cultivation because profits are higher! true you might, but would you, till your population had increased, seeing that the very improvement gave you such an additional supply that you would be induced to take capital from the land to manufactures? But how would the profits of manufacturers be increased? By the fall in the price of labour— their commodities would have the same exchangeable value in relation to each other and to money[3] as before, but the price of producing them would be reduced. My conclusion then is in direct opposition to that of Mr. Malthus—profits on all capital employed in agriculture and manufactures would be high, and rents instead of rising would fall, because capital could not be added to the land, but would in all probability be withdrawn from it.

(80) p. 164. *But if these improvements*
  Answered.

[3] Last eight words are ins.

place in this country are clearly demonstrated by the profits of stock being as high now as they were nearly a hundred years ago, when the land supported but little more than half of its present population. And the power of the necessaries of life, when properly distributed, to create their own demand is fully proved by the palpable fact, that the exchangeable value of corn in the command of labour and other commodities is, to say the least, undiminished, notwithstanding the many and great improvements which have been successively introduced in cultivation, both by the introduction of better implements, and by an improved system of managing the land. (81) In fact, these improvements have gone wholly to the increase of rents and the payment of taxes.

It may be added that, when improvements are introduced in particular districts, which tend to diminish the costs of production, the advantages derived from them go immediately, upon the renewal of leases, to landlords, as the profits of stock must necessarily be regulated by competition, according to the general average of the whole country. (82) Thus the very great agricultural improvements which have taken place in some parts of Scotland, the north of England, and Norfolk, have raised, in a very extraordinary manner, the rents of those districts, and left profits where they were.

166   It must be allowed then, that facility of pro-|duction in necessaries,* unlike facility of production in all other commodities, is

---

* Properly speaking, facility of production in necessaries can only be temporary, where there are gradations of land as far as barrenness, except when capital is prevented from increasing by the want of will to save. It may then be permanent. But though corn will, in that case, cost but little labour, its exchangeable value will be high, that is, it will command a great deal.

---

(81) p. 165. *And the power of the necessaries of life &c. &c.*

The proof is very far indeed from satisfactory. To prove that corn raises up demanders it is said that wages have not materially altered. This no more proves that corn has raised up demanders, than it proves that demanders have raised up corn, or been the cause of its being raised up.[1]

[1] Cp. above, I, 405, n. 2.

never attended with a permanent fall of price. They are the only commodities of which it can be said that their permanent value in the command of labour is nearly proportioned to their quantity. And consequently, in the actual state of things, all savings in the cost of producing them will permanently increase the surplus which goes to rent.

The fourth cause which tends to raise rents, is such an increase in the price of agricultural produce from whatever source arising, as will increase the difference between the price of produce, and the costs of production.

We have already adverted to a rise in the price of raw produce, which may take place in consequence of a regular increase of capital and population while money remains nearly of the same value. But this sort of rise is confined within narrow limits, and has little share in those great variations in the price of corn, which are most frequently the subject of observation. The kind of increased price, the effects of which I wish now more particularly to consider, is a rise of price from increased demand, terminating in an alteration in the value of the precious metals. |

If a great and continued demand should arise among sur- 167 rounding nations for the raw produce of a particular country, the price of this produce would of course rise considerably; and the expenses of cultivation rising only slowly and gradually to the same proportion, the price of produce might for a long time keep so much a head as to give a prodigious stimulus to improvement, and encourage the employment of much capital in bringing fresh land under cultivation, and rendering the old much more productive. If however the demand continued, the price of labour would ultimately rise to its former level, compared with corn; a decided fall in the value of money supported by the abundant

---

(82) p. 165. *It may be added* &c.

This must depend upon the degree of improvement in those districts. If the supply from those districts were very greatly increased, rent might be raised on the renewal of leases in them, but it would generally fall in other places, and so would also the price of corn; for the worst land would be thrown out of cultivation.

exportation of raw produce might generally take place; labour would become extremely productive in the purchase of all foreign commodities; and rents might rise without a fall of profits or wages. (83)

The state of money prices, and the rapid progress of cultivation in North America, tend strongly to illustrate the case here supposed. The price of wheat in the eastern states is nearly as high as in France and Flanders; and owing to the continued demand for hands, the money price of day-labour is nearly double what

---

(83) p. 167. *If a great and continued demand &c.*

The price of corn would rise very high, for a time, but whether the rise would be permanent, would depend on the quality of the soil from which the additional quantity should be obtained.

If it were no worse than that already in cultivation, prices would finally settle at their old prices, and profits would only for a time be higher than before. But if worse land was taken into cultivation, the price of corn would rise, and profits would be permanently lower[1]. I do not know how any fall is to take place in the value of money, but I believe Mr. Malthus would call that a fall in the value of money which I call only a rise in the price of a commodity. Every rise in the price of corn he calls a fall in the value of money, altho' money should exchange for precisely the same quantity as before of every other commodity—I should call it a rise in the price of corn, without the slightest variation in the value of money. Money I think only falls in value, when it will exchange for less of all things; not when it will exchange for less of one thing, or of two things, or of a dozen things. There is a marked difference, which Mr. Malthus's language has not provided for, between a rise in the value of a commodity, and a fall in the medium in which value is estimated. Mr. Malthus would

[1] Replaces 'would be lower than before'.

it is in England. But this high price of corn and labour has given great facilities to the farmers and labourers in the purchase of clothing and all sorts of foreign necessaries and conveniences. And it is certain that if the money prices of corn and labour had been both lower, yet had maintained the same proportion to each other, | land of the same quality could not have been cultivated,   168 nor could equal rents have been obtained with the same rate of profits and the same real wages of labour. (84)

Effects of a similar kind took place in our own country from

---

agree that if the demand doubled for hats,[2] though they would at first rise, they would finally be supplied at the old prices in the requisite abundance, unless the expences of production became greater—why would it not be the same with corn?[3] Mr. Malthus concludes this passage by saying that labour would become extremely productive in the purchase of all foreign commodities; and rents might rise without a fall of profits or wages. I think it can be demonstrated that rents could not rise even under the circumstances of this increased demand, unless the expences of production were reduced, or new land of an inferior quality were required to afford the supply.

(84) p. 167. *The state of money prices &c.*

Here is a mixture of facts and of argument. The facts I must take on Mr. M.'s authority—they appear I confess very extraordinary and I cannot help suspecting some mistake in the statement. "The price of wheat in the eastern states of America is nearly as high as in France and Flanders; and owing to the continued demand for hands, the money price of day labour is nearly double what it is in England." The

---

[2] MS, by a mistake, repeats here 'that'.
[3] First written 'in the requisite abundance at the old prices—why would it not be the same with corn unless the expences of production became greater?'—then rearranged as above.

a similar demand for corn during the twenty years from 1793 to the end of 1813, though the demand was not occasioned in the same way. For some time before the war, which commenced in 1793, we had been in the habit of importing a certain quantity of foreign grain to supply our habitual consumption. The war naturally increased the expense of this supply by increasing the expense of freight, insurance, &c.; and, joined to some bad seasons and the subsequent decrees of the French government, raised the price, at which wheat could be imported, in the quantity wanted to supply the demand, in a very extraordinary manner.

This great rise in the price of imported corn, although the import bore but a small proportion to what was grown at home, necessarily raised in the same proportion the whole mass, and gave the same sort of stimulus to domestic agriculture as would have taken place from a great demand for our corn in foreign countries. In the mean time, the scarcity of hands, occasioned by an extending war, an increasing commerce, and the necessity of raising more food, joined to the ever ready invention of an ingenious people when strongly stimulated, introduced so much

---

land then must be more than[1] doubly productive, with the same quantity of labour employed on it, or profits in those states must be lower than in England, for the price of the produce is considerably lower in France and Flanders[2] than in England.

It is undoubtedly true that if a country is to pay a certain money price for foreign necessaries and conveniences, it is for its interest to sell the commodity which it exports at a high, rather than at a low price; it is desirable that for a given quantity of its own commodity, it should obtain a large rather than a small quantity of foreign commodities in return, but in what way a nation can so regulate its affairs as to accomplish this by any means which it is in its power to adopt, I am totally at a loss to conceive. All trade is in fact a trade of barter, and if money can by any laws be so dis-

[1] 'more than' is ins.   [2] 'in France and Flanders' is ins.

saving of manual labour into every department of industry, that the new | and inferior land taken into cultivation to supply the 169 pressing wants of the society, was worked at a less expense of labour than richer soils some years before. Yet still the price of grain necessarily kept up as long as the most trifling quantity of foreign grain, which could only be obtained at a very high price, was wanted in order to supply the existing demand. With this high price, which at one time rose to nearly treble in paper and above double in bullion, compared with the prices before the war, it was quite impossible that labour should not rise nearly in proportion, and with it, of course, as profits had not fallen, all the commodities into which labour had entered.

We had thus a general rise in the prices of commodities, or fall in the value of the precious metals, compared with other countries, which our increasing foreign commerce and abundance of exportable commodities enabled us to sustain. That the last land taken into cultivation in 1813 did not require more labour to work it than the last land improved in the year 1790, is incontrovertibly proved by the acknowledged fact, that the rate of

---

tributed or accumulated as to raise the price of **exportable** commodities, it will **also raise the** price of imported commodities; so that whether money be of a high or of a low value, it will not affect foreign trade; for a given quantity of a home commodity in either case will be bartered for a given quantity[3] of a foreign commodity: If the exportable commodity wheat[4] had been at a low price in the Eastern States, while the foreign commodities were at a high price, those states would not have been so prosperous, because they would not have made such advantageous exchanges. This appears to me to be the substance of Mr. Malthus's observations. If countries had the power of regulating prices they would all sell at high prices and buy at low ones.[5]

[3] Last ten words, beginning 'in either', replace 'neither more nor less will be received'.

[4] 'wheat' is ins.

[5] The last sentence is ins.

interest and profits was higher in the later period than the earlier. But still the profits were not so much higher as not to have rendered the interval most extremely favourable to the rise of rents. This rise, during the interval in question, was the theme of universal remark; and though a severe and calamitous check, from a combination of unfortunate circumstances, has since oc-170 curred; yet the great drainings and permanent | improvements, which were the effects of so powerful an encouragement to

---

(85) p. 168. *Effects of a similar kind*

The price of grain in England rose from two causes; one, which was common to all other commodities, the fall in the value of the medium in which price was estimated; this rise was merely nominal, and was occasioned by the depreciation of paper money. The other cause was, as Mr. Malthus states, the increased expence of importing corn. On a comparison of the expence of growing our corn, and importing it, it was found cheaper to grow it than to import it, but with a given expence[1] less corn was obtained, than we could before import, and so far the change was highly disadvantageous to England. For a time indeed, from the urgency of the demand for this prime necessary of life, its value might be sustained in the market at a price greatly exceeding its cost of produc-tion,[2] or natural price; and during such time agricultural profits might be high; but it would be very unsafe from such a circumstance to infer any general rule that such a change from importing to growing corn, not from choice, but from necessity, was not very injurious to the interests of the country[3] for it must be remembered that these high profits were and could only be at the expence of the consumer.

But it seems that we derived a compensation from the general rise of the prices of our commodities! By what was

[1] 'expence' is written above 'ex-penditure', which however is not del.

[2] 'of production,' is ins.

[3] The remainder of this sentence is ins.

agriculture, have acted like the creation of fresh land, and have increased the real wealth and population of the country, without increasing the labour and difficulty of raising a given quantity of grain.

It is obvious then that a fall in the value of the precious metals, commencing with a rise in the price of corn, has a strong tendency, while it lasts, to encourage the cultivation of fresh land and the formation of increased rents. (85)

---

this general rise occasioned? Not by our growing our own corn, that may raise the price of corn but will not raise the price of any other commodity [4]. Corn rises [5] comparatively to other things, on account of the increased difficulty of producing it.

Suppose money now to fall in value, not only commodities, but corn also, will rise in price; but the one rise in corn is totally independent of the other. The one rise is owing to the difficulty of production and is confined to corn and agricultural produce, the other is owing to a fall in the value of money and is common to all commodities. This second rise is only nominal, and if it be caused by a depreciation of paper money, which is partial to this country, though goods and corn may rise 20 p.c., bullion will also rise in the same degree, and the exchange will be proportionally against us, so that in all our transactions [6] with foreigners we buy of them as dear and sell to them as cheap as if no such rise had taken place. That rents would rise when we ceased importing

[4] 'but by a fall in the value of money' was ins. here and subsequently del.

[5] 'first' was ins. here and then del.

[6] The first part of this paragraph, beginning 'Suppose', replaces what was originally a continuation of the preceding paragraph: '; commodities rise next, and corn rises still more, on account of the fall in the value of money, which if confined to paper money and not extending to bullion is called depreciation of money. But such a rise is only nominal; if goods rise 20 p.c., the exchange is 20 p.c. against us, bullion is at 20 p.c. premium—so that in all our transactions' etc.

A similar effect would be produced in a country which continued to feed its own people, by a great and increasing demand for its manufactures. These manufactures, if from such a demand the value of their amount in foreign countries was greatly to increase, would bring back a great increase of value in return, which increase of value could not fail to increase the value of the raw produce. The demand for agricultural as well as manufactured produce would be augmented; and a considerable stimulus, though not perhaps to the same extent as in the last case, would be given to every kind of improvement on the land.

Nor would the result be very different from the introduction of new machinery, and a more judicious division of labour in

---

corn is precisely what would be expected—poorer soils would be taken into cultivation which never fails to raise rent.

The peculiar circumstances under which we were placed, sunk, according to Mr. Malthus, the value of the precious metals in this country as compared with their value in other countries[1]. Money was depreciated then, because it was not of equal value with bullion, but it was in addition to this cause of still lower value than before, compared with commodities, because bullion was also lower in comparative value. Now I have always understood that in the differences on the Bullion question Mr. Malthus took a middle course, and ascribed the apparent fall in the value of paper, partly to a real fall in the value of paper and partly to a real[2] rise in the value of the medium (bullion) with which it was compared. He said,[3] that the merchants were partly right, because the difference between bullion and paper was owing partly[4] to a rise of bullion—the bullionists were also partly right because the difference was also owing to the fall of paper; now, how-

---

[1] The last eight words are ins.
[2] 'real fall in the value of paper and partly to a real' is ins.
[3] 'in substance' is del. here.
[4] 'partly' is ins.

manufactures. It almost always happens in this case, not only that the quantity of manufactures is very greatly increased, but that the value of the whole mass is augmented, from the great extension of the demand for them both abroad and at home, occasioned by | their cheapness. We see, in consequence, that in all 171 rich manufacturing and commercial countries, the value of manufactured and commercial products bears a very high proportion to the raw products;* whereas, in comparatively poor countries,

* According to the calculations of Mr. Colquhoun, the value of our trade, foreign and domestic, and of our manufactures, exclusive of raw materials, is nearly equal to the gross value derived from the land. In no other large country probably is this the case.—Treatise on the Wealth, Power, and Resources of the British Empire, p. 96.

---

ever, he tells us that the value of bullion fell in this country, and therefore that the bullionists hardly pushed their argument so far as it would go. How does he reconcile the opinion, given in this passage, to that expressed in Page 6 of the same work. "I have always thought that the late controversy on the bullion question presented a signal instance of this kind of error. Each party being possessed of a theory which would account for an unfavourable exchange and an excess of the market above the mint price of bullion, adhered to that single view of the question, which it had been accustomed to consider as correct; and scarcely one writer seemed willing to admit of the operation of both theories." Now what were the two theories. ["]Bullion has not varied said one party, and the variation in the price of gold has been owing to a fall of paper." "Paper has not varied" said the other party ["]and the variation in the price of gold has been owing to the rise in the value of gold." The truth lies between said [5] Mr. Malthus; yet he now maintains not only that gold had not risen, as some of the bullionists, I think erroneously,[6] contended, but he contends that it actually fell.

[5] Replaces 'says'.

[6] Cp. letter 147 to Trower, 25 Dec. 1815.

without much internal trade and foreign commerce, the value of their raw produce constitutes almost the whole of their wealth.

In those cases where the stimulus to agriculture originates in a prosperous state of commerce and manufactures, it sometimes happens that the first step towards a rise of prices is an advance in the wages of commercial and manufacturing labour. This will naturally have an immediate effect upon the price of corn, and an advance of agricultural labour will follow. It is not, however, necessary, even in those cases, that labour should rise first. If, for instance, the population were increasing as fast as the mercantile and manufacturing capital, the only effect might be an increasing number of workmen employed at the same wages, which would occasion a rise in the price of corn before any rise had taken place in the wages of labour.

We are supposing, however, now, that labour does ultimately rise nearly to its former level compared with corn, that both are 172 considerably higher, | and that money has suffered a decided change of value. Yet in the progress of this change, the other outgoings, besides labour, in which capital is expended, can never all rise at the same time, or even finally in the same proportion. A period of some continuance can scarcely fail to occur when the difference between the price of produce and the cost of production

---

(86)[1] p. 172. *A fall in the value of money cannot indeed be peculiar to one country without the possession of peculiar advantages in exportation.*

In this opinion I partly concur, but it is necessary to understand what the nature of this peculiar advantage is. Competition at home will keep our commodities at the price at which we can afford to sell them, but that price may be much lower particularly with respect to a few commodities[2]

[1] The whole of this Note, with the exception of the two concluding paragraphs, replaces: 'In this opinion I fully concur but does it not overturn Mr. Malthus' theory as explained in the last four pages? What advantages, in exportation, had England which she had not before, in the 20 years from 1793 to 1813 in consequence of being obliged to grow her own corn, that it is to that circumstance Mr. M. ascribes the partial fall in England of the value of money?'
[2] Last seven words are ins.

is so increased as to give a great stimulus to agriculture; and as the increased capital, which is employed in consequence of the opportunity of making great temporary profits, can seldom or ever be entirely removed from the land, a part of the advantage so derived is permanent; together with the whole of that which is occasioned by a greater rise in the price of corn than in some of the materials of the farmer's capital.

Mr. Ricardo acknowledges that, in a fall of the value of money, taxed commodities will not rise in the same proportion with others; and, on the supposition of the fall in the value of money being peculiar to a particular country, the same must unquestionably be said of all the various commodities which are either wholly or in part imported from abroad, many of which enter into the capital of the farmer. He would, therefore, derive an increased power from the increased money price of corn compared with those articles. A fall in the value of money cannot indeed be peculiar to one country without the possession of peculiar advantages in exportation; but with these advantages, which we know are very frequently possessed, and are very frequently increased by stimulants, a fall | in the value of money can scarcely 173 fail permanently to increase the power of cultivating poorer lands, and of advancing rents. (86)

---

than foreigners can make them for, and therefore if they could not obtain them at our cheap prices, they would be willing to pay a much dearer[3] price for them. The great facility of making cotton goods, which cannot perhaps be rivalled in other countries, would, but for our domestic competition, enable us to charge a higher price for them. We may be in possession too of very productive mines, and the metal we obtain from them, may be, from the same cause, sunk below the value which foreigners would readily, and willingly, give for it. What means then have we of charging a higher price for these peculiar commodities. One we have which is evident, and very certain in its effects. Government may[4] lay a duty on the exportation of such commodities,

[3] Replaces 'a dear'.　　　　[4] 'tax' is del. here.

Whenever then, by the operation of the four causes above mentioned, the difference between the price of produce and the cost of the instruments of production increases, the rents of land will rise.

It is, however, not necessary that all these four causes should

---

which will not fail to raise their price to the foreign consumer, without any injury to the home manufacturer.

There is another method which is however doubtful in its effects, and it is to this to which Mr. Malthus refers.

By restrictions on the importation of corn, it is said, great encouragement will be given to the importation of bullion, which will sink its value as compared with corn and labour, and will raise the price of all home made commodities. The natural price of all these commodities will be also raised, while no such rise will take place in the natural price of all foreign commodities;—on the contrary as bullion will be sent from foreign countries, and its value be raised, the natural price of the commodities of those countries will be lowered, and thus in all our foreign trade, which is always finally a trade of barter, we shall obtain more foreign commodities in exchange for a given quantity of ours. Now the justness of this argument depends upon this, whether a low value of money, as compared with corn and labour, peculiar to one country, is necessarily attended with a low value of money, compared with other commodities;—whether, in short, it will raise the natural price of our home made commodities, for it is only in that case that we can be benefited. Money, I think, cannot, from the cause which we are now discussing, be so lowered in value, relatively to our domestic commodities, unless our demand for the commodities of foreign countries is in some degree exhausted, and we therefore refuse to take any more of their commodities in exchange for ours, while they are willing to take more of ours in

operate at the same time; it is only necessary that the difference here mentioned should increase. If, for instance, the price of produce were to rise, while the wages of labour and the price of the other branches of capital did not rise in proportion, and at the same time improved modes of agriculture were coming into

exchange for theirs. In that case money will be imported in unusual quantity, for it is the only condition on which foreigners can obtain the required quantity of English commodities, and they will consequently rise. At the same time corn and labour will have a further rise—they rose first on account of the increased difficulty of producing corn, and secondly on account of the increased quantity and low value of money. On these conditions it is undoubtedly true that by refusing to import so valuable a commodity as corn if its place cannot be supplied by other articles of foreign production, and we have peculiar facilities in the manufacturing of commodities in very general demand the trade of barter, or foreign trade will be peculiarly favourable to England.

We shall sell our goods at a high money price, and buy foreign ones at a low money price,—but it may well be doubted whether this advantage will not be purchased at many times its value, for to obtain it we must be content with a diminished production of home commodities; with a high price of labour, and a low rate of profits.

Such a sacrifice is in every view unpardonable, if, as I have shewn, the same benefit can be obtained, without prohibiting the importation of foreign corn, by simply imposing a duty on the exportation of those commodities, in the production of which we have either peculiar skill, or derive peculiar advantages from climate or situation.

We must not forget too that in imposing restrictions on the importation of corn it is doubtful whether the advantage is obtained at all, because bullion will not as I said before be

general use, it is evident that this difference might be increased, although the profits of agricultural stock were not only un-diminished, but were to rise decidedly higher. (87)

Of the great additional quantity of capital employed upon the land in this country during the last twenty years, by far the greater part is supposed to have been generated on the soil, and not to have been brought from commerce or manufactures. And it was unquestionably the high profits of agricultural stock, occasioned by improvements in the modes of agriculture, and by the constant rise of prices, followed only slowly by a propor-

---

imported—will not sink in general value in this country, while we are disposed to accept foreign goods in payment for our domestic commodities.

The whole argument assumes too that we have com-modities which would bear a high value in foreign trade, but are kept at a low value by the effects of domestic competition.

If then my statement is correct Mr. Malthus proposition is much too general, for money may be, and frequently is peculiarly low in value, compared with corn and labour, in one country, without being low compared with all other things; in which case it would have no advantages whatever, to compensate it for a high value of corn and labour, in the exportation of other commodities.[1]

What is it in the case of the Eastern States of America which gives them the advantages ascribed to a partial fall in the value of money?[2] Is it because their corn is nearly as high as in Europe, and the wages of labour twice as high as in England? These are not circumstances peculiarly favorable to the exportation of the commodity they produce.

It is never the fall in the value of money, but a rise in the value of corn, which will occasion the cultivation of poorer land.

[1] The rewritten section ends here.   [2] Cp. Malthus's p. 167; above, p. 144.

tionate rise in the materials of the farmer's capital, that afforded the means of so rapid and so advantageous an accumulation. |

In this case cultivation has been extended, and rents have risen, 174 although one of the instruments of production, capital, has been dearer. (88)

In the same manner a fall of profits, and improvements in agriculture, or even one of them separately, might raise rents, notwithstanding a rise of wages.

It is further evident, that no fresh land can be taken into

---

(87) p. 173. *If for instance*

Here,[3] two or 3 things must concur, which do not usually happen at the same time. We are to have improved modes of agriculture, which of course will increase the quantity of produce obtained with a given quantity of labour; and yet the labourer is to have less produce[4] given him for wages. We are then to have increased quantity, with a diminished consumption, and a higher price—these are things which I do not know how to reconcile.

(88) p. 174. *In this case &c.*

It must not be supposed from any thing I have said that I deny the possibility of rents being higher, tho' profits may not be lower, than at an antecedent period, when rents were lower. What I say is this, improvements in agriculture raise profits,—population increases, cultivation is extended, and rents rise—profits then fall, perhaps not so low as before perhaps lower[5]; but profits are the fund from which all rent is derived. There is no rent which did not at one time constitute profits.

---

[3] The Note originally opened: 'This would be a common benefit', which was del.

[4] 'produce' is ins.

[5] 'perhaps lower' is ins.

cultivation till rents have risen, or would allow of a rise upon what is already cultivated.

Land of an inferior quality requires a great quantity of capital to make it yield a given produce; and if the actual price of this produce be not such as fully to compensate the cost of production, including profits, the land must remain uncultivated. It matters not whether this compensation is effected by an increase in the money price of raw produce, without a proportionate increase in the money price of the instruments of production; or by a decrease in the price of the instruments of production, without a proportionate decrease in the price of produce. What is absolutely necessary is, a greater *relative* cheapness of the instruments of production, to make up for the quantity of them required to obtain a given produce from poor land.

But whenever, by the operation of one or more of the causes before mentioned, the instruments of production become cheaper, and the difference between the price of produce and the expenses
175 of cultivation increases, rents naturally rise. (89) It fol-|lows therefore as a direct and necessary consequence, that it can never answer to take fresh land of a poorer quality into cultivation till rents have risen, or would allow of a rise, on what is already cultivated.

It is equally true, that without the same tendency to a rise of rents,* it cannot answer to lay out fresh capital in the improvement of old land; at least upon the supposition, that each farm is already furnished with as much capital as can be laid out to advantage, according to the actual rate of profits. (90)

* Rents may be said to have a tendency to rise, when more capital is ready to be laid out upon the old land, but cannot be laid out without diminished returns. When profits fall in manufactures and commerce from the diminished price of goods, capitalists will be ready to give higher rents for the old farms.

---

(89) p. 174. *But whenever by the operation &c. &c. rents naturally rise*

But by no means necessarily; the value of the surplus produce rises, and this may be added to profits. All other profits must increase at the same time.

It is only necessary to state this proposition to make its truth appear. It certainly may happen, (and I fear it happens very frequently) that farmers are not provided with all the capital which could be employed upon their farms at the actual rate of agricultural profits. But supposing they are so provided, it implies distinctly, that more could not be applied without loss, till, by the operation of one or more of the causes above enumerated, rents had tended to rise.

It appears then, that the power of extending cultivation and increasing produce, both by the cultivation of fresh land and the improvement of the old, depends entirely upon the existence of such prices, compared with the expense of pro-|duction, as would   176
raise rents in the actual state of cultivation.

But though cultivation cannot be extended and the produce of a country increased, except in such a state of things as would allow of a rise of rents; yet it is of importance to remark, that this rise of rents will be by no means in proportion to the extension of cultivation or the increase of produce. Every relative fall in the price of the instruments of production may allow of the employment of a considerable quantity of additional capital; and when either new land is taken into cultivation or the old improved, the increase of produce may be considerable, though the increase of rents be trifling. We see, in consequence, that in the progress of a country towards a high state of cultivation, the quantity of capital employed upon the land and the quantity of produce yielded by it bear a constantly increasing proportion to the amount of rents, unless counterbalanced by extraordinary improvements in the modes of cultivation.† |

† To the honour of Scotch cultivators it should be observed, that they have applied their capitals so very skilfully and economically, that at the same time that they have prodigiously increased the produce, they have

---

(90) p. 175. *It is equally true*

In almost all that Mr. Malthus says in this, and the following pages, to the end of the section, I most fully concur. We should agree as to the final results, but we differ greatly in our opinions of the steps by which the final results are brought about.

177   According to the returns lately made to the Board of Agriculture, the average proportion which rent bears to the value of the whole produce seems not to exceed one-fifth;* whereas formerly, when there was less capital employed and less value produced, the proportion amounted to one-fourth, one-third, or even two-fifths. Still, however, the numerical difference between the price of produce and the expenses of cultivation increases with the progress of improvement; and though the landlord has a less *share* of the whole produce, yet this less share, from the very great increase of the produce, yields a larger quantity, and gives him a greater command of corn and labour. If the produce of land be represented by the number six, and the landlord has one-fourth of it, his share will be represented by one and a half. If the produce of land be as ten, and the landlord has one-fifth of it, his share will be represented by two. In the latter case, therefore, though the proportion of the landlord's share to the whole produce is greatly diminished, his real rent, independently of nominal price, will be increased in the proportion of from three to four. And, in general, in all cases of increasing produce, if the landlord's share of this produce do not diminish in the same proportion, which, though it often happens during the currency of leases, rarely or never happens on the renewal of them, the real rents of land must rise. |

178   We see then that a progressive rise of rents seems to be necessarily connected with the progressive cultivation of new land, and the progressive improvement of the old: and that this rise is the natural and necessary consequence of the operation of four causes, which are the most certain indications of increasing prosperity and wealth—namely, the accumulation of capital, the increase of population, improvements in agriculture, and the high market price of raw produce, occasioned either by a great demand for it in foreign countries, or by the extension of commerce and manufactures.

increased the landlord's proportion of it. The difference between the landlord's share of the produce in Scotland and in England is quite extraordinary —much greater than can be accounted for, either by the natural soil or the absence of tithes and poors-rates.—See Sir John Sinclair's valuable Account of the Husbandry of Scotland; and the General Report not long since published—works replete with the most useful and interesting information on agricultural subjects.

* See Evidence before the House of Lords, given by Arthur Young, p. 66.

SECTION IV

Of the Causes which tend to lower Rents

The causes which lead to a fall of rents are, as may be expected, exactly of an opposite description to those which lead to a rise: namely, diminished capital, diminished population, a bad system of cultivation, and the low market price of raw produce. They are all indications of poverty and decline, and are necessarily connected with the throwing of inferior land out of cultivation, and the continued deterioration of the land of a superior quality.* (91)

The necessary effects of a diminished capital and diminished population in lowering rents, are too | obvious to require explanation; nor is it less clear that an operose and bad system of   179

* The effects of importing foreign corn will be considered more particularly in the next section, and a subsequent part of this chapter.

---

(91) p. 178. *They are all indications of poverty and decline*

Not all. To allow the free importation of corn, would lower rents, but would be no indication of poverty and decline. Continued improvements in agriculture might throw lands out of cultivation for years, till the population could come up to[1] the increased means of providing for it. This would be no symptom of decline. The adoption of a cheaper food would throw land out of cultivation, without being necessarily accompanied with poverty, for the people might have a greater desire for articles of dress and furniture, and might expend what they saved in the article of food, on these enjoyments. This would not be poverty and decline.[2]

[1] 'come up to' is written above 'keep pace with', which however is not del.   [2] The last sentence is ins.

cultivation might prevent the formation of rents, even on fertile land, by checking the progress of population and demand beyond what could be supplied from the very richest qualities of soil. I will only therefore advert to the fourth cause here noticed.

We have seen that a rise in the price of corn, terminating in an alteration in the value of the precious metals, would give a considerable stimulus to cultivation for a certain time, and some facilities permanently, and might occasion a considerable and permanent rise of rents. And this case was exemplified by what had happened in this country during the period from 1794 to 1814.

It may be stated in like manner, that a fall in the price of corn terminating in a rise in the value of money, must, upon the same principles, tend to throw land out of cultivation and lower rents. (92) And this may be exemplified by what happened in this country at the conclusion of the war. The fall in the price of corn at that period necessarily disabled the cultivators from employing the same quantity of labour at the same price. Many labourers, therefore, were unavoidably thrown out of employment; and, as the land could not be cultivated in the same way, without the same number of hands, the worst soils were no longer worked, much agricultural capital was destroyed, and rents universally fell; while this great failure in the power of purchasing, among all those who either rented or possessed land, naturally occasioned
180 a | general stagnation in all other trades. In the mean time, the fall in the price of labour from the competition of the labourers joined to the poverty of the cultivators, and the fall of rents both

---

(92) p. 179. *It may be stated in like manner*

It is not necessary to repeat my objection to this theory.[1] Of course I allow that if the fall was occasioned by the free admission of foreign corn, rents would fall; this would not I think be an evil but a benefit.

If the fall took place from a rise[2] in the value of money it would affect every thing alike, and is only injurious as it increases the weight of taxation. This however is not an unmixed evil—the stockholder gains what the other classes

[1] Cp. above, I, 417 ff.   [2] Replaces 'fall'.

from the want of power and the want of will to pay the former rents, restored by degrees the prices of commodities, the wages of labour, and the rents of land, nearly to their former proportions, though all lower than they were before. The land which had been thrown out of tillage might then again be cultivated with advantage; but in the progress from the lower to the higher value of money, a period would have elapsed of diminished produce, diminished capital, and diminished rents. The country would recommence a progressive movement from an impoverished state; and, owing to a fall in the value of corn greater than in taxed commodities, foreign commodities, and others which form a part of the capital of the farmer and of the necessaries and conveniences of the labourer, the permanent difficulties of cultivation would be great compared with the natural fertility of the worst soil then actually in tillage.

It appeared that, in the progress of cultivation and of increasing rents, it was not necessary that all the instruments of production should fall in price at the same time; and that the difference between the price of produce and the expense of cultivation might increase, although either the profits of stock or the wages of labour might be higher, instead of lower.

In the same manner, when the produce of a | country is de- 181 clining, and rents are falling, it is not necessary that all the instruments of production should be dearer. In the natural progress of decline, the profits of stock are necessarily low; because it is specifically the want of adequate returns which occasions this decline. (93) After stock has been destroyed, profits may become

---

lose, and he may if he pleases make as good use of it. Whether he will or no is matter of opinion. Why an alteration in the value of money should impoverish a state, or why it should throw land out of tillage, or diminish corn rents, rents in[3] Mr. M.'s standard, I do not clearly see.

(93) p. 181. *In the natural progress of decline &c. &c.*

All just theory would lead to the very opposite conclusion. Labour would be cheap, because the population could not fail to be redundant. Produce would be dear as compared

[3] 'rents in' is ins.

high and wages low; but the low price of raw produce joined to
the high profits of a scanty capital may more than counterbalance
the low wages of labour, and render it impossible to cultivate land
where much capital is required.

It has appeared also, that in the progress of cultivation, and of
increasing rents, rent, though greater in positive amount, bears
a less and less proportion to the quantity of capital employed
upon the land, and the quantity of produce derived from it.
According to the same principle, when produce diminishes and
rents fall, though the amount of rent will always be less, the proportion which it bears to capital and produce will be greater. And
as, in the former case, the diminished proportion of rent was
owing to the necessity of yearly taking fresh land of an inferior
quality into cultivation, and proceeding in the improvement of
old land, when it would return only the common profits of stock,
with little or no rent; so, in the latter case, the high proportion of
rent is owing to the discouragement of a great expenditure in

---

with labour, because with the diminished capital less would
be produced and the same number of men would be willing
to work for it.[1] Rents would be low, because none but the
best lands would be cultivated. What can be more favorable
to high profits than low wages, and low rent[2]? Be it remembered too that they must be estimated in Mr. Malthus' medium
labour, of which they[3] would then have a great command.

(94) p. 182. *If the doctrine here laid down &c.*

The[4] society is interested in having a large neat surplus
from the land—it is also interested in having this large neat
surplus sold at a cheap price. If corn be sold at a low price
it is a proof that profits are high on the land last taken into

[1] First written simply: 'Produce
would be dear because with the
diminished capital less would be
produced.'
[2] The sentence originally continued 'and high prices'; this
was replaced by 'and the whole
produce of a high value', which
was finally del.
[3] '(the profits of capital)' was
first ins. here, then del.
[4] The Note originally opened:
'Who maintains such an absurd
doctrine', which was del.

agriculture, and the necessity of employing the reduced capital of the country in the exclusive cultivation of the richest lands, and leaving the re-|mainder to yield what rent can be got for them in 182 natural pasture, which, though small, will bear a large *proportion* to the labour and capital employed. In proportion, therefore, as the relative state of prices is such as to occasion a progressive fall of rents, more and more lands will be gradually thrown out of cultivation, the remainder will be worse cultivated, and the diminution of produce will proceed still faster than the diminution of rents.

If the doctrine here laid down respecting the laws which govern the rise and fall of rents, be near the truth, the doctrine which maintains that, if the produce of agriculture were sold at such a price as to yield less neat surplus, agriculture would be equally productive to the general stock, must be very far from the truth. (94) With regard to my own conviction, indeed, I feel no sort of doubt that if, under the impression that the high price of

---

cultivation. If sold at a high price it is equally clear that profits are comparatively low[5], and the high price is the means by which the consumer of corn provides a rent for the landlord.

The landlord can not controul this—he can not make the last land taken into cultivation comparatively poorer than his own, and therefore he is a passive instrument, but nevertheless it is owing to this circumstance that the transfer is made from the consumers pockets to the landlords. In proportion as the last land taken into cultivation is more productive, are the people better off. They[6] are better off because they can purchase the same quantity of produce at a cheaper price,—that is to say with a less quantity, or with the produce of a less quantity of their labour. The capitalists are better off because in proportion as the people are cheaply fed will wages be lower. Low[7] wages are another name for high profits.

[5] Replaces 'high'.   [7] '. Low' replaces ', which'.
[5] Replaces 'The consumers'.

raw produce, which occasions rent, is as injurious to the consumer as it is advantageous to the landlord, a rich and improved nation were determined by law to lower the price of produce, till no surplus in the shape of rent any where remained, it would inevitably throw not only all the poor land, but all except the very best land, out of cultivation, and probably reduce its produce and population to less than one-tenth of their former amount. (95) |

183   SECTION V

On the Dependance of the actual Quantity of Produce obtained from the Land, upon the existing Rents and the existing Prices

From the preceding account of the progress of rent, it follows that the actual state of the natural rent of land is necessary to the actual produce; and that the price of corn, in every progressive country, must be just about equal to the cost of production on

---

(95) p. 182. *With regard to my own conviction*

How[1] can Mr. M. give the interpretation which he does give to the word injurious. My meaning was, and so I am sure was that of the other gentlemen who used this word,[2] that rent was not a clear gain to the nation—it is necessary to the actual supply of corn, but it is derived from a[3] fund, which must diminish if that increases.[4]

(96) p. 183. *Or to the cost of raising &c.*

Why little? No rent would be paid for the additional capital employed on old land. Mr. M. refuses to admit, that any corn would be raised, in which rent did not enter as a component part. If he is correct in saying that a little rent

[1] The Note originally opened: 'My conviction is the same.'; this was del.
[2] See Malthus's p. 149; above, p. 117.
[3] 'a' replaces 'another'.
[4] 'No benefit' is del. here.

land of the poorest quality actually in use, with the addition of the rent it would yield in its natural state; or to the cost of raising additional produce on old land, which additional produce yields only the usual returns of agricultural stock with little or no rent. (96)

It is quite obvious that the price cannot be less; or such land would not be cultivated, nor such capital employed. Nor can it ever much exceed this price, because it will always answer to the landlord to continue letting poorer and poorer lands, as long as he can get any thing more than they will pay in their natural state; and because it will always answer to any farmer who can command capital, to lay it out on his land, if the additional produce resulting from it will fully repay the profits of his stock, although it yields nothing to his landlord.

It follows then, that the price of corn, in reference | to the *whole*   184 *quantity* raised, is sold at the natural or necessary price, that is, at the price necessary to obtain the actual amount of produce, although by far the largest part is sold at a price very much above that which is necessary to its production, owing to this part being

---

would be paid for the last portion of[5] capital employed on the old land, he is right—if no rent would be paid for it he must confess his error. I wish therefore he had given his reason for supposing that any rent would be paid for capital so employed.

Mr. Malthus appears to me to give up the question in the next paragraph for he says "it will always answer to any farmer who can command capital, to lay it out on his land, if the additional produce resulting from it will fully repay the profits of his stock, although it yields nothing to his landlord". There may then be some additional produce which yields no rent to the landlord. In examining the principles of taxation this doctrine is most important, and indeed is material to every part of the science of Political Economy.[6]

[5] 'the last portion of' is ins.
[6] Replaces 'As taxation is con- cerned this doctrine is most im- portant.'

produced at less expense, while its exchangeable value remains undiminished. (97)

The difference between the price of corn and the price of manufactures, with regard to natural or necessary price, is this; that if the price of any manufacture were essentially depressed, the whole manufacture would be entirely destroyed; whereas, if the price of corn were essentially depressed, the *quantity* of it only would be diminished. There would be some machinery in the country still capable of sending the commodity to market at the reduced price. (98)

The earth has been sometimes compared to a vast machine, presented by nature to man for the production of food and raw materials; but, to make the resemblance more just, as far as they admit of comparison, we should consider the soil as a present to man of a great number of machines, all susceptible of continued improvement by the application of capital to them, but yet of very different original qualities and powers.

This great inequality in the powers of the machinery employed in producing raw produce, forms one of the most remarkable features which distinguishes the machinery of the land from the machinery employed in manufactures.

185   When a machine in manufactures is invented, | which will produce more finished work with less labour and capital than before, if there be no patent, or as soon as the patent has expired, a sufficient number of such machines may be made to supply the whole demand, and to supersede entirely the use of all the old machinery. The natural consequence is, that the price is reduced to the price of production from the best machinery, and if the price were to be depressed lower, the whole of the commodity would be withdrawn from the market.

The machines which produce corn and raw materials, on the contrary, are the gifts of nature, not the works of man; and we find, by experience, that these gifts have very different qualities and powers. The most fertile lands of a country, those which, like the best machinery in manufactures, yield the greatest products

---

(97) p. 184. *Owing to this part &c.*

It should be, "produced at the same expence while its exchangeable value considerably increases."

with the least labour and capital, are never found sufficient, owing
to the second main cause of rent before stated, to supply the
effective demand of an increasing population. The price of raw
produce, therefore, naturally rises till it becomes sufficiently high
to pay the cost of raising it with inferior machines, and by a more
expensive process; and, as there cannot be two prices for corn of
the same quality, all the other machines, the working of which
requires less capital compared with the produce, must yield rents
in proportion to their goodness.

Every extensive country may thus be considered as possessing
a gradation of machines for the production of corn and raw
materials, including in this | gradation not only all the various   186
qualities of poor land, of which every large territory has generally
an abundance, but the inferior machinery which may be said to
be employed when good land is further and further forced for
additional produce. As the price of raw produce continues to
rise, these inferior machines are successively called into action;
and as the price of raw produce continues to fall, they are successively thrown out of action. The illustration here used serves
to shew at once the necessity of the actual price of corn to the
actual produce, in the existing state of most of the countries with
which we are acquainted, and the different effect which would
attend a great reduction in the price of any particular manufacture,
and a great reduction in the price of raw produce.

We must not however draw too large inferences from this
gradation of machinery on the land. It is what actually exists in
almost all countries, and accounts very clearly for the origin and
progress of rent, while land still remains in considerable plenty.
But such a gradation is not strictly necessary, either to the original
formation, or the subsequent regular rise of rents. All that is
necessary to produce these effects, is, the existence of the two
first causes of rent formerly mentioned, with the addition of
limited territory, or a scarcity of fertile land.

Whatever may be the qualities of any commodity, it is well
known that it can have no exchangeable value, if it exists in a

---

(98) p. 184. *The difference between the price of corn &c.*
This and the observations in the next two pages are
excellent.

187 great excess above the wants of those who are to use it. But | such are the qualities of the necessaries of life that, in a limited territory, and under ordinary circumstances, they cannot be permanently in excess; and if all the land of such a country were precisely equal in quality, and all very rich, there cannot be the slightest doubt, that after the whole of the land had been taken into cultivation, both the profits of stock, and the real wages of labour, would go on diminishing till profits had been reduced to what were necessary to keep up the actual capital, and the wages to what were necessary to keep up the actual population, while the rents would be high, just in proportion to the fertility of the soil.

Nor would the effect be essentially different, if the quantity of stock which could be employed with advantage upon such fertile soil were extremely limited, so that no further capital were required for it than what was wanted for ploughing and sowing. Still there can be no doubt that capital and population might go on increasing in other employments, till they both came to a stand, and rents had reached the limits prescribed by the powers of the soil, and the habits of the people.

In these cases it is obvious that the rents are not regulated by

---

(99) p. 187. *In these cases it is obvious*

Rents would in this case be regulated by the different products of capital on the same land. With a rise in the price[1] of produce it would be advantageous to employ some more capital on the land[2] with a less return than the capital before employed—this would be limited by the demand for corn, and the most favorable situation would naturally be chosen; I do not see then how my inference has been too large, particularly if it be remembered that I have uniformly contended that one of the main causes of rent is the employment of an additional capital on the old land, without as large a return, as from the capital before employed.

(100) p. 188. *In the progress of cultivation*

Mr. Malthus is mistaken, he has not correctly represented

---

[1] 'in the price' is ins.   [2] 'even' is del. here.

the gradations of the soil, or the different products of capital on the same land; and that it is too large an inference from the theory of rent to conclude with Mr. Ricardo, that "It is only because land is of different qualities with respect to its productive powers, and because in the progress of population, land of an inferior quality, | or less advantageously situated, is called into cultivation, 188 that rent is ever paid for the use of it."* (99)

There is another inference which has been drawn from the theory of rent, which involves an error of much greater importance, and should therefore be very carefully guarded against.

In the progress of cultivation, as poorer and poorer land is taken into tillage, the rate of *profits* must be limited in amount by the powers of the soil last cultivated, as will be shewn more fully in a subsequent chapter. It has been inferred from this, that when land is successively thrown out of cultivation, the rate of profits will be high in proportion to the superior natural fertility of the land which will then be the least fertile in cultivation. (100)

* Principles of Political Economy, ch. ii. p. [70, n.]. This passage was copied from the first edition. It is slightly altered in the second, p. [70]. but not so as materially to vary the sense.

---

the inference. It has been inferred that profits will be high in proportion to the produce obtained by that portion of capital which the cultivator will think it his interest to employ, either on the new land, for which no rent is paid, or on old land, if the additional capital be employed only with a view to profits,[3] and this inference is rigidly true only on the supposition that wages continue unaltered, for with an increased produce and a diminished rent, or a diminished produce and increased rent, a greater or less proportion of the whole may be paid for wages, in which case though profits will rise or fall, they will not rise or fall exactly in proportion to the increased or diminished produce.

[3] Twelve pages of the MS, from here to the end of Note (102), were added later, replacing an original version which (as appears from the gap in the pencil numeration of the sheets) covered only four pages. The pages which contained the original version are wanting.

If land yielded no rent whatever in its natural state, whether it were poor or fertile, and if the relative prices of capital and produce remained the same, then the whole produce being divided between profits and wages, the inference might be just. But the premises are not such as are here supposed. In a civilized country un-cultivated land always yields a rent in proportion to its natural power of feeding cattle or growing wood; and of course, when land has been thrown out of tillage, particularly if this has been occasioned by the importation of cheaper corn from other coun-

189 tries, and consequently without a diminution of population, | the last land so thrown out may yield a moderate rent in pasture, though considerably less than before. As was said in the pre-ceding section, rent will diminish, but not so much in proportion either as the capital employed on the land, or the produce derived from it. No landlord will allow his land to be cultivated by a tillage farmer paying little or no rent, when by laying it down to

---

(101) p. 188. *If land yielded no rent*

But what does Mr. Malthus say to capital withdrawn from land which yet remains in cultivation and for which no rent is paid. By withdrawing this capital will not another capital come under the same condition of not affording a rent although it yields larger returns? On Mr. Malthus own shewing if rent falls, and the land be equally productive, either profits or wages must rise. If this be not true what becomes of the difference between a high and a low rent? Who gets it?

(102)[1] p. 189. *If to this circumstance &c. &c.*

The[2] supposition was that in consequence of importing corn rents fell, and that at any rate the last land in tillage

---

[1] The original and shorter version of this Note is wanting. See above, p. 171, n. 3.
[2] The following is del. here:

'Suppose wages to continue the same and rent to fall profits must depend on the value of the pro-duce.'

pasture, and saving the yearly expenditure of capital upon it, he can obtain a much greater rent. Consequently, as the produce of the worst lands actually cultivated can never be wholly divided between profits and wages, and in the case above supposed, not nearly so, the state of such land or its degree of fertility cannot possibly regulate the rate of profits upon it. (101)

If to this circumstance we add the effect arising from a rise in the value of money, and the probable fall of corn more than of working cattle, it is obvious that permanent difficulties will be thrown in the way of cultivation, and that richer land may not yield superior profits. The higher rent paid for the last land employed in tillage, together with the greater expense of the materials of capital compared with the price of produce, may fully counterbalance, or even more than counterbalance, the difference of natural fertility. (102)

With regard to the capital which the tenant may lay out on his

---

would be more productive, and less rent would be paid for it. Thus much even Mr. Malthus allows. What then can he mean by "the higher rent paid for the last land employed in tillage counterbalancing, or even more than counterbalancing the difference of natural fertility?" Does he mean that if importation of corn [3] were freely allowed, although the last land employed in tillage would be more productive, yet greater profits would not be obtained from it because [4] a greater rent would be paid than before for it? If he means this he must contend that the more free the [5] importation of corn the higher would rents be.

What can the rise [6] in the value of money have to do with this question? What should make it rise? and if it did rise how could that circumstance affect the rate of profit? The simple question is this, with a given expenditure of capital

[3] 'of corn' is ins.
[4] 'the same' is del. here.

[5] 'trade of' was ins. here, then del.
[6] 'rise' replaces 'rise or fall'.

farm in obtaining more produce without paying additional rent
for it, the rate of its returns must obviously conform itself to the
190 general rate of profits. If the prices of manufac-|tured and mer-
cantile commodities were to remain the same notwithstanding the
fall of labour, profits would certainly be raised; but they would
not remain the same, as was shewn in the preceding chapter. The
new prices of commodities and the new profits of stock would be

---

and labour a greater quantity of corn is obtained. Of this
greater quantity the farmer retains a larger proportion because
a less proportion (and indeed a less quantity)[1] is paid to his
landlord for rent. It is therefore true that although he may
sell his corn at a cheaper price he may still obtain greater
profits.

But the rate of his profit "must obviously conform itself
to the general rate of profits. If the prices of manufactured
and mercantile commodities were to remain the same notwithstanding the fall of labour, profits would certainly be
raised; but they would not remain the same, as was shewn in
the preceding chapter." Where shewn in the preceding
chapter? Observe the argument of Mr. Malthus, and the
proposition with which he sets out. "It has been inferred"
he says[2] "that when land is successively thrown out of cultivation, the rate of profits will be high in proportion to the
superior natural fertility of the land which will then be the
least fertile in cultivation."*

This is an incorrect[3] inference says Mr. Malthus. Why?

* This inference has been made only in the case of wages
not absorbing by their rise the whole additional quantity of
produce obtained by the farmer.

[1] The words in brackets are ins.   [3] Replaces 'a wrong'.
[2] Malthus's p. 188; above, p. 171.

determined upon principles of competition; and whatever the
rate was, as so determined, capital would be taken from the land
till this rate was attained. The profits of capital employed in the
way just described must always follow, and can never lead or
regulate.

It should be added, that in the regular progress of a country
towards general cultivation and improvement, and in a natural

---

because though rent may fall in consequence of the importation of cheaper corn from other countries, it will not be
attended with a loss of the whole rent even on those lands
which are the poorest employed in tillage.

Suppose we grant this to Mr. Malthus, yet his admission
that rent will fall, altho' not wholly annihilated on any land
whatever, fully makes out the proposition. But Mr. Malthus
grants a great deal more than this; he says, not only do I
admit that rent will fall, but I think labour will fall, and yet
I contend that the farmer's profits will not rise—[4] because
they must conform to general profits, and with a low price
of labour, other commodities must fall and therefore the
profits on capital employed on their manufacture would not
rise[5]. With a given capital it is admitted that a greater quantity of raw produce will be obtained, that this quantity must
be divided between the landlord, the farmer, and the labourer.
The landlord it is acknowledged will get less, the labourer it
is said will get no more and yet the farmer will have no
greater value. By what is it that Mr. Malthus estimates value?
If he says by that measure which he holds to be the correct
one, "the command of labour," he is evidently maintaining
a contradiction, for he says that labourers will work for the

[4] 'I do more, I maintain they
would positively fall' is del. here.

[5] 'would not rise' replaces 'must
also fall'.

state of things, it may fairly be presumed, that if the last land taken into cultivation be rich, capital is scarce, and profits will then certainly be high; but if land be thrown out of cultivation on account of means being found of obtaining corn cheaper else-

---

same quantity of corn as before, and yet he who has more to bestow on them has no greater value. If he says that his measure of value is [1] "other goods," and that a man has not a greater value, unless he has the power of commanding a greater quantity of those goods, he is still maintaining contradictory propositions [2], for one part of his argument requires him to maintain that the farmer will have the power of commanding a greater quantity of other goods; and another that he will not have the power of commanding so great a quantity as before. If the farmer can command more goods, and goods are the measure of value, then he has a greater value, and his profits will be increased, and the inference Mr. Malthus attacks is a correct one. If he cannot command more goods

[1] 'the power' is del. here.

[2] The remainder of this paragraph replaces: '. If the farmer can not command more goods with his additional quantity of corn, then goods have not fallen in value in consequence of the fall in the value of labour, and ['one of the conditions of the proposition is gone,' is del. here] the profits of the manufacturers of those goods will be higher than before—they will obtain as great a value for their goods in each others commodities ['and in corn' was ins., then del.] as they did previously to the importation of corn, while the value of the labour which they employ to obtain them will be less, and this it is which constitutes high profits. If Mr. Malthus says that corn will fall so much that the farmer will get no additional profits, then he must admit that his profits will not conform to the general rate of profits, because the fall of corn and labour, compared with commodities, is the same thing with him as a high value of commodities, and therefore he gives up his proposition of a fall in the value of commodities and he establishes the necessity of high profits on manufactured goods. "But the rate of returns (from agriculture) must obviously conform itself to the general rate of profits," and therefore profits on agriculture will be also high.'

where, no such inference is justifiable. On the contrary, capital
may be abundant, compared with the demand for corn and commodities, in which case and during the time that such abundance
lasts, whatever may be the state of the land, profits must be low.

---

in consequence of the very low price of his corn then the
manufacturers goods do not fall but rise, and as labour is low
general profits will be high. The manufacturers profits can
be no otherwise than high if he can exchange his goods for
the same quantity of all other commodities, and for a greater
quantity of raw produce, and if at the same time he pays
lower wages of labour, in consequence of the fall of the price
of corn. To me it appears clear that the price of corn will fall,
but that the fall will be more than compensated to the farmer,
by the increase of quantity, and thus his profits will be increased. The profits of the manufacturer will be also augmented, because he will sell his goods at the same price,
while in consequence of the fall in the price of corn, he will
be at less expence in producing them.

Mr. Malthus cannot be allowed to say that corn and manufactured goods would fall as compared with money, because
first he gives no reason for such fall, and secondly if he could
establish it to everybody's satisfaction it would only prove
that money had risen in value and affected every commodity
alike, which would have no influence whatever on the rate
of profits. Its effects would be precisely similar to those which
would follow from the loss of some of the rich mines [3] of
the precious metals, or from the recovery [4] of a paper money
from a great degree of depreciation.

---

[3] Replaces 'from the discovery   [4] Replaces 'depreciation'.
of some rich mine'.

This is a distinction of the greatest practical importance, which it appears to me has been quite overlooked by Mr. Ricardo. (103)

191 It will be observed, that the rents paid for what the land will produce in its natural state, though they make a most essential difference in the questions relating to profits and the component parts of price, in no respect invalidate the important doc-|trine that, in progressive countries in their usual state with gradations of soil, corn is sold at its natural or necessary price, that is, at the price necessary to bring the actual quantity to market. This price must on an average be at the least equal to the costs of its production on the worst land actually cultivated, together with the rent of such land in its natural state: because, if it falls in any degree below this, the cultivator of such land will not be able to pay the landlord so high a rent as he could obtain from the land without cultivation, and consequently the land will be left uncultivated, and the produce will be diminished. The rent of land in its natural state is therefore obviously so necessary a part of the price of all cultivated products, that, if it be not paid they will not come to market, and the real price actually paid for corn is, on an average,

---

(103) p. 190. *It should be added*

No point is more satisfactorily made out to my satisfaction[1] than that high profits have a most intimate connection with the low value of food,—for a low value of food has the greatest influence on the wages of labour, and low wages cannot fail to make high profits.

Suppose I was a manufacturer of cloth, and that I made 100 pieces p^r. Ann., and that food was so high compared with cloth, that it was necessary for me to give 60 pieces to my workmen, to enable them to purchase necessaries; 40 pieces would remain for me. Now suppose the comparative price of food to fall, and that 50 pieces would purchase the necessaries required by my men, would not my portion be increased 10 pieces?

But your 50 pieces of cloth may fall in value, and sell for

[1] Replaces 'to my mind'.

absolutely necessary to the production of the same quantity, or, in the words before stated, corn, in reference to the whole quantity produced, is sold at its necessary price.

I hope to be excused for presenting to the reader in various forms the doctrine, that corn, in reference to the quantity actually produced, is sold at its necessary price, like manufactures; because I consider it as a truth of high importance, which has been entirely overlooked by the Economists, by Adam Smith, and all those writers who have represented raw produce as selling always at a monopoly price. |

SECTION VI

192

Of the Connexion between great comparative Wealth, and a high comparative Price of raw Produce

Adam Smith has very clearly explained in what manner the progress of wealth and improvement tends to raise the price of

---

no more than 40 did before!—this cannot be true with regard to corn and labour, because by the supposition they have fallen in value, and are low compared with cloth; therefore if I wanted to employ labour of any kind with my 50 pieces of cloth, they would go considerably further than even 50 pieces went before. But they will not fall relatively to any other commodity; for the shoemaker, out of a hundred pair of shoes, will retain 50 instead of 40, the brewer out of a hundred barrels of beer, will do the same, and so will every other trade. The cause that operates on one, operates on all; how then can it be said that the relative values of commodities will be affected? But it may be said that though corn falls relatively to all these things, wages will not fall; this is still better, because without lowering profits, the happiness of the most numerous and therefore the most important part of the people will greatly increase.

cattle, poultry, the materials of clothing and lodging, the most useful minerals, &c. compared with corn; but he has not entered into the explanation of the natural causes which tend to determine the price of corn. He has left the reader indeed to conclude, that he considers the price of corn as determined only by the state of the mines, which at the time supply the circulating medium of the commercial world. But this is a cause, which, though it may account for the high or low price of corn positively, cannot account for the relative differences in its price, in different countries, or compared with certain classes of commodities in the same country.

I entirely agree with Adam Smith, that it is of great use to inquire into the causes of high price, as from the result of such inquiries it may turn out, that the very circumstance of which we complain, may be the necessary consequence and the most certain sign of increasing wealth and prosperity. But of all inquiries of this kind, none surely can be so important, or so generally in-
193 teresting, as an inquiry into the causes which affect | the price of corn, and occasion the differences in this price so observable in different countries.

---

(104) p. 193. *A difference in the value of the precious metals,*
in different countries under different circumstances

Nothing seems to me so unimportant as this cause. The value of money cannot alter, without affecting, in the same degree, the prices of[1] all things; and provided we have the same quantity of all commodities, and that they bear the same relative value to each other, what can it signify what the value of money is?

(105) p. 193. *A difference in the quantity of labour and capital*
necessary to produce corn

I agree with Mr. Malthus in these two causes of the high price of corn, but while I deem the first unimportant, I attach the greatest consequence to the second;—the abundance of the most important commodity of all others, depends upon

---

[1] 'the prices of' is ins.

These causes, in reference to the main effects observed, seem to be two:

1. A difference in the value of the precious metals, in different countries under different circumstances. (104)

2. A difference in the quantity of labour and capital necessary to produce corn. (105)

[To the first cause is to be attributed the main differences in the prices of corn in different countries, particularly in those situated at a great distance from each other.

If the value of money were the same in all countries, then 194. the differences of price would arise exclusively from the different costs of production, under all the actual circumstances of each country.

Nations richer than others must, under similar circumstances, 195 either have their corn at a higher price, or be dependent upon their neighbours for their support.

High price, or the importation of necessaries, are the natural 196 alternatives belonging to a great increase of wealth, though liable to various modifications from circumstances.

Corn has a natural tendency to rise in the progress of society, 197

---

the judicious application of labour and capital to its production—my enquiry then is, in what way can we bestow these most judiciously in order to obtain an abundant supply of this chief necessary of life? and if I find that a given quantity of capital and labour, when applied to manufactures, will procure by means of barter a greater quantity of corn from abroad,[2] than when applied to our own land, I decide in favor of that mode of obtaining it; and on the contrary, if labour and capital can be made more productive when directly applied to our own land, I am equally strenuous that no obstacle should be opposed to such an application of it. I am happy to say that I agree with Mr. Malthus in everything he says in the remainder of this section.

[2] First written 'a given quantity of capital and labour will procure a greater quantity of corn from abroad, when applied to manufactures', then revised as above.

from the increasing cost of production, and manufactures have a constant tendency to fall from an opposite cause.

198   Whichever of the two causes of the high price of corn we consider, this high price is generally connected with wealth, contrary to the statement of Adam Smith.]

199   SECTION VII

On the Causes which may mislead the Landlord in letting his Lands, to the Injury both of himself and the Country

In the progress of a country towards a high state of improvement, the positive wealth of the landlord ought, upon the principles which have been laid down, gradually to increase; although his relative condition and influence in society will probably rather diminish, owing to the increasing number and wealth of those who live upon a still more important surplus*—the profits of stock. (106)

The progressive fall, with few exceptions, in the value of the precious metals throughout Europe; the still greater fall, which has occurred in the richest countries, together with the increase of
200 produce which has been obtained from the soil, | must all conduce to make the landlord expect an increase of rents on the renewal

---

* I have hinted before, that profits may, without impropriety, be called a surplus. But, whether surplus or not, they are the most important source of wealth, as they are, beyond all question, the main source of accumulation.

---

(106) p. 199. *In the progress of a country*

I think the landlords relative condition to the capitalists will gradually improve with the progress of a country, although his rent will certainly not increase in the proportion of the gross produce.

(107) p. 201. *There is no just reason to believe &c.*

This is my opinion, but ought not to be that of Mr. Malthus;[1] who contends that rent enters for something into

[1] Cp. above, pp. 117–18.

of his leases. But, in re-letting his farms, he is liable to fall into two errors, which are almost equally prejudicial to his own interests, and to those of his country.

[By letting his lands to the best bidder, without any further attention; or by mistaking a temporary for a permanent rise of price, he may prevent the improvement of his farms.]

A similar caution is necessary in raising rents, even when the rise of prices seems as if it would be permanent. In the progress of prices and rents, rent ought always to be a little behind; not only to afford the means of ascertaining whether the rise be temporary or permanent, but even in the latter case, to give a little time for the accumulation of capital on the land, of which the landholder is sure to feel the full benefit in the end. 201

There is no just reason to believe, that if the landlords were to give the whole of their rents to their tenants, corn would be more plentiful and cheaper. If the view of the subject, taken in the preceding inquiry, be correct, the last additions made to our home produce are sold at nearly the cost of production, and the same quantity could not be produced from our own soil at a less price, even without rent. (107) The effect of transferring all rents to tenants, would be merely the turning them | into gentlemen, and tempting them to cultivate their farms under the superintendence of careless and uninterested bailiffs, instead of the vigilant eye of a master, who is deterred from carelessness by the fear of ruin, and stimulated to exertion by the hope of a competence. The most numerous instances of successful industry, and well-directed knowledge, have been found among those who have paid a fair 202

---

the price of all corn. However little it might be on the corn last raised; to that degree would corn fall, if all rent were given up.

From what Mr. Malthus says here, and in another place,[2] one would think that he admitted there was some corn always sold, in the price of which no charge for rent entered;—but he more often insists on the contrary.[3]

[2] Malthus's p. 183; above, p. 166.   [3] See *e.g.* Malthus's p. 97; above, p. 68.

rent for their lands; who have embarked the whole of their capital in their undertaking; and who feel it their duty to watch over it with unceasing case, and add to it whenever it is possible.

[But when a proper spirit of industry and enterprize prevails among a tenantry, it is of importance that they should have the means of accumulation and improvement.

203   Irregularities in the currency are another source of error to the landlord. When they continue long he must raise his rents accordingly, and lower them again when the value of money is restored.

With these cautions, the landlord may fairly look to a permanent increase of rents, and if in a country, the cultivation of which is extending, they do not rise more than in proportion to the price of corn, it can only be owing to taxation.]

204   Though it is by no means true, as stated by the Economists, that all taxes fall on the neat rents of the landlords, yet it is certainly true that they have little power of relieving themselves. It is also true that they possess a fund more disposable, and better adapted for taxation than any other. They are in consequence more frequently taxed, both directly and indirectly. And if they pay, as they certainly do, many of the taxes which fall on the capital of the farmer and the wages of the labourer, as well as those directly imposed on themselves, they must necessarily feel it in the diminution of that portion of the whole produce, which under other circumstances would have fallen to their share. (108)

---

(108) p. 204. *They are in consequence more frequently &c.*

Mr. Malthus would find it difficult to prove this. What taxes on the capital[1] of the farmer do they pay?

(109) p. 205. *Yet it has been said*

I have answered this   [2] to which I refer the reader. I will only observe here that Mr. Malthus must recollect the

---

[1] 'capital' replaces 'profits'.   [2] Blank in MS. The reference is no doubt to Note (58).

SECTION VIII

On the strict and necessary Connexion of the Interests of the Landlord and of the State in a Country which supports its own Population

It has been stated by Adam Smith, that the interest of the landholder is closely connected with that of the state;* and that the prosperity or adversity of the one involves the prosperity or adversity of the other. The theory of rent, as laid down in the present chapter, seems strongly to confirm | this statement. If under any given natural resources in land, the main causes which conduce to the interest of the landholder are increase of capital, increase of population, improvements in agriculture, and an increasing demand for raw produce occasioned by the prosperity of commerce, it seems scarcely possible to consider the interests of the landlord as separated from those of the state and people.

Yet it has been said by Mr. Ricardo that, "the interest of the landlord is always opposed to that of the consumer and the manufacturer,"† that is, to all the other orders in the state. To this opinion he has been led, very consistently, by the peculiar view he has taken of rent, which makes him state, that it is for the interest of the landlord that the cost attending the production of corn should be increased,‡ and that improvements in agriculture tend rather to lower than to raise rents. (109)

* Wealth of Nations, Book I. c. xi. p. 394. 6th edit.
† Princ. of Polit. Econ. c. xxiv. p. [335]. 2d edit.   ‡ Ibid.

---

qualification which I give to the opinion which he has quoted from my work—I have said that it is only the immediate interest of the landlord which is at variance with improvements in agriculture, and the reduction in the cost of production of corn. Inasmuch as the power of the land, as a machine, is improved, the landlord will be benefited when it is again called into action; and that it infallibly will be after the population has increased in proportion to the increased facility of producing food.

If this view of the theory of rent were just, and it were really true, that the income of the landlord is increased by increasing the difficulty, and diminished by increasing* the facility, of production, the opinion would unquestionably be well founded. But if, on the contrary, the landlord's income is practically found to depend upon natural fertility of soil, improvements in agriculture, and inventions to save labour, we may still think, with Adam Smith, that the landlord's interest is not opposed to that of the country.|

It is so obviously true, as to be hardly worth stating, that if land of the greatest fertility were in such excessive plenty compared with the population, that every man might help himself to as much as he wanted, there would be no rents or landlords properly so called. It will also be readily allowed, that if in this or any other country you could suppose the soil suddenly to be made so fertile, that a tenth part of the surface, and a tenth part of the labour now employed upon it, could more than support the present population, you would for some time considerably lower rents.

But it is of no sort of use to *dwell upon*, and draw general inferences from suppositions which never can take place.

What we want to know is, whether, living as we do in a limited world, and in countries and districts still more limited, and under such physical laws relating to the produce of the soil and the increase of population as are found by experience to prevail, the interests of the landlord are generally opposed to those of the society. (110) And in this view of the subject, the question may be settled by an appeal to the most incontrovertible principles confirmed by the most glaring facts.

Whatever fanciful suppositions we may make about sudden improvements in fertility, nothing of this kind which we have ever seen or heard of in practice, approaches to what we know of

* [In original, 'diminishing'.]

---

(110) p. 206. *But it is of no sort of use*

A principle is either true or false—if true it is as applicable to a limited society as to a large one.[1] It is my opinion that rent is never derived from any other source than from the

[1] '— to a small' is del. here.

the power of population to increase up to the additional means of subsistence.

Improvements in agriculture, however consi-|derable they may 207 finally prove, are always found to be partial and gradual. And as, where they prevail to any extent, there is always an effective demand for labour, the increase of population occasioned by the increased facility of procuring food, soon overtakes the additional produce. Instead of land being thrown out of employment, more land is cultivated, owing to the cheapness of the instruments of cultivation, and under these circumstances rents must rise instead of fall. These results appear to me to be so completely confirmed by experience, that I doubt, if a single instance in the history of Europe, or any other part of the world, can be produced, where improvements in agriculture have been practically found to lower rents.

I should further say, that not only have improvements in agriculture never lowered rents, but that they have been hitherto, and may be expected to be in future, the *main* source of the increase of rents, in almost all the countries with which we are acquainted.

It is a fundamental part of the theory which has been explained in this chapter, that, as most countries consist of a gradation of soils, rents rise as cultivation is pushed to poorer lands; but still the connexion between rent and fertility subsists in undiminished force. The rich lands are those which yield the rents, not the poor ones. The poor lands are only cultivated, because the increasing population is calling forth all the resources of | the country, and 208 if there were no poor soils, these resources would still be called forth; a limited territory, however fertile, would soon be peopled; and without any increase of difficulty in the production of food, rents would rise.

It is evident then, that difficulty of production has no kind of connexion with increase of rent, except as, in the actual state of most countries, it is the natural consequence of an increase of

---

fund which once formed profit, and therefore that every improvement—every reduction in cost of production, whether they be great, or small, either go to wages, or profit, and never to rent. After constituting profits, they may be, in the further progress of society, transferred to rent.

capital and population, and a fall of profits and wages; or, in other words, of an increase of wealth.

· But after all, the increase of rents which results from an increase of price occasioned solely by the greater quantity of labour and capital necessary to produce a given quantity of corn on fresh land, is very much more limited than has been supposed; and by a reference to most of the countries with which we are acquainted, it will be seen that, practically, improvements in agriculture and the saving of labour on the land, both have been, and may be expected in future to be, a much more powerful source of increasing rents.

It has already been shewn, that for the very great increase of rents which have taken place in this country during nearly the last hundred years, we are mainly indebted to improvements in agriculture, as profits have rather risen than fallen, and little or nothing has been taken from the wages of families, if we include parish allowances, and the earnings of women and children. Conse-
209 quently these rents must have been a creation from the | skill and capital employed upon the land, and not a transfer from profits and wages, as they existed nearly a hundred years ago. (111)

[This position may be illustrated by the state of England, Scotland, Ireland, Poland, India, and South America.

In all these countries the future increase of rents will depend mainly upon an improved system of agriculture.

210   The United States of America seem to be the only country which would admit of any considerable rise of rents by a mere transfer from profits and wages.

In old states, an operose and ignorant system of cultivation may keep the profits of stock and the wages of labour low with much good land remaining uncultivated; and this seems to be a very frequent case.

---

(111) p. 208.[1] *Consequently these rents &c. &c.*

Who said that the present rents were a transfer from profits and wages, as they existed nearly a century ago?—they may be a transfer from profits of 10, 5 or 3 years ago. The question is, are they a transfer from profits? There is much in this

[1] In MS, '209'.

But if, independently of importation, every thing which tends 211
to enrich a country increases rents, and every thing which tends
to impoverish it, diminishes them; it must be allowed that the
interests of the landlord and of the state are closely united.]

Mr. Ricardo, as I have before intimated, takes only one simple
and confined view of the progress of rent. (112) He considers it
as occasioned solely by the increase of price, arising from the
increased | difficulty of production.* But if rents in many 212
countries may be doubled or trebled by improvements in agriculture, while in few countries they could be raised a fourth or a
fifth, and in some not a tenth, by the increase of price arising from
the increased difficulty of production, must it not be acknowledged, that such a view of rent embraces only a very small part
of the subject, and consequently that any general inferences from
it must be utterly inapplicable to practice?

It should be further observed, in reference to improvements in
agriculture, that the mode in which Mr. Ricardo estimates the
increase or decrease of rents is quite peculiar; and this peculiarity
in the use of his terms tends to separate his conclusions still
farther from truth as enunciated in the accustomed language of
political economy.

In speaking of the division of the whole produce of the land
and labour of the country between the three classes of landlords,
labourers, and capitalists, he has the following passage.

"It is not by the absolute quantity of produce obtained by
either class, that we can correctly judge of the rate of profit, rent,

---

* Mr. Ricardo always seems to assume, that increased difficulties thrown
in the way of production will be overcome by increased price, and that the
same quantity will be produced. But this is an unwarranted assumption.
Where is the increased price to come from? An increase of difficulty in the
actual state of a country's resources will always tend to diminish produce.

---

section in which I agree, but it appears to me that Mr. Malthus
endeavors to magnify the difference between us.

(112) p. 211. *Mr. Ricardo &c.*

I do not think that a fair construction of what I have
written will justify this charge.

and wages, but by the quantity of labour required to obtain that
213 produce. | By improvements in machinery and agriculture the
whole produce may be doubled; but if wages, rent and profits be
also doubled, they will bear the same proportions to one another
as before. But if wages partook not of the whole of this increase;
if they, instead of being doubled, were only increased one half;
if rent, instead of being doubled, were only increased three-
fourths, and the remaining increase went to profit, it would,
I apprehend, be correct for me to say, that rent and wages had
fallen while profits had risen. For if we had an invariable standard
by which to measure the value of this produce, we should find
that a less value had fallen to the class of labourers and landlords,
and a greater to the class of capitalists than had been given
before." *

A little farther on, having stated some specific proportions, he
observes, "In that case I should say, that wages and rent had
fallen and profits risen, though, in consequence of the abundance
of commodities, the *quantity* paid to the labourer and landlord
would have increased in the proportion of 25 to 44."†

* Princ. of Polit. Econ. chap. i. p. [64]. 2d edit.
† Id. p. [65].

---

(113) p. 213. *In reference to this statement &c.*

It is odd enough that Mr. Malthus most frequently uses
this very standard which he thus reprobates;—he invariably
speaks of the fall of rents, rise of profits, and rise of wages:
meaning a fall or rise in money rents, profits and wages,
which money¹ of course he supposes not to have varied.
Now if the quantity of corn produced by a given quantity of
labour were doubled, (a very extravagant supposition), its
price would fall to one half, and consequently the money
rent of the landlord would fall, unless he had double the
quantity; the profits of the capitalist would be reduced, unless
he had also double; and so would the wages of the labourer,

¹ Last six words replace 'which'.

In reference to this statement, I should observe, that if the application of Mr. Ricardo's invariable standard of value naturally leads to the use of such language, the sooner the standard is got rid of, the better, as in an inquiry into the nature and causes of the wealth of nations, it must necessarily occasion perpetual confusion and error. For what does | it require us to say? We must say that the rents of the landlord have fallen and his interests have suffered, when he obtains as rent above three-fourths more of raw produce than before, and with that produce will shortly be able, according to Mr. Ricardo's own doctrines, to command three-fourths' more labour. In applying this language to our own country, we must say that rents have fallen considerably during the last forty years, because, though rents have greatly increased in exchangeable value,—in the command of money, corn, labour and manufactures, it appears, by the returns to the Board of Agriculture, that they are now only a fifth of the gross produce,‡ whereas they were formerly a fourth or a third. (113)

In reference to labour, we must say that it is low in America, although we have been hitherto in the habit of considering it as very high, both in money value and in the command of the

‡ Reports from the Lords on the Corn Laws, p. 66.

---

if he had a less portion than double also[2]. That the labourers wages would be reduced in money value I can have no doubt, and the chief advantages to the capitalist arise from that circumstance.

But the landlord can with his double produce command more labour than before. So he can,—but is labour the only thing he wants? can he command with his double quantity of corn more iron, copper, gold, tea, sugar, hats, coaches, silks, wine, and every other commodity? Not the least particle more. Am I not then justified in saying that he receives no greater value, though he may receive double the quantity? "In applying this language to our own country, says Mr. M.,

[2] 'than double also' is ins.

214

necessaries and conveniences of life. And we must call it high in Sweden; because, although the labourer only earns low money

---

we must say that rents have fallen considerably during the last forty years, because though rents have greatly increased in exchangeable value,—in the command of money, corn, labour and manufactures it appears, by the returns to the Board of Agriculture, that they are now only a fifth of the gross produce, whereas they were formerly a fourth or a third." [1] Mr. Malthus has not read what I have said on this subject with his usual attention, or, in the first place, he would not have said that my language "requires us to say, that the rents of the landlord have fallen, and his interests have suffered, when he obtains as rent above three fourths more of raw produce than before." If I estimated the riches of individuals, by the value of their incomes—there would be some foundation for the charge, but I have taken great pains to explain my views, and to shew that I think it quite consistent to say that the riches of a man have increased, viz. the quantity of the conveniences and necessaries of life, which he can

[1] The remainder of the Note replaces an earlier version which read: 'Mr. Malthus has either not read what I have said with his usual attention or has not interpreted me with his usual candour ['either' is del., and the last nine words are replaced by 'or he could not suppose that I was of opinion that the landlords rent increased in proportion to the gross produce']. If with a certain capital 180 qts. of corn are raised and the landlord obtains 10 qts. for rent, I say if the quantity obtained with the same capital be increased to 360 qts. he will not have a rent of the same value unless he have 20 qts. or one eighteenth as before ['because 20 qts. will be of no more value in exchange than 10 were before' is ins. here]. If with a second capital only 340 qts. be raised, which is the reason of his obtaining 20 qts. as rent, I do not say he is to have an eighteenth part of the 340 qts. also, ['and of all the produce which can be employed on the land with such a rate of return,' is ins. here] and of the 320 which may be the produce'. The rest of this version is missing.

wages, and with these low wages can obtain but few of the necessaries and conveniences of life; yet, in the division of the whole

command, at the same time that the value of those riches may
have[2] fallen.

Besides, I have never maintained that in order to give the
landlords rents of the same value, they must always bear the
same proportion to the value of the gross produce obtained
from the land, as the argument from the returns of the Board
of Agriculture would imply. I do not say that rents have
fallen *in value*, because they were formerly a fourth or a third
of the gross produce, and are now only one fifth. I have a
farm from which I obtain 360 qrs. of corn, and I pay one
fourth for rent, or 90 qrs. By employing more capital on
inferior land, instead of 360 qrs. being obtained with the
same quantity of labour, only 340 can[3] be got, and therefore
the rent of the land on which 360 were obtained, would rise
from 90 to 110 qrs.; the rent on that particular farm would
be a greater proportion of the gross produce than before, but
it by no means follows that it would be a greater proportion
of the whole gross produce of the country; for instead of one
capital being employed to obtain 340 qrs. one hundred equal
capitals may be so employed. It is possible then that the
gross produce may be increased 34,000 quarters, and rent
rise only 20 qrs. Because the landlord had one fourth of the
gross produce, and has increased that proportion on all lands
before cultivated, does it follow that I am bound to maintain
that rents are also a larger proportion of the whole gross
produce from all the lands in the country?

---

[2] 'may have' replaces 'has'.   [3] 'can' is written above 'may',
which however is not del.

produce of a laborious cultivation on a poor soil, a larger proportion may go to labour.* (114) |

215   Into this unusual language Mr. Ricardo has been betrayed by the fundamental error of confounding cost and value, and the further error of considering raw produce in the same light as manufactures. It might be true, that if, by improvements in machinery, the produce of muslins were doubled, the increased quantity would not command in exchange a greater quantity of labour and of necessaries than before, and would have little or no effect therefore on population. But Mr. Ricardo has himself said, that "if improvements extended to all the objects of the labourer's consumption, we should find him probably, at the end of a very few years, in possession of only a small, if any addition to his enjoyments."† Consequently, according to Mr. Ricardo, population will increase in proportion to the increase of the main articles consumed by the labourer.

But if population increases according to the necessaries which

* It is specifically this unusual application of common terms which has rendered Mr. Ricardo's work so difficult to be understood by many people. It requires indeed a constant and laborious effort of the mind to recollect at all times what is meant by high and low rents, and high or low wages. In other respects, it | has always appeared to me that the style in which the work is written, is perfectly clear. It is never obscure, but when either the view itself is erroneous, or terms are used in an unusual sense.

† Princ. of Polit. Econ. ch. i. p. [16].

---

(114) p. 214. *In reference to labour, we must say it is low in America &c.*

To obtain 180 quarters of corn in England worth £700 on the land last cultivated [1]—I may require the labour of 20 men for a year at 10/- a week altogether £520 per ann. To obtain the same quantity in America where it might sell for £600, might require only the labour of 15 men, wages might in America be also 10/- p^r week, but the farmer in England would pay £520 p^r ann. for wages, and the farmer in America only £390. In one country England the proportion of the whole produce paid to the labourers is $\frac{743}{1000}$.—In the

[1] Last five words are ins.

the labourer can command, the increased quantity of raw produce which falls to the share of the landlord must increase the exchangeable value of his rents estimated in labour, corn and commodities. And it is certainly by real value in exchange, and not by an imaginary standard, which is to measure *proportions* or cost in labour, that the rents and interests of landlords | will be estimated.   216
It would often happen, that after improvements had been taking place, rents would rise according to the accustomed and natural meaning attached to the term, while they might fall according to the new mode of estimating them adopted by Mr. Ricardo.

I need hardly say, that, in speaking of the interests of the landlord, I mean always to refer to what I should call his real rents and his real interests; that is, his power of commanding labour, and the necessaries and conveniences of life, whatever proportion these rents may form of the whole produce, or whatever quantity of labour they may have cost in producing.‡

‡ This interpretation of the term rent is, I conceive, strictly consistent with my first definition of it. I call it that *portion* (not *proportion*) of the value of the produce which goes to the landlord; and if the value of the whole produce of any given quantity of land increases, the *portion* of value which goes to the landlord may increase considerably, although the *proportion* which it bears to the whole may diminish. Mr. Ricardo has himself expressly stated, p. [401]. that whatever sum the produce of land sells for above the costs of cultivating it, is money rent. But if it continually happens that money rent rises, and is at the same time of greater real value in

---

other America it is $\frac{650}{1000}$. Tho' the money wages to each individual is the same, the aggregate of wages paid is greatest in England, and so also is the proportion of the produce. Apply the same statement to Sweden and it will be found quite consistent with my principle.[2]

[2] An unfinished paragraph is del. here: 'It is according to the division of the produce of any given capital between the 3 classes that we are to judge of rent, profit, and wages. Suppose on a given farm with a given capital 100 qrs. of corn are raised and that the land-lord receives one fourth or 25 qrs. the farmer one half 50 & the labourers one fourth 25

——— 100

and that next year, owing to new lands being taken into cultivation elsewhere, these 100 qrs. are differently divided and the landlords receive one third—33 the farmer—

But in fact, improvements in agriculture tend, in a moderate time,

exchange, although it bears a less *proportion* to the value of the whole produce from the land in question, it is quite obvious that neither money rent
nor real rent is regulated by this proportion. (115)

---

(115) p. 216. *Mr. Ricardo has himself expressly stated*

It is very probable that my language about proportions
may not have been so clear as it ought to have been. I will
endeavor now to explain it.

Suppose the last land now in cultivation yields 180 qrs. of
corn with the employment of a given quantity of labour, and
in consequence of the rise of the price of corn a still inferior
quantity of land shall be cultivated next year which shall
yield only 170 qrs. If this year the labourer shall have one
third of the 180 quarters, and next year he shall have one
third of the 170 quarters, I say his wages will be of the same
value next year, as this, because the whole 170 quarters next
year will be of the same value as the 180 quarters are this
year, and consequently $\frac{1}{2}$, a fourth, or a third of either of
these quantities will be also of the same value.

When I speak of this division by proportions I always
apply it, or ought to apply it, (and if I have done otherwise,
it has been from inadvertence), to the produce obtained with
the last capital employed on the land, and for which no rent
is paid. Now in fact the labourer will get a larger proportion
of the 170 qrs., than he got of the 180 qrs., he will get a larger
proportion of this equal value, and therefore it is that I say
his wages have risen. Whatever may be the quantity of corn
obtained by the last capital employed on the land, it will be
of the same value, because it is the produce of the same
quantity of labour. A larger proportion of this equal value
must itself be a larger value.[1]

[1] A paragraph is del. here: 'Rent
is not a proportion of the produce obtained—it is not governed
like wages or profits by proportions—depending as it does
on the difference between the
quantity of produce obtained by
two equal capitals. If therefore

even according to the concessions of Mr. Ricardo, to increase the *proportion* of the whole produce which falls to the landlord's share; so that in any way we can view the subject, we must allow that, in-|dependently of the question of importations, the interest of 217

My measure of value is quantity of labour—rent rises only when the sum paid requires more labour to produce it. Ten men on the fertile land can produce 180 qrs.—on land less fertile only 170—if the 10 labourers then receive one half of the latter quantity, or 85 quarters, they receive what 5 men's labour can produce; the 10 men producing the 180 quarters receive no more; but 85 quarters on that land is produced with less labour, than that of 5 men. True, but the value of corn is regulated by the quantity produced with the capital least advantageously, and last employed on the land[2]; the advantage possessed by the holder of the better land, partakes of the nature of a monopoly, and therefore the value of the reward to the labourer must be measured not by the quantity of labour required to produce 85 quarters on the better land, but by the quantity required to produce it on the worse. Mr. Malthus says "Improvements in agriculture tend even according to the concessions of Mr. Ricardo to increase the *proportion* of the whole produce which falls to the landlord's share" I do not know where I have said this, but I wish to correct the passage if I have fallen into this error[3] by substituting the word used by Mr. Malthus "portion" for *proportion*[4], or if the word proportion be retained, it must be the proportion of the produce obtained on the more fertile lands.[5]

I have anywhere said that rent rises or falls in the proportion that the produce obtained is increased or diminished I have committed an error. I am not however conscious of having so done.'

[2] Replaces 'But value is regulated by the quantity last produced'.

[3] Replaces 'if I have said so'.

[4] Replaces 'substituting the word "portion", instead of *proportion*'.

[5] Cp. the alteration in ed. 3 of Ricardo's *Principles*, above, I, 83, n. 1, and cp. 402–3.

the landlord is strictly and necessarily connected with that of
the state. (116)

SECTION IX

On the Connexion of the Interests of the Landlord and of the State, in Countries which import Corn

The only conceivable doubt which can arise respecting the
strictest union between the interest of the landlord and that of the
state, is in the question of importation. And here it is evident,

---

(116) p. 216. *But in fact, &c. &c.*

After saying so often as Mr. Malthus has done, that I have
represented improvements in agriculture, as hurtful to the
interests of the landlord, and that on this opinion I have
grounded my assertion that the interests of landlords are
opposed to those of the other classes of society, he here [1]
states that I have admitted that improvements in agriculture
tend, *in a moderate time*, to increase the *proportion* of the
whole produce which falls to the landlord's share. Why then
have I been charged with holding a different doctrine? [2]

[1] 'admits' is del. here.
[2] An unfinished paragraph is del.
here: 'Mr. Malthus as I before observed does not appear to understand what I have said about
proportions and it is important
that I should not be misunderstood on that subject. Suppose I
employ 3 equal quantities of capital
successively on the same land as
the prices rise. I say when the
second quantity is applied, the
proportion ['paid to the landlord' is ins. here] of the quantity
obtained by the first will be increased—he will have no portion
whatever of the second. When

the third quantity of capital is
applied he will get a still larger
proportion of the quantity obtained by the first capital, a small
proportion of the quantity obtained by the second, and no
portion of the third. Though the
proportion of each quantity before
obtained will be increased, the
proportion of the whole quantity
obtained allotted to the landlord
will be diminished. Suppose the
quantity obtained by the 1st
capital were 1800 qrs. by the
second 1780 and by the third
1760. When the 2d capital was
employed he would have 20 qrs.

that at all events the landlord cannot be placed in a worse situation than others, and by some of the warmest friends of the freedom of trade, he has justly been considered as placed in a much better. No person has ever doubted that the individual interests of the manufacturers of woollen, silk, or linen goods, might be injured by foreign competition; and few would deny that the importation of a large body of labourers would tend to lower wages. Under the most unfavourable view, therefore, that we can take of the subject, the case of the landlord with regard to importation is not separated from that of the other classes of society. (117)

[Adam Smith was of opinion that the landlords were not

---

(117) p. 217. *Under the most unfavourable*

There is this manifest and³ important difference. The individual interests of the manufacturer of woollen, silk, or linen goods, might be injured by foreign competition, and they might be obliged with a⁴ loss to remove their capitals to other branches of trade, but still they would have a capital and a⁵ revenue, not much inferior to what they had before. The rent of the landlords of the inferior lands would cease altogether, and those of the landlords on the better lands, would be much reduced, if the utmost freedom were allowed to the importation of corn.⁶

There cannot be a greater mistake than to suppose there is any analogy between the interests of landlords, and those of manufacturers, as they are respectively affected by restrictions on the importation of raw produce, and restrictions on the importation of manufactured goods. Their interests

as rent or 1/90 of the quantity obtained by the first capital, but this would be only 1/179 of the whole. When the 3d capital was employed he would get 40 qrs. on No. 1 or one 1/9, and 20 qrs. of No. 2 or 1/17.'

The incorrectness of these calculations is partly due to an alteration of the figures which was not completely carried through.

³ 'manifest and' is ins.
⁴ 'great' is del. here.
⁵ 'capital and a' is ins.
⁶ The remainder of the Note is ins.

injured by foreign competition, though he allowed that manufacturers were.

218   The statement of Adam Smith is too strong; but it is certainly true that the producers of corn and cattle are less injured by foreign competition than the producers of particular manufactures.

On the question of importation it is important to remark that, in the way in which capital is practically employed upon the land, the interests of the state and the cultivator are not proportioned to each other.

219   The cultivation of the country is chiefly carried on by tenants, and a large part of the permanent improvements in agriculture, of late years, has been effected by the capitals of the same class of people.]

But if it be true, as I fully believe it is, that a very large part of the improvements which have taken place on the soil, has been derived from the capital, skill and industry of tenants, no truth
220 can | be more distinct and incontrovertible than that the advantage which such individuals have derived from a capital employed in agriculture, compared with a capital employed in commerce and manufactures, cannot have been proportioned to the advantages derived by the country; or, in other words, that the interests of individuals in the employment of capital, have not in this case been identified with the interest of the state.

This position will be made perfectly clear, if we examine

---

rest on totally different grounds. A manufacturer never can, whatever may be the restriction on importation, get, for any length of time, more than the general and ordinary rate of profit on his capital, and therefore [1] if he could easily remove his capital from one trade to another his loss would be inconsiderable, from the removal of restrictions.

But to the landlord it is a question of rent or no rent—of the possession of a useful machine, or one of no use whatever. It is not the situations of the landlord and manufacturer that are in the least analogous, but the situations of the farmer and manufacturer. In their cases indeed the analogy holds good.

[1] 'he is only permanently' is del. here.

attentively what would be the relative effect to the individual and the state of the employment of a capital of 10,000 *l.* in agriculture, or in manufactures under the circumstances described.

Let us suppose that a capital of 10,000 *l.* might be employed in commerce or manufactures for twenty years, at a profit of about twelve per cent., and that the capitalist might retire, at the end of that term, with his fortune doubled. It is obvious that, to give the same encouragement to the employment of such a capital in agriculture, the same or nearly the same advantages must be offered to the individual. But in order to enable a person who employs his capital on rented land to convert his 10,000 *l.* in the course of twenty years into 20,000 *l.* it is certain that he must make annually higher profits, in order to enable him to recover that part of his capital which he has actually sunk upon the land, and cannot withdraw at the end of the term; and then, if he has been an essential improver, he must necessarily leave the land to his | landlord, at the end of the lease, worth a considerably higher rent, independently of any change in the value of the circulating medium, than at the commencement of it. But these higher annual returns, which are necessary to the farmer with a temporary tenure to give him the common profits of stock, are continued, in part at least, in the shape of rent at the end of the lease, and must be so much gained by the state. (118)

In the case of the capital employed in commerce and manu-

221

---

(118) p. 220². *Let us suppose &c.*—

Mr. Malthus is here a little inconsistent with himself. He estimates the advantage to the state by money value, and will not employ, as he ought to do, on this occasion, his own measure of value, corn and labour. Suppose Mr. Malthus could demonstrate, which he cannot do, that we have made the same money profits by employing a given capital at home in agriculture as we should have done with the same capital³ if importation had been freely allowed. I might answer him; "if importation had been permitted and you had allowed corn to be cheap; with the same money capital I could have

² In MS, '221'.   ³ 'with the same capital' is ins.

factures, the profit to the state is proportioned to the profit derived by the individual; in the case of the capital employed in agriculture it is much greater; and this would be true, whether the produce were estimated in money, or in corn and labour. In either way, under circumstances which in all probability have actually occurred, the profits to the state derived from the capital employed in agriculture might be estimated perhaps at fourteen or fifteen per cent., while the profits to the individuals, in both cases, may have been only twelve per cent.

Sir John Sinclair, in his Husbandry of Scotland, has given the particulars of a farm in East Lothian, in which the rent is nearly half the produce; and the rent and profits together yield a return of fifty-six per cent. on the capital employed. But the rent and profits together are the real measure of the wealth derived by the country from the capital so employed; and as the farm described is one where the convertible husbandry is practised, a system in
222 which the greatest improvements have been made | of late years, there is little doubt that a considerable part of this increase of

---

employed much more labour—I could also have done the same with the same money revenue, therefore by not permitting free importation you have deprived us of all the commodities which this additional quantity of labour could employ." [1] Against this solid advantage Mr. Malthus puts the permanent [2] improvements which tenants make to the lands they rent, and which they cannot again take away, as they become permanently fixed on the soil. It may be doubted whether the expectation of these trifling advantages are not always allowed for in agreeing for rent, and whether they do not [3] really constitute a portion of the landlord's rent.

Others can judge better than I can do of the value thus left on the lands by tenants at the expiration of their leases. I am not disposed to estimate it very highly. If the power of commanding labour be the measure of value, value must

[1] Should probably be 'which this additional quantity of labour employed could produce.'

[2] 'permanent' is ins.

[3] 'whether they do not' is ins.

wealth had been derived from the capital of the tenant who held the farm previous to the renewal of the lease, although such increase of wealth to the state could not have operated as a motive of interest to the individual so employing his stock. (119)

If then during the war no obstacles had occurred to the importation of foreign corn, and the profits of agriculture had in consequence been only ten per cent. while the profits of commerce and manufactures were twelve, the capital of the country would of course have flowed towards commerce and manufactures; and measuring the interest of the state, as usual, by the interest of individuals, this would have been a more advantageous direction of it, in the proportion of twelve to ten. But, if the view of the subject just taken be correct, instead of a beneficial direction of it to a profit of twelve per cent. from a profit of ten per cent. as measured by the interests of the individuals concerned, it might have been a disadvantageous direction of it to a profit of only twelve per cent. from a profit of fourteen per cent. as measured by the interest of the state. (120)

---

depend on the *quantity* of necessaries, and not on their money value.

(119) p. 221. *Sir John Sinclair, &c.*

Does Mr. Malthus believe that the freest importation of corn would deprive us of any particle of the quantity which we now derive from that farm? As for the great rent upon it being derived from capital accumulated upon it by tenants I cannot help being sceptical on this subject.

(120) p. 222. *If then during the war*

Here again the estimate is made of money profits, but I require that in both instances the money profits should be reduced into the power of commanding labour and commodities[4]. I do not want to know what value we could[5] have obtained in the two cases, but what riches we might have got,—what means of happiness to the community!

---

4 'and commodities' is ins.   5 'could' is ins.

It is obvious therefore that the natural* restrictions upon the importation of foreign corn during the war, by forcibly raising
223 the profits of domestic | cultivation, may have directed the capital of the country into a channel more advantageous than that into which it would otherwise have flowed, and instead of impeding the progress of wealth and population, as at first one should certainly have expected, may have decidedly and essentially promoted it.

And this, in fact, such restrictions not only may, but must do, whenever the demand for corn grown at home is such, that the profits of capitals employed on the new lands taken into cultivation, joined to the rents which they generate, form together greater returns in proportion to the stock employed, than the returns of the capitals engaged in commerce and manufactures; because, in this case, though foreign corn might be purchased, without these restrictions, at a cheaper money price than that at which it could be raised at home, it would not be purchased at so small an expense of capital and labour†, which is the true proof of the advantageous employment of stock. (121)

* It is of great importance always to recollect that the high price of corn from 1798 to 1814 was occasioned by the war and the seasons,—not by corn-laws; and that a country with open ports may be subjected to very great alternations of price in war and in peace.

† If restrictions upon importation necessarily increased the quantity of labour and capital required to obtain corn, (122) they could not of course

---

(121) p. 223. *And this in fact*

True if estimated in corn returns, and not in money returns. The only question of importance, in fact, is, whether we could buy our corn at home or abroad at the least expence of capital and labour—[1] and we are to judge of this only by a comparison of the quantity we can import with a given capital and the quantity we can grow with an equal amount of capital. It is by quantity and not by money value that we must judge. We may make any thing of a high money value, by rendering it scarce.

[1] 'Mr. Malthus thinks this would not be the case' is del. here.

But if the progress of wealth has been rather accelerated than retarded by such restrictions upon | the importation of foreign 224 corn, on account of the greater quantity of raw produce that has been purchased by a given quantity of capital and labour at home, than could have been purchased by the same quantity of capital and labour from abroad, (123) it is quite obvious that the population must have been accelerated rather than retarded; and certainly the unusually rapid increase of population which is known to have taken place during the last ten or fifteen years of the war so much beyond the average of the century, tends strongly to confirm this conclusion.

The position here laid down may appear to be rather startling; but the reader will see how it is limited. (124) It depends for its general effects upon permanent improvements being made by a capital which has only a temporary interest in the fruits of such improvements; and, in reference to restrictions upon importation, it depends upon the circumstance that these restrictions by the increased demand for the products of domestic agriculture which

be defended for a moment, with a view to wealth and productive power. But if by directing capital to the land they occasion permanent improvements, the whole question is changed. Permanent improvements in agriculture are like the acquisition of additional land. Even however, if they had no effect of this kind, they might be desirable on other grounds yet more important. Late events must make us contemplate with no small alarm a great increase in the *proportion* of our manufacturing population, both with reference to the happiness and to the liberty of our country.

---

(122) p. 223. *If restrictions upon importation &c.*

It is only because they do so, that they are attacked. Can any man doubt of their having this effect?

Their policy on other grounds is a different question. I confess on those other grounds the arguments in favour of restrictions have[2] very little solidity in my view of the subject.

(123) p. 223. *But if the progress of wealth &c.*

Grant this indeed, and the conclusion follows.

(124) p. 224. *The position here laid down*

To me it is very startling, and I believe wholly unfounded.

[2] Replaces 'I confess those grounds have'.

they create, should have the effect of occasioning improvements which would otherwise not have taken place. But neither of these usual concomitants are absolutely necessary.

Considerable quantities of capital might be employed upon the land, and a temporary increase of demand for domestic produce might take place, without permanent improvements in agriculture. All that is meant to be said is, that when, under such circumstances, permanent improvements in agriculture are really made, and rent is created, it is impossible to resist the conclusion, that to such | extent the interest of the state in the exchangeable value created by such capital,* is decidedly greater than the interest of the individual.

225

* I refer to exchangeable value and rate of profits, not to abundance of

---

(125) p. 225. *I refer to exchangeable value and rate of profits, not to abundance of conveniences and luxuries*

If this be the case, if you even made out your proposition it ought to have no effect on our practice. We care little what the nominal exchangeable value of our goods may be, (and I should say, their real value[1] either;) what we are anxious about is to possess an abundance of conveniences and luxuries. If then every word you have said be true, we are for an unrestricted corn trade, if it is to give us a value no matter, whether high or low, which will give us an abundance of conveniences and luxuries.

But again I ask what is become of Mr. Malthus's measure of real value in exchange—we were told that it implied a certain quantity of necessaries and conveniences and that things rose and fell in exchangeable real value as they would sell for more or less of these conveniences and necessaries— then as it was supposed that a certain quantity of necessaries and conveniences would command always a certain quantity of labour—labour was selected as the measure of value:— this underwent another correction, as labour was acknow-

[1] Replaces 'real exchangeable value'.

This consideration, combined with those before adverted to, may make it at least a matter of doubt, whether even in the case of restrictions upon the importation of foreign corn, the interest of the state may not sometimes be the same as that of the landlords. But no such doubt exists respecting a restriction upon the importation of other commodities. And when we add, that in a state of perfectly free intercourse, it is eminently the interest of those who live upon the rents of land, that capital and population should increase, while to those who live upon the profits of stock and the wages of labour, an increase of capital and population is,

conveniences and luxuries. (125) In almost all improvements in machinery, the state is ultimately more benefited than the producers, but not in reference to rate of profits and real value in exchange.

---

ledged to be variable; it was desirable to introduce another commodity, which it was alleged was also variable, but variable in another direction, and therefore as the variation of one would correct that of the other, a mean between the two it was said would give us an unvarying measure of value[2], accordingly the final measure of real value in exchange was settled to be a mean between corn and labour.

It must be confessed that it has not hitherto been often referred to, and in the present argument it appears to be given up altogether for we are told that exchangeable value is referred to, not abundance of conveniences and luxuries.[3] We are quite at a loss to know what is here meant by exchangeable value. It cannot be corn and labour, for they are considered as I have just shewn, of exactly the same nature as conveniences and luxuries. I strongly suspect that the reprobated money value is meant, if so, Mr. Malthus must agree with me that there is a very marked distinction between value and riches: value depends on the cost of production, riches on the abundance of productions.

[2] 'of value' is ins.
[3] The MS has here a cross, perhaps a reference to a footnote on a lost slip.

to say the least of it, a much more doubtful benefit; it may be most safely asserted, that the interest of no other class in the state is so nearly and necessarily connected with its wealth and power, as the interest of the landlord. |

226   SECTION X

General Remarks on the Surplus Produce of the Land.

It seems rather extraordinary that the very great benefit which society derives from that surplus produce of the land which, in the progress of society, falls mainly to the landlord in the shape of rent, should not yet be fully understood and acknowledged. I have called this surplus a bountiful gift of Providence, and am most decidedly of opinion, that it fully deserves the appellation. But Mr. Ricardo has the following passage:—

"Nothing is more common than to hear of the advantages which the land possesses over every other source of useful produce, on account of the surplus which it yields in the form of rent. Yet when land is most abundant, when most productive and most fertile, it yields no rent; and it is only, when its powers decay, and less is yielded in return for labour, that a share of the original produce of the more fertile portions is set apart for rent. It is singular that this quality in the land, which should have been noticed as an imperfection, compared with the natural agents by which manufactures are assisted, should have been pointed out as constituting its peculiar pre-eminence. If air, water, the elasticity of steam, and the pressure of the atmosphere were of various qualities, if they could be appropriated, and each quality existed |
227 only in moderate abundance, they, as well as the land, would afford a rent, as the successive qualities were brought into use. With every worse quality employed, the value of the commodities in the manufacture of which they were used would rise, because equal quantities of labour would be less productive. Man would do more by the sweat of his brow, and nature perform less, and the land would be no longer pre-eminent for its limited powers."

"If the surplus produce which the land affords in the form of rent be an advantage, it is desirable that every year the machinery newly constructed should be less efficient than the old, as that

would undoubtedly give a greater exchangeable value to the
goods manufactured, not only by that machinery, but by all the
other machinery in the kingdom; and a rent would be paid to all
those who possessed the most productive machinery." *

Now, in referring to a gift of Providence, we should surely
speak of its value in relation to the laws and constitution of our
nature, and of the world in which we live. But, if any person will
take the trouble to make the calculation, he will see that if the
necessaries of life could be obtained without limit, and the number
of people could be doubled every twenty-five years, the population which might have been produced from a single pair since the
Christian æra, would have been sufficient, not only to fill the
earth quite full of people, so that | four should stand in every 228
square yard, but to fill all the planets of our solar system in the
same way, and not only them, but all the planets revolving round
the stars which are visible to the naked eye, supposing each of
them to be a sun, and to have as many planets belonging to it as
our sun has. Under this law of population, which, excessive as
it may appear when stated in this way, is, I firmly believe, best
suited to the nature and situation of man, it is quite obvious that
some limit to the production of food, or some other of the necessaries of life, must exist. Without a total change in the constitution of human nature, and the situation of man on earth, the whole
of the necessaries of life could not be furnished in the same plenty
as air, water, the elasticity of steam, and the pressure of the atmosphere. It is not easy to conceive a more disastrous present—one
more likely to plunge the human race in irrecoverable misery,
than an unlimited facility of producing food in a limited space.
A benevolent Creator then, knowing the wants and necessities of
his creatures, under the laws to which he had subjected them,
could not, in mercy, have furnished the whole of the necessaries
of life in the same plenty as air and water. This shews at once the
reason why the former are limited in quantity, and the latter
poured out in profusion. But if it be granted, as it must be, that
a limitation in the power of producing food is obviously necessary
to man confined to a limited space, then the value of the actual
quantity of land which he has received, depends upon the small
quantity of labour neces-|sary to work it, compared with the 229

* Princ. of Polit. Econ. ch. ii. p. [75].

number of persons which it will support; or, in other words, upon that specific surplus so much under-rated by Mr. Ricardo, which by the laws of nature terminates in rent. (126)

If manufactured commodities, by the gradations of machinery supposed by Mr. Ricardo, were to yield a rent, man, as he observes, would do more by the sweat of his brow;* and supposing him

* That is, supposing the gradations were towards worse machinery,

---

(126) p. 227. *Now in referring to a gift of Providence*

I do not agree that in a treatise on Political Economy it should be so considered. The gift is great or little according as it is more or less, not according as it may be more or less morally useful. It may be better for the health of my friend, that I should restrict him to a pint of wine a day, but my gift is most valuable if I give him a bottle a day. The question is not whether the Creator did not consult our real happiness by limiting the productive powers of the land, but whether the fact be not, that he has so limited it,—while He[1] has given us an unbounded supply of water, of air, and has set no limits to the use we may make of[2] the pressure of the atmosphere, the elasticity of steam and many other[3] services rendered to us by nature.

Mr. Malthus says I underrate the specific surplus which by the laws of nature terminate in rent. In the beginning of the very paragraph in which this observation occurs the charge brought against me is that I am not satisfied with the prolific power of the earth, because it is not boundless, as are many others of the gifts of nature, and the conclusion is that I underrate all prolific power in the earth. I complain in short of its not yielding enough[4] of what Mr. Malthus justly calls surplus produce, and at the same time I complain of its yielding more than is serviceable.

[1] Replaces 'he'.
[2] Last twelve words are ins.
[3] 'natural prod...' is del. here.
[4] 'surplus' is del. here.

still to obtain the same quantity of commodities, (which, however,
some of which it was necessary to use, but not otherwise. The reason why
manufactures and necessaries will not admit of comparison with regard to
rents is, that necessaries, in a limited territory, are always tending to the
same exchangeable value, whether they have cost little or much labour;
but manufactures, if not subjected to an artificial monopoly, must fall with
the facility of producing them. We cannot therefore suppose the price to
be given; but if we could, facility of production would, in both cases, be
equally a measure of relief from labour.

Against two such contrary accusations I cannot defend
myself, and as I plead guilty only to one, I shall say little
of the other. Here then once for all let me declare that I
estimate as the source from which we derive [5] all we possess
the power which the earth has of yielding a surplus produce.
In proportion to this power we enjoy leisure for study and
the obtaining of that knowledge which [6] gives dignity to life.
Without it we could neither possess arts or manufactures,
and our whole time would be devoted to the procuring food
to support a miserable existence.

It is only because the prolific powers of land in other
countries are greater than those on which we must draw for
our last supplies, that I would have recourse to those lands,
and would consent to import corn, because as less labour
would be devoted to the obtaining of food, more might be
employed in getting other gratifications.

With respect to the other point, I repeat confidently that
rent is owing to the limit which nature has set to her present,
and not to the unbounded extent of it. If there had been no
limits to fertility, if one capital after another had been equally
productive, of produce, no rent could have been generated.
"But the earth could not contain the population that might
have been born under such circumstances"!—I do not deny

[5] 'from which we derive' replaces 'of'.

[6] Last seven words replace 'and all that'.

he would not,) the increase of his labour would be in proportion to the greatness of the rent so created. (127) But the surplus, which a given quantity of land yields in the shape of rent, is totally different. Instead of being a measure of the increase of labour, which is necessary altogether to produce the quantity of corn which the land can yield, it is finally an exact measure of the *relief* from labour in the production of food granted to him by a kind Providence. If this final surplus be small, the labour of a large portion of the society must be constantly employed in procuring, by the sweat of their brows, the mere necessaries of 230 life, and so-|ciety must be most scantily provided with convenient

---

this—neither does the observation refute[1] any of the statements I have made.

Is my proposition true or not true? Not true says Mr. Malthus. Your proof? The present would be a disastrous present and the human race would be plunged in irrecoverable misery. Now I ask whether this is an answer. If I murmured against Providence, and reproached Nature for a want of liberality, Mr. Malthus might have shewn my complaint to be unfounded, and unreasonable. But have I done this? Certainly not, I have only said that if she had not limited her present there would be no rent, and Mr. Malthus observation in answer is that it seems rather extraordinary that the very great benefit which society derives from that surplus produce of the land, which in the progress of society, falls mainly to the landlord, in the shape of rent, should not yet be fully understood and acknowledged. Now I humbly contend that he has not brought forward one fact, or one argument, to shew that I have either misunderstood it, or failed to acknowledge it.

(127) p. 229. *If manufactured commodities &c.*

True, but would not the same be the case if you diminished

---

[1] Replaces 'answer'.

luxuries and leisure; while if this surplus be large, manufactures, foreign luxuries, arts, letters and leisure may abound.

It is a little singular, that Mr. Ricardo, who has, in general, kept his attention so steadily fixed on permanent and final results, as even to define the *natural* price of labour to be that price which would maintain a stationary population, although such a price cannot generally occur under moderately good governments, and in an ordinary state of things, for hundreds of years, has always, in treating of rent, adopted an opposite course, and referred almost entirely to temporary effects.

It is obviously with this sort of reference, that he has objected

---

the fertility of the earth, and thereby increased rent? Would not the increase of his labour in that case also be in proportion to the greatness of the rent so created? But you may increase rent by increasing the fertility of the land, and so you may in the supposed case of machines by increasing their productive powers, and increasing the difference in those powers. "Rent is finally an exact measure of the relief from labour in the production of food, granted to him by Providence"! Mr. Malthus may call it so if he pleases, but would not the real[2] relief be greater—if the land were more fertile? Would not rent fall as the present became more liberal. But is rent an exact measure of the relief from labour in the production of food? I deny it. The surplus produce is, but rent, and surplus produce, do not mean the same thing. The surplus produce in America, in proportion to the population, is greater than here. Is rent as high there? Mr. Malthus will not say it is. The surplus produce in America shews itself chiefly in profits and[3] in high wages,[4] and contributes much more to the general prosperity in that form, than if it appeared in the form of rent.

---

[2] 'the real' replaces 'that'.
[3] 'sometimes' was ins. here, and then del.

[4] Replaces 'The surplus produce shews itself in profits and wages,'.

to Adam Smith for saying that, in rice countries a greater share of the produce would belong to the landlord than in corn countries, and that rents in this country would rise, if potatoes were to become the favourite vegetable food of the common people, instead of corn.* Mr. Ricardo could not but allow, indeed he has allowed,† that rents would be finally higher in both cases. (128) But he immediately supposes that this change is put in execution at once, and refers to the temporary result of land being thrown out of cultivation. Even on this supposition however, all the lands which had been thrown up, would be cultivated again in a very much less time, than it would take to reduce the price of 231 labour, in a natural state of things, to | the maintenance only of a stationary population. (129) And therefore, with a view to permanent and final results, which are the results which Mr. Ricardo has mainly considered throughout his work, he ought to have allowed the truth of Adam Smith's statements.

But, in point of fact, there is every probability that not even a temporary fall of rent would take place. No nation ever has changed or ever will change the nature of its food all at once. The process, both in reference to the new system of cultivation to be adopted, and the new tastes to be generated, must necessarily be very slow. In the greater portion of Europe, it is probable, that a change from corn to rice could never take place; and where it could, it would require such great preparations for irrigation, as

* Wealth of Nations, vol. i. Book I. c. xi. pp. 248–250. 6th edit.
† Princ. of Polit. Econ. ch. xxiv. p. [334].

---

(128) p. 230. *Mr. Ricardo could not but allow indeed he has allowed &c. &c.*

And yet "that specific surplus is so much underrated by Mr. Ricardo which by the laws of nature terminates in rent." [1] Can these passages be consistent?

(129) p. 230. *Even on this supposition &c. &c.*

Does it take a very little time to reduce the price of labour, "in a natural state of things," to the maintenance only of a stationary population?

[1] Malthus's p. 229; above, p. 210.

to give ample time for an increase of population fully equal to the increased quantity of food produced. In those countries where rice is actually grown, the rents are known to be very high. Dr. Buchanan, in his valuable travels through the Mysore, says, that in the watered lands below the Ghâts, the government was in the habit of taking two-thirds of the crop.‡ This is an amount of rent which probably no lands cultivated in corn can ever yield; and in those parts of India and other countries, where an actual change has taken place from the cultivation of corn to the cultivation of rice, I have little doubt that rents have not only finally risen very considerably, but have risen even during the progress of the change. (130) |

With regard to potatoes, we have very near to us an oppor-   232
tunity of studying the effects of their becoming the vegetable food of the great mass of a people. The population of Ireland has increased faster, during the last hundred years, than that of any other country in Europe; and under its actual government, this fact cannot be rationally accounted for, but from the introduction and gradual extension of the use of the potatoe. I am persuaded, that had it not been for the potatoe, the population of Ireland would not have more than doubled, instead of quadrupled, during the last century. This increase of population has prevented lands from being thrown out of cultivation, or given greater value to natural pasture, at the same time that it has occasioned a great fall in the comparative money wages of labour. This fall, experience

‡ Vol. ii. p. 212.

---

(130) p. 231. *And in those parts of India &c.*

That is to say the surplus produce has risen very considerably, and the government has seized upon it—this is very[2] different from rent rising. If the taxes were remitted would not the price of produce fall? If you say it would the tax not only takes all the rent but also a part of the profits, which is repaid by the consumer in the advanced price of produce.[3]

[2] 'very' is ins.

[3] The last two sentences, beginning 'If the taxes', are ins.

tells us, has not been accompanied by a proportionate rise of profits, and the consequence is a considerable rise of rents. (131) The wheat, oats and cattle of Ireland are sold to England and bear English money prices, while they are cultivated and tended by labour paid at half the money price; a state of things which must greatly increase either the revenue derived from profits, or the revenue derived from rents; and practical information assures us, that it is the latter which has derived the greatest benefit from it.

I think, therefore, that though it must lead to great errors, not to distinguish very decidedly the temporary rates of wages from their final rates, it would lead to no such error to consider the 233 tempo-|rary effects of the changes of food which have been referred to, as of the same kind with their final effects, that is, as tending always to raise rents. And I am convinced, that if we make our comparisons with any tolerable fairness, that is, if we compare countries under similar circumstances, with respect to extent, and the quantity of capital employed upon the soil, which is obviously the only fair mode of comparing them, we shall find that rent will be in proportion to the natural and acquired fertility of the land. (132)

If the natural fertility of this island had been double what it is, and the people had been equally industrious and enterprising, the country would, according to all just theory, have been at this

---

(131) p. 232.

At first the advantage will go to profit, afterwards to rent—The time when it will do so[1] depends on the increase of population, and the consequent[2] demand for the increased raw produce that can be yielded.

(132) p. 233. *And I am convinced &c.*

[Mr. Malthus often refers me to South America, to shew me that some of my results do not agree with facts,—[3] it would hardly be fair to refer any one else to that country to shew that with a most fertile soil rents are low.][4]

[1] Last seven words replace 'it'.
[2] 'consequent' is ins.
[3] 'to any one else' is del. here, and 'any one else' is ins. seven words below.
[4] The whole Note is del.

time doubly rich and populous, and the rents of land much more than double what they are now. On the other hand, if the soil of the island had possessed only half its present fertility, a small portion of it only, as I stated on a former occasion, would have admitted of corn cultivation, the wealth and population of the country would have been quite inconsiderable, and rents not nearly one half of what they are now. But if, under similar circumstances, rent and fertility go together, it is no just argument against their natural connexion to say that rent is higher in England, where a great mass of capital has been employed upon the land, than in the more fertile country of South America, where, on the same extent of territory, not a twentieth part has been employed, and the population is extremely scanty. (133) |

The fertility of the land, either natural or acquired, may be   234
said to be the only source of permanently high returns for capital. If a country were exclusively manufacturing and commercial, and were to purchase all its corn at the market prices of Europe, it is absolutely impossible that the returns for its capital should for any great length of time be high. (134) In the earlier periods of history, indeed, when large masses of capital were extremely rare, and were confined to a very few towns, the sort of monopoly which they gave to particular kinds of commerce and manufactures tended to keep up profits for a much longer time; and great and brilliant effects were undoubtedly produced by some

---

(133) p. 233. *If the natural fertility*

No one denies the natural and ordinary, but not necessary[5] connection between rent and fertility.

(134) p. 234. *If a country were exclusively &c. &c.*

The rate of profits in[6] such a country would depend, as the rate of profits in all countries depend, on the[7] quantity of labour necessary to provide for the wages of the labourer. If the[8] price of corn is low as compared with the prices of[9] all other things with which corn is purchased, profits will

5 Last six words are ins.
6 'The rate of profits in' replaces 'The profits of', here and six words below.
7 'proportional' was ins. here, and then del.
8 'relative' is del. here.
9 'the prices of' is ins.

states which were almost exclusively commercial. (135) But in modern Europe, the general abundance of capital, the easy intercourse between different nations, and the laws of domestic and foreign competition prevent the possibility of large permanent returns being received for any other capitals than those employed on the land. No great commercial and manufacturing state in modern times, whatever may have been its skill, has yet been known permanently to make higher profits than the average of the rest of Europe. (136) But the capitals successfully employed on moderately good land, may permanently and without fear of interruption or check, sometimes yield twenty per cent., sometimes thirty or forty, and sometimes even fifty or sixty per cent.

235   A striking illustration of the effects of capitals employed on land compared with others, appeared in | the returns of the property-tax in this country. The taxable income derived from the capitals employed on land, was such as to yield to the property-tax nearly $6\frac{1}{2}$ millions, while the income derived from the capitals employed in commerce and manufactures was only such as to

---

naturally be high, whether the country grows its own corn, or imports it.[1]

The real cheapness of corn, its cheap labour price, whether obtained directly from the land, or by means of importation, is the efficient cause of high profits. Without cheapness of corn, that is to say, without a great surplus produce in return[2] for labour, profits cannot be high—with it, they may not be high, because the labourers position may chance to be such that he may have the power of commanding a great portion of this surplus produce—that is to say, he may have high wages.

(135) p. 234. *In the earlier periods of history &c.*

These states had no close monopoly; there was competition amongst the citizens—they might undersell each other,

[1] An unfinished paragraph is del. here: 'The relative cheapness of corn to manufactures ['particularly' ins., then del.] if the goods are made in the country, and are made with the usual and ordinary quantity of labour,'.
[2] 'in return' is ins.

yield two millions.* It is probably true, that a larger proportion of the incomes derived from the capitals employed in trade and manufactures, escaped the tax, partly from their subdivision, and partly from other causes; but the deficiency so occasioned could in no respect make up for the extraordinary productiveness of the capitals employed in agriculture.† And indeed it is quite obvious that, in comparing two countries together with the *same* capitals and the *same* rate of profits, one of which has land on which to grow its corn, and the other is obliged to purchase it, that which has the land, particularly if it be fertile, must be much richer, more populous, and have a larger disposable income for taxation. (137)

Another most desirable benefit belonging to a fertile soil is, that states so endowed are not obliged to pay much attention to

* The Schedule D. included every species of professions. The whole amounted to three millions, of which the professions were considered to be above a million.

† It must always be recollected, that the national profits on land must be considered as including rents as well as the common agricultural profits.

---

and consequently they must have reduced the price of their goods[3] to their cost of production, or natural price.

(136) p. 234. *No great commercial and manufacturing*

Because the labour price of corn has not differed much in those countries—or because the labourers were better paid in some than others.

(137) p. 235. *And indeed it is quite obvious &c.*

We say if corn could have been imported into England at a low price, profits would have been very high. We say that the present rents and all rent once constituted profits and therefore must be a deduction, from them.[4] Mr. Malthus answers, if profits had been the same, and you had imported corn, you would obviously have been poorer by all your rents. True, *if profits had been the same* ! but that is precisely the subject in dispute.

[3] 'the price of their goods' replaces 'prices'.

[4] Replaces: 'The present rents once constituted profits.'

that most distressing and disheartening of all cries to every man
of humanity—the cry of the master manufacturers and merchants
236 for low wages, to enable them to find a market for | their exports.
If a country can only be rich by running a successful race for
low wages, I should be disposed to say at once, perish such
riches! (138) But, though a nation which purchases the main part
of its food from foreigners, is condemned to this hard alternative, it
is not so with the possessors of fertile land. The peculiar products
of a country, though never probably sufficient to enable it to
import a large proportion of its food* as well as of its conveniences
and luxuries, will generally be sufficient to give full spirit and
energy to all its commercial dealings, both at home and abroad;
while a small sacrifice of produce, that is, the not pushing cultivation too far, would, with prudential habits among the poor,†
enable it to maintain the whole of a large population in wealth

---

* Cottons are no more a peculiar product of this country than silks: and
woe will, I fear, befal us, greater than ever we have yet experienced, if the
prosperity of our cotton trade should become necessary to purchase the
food of any considerable body of our people!

† Under similar circumstances, with respect to capital, skill, &c., it is
obvious that land of the same degree of barrenness could not be cultivated,
if by the prevalence of prudential habits the labourers were well paid; but
to forego the small increase of produce and population arising from the
cultivation of such land, would, in a large and fertile territory, be a slight
and imperceptible sacrifice, while the happiness which would result from
it to the great mass of the population, would be beyond all price. (139)

---

(138) p. 236. *If a country can only be rich by running*

So would I. We want the labourer to be abundantly provided, and maintain that the way to effect it is, by making
the labour price of the chief commodity he consumes cheap.
Mr. Malthus says, a nation which purchases the main part
of its food from foreigners is condemned to the hard alternative of allowing the lowest wages to its labouring classes.
This is begging the question. We answer that it is not on
the circumstance of its buying[1] its food that this must
depend, but on the terms on which it is bought—no nation
will buy abroad if they can buy cheaper at home.

[1] 'or growing' is del. here.

and plenty. Prudential habits, among the labouring classes of a country mainly depending upon manufactures and commerce, might ruin it. (140) In a country of fertile land, such | habits 237 would be the greatest of all conceivable blessings.

Among the inestimable advantages which belong to that quality in the land, which enables it to yield a considerable rent, it is not one of the least, that in the progress of society it affords the main security to man that nearly his whole time, or the time of nearly the whole society, shall not be employed in procuring mere necessaries. According to Mr. Ricardo, not only will each individual capital in the progress of society yield a continually diminishing revenue, but the whole amount of the revenue derived from profits will be diminished; and there is no doubt that the labourer will be obliged to employ a greater quantity of labour to produce that portion of his wages which must be spent in necessaries. (141) Both these great classes of society, therefore, may be expected to have less power of giving leisure to themselves, or of commanding the labour of those who administer to the enjoyments of society, as contradistinguished from those who administer to its necessary wants. But, fortunately for mankind, the neat rents of the land, under a system of private property, can never be diminished by the progress of cultivation. Whatever proportion they may bear to the whole produce, the actual amount must always go on increasing, and will always afford a

---

(139) p. 236. *To forego the small increase &c.*

Any people almost might be happy on any territory, if they carried their prudential habits far enough, and restricted their population to the provision which they were easily able to make for them.

(140) p. 236. *Prudential habits among the labouring classes &c. &c.*

This is quite a new doctrine—I shall have other opportunities of examining whether it be a true one.

(141) p. 237. *According to Mr. Ricardo &c. &c.*

I am not fairly quoted—I have said this will be the case if you are obliged to have recourse to worse land to feed your

fund for the enjoyments and leisure of the society, sufficient to leave and animate the whole mass.

If the only condition on which we could obtain lands yielding 238 rent were, that they should remain | with the immediate descendants of the first possessors, though the benefits to be derived from the present would no doubt be very greatly diminished, yet from its general and unavoidable effects on society, it would be most unwise to refuse it as of little or no value. But, happily, the benefit is attached to the soil, not to any particular proprietors. Rents are the reward of present valour and wisdom, as well as of past strength and cunning. Every day lands are purchased with the fruits of industry and talents.* They afford the great prize, the "*otium cum dignitate*" to every species of laudable exertion;

* Mr. Ricardo himself is an instance of what I am stating. He is now become, by his talents and industry, a considerable landholder; and a more honourable and excellent man, a man who for the qualities of his head and heart more entirely deserves what he has earned, or employs it better, I could not point out in the whole circle of landholders.

It is somewhat singular that Mr. Ricardo, a considerable receiver of rents, should have so much underrated their national importance; while I, who

---

increasing population,—the consequence of the accumulation of your capital; but, I have added this will not be the case if you can and will get cheap food from abroad.[1]

On my plan there will be no transfer neither from profits or wages to rent, prohibit importation and there will, while the actual produce will be less. "See the advantages of growing corn over importing it" says Mr. Malthus, "with the progress of capital, profits and wages will fall, but if you grow your own corn, you will have rents to compensate you for this loss.["] I answer refuse to grow your own corn, and profits will not fall, and you will not want an inadequate compensation for a loss which you will not suffer. It was hardly fair to quote me to shew[2] that profits would fall whether you imported or grew corn.

[1] Above, I, 126.   [2] Replaces 'prove'.

and, in the progress of society, there is every reason to believe, that, as they become more valuable from the increase of capital and population, and the improvements in agriculture, the benefits which they yield may be divided among a much greater number of persons. |

In every point of view, then, in which the subject can be 239 considered, that quality of land which, by the laws of our being, must terminate in rent, appears to be a boon most important to the happiness of mankind; and I am persuaded, that its value can only be underrated by those who still labour under some mistake, as to its nature, and its effects on society. (142)|

never received, nor expect to receive any, shall probably be accused of overrating their importance. Our different situations and opinions may serve at least to shew our mutual sincerity, and afford a strong presumption, that to whatever bias our minds may have been subjected in the doctrines we have laid down, it has not been that, against which perhaps it is most difficult to guard, the insensible bias of situation and interest.

---

(142) p. 239. *In every point of view then*

There is a surplus produce from the land from which profits and rents are taken. I am of opinion that the interests of society are best promoted by allowing the free importation of corn, the consequence of which is that the surplus produce from the land in cultivation at home will be divided in proportions more favorable to the farmer and capitalist, and less favorable to the landholder. Mr. Malthus appears to differ from me, but instead of shewing that society would be benefited by taking from the capitalist and giving to the landlord, he considers rent as a clear gain and accuses me of underrating its value because I am not willing to allow that the surplus produce increases or diminishes as rent rises or falls.

CHAPTER IV

OF THE WAGES OF LABOUR

SECTION I

On the Dependance of the Wages of Labour upon Supply and Demand

240   [The wages of labour are the remuneration to the labourer for his personal services, and may be distinguished into nominal and real.

Nominal wages are the money earned by the labourer. Real wages are the necessaries and conveniences which that money will command.

Wages are determined by the demand and supply of labour, compared with the demand and supply of what is paid for labour.]

241   The principle of demand and supply is the paramount regulator of the prices of labour as well as of commodities, not only temporarily but permanently; and the costs of production affect these prices only as they are the necessary condition of the permanent supply of labour, or of commodities.

It is as the condition of the supply, that the prices of the necessaries of life have so important an influence on the price of labour. A certain portion of these necessaries is required to enable the labourer to maintain a stationary population, a greater portion to maintain an increasing one; and consequently, whatever may be the prices of the necessaries of life, the money wages of the

---

(143) p. 241. *To shew that what may be called &c. &c.*

In many parts of Mr. M's work this opinion as applied to commodities is enforced, but I do not know by whom it is called in question. Natural price is another name for cost of production—while a commodity will sell in the market for its natural price or above it, it will be supplied, the cost

labourer must be such as to enable him to purchase these portions, or the supply cannot possibly take place in the quantity required.

To shew that what may be called the cost of producing labour only influences wages as it regulates the supply of labour, it is sufficient to turn our attention to those cases, where, under temporary circumstances, the cost of production does not regulate the supply; and here we shall always find that this cost immediately ceases to regulate prices. (143)

When, from a course of abundant seasons, or any cause which does not impair the capitals of the farmers, the price of corn falls for some time to-|gether, the cost of producing labour may be   242 said to be diminished, but it is not found that the wages of labour fall;* and for this obvious reason, that the reduced cost of production cannot, under sixteen or eighteen years, materially influence the *supply* of labour in the market. On the other hand, when the prices of corn rise from a succession of indifferent seasons, or any cause which leaves the demand for labour nearly the same as before, wages will not rise: because the same number of labourers remain in the market; and though the price of production has risen, the supply is not for some time affected by it. So entirely, indeed, does the effect of the cost of production on price depend upon the manner in which it regulates supply, that if in this, or any other country during the last twenty years, the production of labour had cost absolutely nothing, but had still been supplied in exactly the same proportion to the demand, the wages of labour would have been in no respect different. Of the truth of this position, we may be quite assured, by the instance alluded to in a former chapter, of a paper currency so limited in quantity as not to exceed the metallic money, which would other-

* The fall in the price of labour which took place in 1815 and 1816 was occasioned solely by the diminution of demand, arising from the losses of the farmers, and in no respect by the diminished cost of production.

---

of production therefore regulates its supply. Mr. Malthus says the demand compared to the supply regulates price [1], and the cost of producing the commodity regulates the supply. This is a dispute about words—whatever regulates the supply regulates the price.

[1] Replaces 'the demand regulates the supply'.

wise have circulated, in which case, though the cost of the paper
is comparatively nothing, yet, as it performs the same function,
243 and is supplied | only in the same quantity as the money, it
acquires the same value in exchange.

[Adam Smith's position, that the money price of labour is
regulated by the demand for labour, and the price of necessaries,
is practically quite true; but it is of importance to keep constantly
in view the mode in which the price of necessaries affects the
price of labour.

244   In all the cases of different prices of labour in different employments, which Adam Smith has illustrated, the effect obviously
depends upon causes which affect the supply of labour.]

245   Adam Smith has in general referred to the principle of supply
and demand in cases of this kind, but he has occasionally forgotten
it:—"If one species of labour," he says, "requires an uncommon
degree of dexterity and ingenuity, the *esteem* which men have for
such talents will give a value to their produce, superior to what
would be due to the time employed about it."* (144) And in
another place, speaking of China, he remarks, "That if in such
a country, (that is, a country with stationary resources,) wages
had ever been more than sufficient to maintain the labourer, and
enable him to bring up a family; the competition of the labourers |
246 and the interest of the masters, would soon reduce them to the
lowest rate which is consistent with *common humanity*."† The
reader will be aware, from what has been already said, that in the
first case here noticed, it is not the esteem for the dexterity and
ingenuity referred to, which raises the price of the commodity,

* Wealth of Nations, Book I. ch. vi. p. 71. 6th edit.
† Wealth of Nations, Book I. chap. vii. p. 108.

---

(144) p. 245. *If one species of labour &c. &c.*

That is to say will make men willing to give more for it,
but its value will not be regulated by this willingness but by
the supply which will again depend upon the interest which
fathers may feel to give their children this dexterity and
ingenuity and the cost of giving it.[1] If it could easily be
given by labourers to their children and at little cost, it
would have little value however much it might be esteemed.

[1] Last six words are ins.

but their scarcity, and the consequent scarcity of the articles produced by them, compared with the demand. And in the latter case, it is not common humanity which interferes to prevent the price of labour from falling still lower. If humanity could have successfully interfered, it ought to have interfered long before, and prevented any premature mortality from being occasioned by bad or insufficient food. But unfortunately, common humanity cannot alter the resources of a country. While these are stationary, and the habits of the lower classes prompt them to supply a stationary population cheaply, the wages of labour will be scanty; but still they cannot fall below what is necessary, under the actual habits of the people, to keep up a stationary population; because, by the supposition, the resources of the country are stationary, not increasing or declining, and consequently the principle of demand and supply would always interfere to prevent such wages as would either occasion an increase or diminution of people. |

SECTION II

Of the Causes which principally affect the Habits of the Labouring Classes

247

Mr. Ricardo has defined the natural price of labour to be "that price which is necessary to enable the labourers one with another to subsist, and to perpetuate their race, without either increase or diminution."‡ (145) This price I should really be disposed to call

‡ Polit. Econ. c. v. p. [93]. 2d edit.

---

(145) p. 247. *Mr. Ricardo has defined &c. &c.*

I have done so that we may have one common language to apply to all cases which are similar. By natural price I do not mean the usual price, but such a price as is necessary to supply constantly[2] a given demand. The natural price of corn is the price at which it can be supplied affording the usual profits. With every demand for an increased quantity the market price of corn will rise above this price and prob-

² 'constantly' is ins.

a most unnatural price; because in a natural state of things, that is, without great impediments to the progress of wealth and population, such a price could not generally occur for hundreds of years. But if this price be really rare, and, in an ordinary state of things, at so great a distance in point of time, it must evidently lead to great errors to consider the market-prices of labour as only temporary deviations above and below that fixed price to which they will very soon return.

The natural or necessary price of labour in any country I should define to be, "that price which, in the actual circumstances of the society, is necessary to occasion an average supply of labourers, sufficient to meet the average demand." And the market-price I should define to be, the actual price in the market, which from 248 temporary causes is sometimes | above, and sometimes below, what is necessary to supply this average demand.

[The condition of the labouring classes depends partly upon the rate at which the resources of the country are increasing, and partly upon the habits of the people.

Both these causes are subject to change, and often change together.

249 Still, however, habits are different with the same increase of resources; and an inferior mode of living is a cause as well as a consequence of poverty.

It would be desirable, though difficult, to ascertain the principal causes of the different modes of subsistance which prevail among the poor of different countries.

250 From high wages two results may arise—either a rapid increase of population, or a decided improvement in the mode of living.

Whatever tends to depress the character of the poor, contributes to the first of these results; whatever tends to elevate them, to the second.

---

ably is never at the natural price but either above or below it,—the same may be said of the natural price of labour.[1]

[1] Replaces: 'With every demand for an increased quantity it will rise above this price therefore if capital and population regularly increase the market price may for years exceed its natural price. I am however very little solicitous to retain my definition of the natural price of labour—Mr. Malthus's will do ['nearly' is ins. here] as well for my purpose.'

The most efficient causes of depression are, despotism, op- 251
pression and ignorance; the most efficient causes of elevation are,
civil and political liberty and education.

Of the causes which tend to generate prudential habits, the
most essential is civil liberty; and to the maintenance of civil
liberty, political liberty is generally necessary.

Education may prevail under a despotism, and be deficient
under a free constitution; but it can do little under a bad government, though much under a good one.

Ireland is an instance where increasing produce has occasioned 252
a rapid increase of population, without improving the condition
of the people.

England, in the first half of the last century, is an instance of 253
high wages leading to an improved mode of living, without a
rapid increase of population.

The change from bread of an inferior quality to the best 254
wheaten bread was probably aided by a change in the relative
values of wheat, oats and barley, occasioned by adventitious 255
circumstances.

When wheaten bread had become customary in some districts, 256
it would spread into others, even at the expense of comforts of
a different description.]

SECTION III   257

*Of the Causes which principally influence the Demand for
Labour, and the Increase of the Population*

There is another cause, besides a change in the habits of the
people, which prevents the population of a country from keeping
pace with the apparent command of the labourer over the means
of subsistence. It sometimes happens that wages are for | a time 258
rather higher than they ought to be, in proportion to the demand
for labour. This is the most likely to take place when the price of
raw produce has fallen in value, so as to diminish the power of
the cultivators to employ the same or an increasing number of
labourers at the same price. If the fall be considerable, and not
made up in value by increase of quantity, so many labourers will

be thrown out of work that wages, after a period of great distress, will generally be lowered in proportion. (146) But if the fall be gradual, and partly made up in exchangeable value by increase of quantity, the money wages of labour will not necessarily sink; and the result will be merely a slack demand for labour, not sufficient perhaps to throw the actual labourers out of work, but such as to prevent or diminish task-work, to check the employment of women and children, and to give but little encouragement

---

(146) p. 258. *If the fall be considerable*

How can it fall unless from increased supply, diminished demand or cheaper cost of production?[1] If it be from diminished demand, the labourers must have been thrown out of work before, and their not being employed cannot be attributed to this cause. If the supply be increased without any diminution of the supply of other things, it cannot diminish the power of the country generally to employ labour, but on the contrary must increase it.

It may diminish the power of the farmer because he must make good a money rent, and therefore with an increased quantity of produce he may have less power of commanding labour, after the payment of his rent, than he had before. But if he have less, someone must have more. The landlords rent would enable him to employ more labour. If the capitalists retained the same money capitals[2] they might with the same money employ more people if wages fell, and yet the labourers might be better off than before. If money wages did not fall, still, more labour would be demanded, because the same money wages would purchase more commodities and food together and therefore give more encouragement to labour. If nothing else were required more millers would be wanted to grind the corn, more bakers to

[1] Replaces 'increased supply and diminished demand?'   [2] 'capitals' replaces 'profits'.

to the rising generation of labourers. In this case the quantity of the necessaries of life actually earned by the labourer and his family, may be really less than when, owing to a rise of prices, the daily pay of the labourer will command a smaller quantity of corn. The command of the labouring classes over the necessaries of life, though apparently greater, is really less in the former than in the latter case, and, upon all general principles, ought to produce less effect on the increase of population. (147)

---

bake bread, and more cooks to make pastry. If the cost of production of corn were reduced, it would fall, without an increased supply, but less[3] labour could not be required in the country[4]—because in proportion as less labour was bestowed on the production of corn more would be devoted to the production of other things.[5]

(147) p. 258. *The command of the labouring classes*

If it be meant that a mere fall in the *price* of necessaries is not of itself a cause of an increased demand for labour, and of placing the labourer in a situation really better than before, there can be no dispute about it, because money may alter in value and corn may at the same time become scarcer. The money price of corn would fall but the money price of labour[6] would fall still more.

If money does not alter in value—the fall in the money price of corn must be favorable to the labourer. It can only be caused by abundance and that abundance must be temporary, and[7] in consequence of an accidental good season, or it must arise from a more permanent cause[8] and in consequence of a cheaper mode of production. A temporary

3 Replaces 'more'.
4 'in the country' is ins.
5 A footnote written on a loose slip is printed here in the Johns Hopkins ed., but it properly belongs to Note (208), p. 320 below.

6 Replaces 'the money price of wages'.
7 'temporary, and' is ins.
8 Replaces 'or it must be permanent'.

This disagreement between apparent wages and the progress of population will be further aggravated in those countries where poor laws are es-|tablished, and it has become customary to pay a portion of the labourers' wages out of the parish rates. If, when corn rises, the farmers and landholders of a parish keep the wages of labour down, and make a regular allowance for children, it is obvious that there is no longer any necessary connexion between the wages of day labour and the real means which the labouring classes possess of maintaining a family. When once the people are reconciled to such a system, the progress of population might be very rapid, at a time when the

abundance from a very good harvest is not favorable to the[1] farmer, but it is favorable to all other classes. The farmer may have a diminished revenue, and even a diminished capital, because his engagements to his landlord are made in money, and a very abundant crop will be worth less money than a scanty one. The landlord will receive no more money rent, but the corn he consumes for his own family and in the support of his horses and cattle will be at a lower price, and he will be benefited by the difference of price. If wages fall, the manufacturers will be benefited, by getting increased profits, as well as by getting the same advantage in their expenditure as that obtained by the landlords. Even the farmer will be in some degree compensated by paying[2] lower wages. If wages do not fall the labourers will have many increased means of enjoyment; the chief article of expence with them being cheap, they will have the difference between the sum they before expended on corn, and the sum now required for that purpose, to expend on other things, or to save. If as much is saved by them as is lost by the farmer, the society will be no poorer than before, and even at the former[3] average price of corn, in future, the same

[1] 'capitalist' is del. here. [3] 'former' is ins.
[2] 'paying' is ins.

wages of labour, independently of parish assistance, were only sufficient to support a wife and one child, or even a single man without either wife or child, because there might still be both encouragement to marriage, and the means of supporting children.

[The actual application of a greater quantity of food of some 260 kind or other, to the maintenance of labouring families, is necessary to an increase of population; and may generally be traced.

The increase of population in America, Ireland, England and Scotland, of late years, may be traced to this cause.]

What is mainly necessary to a rapid increase of population, is 261 a great and continued demand for labour; and this is occasioned

---

quantity of labour will be in demand. But if no saving is made by labourers and wages do not fall[4] it must I think be admitted that a temporary abundance of corn from a good harvest has a tendency to diminish the effective capital of the country. Not so will a low price of corn caused by the permanently diminished cost of its production. That may also be injurious to farmers,—will also be injurious for a time to landlords, but all other classes receive such permanent benefits from it that the society altogether is more than compensated for these trifling drawbacks.

On this part of the subject it will not be necessary to dwell as I have explained my views on several other occasions.

Mr. Malthus appears to think that under all circumstances, and however caused, a fall in the price of raw produce will be attended with a diminished demand for labour. In one case "so many labourers will be thrown out of work that wages after a period of great distress, will generally be lowered in proportion." In another "the quantity of the necessaries of life actually earned by the labourer and his family, may be really less than when, owing to a rise of prices, the daily pay of the labourer will command a smaller quantity of corn."

[4] 'and wages do not fall.' is ins.

by, and proportioned to, the rate at which the whole value of the capital and revenue of the country increases annually; because, the faster the value of the annual produce increases, the greater will be the power of purchasing fresh labour, and the more will be wanted every year. (148)

It has been sometimes thought, that the demand for labour can only be in proportion to the increase of the circulating, not the fixed capital; and this is no doubt true in individual cases:* but

* See an ingenious pamphlet on the condition of the labouring classes by Mr. Barton.

---

(148) p. 261. *What is mainly necessary to a rapid increase of population*

The truth of this proposition depends on the meaning which is attached to the word value. According to my view[1] the power of commanding labour may increase although the value of the capital of the country may diminish—it depends mainly on the quantity of capital—or that portion of capital which employs labour. Now value according to Mr. Malthus depends on the quantity of necessaries and conveniences. His proposition then is "that population will increase with a demand for labour, and with the means of supporting the labourers"—a proposition that cannot be controverted.

(149) p. 261. *It has been sometimes thought*

The effective[2] demand for labour must depend upon the increase of that part of capital, in which the wages of labour are paid.[3] If I have a revenue of £2000—in the expenditure of that revenue I necessarily employ labour. If I turn this revenue into capital, I at first employ the same labour as before, but productively instead of unproductively. This labour may be

[1] Above, I, 95.
[2] 'effective' is ins.
[3] A sentence is del. here: 'Fixed capital cannot be increased, but through the means of labour—and therefore there must previously be an increase of circulating capital, or which is the same thing, a diminution of unproductive, and an increase of productive consumption.'

it is not necessary to make the distinction in reference to a whole nation; because where the substitution of fixed capital saves a great quantity of labour, which cannot be employed elsewhere, it diminishes the value of the annual produce, and retards the increase of the capital and revenue taken together. (149)

If, for instance, a capitalist who had employed £20,000 in productive labour, and had been in the habit of selling his goods for £22,000, making | a profit of 10 per cent., were to employ 262 the same quantity of labour in the construction of a machine worth £20,000, which would enable him to carry on his business

---

employed in making a machine, the machine becomes a capital, and all that it produces is the revenue derived from that capital. Or this labour may be employed on the land, and the corn which it produces may be a capital to enable me to employ an additional quantity of labour[4]. A society does one or the other in proportion to the demand for either the objects of men's work; or for objects which are almost exclusively produced by machinery:—in general the capital accumulated will consist of a mixture of both, of fixed and of circulating capital. It appears then that to the person saving capital, it. can be of no importance whether it be employed as fixed or as circulating capital; if profits be 10 p.c. they will equally yield a revenue of £200 on £2000 capital, but if it be employed as fixed capital[,] goods to the amount of £250 or £300 may replace the capital, and give the £200 profit—if it be employed as circulating capital it may be necessary to sell the goods produced for £2200, to replace the capital and give the £200 profit. The country, which is enriched only by the net income, and not by the gross income, will be equally powerful in both cases:—to the capitalist it can be of no importance whether his capital consists of fixed or of circulating capital, but it is of the

[4] 'an additional quantity of labour' replaces 'this additional capital in the support of labour'.

without labour in future, except as his machine might require repair, it is obvious that, during the first year, the same value of the annual produce and the same demand for labour would exist; but in the next year, as it would only be necessary for the capitalist, in order to obtain the same rate of profits as before, to sell his goods for a little more than £2,000 instead of £22,000, the value of the annual produce would fall, the capital would not be increased, and the revenue would be decidedly diminished; and upon the principle that the demand for labour depends upon the rate at which the value of the general produce, or of the capital and revenue taken together, increases, the slackness of the demand for labour under such circumstances would be adequately accounted for. (150)

In general, however, the use of fixed capital is extremely favourable to the abundance of circulating capital; and if the market for the products can be proportionally extended, the whole value of the capital and revenue of a state is greatly increased by it, and a great demand for labour created.

The increase in the whole value of cotton products, since the introduction of the improved machinery, is known to be prodigious; and it cannot for a moment be doubted that the demand for labour in the cotton business has very greatly increased during

---

greatest importance to those who live by the wages of labour; they are greatly interested in increasing the gross revenue, as it is on the gross revenue that[1] must depend the means of providing for the population. If capital is realized in machinery, there will be little demand for an increased quantity of labour,—if it create an additional demand for labour it will necessarily be realized in those things which are consumed by the labourer.

(150) p. 261.[2] *If for instance, a capitalist who had*

[There appears to me to be a fallacy in the whole of this argument. I have a circulating capital of £20000 with which I make goods that sell for £22000—. I all at once dis-

[1] 'they' was ins. here, and then del.   [2] In MS, '262'.

the last forty years. This is indeed | sufficiently proved by the 263
greatly increased population of Manchester, Glasgow, and the
other towns where the cotton manufactures have most flourished.

A similar increase of value, though not to the same extent, has
taken place in our hardware, woollen, and other manufactures,
and has been accompanied by an increasing demand for labour,
notwithstanding the increasing use of fixed capital.

Even in our agriculture, if the fixed capital of horses, which,
from the quantity of produce they consume, is the most disadvantageous description of fixed capital, were disused, it is
probable, that a great part of the land which now bears corn
would be thrown out of cultivation. Land of a poor quality
would never yield sufficient to pay the labour of cultivating with
the spade, of bringing manure to distant fields in barrows, and
of carrying the products of the earth to distant markets by the
same sort of conveyance. Under these circumstances, as there
would be a great diminution in the quantity of corn produced,
there would be a great diminution in the whole value of the
produce; and the demand for labour and the amount of the
population would be greatly diminished. (151)* |

* It has lately been stated, that spade cultivation will yield both a greater
gross produce and a greater neat produce. I am always ready to bow to

---

continue my trade and instead of making these goods I make
a machine worth £22,000;—I shall neither be richer nor
poorer, for my goods in the one case, and the machine in
the other, are of equal value][3]

(151) p. 263. *Even in Agriculture, if the fixed capital*—to the
end of the paragraph.

It does not appear to me as a necessary consequence "that
the demand for labour and the amount of the population
would be greatly diminished."

Suppose that 1000 qrs. of corn were raised, of which 200 qrs.

[3] The whole Note is del. The
above is only a fragment: the
original Note must have covered
over six pages of the MS, as it
appears from the gap in the pencil
numeration of the sheets.

264   On the other hand, if, by the gradual introduction of a greater
quantity of fixed capital, we could cultivate and dress our soil and
carry the produce to market at a much less expense, we might

well established experience; but if such experience applies in the present
case, one cannot sufficiently wonder at the continued use of ploughs and
horses in agriculture. Even | supposing however that the use of the spade
might, on some soils, so improve the land, as to make the crop more than
pay the additional expense of the labour, taken separately; yet, as horses
must be kept to carry out dressing to a distance and to convey the produce
of the soil to market, it could hardly answer to the cultivator to employ men in digging his fields, while his horses were standing idle in his
stables. (152) As far as experience has yet gone, I should certainly say,
that it is commerce, price and skill, which will cultivate the wastes of large
and poor territories—not the spade.

---

might be considered as the surplus produce and that of
the remaining 800—four hundred were paid to the labourers
for their work, and four hundred were used in feeding the
horses and oxen employed in the business of the farm. Suppose now, that instead of 1000 qrs., only 900 [1] were produced,
in consequence of the adoption of spade husbandry, and
the dismissal of the horses and oxen from the work of the
farm.

Of this 950, let 150 [2] qrs. only be the surplus produce, and
let the remaining 800 be given to the labourers in husbandry
for their work. Under these circumstances there might be
an increased demand for labour with a diminution in the
gross and net produce. Whether there would be or not would
depend on the quantity of land which such a low rate of
profits might throw out of cultivation. It must however be
allowed that [3] a diminished production is compatible with an
increased consumption, *by human beings* and as in this case
the whole quantity produced would be consumed by man,
there might be an increased demand for labour although

[1] Should be 950, as below.
[2] '950' and '150' replace respectively '900' and '100'.

[3] 'it is quite possible that' is del.
here.

increase our produce very greatly by the cultivation and improvement of all our waste lands; and if the substitution of this fixed capital were to take place in the only way in which we can suppose it practically to take place, that is, gradually, there is no reason to doubt that the value of raw produce would keep up nearly to its former level; and its greatly increased quantity, combined with the greater proportion of the people which might be employed in manufactures and commerce, would unquestionably occasion a very great increase in the exchangeable value of the general produce, and thus cause a great demand for labour and a great addition to the population. (153)

In general, therefore, there is little to fear that the introduction

---

corn should be higher in price and require an increased cost for its production.[4]

(152) p. 264 note. *Yet as horses must be kept to*

I mean to give no opinion on the subject of spade husbandry—I am not qualified to do so, but I do not see the necessity of horses standing idle in the stable. The same horses might do the work of various farms—they might be let out for other purposes to which the work of horses is applicable or they might be hired on occasion by the farmer.

(153) p. 264. *On the other hand*

It might be possible to do almost all the work performed by men with horses, would the substitution of horses in such case, even if attended with a greater produce, be advantageous to the working classes, would it not on the contrary very materially diminish the demand for labour? All I mean to say is that it *might* happen with a cheaper mode of cultivation the demand for labour *might* diminish, and with a dearer it might increase.

[4] A sentence is del. here: 'This is perhaps the only case in which the substitution of labour for fixed capital, if horses can be so called, is not attended with advantage to the capitalist yet is nevertheless beneficial to the working classes.'

of fixed capital, as it is likely to take place in practice, will diminish the effective demand for labour; indeed it is to this

265   source that we are to look for the main cause of its future in-|crease. At the same time, it is certainly true, as will be more fully stated in a subsequent part of this volume, that if the substitution of fixed capital were to take place very rapidly, and before an adequate market could be found for the more abundant supplies derived from it and for the new products of the labour that had been thrown out of employment, a slack demand for labour and great distress among the labouring classes of society would be universally felt. (154) But in this case, the general produce, or the capital and revenue of the country taken together, would certainly

---

(154) p. 265. *At the same time it is certainly true*

Mr. Malthus's peculiar theory is that supplies may be so abundant, that they may not find a market. This is insisted on in various parts of his work. A very great facility of production, might, under certain circumstances, encourage a habit of indolence, and therefore might be a reason for commodities not being produced abundantly, but it can be no reason, when they are produced, for their not being exchanged against each other. We all like to buy and consume, the difficulty is in the production. One product is bought by another[;] every man will buy if he has a product to give in exchange, and does not value that higher than the commodity offered.

(155) p. 265. *But in this case the general produce*

That is to say they might fall in [1] I suppose Mr. Malthus measure of real value in exchange, namely, in conveniences and necessaries, but suppose this increased produce consisted of conveniences and necessaries, then they must rise in value, for the value of a standard measure depends upon its quantity.[2]

[1] 'a money' was ins. here, then   [2] Replaces 'for value depends
del.   upon quantity.'

fall in value, owing to a temporary excess of supply compared with the demand, and would shew that the variations in this value, compared with the previous value paid in wages, are the main regulators of the power and will to employ labour. (155)

In the formation of the value of the whole produce of a country, a part depends upon price, and a part upon quantity. That part which depends merely upon price is in its nature less durable and less effective than that which depends upon quantity. An increase of price, with little or no increase of quantity, must be followed very soon by a nearly proportionate increase of wages; while the command of these increased money wages over the necessaries of life going on diminishing, the population must

---

Neither could it be said that they would command less labour, unless labour rose in value, because the command of labour must depend on the means of paying for it, and these means would be increased by the increased quantity of conveniences and necessaries. If less labour could be commanded it would only be because labour rose as compared with necessaries, a reason why profits should fall, and [3] capital be less rapidly accumulated, but low profits would only exist while labour continued high. Increase population and sink the value of labour as compared with necessaries, and profits would again be high and afford an inducement to new accumulations. I must repeat here what I have often said elsewhere that capital [4] and labour could not both be abundant [5] at the same time, for the one will always purchase the other, however they may be multiplied.

To say that I have a very abundant capital is to say that I have a great demand for labour. To say that there is a great abundance of labour, is to say that there is not an adequate capital to employ it.

---

[3] 'less' is del. here.   [5] Replaces 'redundant'.
[4] 'capital' replaces 'profits'.

come to a stop, and no further rise of prices can occasion an effective demand for labour. (156)

---

(156) p. 265. *In the formation of the value of the whole pro-duce of a country, a part depends upon price, and a part upon quantity* [1]

If price be estimated in a medium unvarying in value, price and value mean the same thing, and then I understand the proposition to be this. Either the whole quantity of produce may have increased, each particular thing remaining at the same price; or the quantity may not have increased and each individual thing may be at a higher price. The whole price of 150 qrs. of wheat, may be greater than the

[1] There are three versions of this Note, of which the final one is printed above. The earliest attempt began as follows: 'By price Mr. Malthus means money price and of course at a time when money is not varying in value. This it must be remembered is my measure of value which Mr. Malthus so loudly condemns. In this passage he proposes a compromise with me, he will admit one half of my measure of value if I will admit one half of his. I cannot consent'—here Ricardo broke off and started again:

'Mr. Malthus must mean price in a money stationary, or varying in value. If the former, I say that the whole value depends upon price [replaced by 'upon price and not upon quantity'; which in its turn is replaced by 'upon the price of the whole quantity']; and that it will be durable; and with little or no increase of quantity, there will be no increase of wages because the demand for labour depends on quantity. Though the whole produce may be at a greater price taken collectively every thing may be at its former price. The price of 150 qrs. of wheat may be greater than the price of 100 qrs. and yet each individual quarter may be at the same price. If Mr. Malthus means that the value of the whole produce depends in any degree upon price in a varying medium, I do not know how to argue with him, for then our notions of value are so different that we clearly do not understand the terms used by each other. In such a medium an increase of price may take place without any increase of quantity, ['and even with a diminished quantity' is ins. here] or the contrary may be the fact, the quantity and price may both rise, or both fall.' This again was superseded, but two concluding sentences, which followed here, are preserved at the end of the final version of the Note.

On the other hand, if the quantity of produce be increased so fast that the value of the whole | diminishes from excessive supply, 266

---

whole price of 100 qrs. yet each individual quarter may be of the same value as before or the 100 qrs. may be of equal value with that which 150 qrs. bore before, because each individual quarter may have risen in value. The increase in the price of each individual quarter, in an unvarying medium, must be owing, if it have any duration, to an increased cost of production; but the increase in the price of the larger quantity, is compatible with a diminished cost of production.

Mr. Malthus says that "an increase of price, with little or no increase of quantity, must be followed very soon by a nearly proportionate increase of wages." I should very much doubt if the increase of wages would be proportionate to the rise in the price of corn, for if corn can only rise in an unvarying medium on account of an increased cost of production, more labour must be bestowed to obtain the same quantity.

With more labour, there will be more labourers, and if more labourers only get the same quantity of corn, less of course will be the portion of each individual labourer, and therefore labour cannot rise in the same proportion as corn. I agree with Mr. Malthus "that the command of the labourer over the necessaries of life would go on diminishing, and the population must come to a stop" and therefore I cannot agree with him that the labourers wages would increase proportionably with the price of corn—if they did—population never could come to a stop. If the rise in the whole value of produce is owing to the increased quantity, then indeed wages would probably rise, because there would be an increased demand for labour.

As money wages would rise, and the commodities on

it may not command so much labour this year as it did in the last, and for a time there will be no demand for workmen. (157)

These are the two extremes, one arising from increased value without increased quantity; and the other from increased quantity without increased value.

It is obvious that the object which it is most desirable to attain is the union of the two. There is somewhere a happy medium, where, under the actual resources of a country, the increase of wealth and the demand for labour are a maximum; but this point cannot be ascertained. An increase of quantity with steady prices, or even slightly falling, is consistent with a considerable increase of the general value of produce, and may occasion a considerable demand for labour; but in the actual state of things, and in the way in which the precious metals are actually distributed, some increase of prices generally accompanies the most effective demand for produce and population. It is this increase both of quantity and price which most surely creates the greatest demand

---

which wages were expended would not rise, the labourer would command an additional quantity of commodities, and the population instead of coming to a stop would go on increasing; and another rise of prices, under the same circumstances, would occasion a further effective demand for labour.

This is on the supposition always that money in which price is estimated is at the time of an unvarying value; but if this be not a condition of the proposition, if Mr. Malthus means that the value of the whole produce increases in a money of varying value, I do not know how to deal with him, for[1] we may suppose the medium itself to become more valuable, or less valuable. In such a medium an increase of price may take place with the same,[2] with a larger, or with a smaller quantity of produce. Quantity and price may both rise, or both fall.[3] Each individual thing may rise

[1] 'then' is del. here.
[2] 'quantity of produce' is del. here.
[3] Here ends the re-written section; cp. above p. 242, n. 1.

for labour, excites the greatest quantity of industry, and generally occasions the greatest increase of population. |

SECTION IV   267

On the Effect of a Fall in the Value of Money upon the Demand for Labour, and the Condition of the Labourer

[The unfavourable effects of a fall in the value of money on the condition of the labourer, are not so certain as have been supposed.

The fall in the real wages of labour, from the end of the 15th to   268
the end of the 16th century, contemporary with the fall in the   269
value of money, is proved from authentic documents.

But the question is, which wages were the most extraordinary,   270
the high or the low.

---

or fall and may be followed by a rise or fall of wages. It is impossible to deny any proposition which may be advanced respecting price, unless it be previously determined whether the person advancing it regards money at the time as stationary, or variable in value, and if variable in what degree and in what direction.

(157) p. 265. *On the other hand*

By increasing the quantity of commodities, they may not be able to command so much labour as before. This I understand, because in proportion as commodities are low as compared with labour, labour is high as compared with commodities. Labour then is in great demand, it is paid for at a high value, and the labourer has an abundance of enjoyments:—there are plenty of commodities, and he has a large share of them: no such thing says Mr. Malthus "for a time there will be no demand for workmen." How are these propositions to be reconciled?

271   During the reign of Edward III. the real wages of labour seem to have been as low as in the reign of Elizabeth.

272   In the intermediate period, they varied considerably with the
273   varying prices of corn and labour; but from 1444 they were uniformly very high to the end of the century.

274   The very slight rise in the nominal price of grain, from the middle of the 14th to the end of the 15th century, in no respect made up for the diminished quantity of silver in the coin, so that the bullion price of corn fell considerably.

But the bullion price of labour rose considerably during the time that the bullion price of corn fell; and if Adam Smith had taken either labour or a mean between corn and labour as his measure, instead of corn, his conclusions respecting the value of silver would have been very different.

275   But to shew that the wages of labour were peculiar during the last sixty years of the 15th century, it is necessary further to compare them with periods after the depreciation of money had ceased.

276   The earnings of the labourer, during the last sixty years of the
277   17th century, after the depreciation of money had ceased, were
278   lower than in the reigns of Elizabeth and Edward III.

279   From 1720 to 1750 the price of corn fell and the wages of labour rose, but still they could command but little more than the half of what was earned in the 15th century.

280   From this period corn began to rise, and labour not to rise quite in proportion; but during the forty years from 1770 to 1810 and 11, the wages of labour in the command of corn seem to have been nearly stationary.]

281   SECTION V

*On the Conclusions to be drawn from the preceding Review
    of the Prices of Corn and Labour during the Five
    last Centuries*

[From this review it appears, that the great fall of labour in the 16th century must have been occasioned more by the unusual elevation it had before attained, than by the discovery of the American mines; and that the high wages of the 15th century could only have been occasioned by some temporary causes, which increased the relative supply of corn compared with labour.

Such high wages, whatever might have been their causes, 282 must have fallen during the next century, if the American mines had not been discovered.

There is reason to think that a rise in the price of corn, occa- 283 sioned merely by a fall in the value of money, would not injure the labouring classes for more than a few years.

Another inference which we may draw from this review is, that, 284 during the last 500 years, the corn wages of labour in England have been more frequently under than above a peck of wheat.

A third inference is, that the seasons have a very great influence 285 on the prices of corn, and the real wages of labour, not only for two or three years occasionally, but for fifteen or twenty years together.

The periods of the lowest wages have generally occurred when 286 a rise in the price of corn has taken place under circumstances not favourable to a rise in the price of labour; it was the rapid increase of population during the reigns of Henry VIII. and Elizabeth, which prevented wages from rising with the price of corn.

If the discovery of the American mines had found the people 287 earning less than a peck of wheat instead of half a bushel, the increase of resources, during the 16th century, would have raised the corn price of labour, notwithstanding the increasing money price of corn.

If the price of labour from 1793 to 1814 had not been kept 288 down by artificial means, it would have risen quite in proportion to the price of corn.]

In considering the corn wages of labour in the course of this review, it has not been possible to | make any distinction between 289 the effects of a fall in the price of corn and a rise in the price of labour. In merely comparing the two objects with each other, the result is precisely similar; but their effects in the encourage-ment of population are sometimes very dissimilar, as I have before intimated. There is no doubt that a great encouragement to an increase of population is consistent with a fall in the price of raw produce, because, notwithstanding this fall, the exchangeable value of the whole produce of the country may still be increasing compared with labour; but it may sometimes happen that a fall in the price of raw produce is accompanied by a diminished power and will to employ labour; and in this case the demand for labour and the encouragement to population will not be in proportion to the apparent corn wages of labour.

If a labourer commands a peck instead of $\frac{3}{4}$ of a peck of wheat a day in consequence of a rise of wages occasioned by a demand for labour, it is certain that all labourers may be employed who are willing and able to work, and probably also their wives and children; but if he is able to command this additional quantity of wheat on account of a fall in the price of corn which diminishes the capital of the farmer, the advantage may be more apparent than real, and though labour for some time may not nominally fall, yet as the demand for labour may be stationary, if not retrograde, its current price will not be a certain criterion of what **290** might be earned by the united labours of a large | family, or the increased exertions of the head of it in task-work. (158)

It is obvious, therefore, that the same current corn wages will, under different circumstances, have a different effect in the encouragement of population. (159)

[Wheat has been taken, as the usual grain consumed in this country, but wherever or whenever that is not the case, wheat

---

(158) p. 289. *But if he is able to command this additional*

Every thing in this argument must depend on the cause of the fall of the price of wheat. Is the cause temporary, or permanent? Is it occasioned by facility of production, or by temporary glut? Has money risen in value as compared with corn, and other things, or has the rise in the money price of corn been confined to corn only? Accordingly as the fall might be owing to one or other of these causes, would the effects be different.

I do not understand how the demand for labour may be stationary, if not retrograde, without any alteration in its price.

The current price of labour is the best criterion we can possess of the condition of the labourer and his family. What can prevent competition from acting on the price when the demand slackens or the supply increases?

wages are not the proper criterion of the encouragement given to population.

The quantity of the customary food which a labouring family 291 can actually earn throughout the year, is at once the measure of the encouragement to population, and of the condition of the labourer.

The prudential habits of the poor can alone give them the command over a fair proportion of the necessaries and conveniences of life, from the earliest stage of society to the latest.]

I have said nothing of the value of labour as measured by the criterion assumed by Mr. Ricardo, that is, by the labour which has been expended in procuring the earnings of the labourer, or the cost in labour of the labourer's wages; because it appears to me, that what I have called the real and nominal wages of labour include every thing which relates to the condition of the labourer, the encouragement to population, and the value of money, the three great points which chiefly demand our attention. According to Mr. Ricardo's view of the subject, nothing can be inferred on these points either from high or from low | wages. (160) Such 292

---

(159) p. 290. *It is obvious therefore*

This conclusion is not made out, at least, to my satisfaction.

(160) p. 291. *I have said nothing of the value of labour &c.*

Mr. Malthus thinks that what[1] he calls nominal and real wages of labour include every thing which relates to the condition of the labourer, and the encouragement to population. But according to my view of the subject, he says, nothing can be inferred on these points. Does my view prevent an examination into the real condition of the labourer? It is true that I say the labourers wages are high if he receives a high value for his work, that is to say if he receive the produce of a great deal of labour. To know his real condition we must still enquire what this produce is in quantity,

[1] Replaces 'whatever'.

high or low wages serve only to determine the rate of profits, and their influence in this respect will be fully considered in the next chapter. |

---

the very enquiry made by Mr. Malthus. Because I give different names to Mr. Malthus nominal, and real price, he thinks there is a real difference between us—in this case I think there is none. I should first enquire what the labourers money wages were, and should estimate his[1] condition by the abundance of necessaries which those money wages would procure him.

[1] 'real' is del. here.

CHAPTER V

OF THE PROFITS OF CAPITAL

SECTION I

Of Profits as affected by the increasing Difficulty of procuring the Means of Subsistence

It has been usual, in speaking of that portion of the national revenue which goes to the capitalist in return for the employment of his capital, to call it by the name of the profits of stock. But stock is not so appropriate an expression in this case, as capital. Stock is a general term, and may be defined to be all the material possessions of a country, or all its actual wealth, whatever may be its destination; while capital is that particular portion of these possessions, or of this accumulated wealth, which is destined to be employed with a view to profit. They are often, however, used indiscriminately; and perhaps no great error may arise from it; but it may be useful to recollect that all stock is not properly speaking capital, though all capital is stock.

The profits of capital consist of the difference between the value of the advances necessary to produce a commodity, and the value of the commodity when produced; and these advances are generally | composed of accumulations which have previously cost in their production a certain quantity of wages, profit and rent, exclusive of the rent which, in the case of landed products, is paid directly.

The *rate* of profits is the proportion which the difference between the value of the advances and the value of the commodity produced bears to the value of the advances, and it varies with the variations of the value of the advances compared with the value of the product. When the value of the advances is great compared with the value of the product, the remainder being small, the rate of profits will be low. When the value of the advances is inconsiderable the remainder being great, the rate of profits will be high.

The varying rate of profits, therefore, obviously depends upon the causes which alter the proportion between the value of the advances and the value of the produce; and this proportion may be altered either by circumstances which affect the value of the advances, or the value of the product.

Of the advances necessary to production, the means of supporting labour are generally the greatest and most important. These means, therefore, will have the greatest influence on the value of the advances.

---

(161) p. 294. *The difficulty or facility of production*

 p. 295. *The varying relation*

These two causes may both be classed under the name of high or low wages. Profits in fact depend on high or low wages, and on nothing else.

The greater the proportion of the value of the whole produce necessary to support the labourer, the higher will be wages.

The greater the quantity of capital is, compared with the labour which it is to employ, the higher will wages be.

In all this Mr. Malthus and I appear to concur. Whenever the difficulty of production on the land is such that a greater proportion of the value of the whole produce is employed in supporting labour, I call wages high, for I measure value by these proportions; and from Mr. Malthus language here, everybody would think he agreed with me, yet in page 291 he says "I have said nothing of the criterion assumed by Mr. Ricardo, that is, by the labour which has been expended in procuring the earnings of the labourer, or the cost in labour of the labourers wages."[1] In what does this differ from Mr. Malthus' criterion? One hundred quarters of corn are produced on the last land taken into cultivation, and with

---

[1] 'This is only saying' is del. here.

The two main causes which influence the means of supporting labour, are

1st. The difficulty or facility of production on the land, by which a greater or less proportion of the value of the whole produce is capable of supporting the labourers employed. |

And 2dly, The varying relation of the quantity of capital to the quantity of labour employed by it, by which more or less of the necessaries of life may go to each individual labourer. (161)

Each of these causes is alone sufficient to occasion all the

295

---

so much increased difficulty,[2] that the labourers portion of these 100 quarters is 65 quarters. On the land which before that was cultivated, as the last, 110 quarters were produced with the same quantity of labour and the labourers then[3] obtained 70 quarters for their share. The portion now paid to the labourers is less, but the proportion of the whole produce obtained by their labour is greater, for they before had 63 p.c. now they have 65, and as the 100 qrs. will now rise to the same value that 110 qrs. were of before, by having a larger proportion of the quantity produced, they will also have a larger value, and that value will be the produce of a greater quantity of labour than the smaller value was of before. I contend then that a greater proportion and a greater value mean the same thing. I allow Mr. Malthus to chuse any medium he pleases for measuring value except raw produce itself whose value is to be measured, and he will find my proposition true. Of course the measure itself must not have varied in value between the two periods of comparison.

---

[2] The remainder of the sentence replaces 'that tho' the labourers portion of these 100 quarters before produced was 70 quarters and is now reduced to 65 quarters yet the latter quantity may be a larger proportion of the whole value. Corn may have risen in value in any measure Mr. Malthus will name, and therefore if 65 qrs. be a greater proporti...'

[3] 'with the same quantity of labour' and 'then' are ins.

variations of which profits are susceptible. If one of them only acted, its operation would be simple. It is the combination of the two, and of others in addition to them, sometimes acting in conjunction and sometimes in opposition, which occasions in the progress of society those varied phenomena which it is not always easy to explain.

If the first cause operated singly, and the wages of the individual labourer were always the same, then supposing that the skill in agriculture were to remain unchanged, and that there were no means of obtaining corn from foreign countries, the rate of profits must regularly and without any interruption fall, as the society advanced, and as it became necessary to resort to inferior machines which required more labour to put in action.

It would signify little, in this case, whether the last land taken into cultivation for food had yielded a rent in its uncultivated state. It is certain that the landlord would not allow it to be cultivated, unless he could, at the least, obtain the same rent for it as before. This must be considered as an absolute condition on the worst lands taken into cultivation in an improved country. After this payment was made, the remainder of | the produce would be divided chiefly* between the capitalist and the labourers, and it is evident that if the number of labourers necessary to obtain a given produce were continually increasing, and the wages of each labourer remained the same, the portion destined to the payment of labour would be continually encroaching upon the portion destined to the payment of profits; and the rate of profits would of course continue regularly diminishing till, from the want of power or will to save, the progress of accumulation had ceased.

In this case, and supposing an equal demand for all the parts of the same produce,† it is obvious that the profits of capital in

* I say *chiefly*, because, in fact, some rent, though it may be trifling, is almost always paid in the materials of the farmer's capital.

† It is necessary to qualify the position in this way, because, with regard to the main products of agriculture, it might easily happen that all the parts were not of the same value. If a farmer cultivated his lands by means of domestics living in his house whom he found in food and clothing, his advances might always be nearly the same in quantity and of the same high value in use; but in the case of a glut from the shutting up of an accustomed market, or a season of unusual abundance, a part of the crop might be of no value either in use or exchange, and his profits could by no means be determined, by the excess of the *quantity* produced, above the advances necessary to produce it.

agriculture would be in proportion to the fertility of the last land taken into cultivation, or to the amount of the produce obtained by a given quantity of labour. And as profits in the same country tend to an equality, the general rate of profits would follow the same course. (162) |

But a moment's consideration will shew us, that the supposi-   297 tion here made of a constant uniformity in the real wages of labour is not only contrary to the actual state of things, but involves a contradiction. (163)

The progress of population is almost exclusively regulated by the quantity of the necessaries of life actually awarded to the labourer; and if from the first he had no more than sufficient to keep up the actual population, the labouring classes could not increase, nor would there be any occasion for the progressive cultivation of poorer land. On the other hand, if the real wages of labour were such as to admit of and encourage an increase of population, and yet were always to remain the same, it would involve the contradiction of a continued increase of population after the accumulation of capital, and the means of supporting such an increase had entirely ceased.

We cannot then make the supposition of a *natural* and *constant* price of labour, at least if we mean by such a price, an unvarying quantity of the necessaries of life. And if we cannot fix the real price of labour, it must evidently vary with the progress of capital and revenue, and the demand for labour compared with the supply.

We may however, if we please, suppose a uniform progress of capital and population, by which is not meant in the present case

---

(162) p. 296. *In this case &c.*

I quite agree with Mr. Malthus in this explanation of profits.

(163) p. 297. *But a moment's consideration &c.*

And yet the value of labour is Mr. Malthus standard measure of real value in exchange. See the following paragraphs.

the same *rate* of progress permanently, which is impossible; but a uniform progress towards the greatest practicable amount, without temporary accelerations or retardations. | And before we proceed to the actual state of things, it may be curious to consider in what manner profits would be affected under these circumstances.

At the commencement of the cultivation of a fertile country by civilized colonists, and whole rich land was in great plenty, a small portion only of the value of the produce would be paid in the form of rent. Nearly the whole would be divided between profits and wages; and the proportion which each would take, as far as it was influenced by the share of each individual labourer, must be determined by the demand and supply of capital compared with the demand and supply of labour.

As the society continued to proceed, if the territory were limited, or the soil of different qualities, it is quite obvious that the productive powers of labour as applied to the cultivation of land must gradually diminish; and as a given quantity of capital and of labour would yield a smaller and smaller return, there would evidently be a less and less produce to be divided between labour and profits.

If, as the powers of labour diminished, the physical wants of the labourer were also to diminish in the same proportion, then the same share of the whole produce might be left to the capitalist, and the *rate* of profits would not necessarily fall. But the physical wants of the labourer remain always the same; and though in the progress of society, from the increasing scarcity of provisions compared with labour, these wants are in general less fully supplied, and the real wages of labour | gradually fall; yet it is clear that there is a limit, and probably at no great distance, which cannot be passed. The command of a certain quantity of food is absolutely necessary to the labourer in order to support himself, and such a family as will maintain merely a stationary population. Consequently, if poorer lands which required more labour were successively taken into cultivation, it would not be possible for the corn wages of each individual labourer to be diminished in proportion to the diminished produce; a greater proportion of the whole would necessarily go to labour; and the rate of profits would continue regularly falling till the accumulation of capital had ceased.

Such would be the necessary course of profits and wages in the progressive accumulation of capital, as applied to the progressive cultivation of new and less fertile land, or the further improvement of what had before been cultivated; and on the supposition here made, the rates both of profits and of real wages would be highest at first, and would regularly and gradually diminish together, till they both came to a stand at the same period, and the demand for an increase of produce ceased to be effective.

In the mean time, it will be asked, what becomes of the profits of capital employed in manufactures and commerce, a species of industry not like that employed upon the land, where the productive powers of labour necessarily diminish; but where these powers not only do not necessarily diminish, but very often greatly increase? |

In the cultivation of land, the immediate and main cause of the 300 necessary diminution of profits appeared to be the increased quantity of labour necessary to obtain the same produce. In manufactures and commerce, it is the fall in the exchangeable value of the products of industry in these departments, compared with corn and labour.

The cost of producing corn and labour continually increases from inevitable physical causes, while the cost of producing manufactures and articles of commerce sometimes diminishes, sometimes remains stationary, and at all events increases much slower than the cost of producing corn and labour. Upon every principle therefore of demand and supply, the exchangeable value of these latter objects must fall, compared with the value of labour. But if the exchangeable value of labour continues to rise, while the exchangeable value of manufactures either falls, remains the same, or rises in a much less degree, profits must continue to fall; and thus it appears that in the progress of improvement, as poorer and poorer land is taken into cultivation, the rate of profits must be limited by the powers of the soil last cultivated. If the last land taken into cultivation can only be made to yield a certain excess of value above the value of the labour necessary to produce it, it is obvious that, upon the principles of competition, profits, generally, cannot possibly be higher than this excess will allow. In the ascending scale, this is a barrier which cannot be passed. But limitation is essentially different from regulation. In the de-|scending scale, profits may be lower in any degree. There is 301 here no controlling necessity which determines the rate of profits; and below the highest limit which the actual state of the land will allow, ample scope is left for the operation of other causes. (164)

SECTION II

Of Profits as affected by the Proportion which Capital bears to Labour

The second main cause which, by increasing the amount of advances, influences profits, is the proportion which capital bears to labour.*

This is obviously a cause which alone is capable of producing the very greatest effects; and on the supposition of adequate variations taking place between the supplies of capital and the supplies of labour, all the same effects might be produced on profits as by the operation of the first cause, and in a much shorter time.

When capital is really abundant compared with labour, nothing 302 can prevent low profits; and the | greatest facility of production is incapable of producing high profits, unless capital is scarce compared with labour.

* I have stated in a former chapter, that the demand for labour does not depend upon capital alone, but upon capital and revenue together, or the value of the whole produce; but to illustrate the present *supposition*, it is only necessary to consider capital and labour. We may allow that no difficulty will occur with respect to demand.

---

(164) p. 300. *The cost of producing corn &c. &c.*

I agree throughout this section with Mr. Malthus in principle, we only differ in our ideas of what constitutes a real[1] measure of value.

(165) p. 302. *If, in an early stage of improvement*

I am glad to observe that Mr. Malthus estimates profits by proportions, I only require him to estimate wages by the same rule. If he did he would not say that high profits and

[1] Last six words are ins.

But in order to see more clearly the powerful effects of the second cause on profits, let us consider it for a moment as operating alone; and suppose, that while the capital of a country continued increasing, its population were checked and kept short of the demand for it, by some miraculous influence. Under these circumstances, every sort of gradation might take place in the proportion which capital would bear to labour, and we should see in consequence every sort of gradation take place in the rate of profits.

If, in an early period of improvement, capital were scarce compared with labour, the wages of labour being on this account low, while the productive powers of labour, from the fertility of the land, were great, the proportion left for profits would necessarily be very considerable, and the rate of profits would be very high.

In general, however, though capital may be said to be scarce in the early periods of cultivation, yet that particular portion of capital, which resolves itself into food, is often plentiful compared with the population, and high profits and high real wages are found together. (165) In the most natural state of things this is generally the case, though it is not so when capital is prematurely checked by extravagance, or other causes. But whether we set out from low or high corn wages, the diminution in the rates of profits, from the gradual in-|crease of capital compared with labour, will remain undisturbed. 303

As capital at any time increases faster than labour, the profits of capital will fall, and if a progressive increase of capital were to

---

high real wages are found together in the early periods of cultivation. Our only difference here is in the names we give to the same thing, we both agree that the labourer will have high corn wages, Mr. Malthus therefore calls his wages high real wages. As it is acknowledged that corn will be at a low value, when it is so easily produced, I say his high corn wages will be of a low value, and therefore his real wages will be low; and the proof is, that he has but a small proportion of the produce.

take place, while the population, by some hidden cause, were prevented from keeping pace with it, notwithstanding the fertility of the soil and the plenty of food, then profits would be gradually reduced, until, by successive reductions, the power and will to accumulate had ceased to operate. (166)

Profits in this case would experience exactly the same kind of progressive diminution as they would by the progressive accumulation of capital in the present state of things; but rent and wages would be very differently affected. From what has before been stated on the subject of rent, the amount of it in such a country could not be great. According to the supposition, the progress of the population is retarded, and the number of labourers is limited, while land of considerable fertility remains uncultivated. The demand for fertile land therefore, compared with the supply, would be comparatively inconsiderable; and in reference to the whole of the national produce, the portion which would consist of rent would depend mainly upon the gradations of more fertile land that had been cultivated before the population had come to a stop, and upon the value of the produce to be derived from the land that was not cultivated.

With regard to wages they would continue progressively to 304 rise, and would give the labourer a | greater command not only of manufactures and of the products of foreign commerce (as is generally the case in the present state of things) but of corn and all other necessaries, so as to place him in a condition continually and in all respects improving, as long as capital continued to increase.

In short, of the three great portions into which the mass of produce is divided, rent, profits, and wages, the two first would be low, because both the supply of land and the supply of capital would be abundant compared with the demand; while the wages

---

(166) p. 303. *As Capital at any time*

The labourers would have a monopoly, and the price of their labour would depend solely on the demand.

(167) p. 305. *The money price of corn and money wages would perhaps be as high as when their cost in labour had been double or treble*

Is it possible to believe that money would so fall in value

of labour would be very high, because the supply of labourers would be comparatively scanty; and thus the value of each would be regulated by the great principle of demand and supply.

If, instead of supposing the population to be checked by some peculiar influence, we make the more natural supposition of a limited territory, with all the land of nearly equal quality, and of such great fertility as to admit of very little capital being laid out upon it, the effects upon the profits of capital would be just the same as in the last instance, though they would be very different on rents and wages. After all the land had been cultivated, and no more capital could be employed on it, there cannot be a doubt that rents would be extremely high and profits and wages very low. The competition of increasing capital in manufactures and commerce would reduce the rate of profits, while the principle of population would continue to augment the number of the | labouring classes, till their corn wages were so low as to check their further increase. It is probable that, owing to the facility of production on the land and the great proportion of persons employed in manufactures and commerce, the exports would be great and the value of money very low. The money price of corn and money wages would perhaps be as high as when their cost in labour had been double or treble; (167) rents would rise to an extraordinary pitch without any assistance from poor lands, and the gradations of soil; and profits might fall to the point only just sufficient to keep up the actual capital without any additional labour being necessary to procure the food of the labourer.

The effects which would obviously result from the two suppositions just made, clearly shew that the increasing quantity of labour required for the successive cultivation of poorer land is not theoretically necessary to a fall of profits from the highest rate to the lowest. (168)

---

from such a cause: If it did, of what importance would it be?[1]

(168) p. 305. *The effects which would obviously*

In this case the landlords would have a strict monopoly, and the price of corn would rise to the limit of[2] the ability of the consumers to pay for it.

[1] The whole Note replaces: 'I do not understand what the author means by these words.'

[2] 'to the limit of' replaces 'in proportion as'.

The former of these two suppositions further shews the extraordinary power possessed by the labouring classes of society, if they chose to exercise it. The comparative check to population, which was considered as occasioned by some miraculous influence, might in reality be effected by the prudence of the poor; and it would unquestionably be followed by the result described. It may naturally appear hard to the labouring classes that, of the vast mass of productions obtained from the land, the capital, and 306 the labour of the | country, so small a portion should individually fall to their share. But the division is at present determined, and must always in future be determined, by the inevitable laws of supply and demand. If the market were comparatively understocked with labour, the landlords and capitalists would be obliged to give a larger share of the produce to each workman. But with an abundant supply of labour, such a share, for a permanence, is an absolute impossibility. The rich have neither the power, nor can it be expected that they should all have the will, to keep the market understocked with labour. Yet every effort to ameliorate the lot of the poor generally, that has not this tendency, is perfectly futile and childish. It is quite obvious therefore, that the knowledge and prudence of the poor themselves, are absolutely the *only* means by which any general improvement in their condition can be effected. They are really the arbiters of their own destiny; and what others can do for them, is like the dust of the balance compared with what they can do for themselves. These truths are so important to the happiness of the great mass of society, that every opportunity should be taken of repeating them. (169)

But, independently of any particular efforts of prudence on the part of the poor, it is certain that the supplies of labour and the supplies of capital do not always keep pace with each other. They are often separated at some distance, and for a considerable 307 period; and sometimes population in-|creases faster than capital, and at other times capital increases faster than population.

---

(169) p. 305. *It may naturally appear hard &c.*

The whole of this is excellent and cannot be too often and too clearly inculcated on the minds of the labouring classes.

It is obvious, for instance, that from the very nature of population, and the time required to bring full-grown labourers into the market, a sudden increase of capital cannot effect a proportionate supply of labour in less than sixteen or eighteen years; and, on the other hand, when capital is stationary from the want of will to accumulate, it is well known that population in general continues to increase faster than capital, till the wages of labour are reduced to that standard which, with the actual habits of the country, are no more than sufficient to maintain a stationary population.

These periods, in which capital and population do not keep pace with each other, are evidently of sufficient extent to produce the most important results on the rate of profits, and to affect in the most essential manner the progress of national wealth.

The value of the government long annuities has a natural and inevitable tendency to diminish as they approach nearer and nearer to the end of the term for which they were granted. This is a proposition which I conceive no person is inclined to doubt; but under the fullest acknowledgment of its truth, it would be a most erroneous calculation to estimate the value of this kind of stock solely by the number of years which it would have to run. It is well known that out of the comparatively short term of ninety years, so large a propor-|tion as twenty has sometimes 308 elapsed, not only without any diminution, but with an actual increase of value. (170)

In the same manner, the natural and necessary tendency of profits to fall in the progress of society, owing to the increasing difficulty of procuring food, is a proposition which few will be disposed to controvert; but to attempt to estimate the rate of profits in any country by a reference to this cause alone, for ten, twenty, or even fifty years together, that is for periods of sufficient length to produce the most important effects on national prosperity, would inevitably lead to the greatest practical errors.

Yet notwithstanding the utter inadequacy of this single cause

---

(170) p. 307. *The value of the Government*

Does Mr. Malthus conceive that any one doubts the truth of the variableness of profits?

to account for existing phenomena, Mr. Ricardo, in his very ingenious chapter on profits, has dwelt on no other. (171)

If the premises were all such as he has supposed them to be, that is, if no other cause operated on profits than the increasing difficulty of procuring the food of the labourer, and no other cause affected the exchangeable and money value of commodities than the quantity of labour which they had cost in production, the conclusions which he has drawn would be just, and the rate of

---

(171) p. 308. *Yet notwithstanding the utter inadequacy*

Mr. Malthus here brings a charge against me which he would find it very difficult to prove. He has himself Page 294 Section 1 of this Chap. stated two causes for the fall of profits. I fully concur[1] with him in thinking that profits never vary but from one or other of those causes. I however endeavored to shew that they might be classed under one head, as in both cases the labourer received either a larger, or a smaller proportion of the whole produce. If a larger I called his wages higher, if a smaller lower.

Profits then were high when wages were low, and low when wages were high. Now Mr. Malthus will not deny that both the causes he mentions for high or low profits resolve themselves into the allottment of a larger or a smaller proportion of the produce to the workman.—When the workman has a large proportion of the produce he will not call it high wages because he measures value by quantity and not by proportions—but here he differs only about a name; we mean, and he knows we mean, the same thing. Now I have invariably insisted that high or low profits depended on low and high wages, how then can it be justly said of me that the only cause which I have recognized of high or low profits is the facility or difficulty of providing food for the labourer. I contend that I have also recognized the other cause, the

[1] 'in those two causes' is del. here.

profits would certainly be regulated in the way which he has described. But, since in the actual state of things the premises are most essentially different from those which he has supposed; since another most powerful cause operates upon profits, as I have endeavoured to shew in the present section; and since | the exchangeable value of commodities is not determined by the labour they have cost, as I endeavoured to shew in a former chapter, the conclusion drawn by Mr. Ricardo must necessarily

309

---

relative amount of population to capital, which is another of the great regulators of wages.

In my chapter on Profits, Page [110–111] 2nd ed. I say "If then wages continued the same, the profits of manufacturers would remain the same; but if, as is absolutely certain, wages would rise with the rise of corn, then their profits would necessarily fall." In page [115], I say "Thus in every case, agricultural, as well as manufacturing profits are lowered by a rise of raw produce, *if it be accompanied by a rise of wages.*["]

I have read the 1 and 2d sections of Chap. 5 of Mr. Malthus work with great pleasure they express with great clearness and ability the doctrines which appear to me to be true respecting profits—I had, very imperfectly indeed, attempted to explain the same principles myself, in my work, and therefore I received great satisfaction on seeing so able an exposition of them by Mr. Malthus.

I was a little disappointed however[2] at finding, towards the end of the section, that Mr. Malthus thought that the doctrine he had been laying down was essentially different from mine. In page 308 he says that there are two causes which operate on profits, and I have exclusively dwelt on one, which is inadequate to the effects actually produced— this accusation I hope I have already satisfactorily answered. In page 309 he says, ["] It is impossible then to agree in the

[2] 'however' replaces 'then'.

contradict experience; not slightly, and for short periods, as the
market prices of some articles occasionally differ from the natural
or necessary price, properly explained; but obviously and broadly,
and for periods of such extent, that to overlook them, would not
be merely like overlooking the resistance of the air in a falling
body, but like overlooking the change of direction given to a ball
by a second impulse acting at a different angle from the first.

It is impossible then to agree in the conclusion at which

---

conclusion at which Mr. Ricardo arrives in his chapter on
profits, that in all countries, and at all times, profits depend
upon the quantity of labour required to provide necessaries
for the labourer on that land, or with that capital which
yields no rent." Now this is no other than Mr. Malthus
doctrine expressed in other words. I do not say that the
labourers earnings will always be the same, but whatever
they may be, profits will depend on the[1] proportion which
their value bears, to the whole value produced on the last
land. A certain quantity of labour is necessary to obtain the
whole produce, and profits depend on the proportion of the
whole quantity which may be[2] necessary to provide the
labourers earnings, the rest only is profits.

"It is, says Mr. Malthus, merely a truism to say that if
the value of commodities be divided between labour and
profits, the greater is the share taken by one, the less will be
left for the other; or in other words, that profits fall as labour
rises, or rise as labour fall."[3]

If it is a truism it is not an error, why then notice it as
such? It is a truism however which Mr. Malthus to ones
great astonishment does not uniformly admit. Sometimes
he is at variance with the principle, as I shall hereafter shew:
but generally his objection is to the language. He for ex-

[1] 'quantity' is del. here.   [3] Malthus's p. 310; below, p. 269.
[2] 'which may be' is ins.

Mr. Ricardo arrives in his chapter on profits, "that in all countries, and at all times, profits depend upon the quantity of labour required to provide necessaries for the labourer on that land, or with that capital which yields no rent."*

If by the necessaries of the labourer be meant, such wages as will just keep up the population, or what Mr. Ricardo calls the natural wages of labour, it is the same as saying that land of equal

* Princ. of Polit. Econ. c. vi. p. [126]. 2d edit.

---

ample says that profits and wages may, and frequently do, rise at the same time. This I say never can be true, Why? because value is measured by proportions, and a high value means a large⁴ proportion of the whole produce. As one proportion of a whole increases the other must diminish. Mr. Malthus says value is not measured by proportions it is measured by quantity—Increase the quantity then, and though you alter the proportions, both parties may get more. "We can know little of the laws which determine profits, unless, in addition to the causes which increase the price of necessaries we explain the causes which award a larger or a smaller share of these necessaries to each labourer."⁵ True, this is the important principle which I wish to establish, and I do not plead guilty to the charge that I attribute to one cause only, namely the diminished power of production, the greater or smaller share of the⁶ necessaries awarded to the labourer.

Mr. M's charge really comes to this. ["]You have acknowledged that profits depend upon wages—you have said too that wages are affected by two causes, by the difficulty of furnishing a continued increasing supply of food for an increasing population; and by the varying proportions of capital to population which must necessarily have an effect

⁴ Replaces 'high'.   ⁶ 'whole' is del. here.
⁵ Malthus's p. 310.

fertility will always yield the same profits—a proposition which must necessarily be untrue.

If, for instance, in one country, with the last land taken into cultivation of a given fertility, capital were stationary, not from want of demand, | but from great expenditure and the want of saving habits, it is certain that labour, after a time, would be paid very low, and profits would be very high.

If, in another country with similar land in cultivation, such a spirit of saving should prevail as to occasion the accumulation of capital to be more rapid than the progress of population, it is as certain that profits would be very low.

---

on wages,—but you have attached too much weight to the first cause, and too little to the last." My principles are right then, but I have not weighed the force of each with sufficient nicety.*

[*] Note. Looking to my Chap. on Wages I see

page [94]. The market price of labour is the price which is really paid for it, from the natural operation of the proportion of the supply to the demand; labour is dear when it is scarce, and cheap when it is plentiful.

page [94–95]. "Notwithstanding the tendency of wages to conform to their natural rate, their market rate may, in an improving society, for an indefinite period, be constantly above it."

page [97]. ["]Independently of the variations in the value of money, which necessarily affect wages, but which we have here supposed to have no operation, as we have considered money to be uniformly of the same value, it appears then that wages are subject to a rise or fall from *two* causes:

1st. The supply and demand of labourers.

2dly. The price of the commodities on which the wages of labour are expended."

Now be it observed that these two causes are the very same as those mentioned by Mr. Malthus as operating on profits in Page 294 of his work.

See also pages [215] and [216] Chap. 16.

So understood therefore, the proposition cannot for a moment be maintained.

If, on the other hand, by necessaries be meant the actual earnings of the labourer, whatever they may be, the proposition is essentially incomplete. Even allowing that the exchangeable value of commodities is regulated by the quantity of labour that has been employed in their production, (which it has been shewn is not so,) little is done towards determining the rate of profits. It is merely a truism to say that if the value of commodities be divided between labour and profits, the greater is the share taken by one, the less will be left for the other; or in other words, that profits fall as labour rises, or rise as labour falls. We can know little of the laws which determine profits, unless, in addition to the causes which increase the price of necessaries, we explain the causes which award a larger or a smaller share of these necessaries to each labourer. And here it is obvious that we must have recourse to the great principles of demand and supply, or to that very principle of competition brought for-|ward by Adam Smith, 311 which Mr. Ricardo expressly rejects, or at least considers as of so temporary a nature as not to require attention in a general theory of profits.*

And yet in fact there is no other cause of permanently high profits than a deficiency in the supply of capital; and under such a deficiency, occasioned by extravagant expenditure, the profits of a particular country might for hundreds of years together continue very high, compared with others, owing solely to the different proportions of capital to labour.

In Poland, and some other parts of Europe, profits are said to be higher than in America; yet it is probable that the last land taken into cultivation in America is richer than the last land taken into cultivation in Poland. But in America the labourer earns perhaps the value of sixteen or eighteen quarters of wheat in the year; in Poland only the value of eight or nine quarters of rye. This difference in the division of the same or nearly the same produce, must make an extraordinary difference in the rate of profits; yet the causes which determine this division can hardly be said to form any part of Mr. Ricardo's theory of profits, although, far from being of so temporary a nature that they may be safely overlooked, they might contribute to operate most powerfully

---

* Princ. of Polit. Econ. chap. vi. p. [125–6]. and ch. xxi. 2d edit.

for almost any length of time. Such is the extent of America, that the price of its labour may not essentially fall for hundreds of 312 years; and | the effects of a scanty but stationary capital on an overflowing but stationary population might last for ever.

In dwelling thus upon the powerful effects which must inevitably be produced by the proportion which capital bears to labour, and upon the necessity of giving adequate weight to the principle of demand and supply or competition in every explanation of the circumstances which determine profits, it is not meant to underrate the importance of that cause which has been almost exclusively considered by Mr. Ricardo. It is indeed of such a nature as finally to overwhelm every other. To recur to the illustration already used—as the Long Annuities approach nearer and nearer to the term at which they expire, their value must necessarily so diminish, on this account alone, that no demand arising from plenty of money could possibly keep up their value. In the same manner, when cultivation is pushed to its extreme practical limits, that is, when the labour of a man upon the last land taken into cultivation will scarcely do more than support such a family as is necessary to maintain a stationary population, it is evident that no other cause or causes can prevent profits from sinking to the lowest rate required to maintain the actual capital.

But though the principle here considered is finally of the very greatest power, yet its progress is extremely slow and gradual; and while it is proceeding with scarcely perceptible steps to its final destination, the second cause, particularly when combined 313 with others which will be noticed | in the next section, is producing effects which entirely overcome it, and often for twenty or thirty, or even 100 years together, make the rate of profits take a course absolutely different from what it ought to be according to the first cause.

SECTION III

Of Profits as affected by the Causes practically in operation

We come now to the consideration of the causes which influence profits in the actual state of things. And here it is evident that we shall have in operation not only both the causes already stated, but others which will variously modify them.

In the progressive cultivation of poorer land for instance, as capital and population increase, profits, according to the first cause, will regularly fall; but if at the same time improvements in agriculture are taking place, they may certainly be such as, for a considerable period, not only to prevent profits from falling, but to allow of a considerable rise. To what extent, and for what length of time, this circumstance might interrupt the progress of profits arising from the first cause, it is not easy to say; but, as it is certain that in an extensive territory, consisting of soils not very different in their natural powers of production, the fall of profits arising | from this cause would be extremely slow, it is   314
probable that for a considerable extent of time agricultural improvements, including of course the improved implements and machinery used in cultivation, as well as an improved system of cropping and managing the land, might more than balance it.

A second circumstance which would contribute to the same effect is, an increase of personal exertion among the labouring classes. This exertion is extremely different in different countries, and at different times in the same country. A day's labour of a Hindoo, or a South-American Indian, will not admit of a comparison with that of an Englishman; and it has even been said, that though the money price of day-labour in Ireland is little more than the half of what it is in England, yet that Irish labour is not really cheaper than English, although it is well known that Irish labourers when in this country, with good examples and adequate wages to stimulate them, will work as hard as their English companions.

This latter circumstance alone clearly shews how different may be the personal exertions of the labouring classes in the same country at different times; and how different therefore may be the products of a given number of days labour, as the society proceeds from the indolence of the savage to the activity of the civilized state. This activity indeed, within certain limits, appears almost always to come forward when it is most called for, that is, when there is much work to be done without | a full supply of persons to do it. The personal exertions of the South American Indian, the Hindoo, the Polish boor, and the Irish agricultural labourer, may be very different indeed 500 years hence. (172)

The two preceding circumstances tend to diminish the expenses of production, or to reduce the relative amount of the advances necessary to obtain a certain value of produce. But it was stated at the beginning of this chapter, that profits depend upon the prices of products compared with the expenses of production, and must vary therefore with any causes which affect prices without proportionally affecting costs, as well as with any causes which affect costs without proportionally affecting prices. (173)

A considerable effect on profits may therefore be occasioned by a third circumstance which not unfrequently occurs, namely,

---

(172) p. 314. *A second circumstance &c.*

All these circumstances come under the general cause already noticed, namely the "proportion of the produce that is given to the labourer."[1] The circumstances here enumerated undoubtedly affect wages, and therefore affect profits.

A day's labour of a Hindoo or a South American it is admitted cannot be compared with that of an Englishman—was it fair then in Mr. Malthus to suppose that when I was talking of the quantity of labour regulating price and profits I considered it as of no importance whether it was the labour for a given time of a Hindoo, an Irishman, or an Englishman. I apply my doctrine to the same country only, and fix on a standard which is common in that country. I should not estimate profits in England, by the labour of a Hindoo; nor

[1] Replaces: 'All these circumstances come under the general one of "what proportion of the produce shall be given to the labourer". Profits depend on wages'.

the unequal rise of some parts of capital, when the price of corn
is raised by an increased demand. I was obliged to allude to this
cause, and indeed to the two preceding ones, in the chapter on
rents. I will only therefore add here, that when the prices of corn
and labour rise and terminate in an altered value of money, (174)
the prices of many home commodities will be very considerably
modified for some time, by the unequal pressure of taxation, and
by the different quantities of fixed capital employed in their
production; and the prices of foreign commodities and of the
commodities worked up at home from foreign | materials, will   316
permanently remain comparatively low. The rise of corn and
labour at home will not proportionally raise the price of such
products; and as far as these products form any portion of the
farmer's capital this capital will be rendered more productive;
but leather, iron, timber, soap, candles, cottons, woollens, &c. &c.
all enter more or less into the capitals of the farmer, or the wages
of the labourer, and are all influenced in their prices more or less
by importation. While the value of the farmer's produce rises,

---

in India by the labour of an Englishman,—unless I had the
means of reducing them to one common standard.

(173) p. 315. *But it was stated at the beginning of*

Mr. Malthus use of the word cost is throughout this work
very ambiguous. In the cost of a commodity does he include
or exclude the profits of stock. Here he evidently excludes it.

(174) p. 315. *I will therefore only add here*

I do not understand what is meant by the prices of corn
and labour rising and terminating in an altered value of
money. The price of corn may rise on account of increased
difficulty of producing it—this will raise corn relatively to
other things, but money will continue unaltered in value.
The price of corn may rise because money falls in value,
every thing else will then rise, and no effect will be produced
on real[2] wages and profits, the rise will be altogether nominal.

[2] 'real' is ins.

these articles will not rise in proportion, and consequently a given value of capital will yield a greater value of produce. (175)

All these three circumstances, it is obvious, have a very strong tendency to counteract the effects arising from the necessity of taking poorer land into cultivation; and it will be observed that, as they are of a nature to increase in efficiency with the natural progress of population and improvement, it is not easy to say how long and to what extent they may balance or overcome them.

The reader will be aware that the reason why, in treating of profits, I dwell so much on agricultural profits is, that the whole stress of the question rests upon this point. The argument against the usual view which has been taken of profits, as depending principally upon the competition of capital, is founded upon the physical necessity of a fall of profits in agriculture, arising from 317 the in-|creasing quantity of labour required to procure the same food; and it is certain that if the profits on land permanently fall from this or any other cause, profits in manufactures and commerce must fall too, as it is an acknowledged truth that in an improved and civilized country the profits of stock, with few and temporary exceptions which may be easily accounted for, must be nearly on a level in all the different branches of industry to which capital is applied.

Now I am fully disposed to allow the truth of this argument, as applied to agricultural profits, and also its natural consequences on all profits. This truth is indeed necessarily involved both in the *Principle of Population* and in the theory of rent which I published separately in 1815. But I wish to shew, theoretically as well as practically, that powerful and certain as this cause is, in its final operation, so much so as to overwhelm every other; yet in the actual state of the world, its natural progress is not only

---

(175) p. 316. *The rise of corn and labour at home*

If it be a real rise of corn and labour, and not a fall in the value of money, it will not raise the price of foreign products. But how will it affect the price of home products? it will raise some, and lower others, according as more or less fixed capital may be employed on their production. See Page ¹

¹ Blank in MS. See Malthus's p. 91 ff; above, p. 60 ff.

extremely slow, but is so frequently counteracted and overcome by other causes as to leave very great play to the principle of the competition of capital; so that at any one period of some length in the last or following hundred years, it might most safely be asserted that profits had depended or would depend very much more upon the causes which had occasioned a comparatively scanty or abundant supply of capital than upon the natural fertility of the land last taken into cultivation.

The facts which support this position are obvious | and in-   318 controvertible. Some of them have been stated in the preceding section, and their number might easily be increased. I will only add however one more, which is so strong an instance as to be alone almost decisive of the question, and having happened in our own country, it is completely open to the most minute examination.

From the accession of George II. in 1727 to the commencement of the war in 1739, the interest of money was little more than 3 per cent. The public securities which had been reduced to 4 per cent. rose considerably after the reduction. According to Chalmers, the *natural* rate of interest ran steadily at 3 per cent.;* and it appears by a speech of Sir John Barnard's that the 3 per cent. stocks sold at a premium upon Change. In 1750, after the termination of the war, the 4 per cent. stocks were reduced to $3\frac{1}{2}$, for seven years, and from that time to 3 per cent. permanently.†

Excluding then the interval of war, we have here a period of twenty-two years, during which the general rate of interest was between $3\frac{1}{2}$ and 3 per cent.

* Estimate of the Strength of Great Britain, c. vii. p. 115.
† Id. ch. vii. p. 120.

What Mr. Malthus says in this paragraph is shortly this "profits will not fall so much as might be expected from a rise of corn, because the labourers wages, though they will rise, will be kept from rising much[2] by the comparatively cheaper price of the other necessaries which he consumes. ["] This can not nor has not been disputed.

[2] 'from rising much' replaces 'down'.

The temporary variations in the value of government securities will not certainly at all times be a correct criterion of the rate of profits or even of the rate of interest; but when they remain nearly steady for some time together, they must be considered as 319 a fair approximation to a correct mea-|sure of interest; and when the public creditors of a government consent to a great fall in the interest which they had before received, rather than be paid off, it is a most decisive proof of a great difficulty in the means of employing capital profitably, and consequently a most decisive proof of a low rate of profits.

After an interval of nearly seventy years from the commencement of the period here noticed, and forty years from the end of it, during which a great accumulation of capital had taken place, and an unusual quantity of new land had been brought into cultivation, we find a period of twenty years succeed in which the average market rate of interest was rather above than below 5 per cent.; and we have certainly every reason to think, from the extraordinary rapidity with which capital was recovered, after it had been destroyed, that the rate of profits in general was quite in proportion to this high rate of interest. (176)

The difficulty of borrowing on mortgage during a considerable part of the time is perfectly well known; and though the pressure of the public debt might naturally be supposed to create some

---

(176) p. 318. *From the accession of Geo.* 2

Nobody can deny that improvements in Agriculture, and in the application of labour to the land, have the same effect in raising profits, as an increase of fertility in the land.

(177) p. 320. *The different rates of interest &c. &c.*

This is disingenuous. Who has advanced a ["] theory of profits founded on the natural quality of the last land taken into cultivation." The theory is that profits depend on the productiveness of the last land taken into cultivation, whether that productiveness be owing to the natural quality of the land, or the economy and skill with which labour may be applied to it. Profits are increased, either by diminishing the quantity of labour bestowed on the last land which yields

alarm and incline the owners of disposable funds to give a preference to landed security; yet it appears from the surveys of
Arthur Young, that the number of years purchase given for land
was in 1811, 29¼, and forty years before, 32 or 32½,*—the | most 320
decisive proof that can well be imagined of an increase in the
profits of capital employed upon land.

The different rates of interest and profits in the two periods
here noticed are diametrically opposed to the theory of profits
founded on the natural quality of the last land taken into cultivation. The facts, which are incontrovertible, not only cannot be
accounted for upon this theory, but in reference to it, either
exclusively or mainly, they ought to be directly the reverse of
what they are found to be in reality. (177)

The nature of these facts, and the state of things under which
they took place, (in the one case, in a state of peace with a slack
demand for agricultural products, and in the other, a state of war
with an unusual demand for these products,) obviously and
clearly point to the *relative* redundancy or deficiency of capital,
as, according to every probability, connected with them. (178)

* Annals of Agriculture, No. 270. pp. 96. and 97. and No. 271. p. 215.
Mr. Young expresses considerable surprize at these results, and does not
seem sufficiently aware, that the number of | years purchase given for land
has nothing to do with prices, but mainly expresses the abundance or scarcity
of movable capital compared with the means of employing it.

---

a given produce, or by increasing the produce with a given
quantity of labour. Mr. Malthus will I am sure not say that
I have ever denied this principle—he will not say that I have
not distinctly advanced it.

(178) p. 320. *The nature of these facts*

What does Mr. Malthus mean by relative redundancy of
capital? I do not like the term; but waiving that objection,
under every increase of capital, if population increases still
faster, and labour falls, population is redundant as compared
with capital; and if population increases at a slower rate, than
capital, capital is relatively redundant to population. This
is again another way of stating that profits will be high or
low, according as wages are low or high.

And the question which now remains to be considered, is, whether the circumstances which have been stated in this section are sufficient to account theoretically for such a free operation of this principle, notwithstanding the progressive accumulation of capital, and the progressive cultivation of fresh land, as to allow of low profits at an earlier period of this progress and high profits at a later period. At all events, the facts must be accounted for, as they 321 are | so broad and glaring, and others of the same kind are in reality of such frequent recurrence, that I cannot but consider them as at once decisive against any theory of profits which is inconsistent with them.

In the first period of the two which have been noticed, it is known that the price of corn had fallen, but that the wages of labour had not only not fallen in proportion, but had been considered by some authorities as having risen. Adam Smith states the fall of corn and the rise of labour during the first sixty-four years of the last century as a sort of established fact*; but Arthur Young, in his very useful inquiries into the prices of corn and labour published in his Annals of Agriculture, seems to think with some reason, that the fact is not well authenticated, and is besides a little inconsistent with the apparently slack demand for labour and produce and comparatively slow progress of population, which took place during the period in question.† Allowing, however, even a stationary price of labour, with a falling price of corn, and the fall of agricultural profits is at once accounted for.

* Wealth of Nations, Book I. ch. xi. p. 309. 313. 6th edit.
† Annals of Agriculture, No. 270. p. 89.

---

(179) p. 321. *Allowing, however, even a stationary*

Whatever Mr. Malthus may call it this is a high price of labour, because by his own shewing it is an increased proportion of the produce obtained from the last land which is awarded to the labourer.[1] He is particularly bound to call such wages high, because he measures value by quantity, and he tells us the labourer will have an increased quantity of corn, which he calls increased real wages. Profits then

[1] Last six words are ins.

Such a state of prices might alone be much more than sufficient to counteract the effects arising from the circumstance of pretty good land being yet uncultivated. When we add,˙ that the other outgoings belonging to the farmers' capital, such as leather, iron, timber, &c. &c., are | supposed to have risen while his main 322 produce was falling, we can be at no loss to account for a low rate of agricultural profits, notwithstanding the unexhausted state of the country. And as to the low rate of mercantile and manufacturing profits, that would be accounted for at once by the proportion of capital to labour. (179)

In the subsequent period, from 1793 to 1813, it is probable that all the circumstances noticed in this section concurred to give room for the operation of that principle which depends upon the proportion of capital to labour.

In the first place, there can be no doubt of the improvements in agriculture which were going forwards during these twenty years, both in reference to the general management of the land and the instruments which are connected with cultivation, or which in any way tend to facilitate the bringing of raw produce to market. 2dly, the increasing practice of task-work during these twenty years, together with the increasing employment of women and children, unquestionably occasioned a great increase of personal exertion; and more work was done by the same number of persons and families than before.

These two causes of productiveness in the powers of labour were evidently encouraged and in a manner called into action by the circumstances of the times, that is, by the high price of

---

fall because wages rise—circumstances have made the position of the labourer favorable to him. Labour is undersupplied compared with capital.[2] If money wages were higher than before, that would account for a fall in mercantile profits. If they were no higher, money could not be of the same value—it must have risen[3] and the prices of goods have fallen.

[2] 'Under the circumstances mentioned' is del. here.   [3] Replaces 'varied'.

corn, (180) which encouraged the employment of more capital upon the land with the most effective modes of applying it, and
323 by the increasing demand for labour, | owing to the number of men wanted in the army and navy at the same time that more than ever were wanted in agriculture and manufactures.

The third cause, which had a very considerable effect, much more indeed than is generally attributed to it, was a rise in the money price of corn without a proportionate rise in mercantile

---

(180) p. 322. *These two causes of productiveness in the powers of labour were evidently encouraged and in a manner called into action by the circumstances of the times, that is by the high price of corn*

Money, and money unvarying in value, is uniformly referred to by Mr. Malthus, altho' he before so pointedly rejected it as a measure of value. If money prices were as Mr. Malthus calls them always[1] nominal prices, and very different from real prices, high money prices[2] would not afford any encouragement to the increased production of a particular commodity[3]. It is only high real value which affords any such encouragement. I wish Mr. Malthus had kept[4] to his own standard, and[5] explained the principles of political Economy by a reference to it. If corn rises from £4—to £5 p^r. quarter he calls it a rise in the price of corn, if labour rises from 10 to 12/- p^r. week he speaks of the rise in the price of labour, but he sometimes calls the same thing a fall in the real[6] value of labour. True he would say the labourer gets more money but for that money he gets less corn. How am I to know when he talks of the high price of labour whether he means a high or a low real value?

[1] 'always' is ins.
[2] 'high money prices' replaces 'they'.
[3] 'or at least they would only do in proportion' is del. here.
[4] 'uniformly' was ins. here, and then del.
[5] 'not changed from his own to mine and from mine to his own on various occasions' is del. here.
[6] 'real' is ins.

and manufacturing produce. This state of things always allows of some diminution in the corn wages of labour without a proportionate diminution of the comforts of the labourer; and if the money price of the farmer's produce increases without a proportionate increase in the price of labour and of the materials of which his capital consists, this capital becomes more productive and his profits must necessarily rise. (181)

In a country in which labour had been well paid, it is obvious

---

(181) p. 323. *The third cause*

Now this is one of the occasions where it appears to me that Mr. Malthus comes to a wrong conclusion by mixing the two measures of value—corn value—and money price.

He supposes that corn rises relatively to other commodities, and that wages rise relatively to other commodities, but fall in corn, and he concludes that profits will rise.

First how can the manufacturers profit rise? Wages in commodities are higher than before, the manufacturer therefore retains a smaller quantity of manufactured goods for himself after paying the remainder for wages. The relative value of manufactured goods have not altered, therefore with his diminished quantity of goods he can obtain only a diminished quantity of all other manufacturers goods. But the relative value of manufactured goods are lower compared with corn. If he had the same quantity of goods as before he could obtain less corn for them, having a less quantity of those goods this less quantity of corn will still be reduced lower. His profits then estimated in goods or in corn are lower than before.[7] Why does the relative value of corn rise? because it is more difficult to produce it, or the demand has increased compared with the supply. The demand can not have increased, because the labourers by the supposition

---

[7] 'On the land last cultivated the farmer will get a less portion of   corn and the labourer will' is del. here.

that an alteration in the proportion between labour and capital might occasion a rise in the rate of profits without supposing any increase in the productive powers of labour. But all the causes just noticed are of a nature to increase the productive powers both of labour and capital; and if in any case they are of sufficient force to overcome the effect of taking poorer land into cultivation, the rate of profits may rise consistently even with an increase in the real wages of labour.

In the case in question, though it is generally supposed that the money wages of labour did not rise in proportion to the rise in the price of provisions; yet I cannot help thinking, both from 324 the acknowledged demand for labour and the rapid in-|crease of population, that, partly owing to parish assistance and the more extended use of potatoes, and partly to task-work and the increased employment of women and children, the labouring classes had on an average an increased command over the necessaries of life. I am inclined to think, therefore, that the increased rate of profits from 1793 to 1813 did not arise so much from the diminished quantity of agricultural produce given to the labourer's family, as from the increase in the amount of agricultural produce

---

consume less. The supply may have diminished from a bad season, the farmer's profits are then accidental and temporary, and are besides counteracted by his obtaining the increased price for a smaller quantity. The only permanent cause then is increased cost of production. On the land last cultivated, less will be obtained, and notwithstanding the reduction in the quantity given to the labourer, it will be a larger proportion of the whole. The whole quantity obtained by the farmer may and will[1] be of no greater value in manufactured commodities than before—out of that equal[2] value, he is to pay a larger proportion, and therefore a larger value[3] estimated also, if you please, in manufactured goods, to the labourers; how then can his profits have risen? they will fall to the level of the manufacturers profits. On the better lands

[1] 'and will' is ins.   [3] 'value' replaces 'proportion'.
[2] 'equal' is ins.

obtained by the same number of families. As a matter of fact, I have no doubt that, as I stated in the chapter on rent, the capital employed upon the last land taken into cultivation in 1813 was more productive than the capital employed upon the last land taken into cultivation in 1727; and it appears to me that the causes which have been mentioned are sufficient to account for it theoretically, and to make such an event appear not only possible, but probable, and likely to be of frequent recurrence.

It will be said, perhaps, that some of the causes which have been noticed are in part accidental; and that in contemplating a future period, we cannot lay our account to improvements in agriculture, and an increase of personal exertions in the labouring classes. This is in some degree true. At the same time it must be allowed that a great demand for corn of home growth must tend greatly to encourage improvements in agriculture, (182) and a great demand for labour must stimulate the actual population to do more work; and when to these two | circumstances we add the   325 necessary effect of a rising price of corn owing to an increase of wealth, without a proportionate rise of other commodities, (183) the probabilities of an increase in the productive powers of labour

---

rents will rise, which will occasion a like fall in the profits of the cultivators of such lands.

(182) p. 324. *At the same time it must be allowed*

Under a system of free importation, there would be a sufficient demand for corn of home growth, to encourage[4] improvements in Agriculture.

(183) p. 324.

Mr. speaks of a rising price of corn owing to an increase of wealth. If this is not occasioned by an increased cost of production, why should it operate on corn more than on other things. If it did not, either corn would not rise, or there would be a proportionate rise of other commodities, and then the whole might be referred to a fall in the value of money—which produces no effects on profits.

[4] Replaces 'to stimulate to'.

sufficient to counterbalance the effect of taking additional land into cultivation are so strong, that, in the actual state of most countries in the world, or in their probable state for some centuries to come, we may fairly lay our account to their operation when the occasion calls for them.

I should feel no doubt, for instance, of an increase in the rate of profits in this country for twenty years together, at the beginning of the twentieth century, compared with the twenty years which are now coming on; provided this near period were a period of profound tranquillity and peace and abundant capital, and the future period were a period in which capital was scanty in proportion to the demand for it owing to a war, attended by the circumstances of an increasing trade and an increasing demand for agricultural produce similar to those which were experienced from 1793 to 1813. (184)

But if this be so, it follows, that in the actual state of things in most countries of the world, and within limited periods of moderate extent, the rate of profits will practically depend more upon the causes which affect the relative abundance or scarcity of capital, than on the natural powers of the last land taken into cultivation. And consequently, to dwell on this latter point as 326 the sole, or even the main cause which determines profits, | must

---

(184) p. 325. *I should feel no doubt &c.*

What a number of conditions! the only one of importance is the abundance or scarcity of capital compared with the demand for it, which is saying in other words that if in the beginning of the twentieth century the comparative quantity of capital and labour should be such that the labourers should not be able to command so large a[1] proportion of the produce obtained on the last land profits will then be higher. On these conditions there is no denying the conclusion. Whether they will be so or not must depend on improvements in Agriculture—or on the permission by law to import corn[2] without restrictions from other countries.

[1] Last eight words replace 'have   [2] 'freely and' is del. here.
a less'.

lead to the most erroneous conclusions. (185) Adam Smith, in
stating the cause of the fall of profits, has omitted this point, and
in so doing has omitted a most important consideration; but in
dwelling solely upon the abundance and competition of capital,
he is practically much nearer the truth,* than those who dwell
almost exclusively on the quality of the last land taken into
cultivation.

SECTION IV

Remarks on Mr. Ricardo's Theory of Profits

According to Mr. Ricardo, profits are regulated by wages, and
wages by the quality of the last land taken into cultivation. (186)
This theory of profits depends entirely upon the circumstance of
the mass of commodities remaining at the same price, while

* Perhaps it ought to be allowed that Adam Smith, in speaking of the
effects of accumulation and competition on profits, naturally means to refer
to a limited territory, a limited population, and a limited demand; but
accumulation of capital under these circumstances involves every cause that
can affect profits.

---

(185) p. 325. *And consequently to dwell on*
       An unfounded charge—see P.   3

(186) p. 326. *According to Mr. Ricardo &c. &c.*
This account of my opinion differs greatly from that given
by Mr. Malthus Page 309,—but in what he now says he is
not quite correct. I do not say that profits are regulated by
wages, and wages by the quality of the last land taken into
cultivation without any regard to its productiveness, for it
is expressly the productiveness of that land which regulates
profits if wages be supposed of a fixed value.[4]

3 Blank in MS. See Note (171),   on Page 66' [of ed. 2; above, I,
above, p. 264.   79–80]; then replaced by 'that land
4 First written 'that land which   which regulates both wages and
regulates profits. I have said so   profits'; finally altered as above.

money continues of the same value, whatever may be the variations in the price of labour. This uniformity in the value of wages
and profits taken together is indeed assumed by Mr. Ricardo in
all his calculations, from one end of his work to the other; and if
327 it were true, | we should certainly have an accurate rule which
would determine the rate of profits upon any given rise or fall of
money wages. But if it be not true, the whole theory falls to the
ground. We can infer nothing respecting the rate of profits from
a rise of money wages, if commodities, instead of remaining of
the same price, are very variously affected, some rising, some
falling, and a very small number indeed remaining stationary. But
it was shewn in a former chapter* that this must necessarily take
place upon a rise in the price of labour. Consequently the money
wages of labour cannot regulate the rate of profits.

This conclusion will appear still more strikingly true, if we
adopt that supposition respecting the mode of procuring the
precious metals which would certainly maintain them most strictly
of the same value, that is, if we suppose them to be procured by
a uniform quantity of unassisted labour without any advances in
the shape of capital beyond the necessaries of a single day. That
the precious metals would in this case retain, more completely
than in any other, the same value, cannot be denied, as they would
both cost and command the same quantity of labour. But in this
case, as was before stated, the money price of labour could never
permanently rise. We cannot however for a moment imagine that
this impossibility of a rise or fall in the money price of labour
328 could in any respect impede or interrupt the | natural career of
profits. The continued accumulation of capital and increasing
difficulty of procuring subsistence would unquestionably lower
profits. All commodities, in the production of which the same
quantity of labour continued to be employed, but with the
assistance of capitals of various kinds and amount, would fall in
price, and just in proportion to the degree in which the price of
the commodity had before been affected by profits; and with
regard to corn, in the production of which more labour would be
necessary, this article would rise in money price, notwithstanding
the capital used to produce it, just to that point which would so
reduce corn wages as to render the population stationary; and

* Chap. ii. sects. 4 and 5.

thus all the effects upon profits, attributed by Mr. Ricardo to a rise of money wages, would take place while money wages and the value of money remained precisely the same. This supposition serves further to shew how very erroneous it must be to consider the fall of profits as synonymous with a rise of money wages, or to make the money price of labour the great regulator of the rate of profits. It is obvious that, in this case, profits can only be regulated by the principle of competition, or of demand and supply, which would determine the degree in which the prices of commodities would fall; and their prices, compared with the uniform price of labour, would mainly regulate the rate of profits.

But Mr. Ricardo never contemplates the fall of prices as occasioning a fall of profits, although prac-|tically in many cases, 329 as well as on the preceding supposition, a fall of profits must be produced in this way.

Let us suppose a prosperous commercial city, greatly excelling in some manufactures, and purchasing all its corn abroad. At first, and perhaps for a considerable time, the prices of its manufactures in foreign markets might be such as, compared with the price of its imported corn, to yield high profits; but, as capital continued to be accumulated and employed in larger quantities on the exportable manufactures, such manufactures, upon the principles of demand and supply, would in all probability fall in price. A larger portion of them must then be exchanged for a given portion of corn, and profits would necessarily fall. It is true that, under these circumstances, the labouring manufacturer must do more work for his support, and Mr. Ricardo would say that this is the legitimate cause of the fall of profits. In this I am quite willing to agree with him; but surely the specific cause, in this case, of more work being necessary to earn the same quantity of corn is the fall in the prices of the exportable manufactures with which it is purchased, and not a rise in the price of corn, which may remain exactly the same. The fall in these manufactures is the natural consequence of an increase of supply arising from an accumulation of capital more rapid than the extension of demand for its products; and that the fall of profits so occasioned depends entirely upon the principles of demand and supply will be acknowledged, if we | acknowledge, as we certainly must do, 330 that the opening a new market for the manufactures in question would at once put an end to the fall of profits. (187)

---

(187) p. 329. *Let us suppose a prosperous commercial city &c. &c.*

In all the remarks preceding this passage Mr. Malthus has clearly shewn that no medium that can be chosen is or can under any circumstances be even[1] supposed to be an accurate measure of value. I not only admit this but have myself pointed it out.[2] To whatever corrections must be made for this irremediable imperfection in the most perfect measure[3] of value that can be conceived, I have no objections to offer. It may affect some commodities one way, some the contrary way, the general average however will not be much affected. The general principle is not in the slightest degree invalidated by the necessary imperfection of the measure. I maintain no other doctrine than that which has been well explained by Mr. Malthus in the 2 first sections of 5th Chapter. His own statements are sometimes at variance with it, mine I believe never.

I have now however to do with the passage at the head of this remark.

Instead of supposing that all the corn this prosperous and commercial city required[4] was imported let us suppose that three fourths of that quantity was imported, and that no land remained in cultivation but such as afforded so abundant a supply that the farmer could afford to sell it at the low price of importation[5] and obtain the current rate of profits. Mr. Malthus would probably then agree with me that profits could not fall whilst we could import corn at the same price

---

[1] 'even' is ins.
[2] Above, I, 17, n. 3.
[3] Replaces 'in all measures'.

[4] Replaces 'imported'.
[5] 'of importation' is ins.

Upon the same principle, of considering the prices of commodities as constant, Mr. Ricardo is of opinion, that if the prices

---

because till it rose no worse land could be cultivated. If
poorer land were cultivated the quantity of produce on that
land[6] would not bear the same proportion to the labour
employed as before, and therefore either corn must rise or
commodities must fall to preserve the equilibrium of profits.
If poorer land were cultivated I should say that the natural
value[7] of corn had risen, at whatever value in money it
might be rated. If it did not rise in price but commodities
fell in price I should think that money had risen in value.
Now this rise in the value of money is either common to all
countries or particular to this. If common to all countries
while the price of corn was stationary in this country it
would fall in other countries—if it rose in this country it
would remain stationary in other countries. The real cause
of the variation here is that more labour was required to
produce the last portions wanted—no such cause operated
abroad and therefore corn would be exported from abroad
to this country till the relative prices were restored to the
same state at which they were before the worse land had
been taken into cultivation.

Now suppose our demand to increase—to double if you
please—the question is can foreign countries supply this
additional quantity without taking new land into cultivation.
If they can I can see no reason for the rise in the price of
their corn, if they cannot it will rise and the result will be
a fall of profits in both countries. Now while corn remained
at the low price in England commodities could not fall[8]
for the reason already given that if they did agricultural

6 'on that land' is ins.   8 'fall' replaces 'rise'.
7 'value' replaces 'price'.

of our corn and labour were to fall, the profits of our foreign trade would rise in proportion. But what is it, I would ask, that is to fix the prices of commodities in foreign markets? (188)— not merely the quantity of labour which has been employed upon them, because, as was noticed in a former chapter, commodities

---

profits would differ from manufacturing profits and capital would move from one to the other. But the demand for foreign corn may be so great that the foreign country may not be able or willing to supply it—they may refuse to accept of any more of the commodities which alone we can ultimately offer in exchange for them. England however wants the corn and therefore she must consent to export her money for corn. This accumulation of money will raise the price of corn in the foreign country but it will not in the same degree raise the price of English goods and therefore the relation between corn and commodities in the foreign country being no longer the same as before England would have less inducement to buy corn of her.

The exportation of money in England would operate in a reverse order it would lower both[1] the value of corn and commodities. Importation then of corn and exportation of commodities would both be checked for they would be more nearly of a value in both countries. If the wants of England for corn were great she would either consent to import it on the new terms, or she would grow it herself; in either case her profits would fall, for if the same or even a less quantity of corn were given to the labourer it would still be a larger proportion of the quantity obtained by a given quantity of labour.

Now these effects are brought about by the limited demand

---

[1] 'lower both' replaces 'raise'.

will be found selling at the same price in foreign markets, which have cost very different quantities of labour. But if they are determined, as they certainly are, both on an average and at the moment, by supply and demand, what is to prevent a much larger supply, occasioned by the competition of capital thrown out of

---

of the foreign country for the commodities which we could give in exchange for corn. Our demand for their corn was not so limited, and in consequence they become possessed of something like a monopoly against us. Profits in all countries must mainly depend upon the quantity of labour given for corn, either when grown on their own land, or embodied in manufactures and [2] with them bought from other countries. I say mainly depend, because I think wages mainly depend on the price of corn. After the observations of Mr. Malthus on the other causes which may affect labour, I must guard myself against being supposed to deny the effect of those other causes on wages.

The case then put by Mr. Malthus only confirms the general doctrine, it appears clear that what he calls a fall in the price of manufactured goods is in reality an increased labour price of food. I acknowledge the results but I think I have given the fair solution of them.

(188) p. 330. *What is it, I would ask is to &c.*

I answer the cost of production in the foreign country. If England gives this year to Portugal the same quantity of hardware for wine which she gave last year, she will have an increased profit on that trade if the hardware cost her a great deal less labour and the labourer be [3] not more amply remunerated that produces it.

[2] 'exchanged for corn' is del.   [3] 'the labourer be' is ins. here.

employment, from rapidly lowering prices, and with them reducing the rate of profits? (189)

If the price of corn during the last twenty-five years could have
been kept at about fifty shillings the quarter, and the increasing
capital of the country had chiefly been applied to the working
up of exportable commodities for the purchase of foreign corn,
I am strongly disposed to believe that the profits of stock would
have been lower instead of higher. (190) The millions which have
been employed in permanent agricultural improvements* have
331 had | no tendency whatever to lower profits; but if, in conjunction
with a large portion of the common capital employed in domestic
agriculture, they had been added to the already large capitals
applied to the working up of exportable commodities, I can
scarcely feel a doubt that the foreign markets would have been
more than fully supplied; that the prices of commodities would
have been such as to make the profits of stock quite low;† and
that there would have been both a greater mass of moveable

* The millions of capital which have been expended in drainings, and
in the roads and canals for the conveyance of agricul-|tural products, have
tended rather to raise than lower profits; and millions and millions may yet
be employed with the same advantageous effect.

† Our present body of manufacturers, when they call for imported corn,
think chiefly of the additional demand for their goods occasioned by the
increased imports, and seem quite to forget the prodigious increase of
supply which must be occasioned by the competition of so many more
capitals and workmen in the same line of business.

---

(189) p. 330. *But if they are determined &c.*

Because you cannot reduce the profits on agriculture. If
corn and labour be at a low real[1] price the profits on agriculture must be high, and so must also be the profits on all
other capitals—for as Mr. Malthus observes Page 296 "Profits
in the same country tend to an equality." See[2]

(190) p. 330. *If the price of corn*

That is to say we should not have imported our corn
cheap, for by cheapness I mean a cheap price relatively to

[1] 'real' is ins.   [2] Blank in MS. See Note (162),
                                       above, p. 254.

capitals at a loss for employment, and a greater disposition in those capitals to emigrate than has actually taken place.

Mr. Ricardo has never laid any *stress* upon the influence of permanent improvements in agriculture on the profits of stock, although it is one of the most important considerations in the whole compass of Political Economy, as such improvements unquestionably open the largest *arena* for the employment of capital without a diminution of profits. He observes, that "however extensive a country may be, where the land is of a poor quality, and where the importation of food is prohibited, the most moderate accumulations of capital | will be attended with great reductions in the rate of profits, and a rapid rise in rent; and on the contrary, a small but fertile country, particularly if it freely per‐ mits the importation of food, may accumulate a large stock of capital, without any great diminution in the rate of profits, or any great increase in the rent of land." ‡ (191)

Adverting to the known effects of permanent improvements on the land, I should have drawn an inference from these two cases precisely the reverse of that which Mr. Ricardo has drawn. A very extensive territory, with the soil of a poor quality, yet all, or nearly all capable of cultivation, might, by continued improve‐ ments in agriculture, admit of the employment of a vast mass of capital for hundreds of years, with little or with no fall of profits;

‡ Princ. of Pol. Econ. ch. vi. p. [126]. 2d edit.

the commodities exported. If this be true, we should have preferred growing corn, and profits in that case would be just where they are.

(191) p. 331. *Mr. Ricardo has not*

Once more I must say that I lay the very greatest stress upon the influence of permanent improvements in Agricul‐ ture. The passage quoted refers to a state of things when no improvements are taking place, and therefore the argument built upon it which supposes improvements has no founda‐ tion.

while the small but fertile territory, being very soon filled with all the capital it could employ on the land, would be obliged to employ its further accumulations in the purchase of corn with falling manufactures; a state of things which might easily reduce profits to their lowest rate before one-third of the capital had been accumulated that had been accumulated in the former case.

A country, which accumulates faster than its neighbours, might for hundreds of years still keep up its rate of profits, if it were successful in making permanent improvements on the land; but, if with the same rapidity of accumulation it were to depend chiefly on imported corn, its profits could | scarcely fail to fall; and the fall would probably be occasioned, not by a rise in the bullion price of corn in the ports of Europe, but by a fall in the bullion price of the exports with which the corn was purchased by the country in question. (192)

These statements appear to me to accord with the most correct theory of profits, and they certainly seem to be confirmed by experience. I have already adverted to the unquestionable fact of the profits on land being higher in 1813 than they were above eighty years before, although in the interval millions and millions of accumulated capital had been employed on the soil. And the effect of falling prices in reducing profits is but too evident at the present moment. In the largest article of our exports, the wages of labour are now lower than they probably would be in an ordinary state of things if corn were at fifty shillings a quarter. If, according to the new theory of profits, the prices of our exports had remained the same, the master manufacturers would have been in a state of the most extraordinary prosperity, and the rapid accumulation of their capitals would soon have employed all the workmen that could have been found. But, instead of this, we

---

(192) p. 333. *And the fall would probably be occasioned, not by a rise in the bullion price of corn in the Ports of Europe, but by a fall in the bullion prices of the exports with which the corn was purchased by the country in question.*

The question is one of trifling importance, but I have little doubt that it would be occasioned by a rise in the bullion

NOTES 192-193] PROFITS OF CAPITAL 295

hear of glutted markets, falling prices, and cotton goods selling at Kamschatka lower than the costs of production.

It may be said, perhaps, that the cotton trade happens to be glutted; and it is a tenet of the new doctrine on profits and demand, that if one trade be overstocked with capital, it is a certain sign that some other trade is understocked. But where, | I would 334 ask, is there any considerable trade that is confessedly understocked, and where high profits have been long pleading in vain for additional capital? The war has now been at an end above four years; and though the removal of capital generally occasions some partial loss, yet it is seldom long in taking place, if it be tempted to remove by great demand and high profits; but if it be only discouraged from proceeding in its accustomed course by falling profits, while the profits in all other trades, owing to general low prices, are falling at the same time, though not perhaps precisely in the same degree, it is highly probable that its motions will be slow and hesitating.

It must be allowed then, that in contemplating the altered relation between labour and the produce obtained by it which occasions a fall of profits, we only take a view of half the question if we advert exclusively to a rise in the wages of labour without referring to a fall in the prices of commodities. Their effects on profits may be precisely the same; but the latter case, where there is no question respecting the state of the land, shews at once how much profits depend upon the prices of commodities, and upon the cause which determines these prices, namely the supply compared with the demand. (193)

[On every supposition, however, the great limiting principle, which depends upon the increasing difficulty of procuring subsistence, is always ready to act, and must finally lower profits;

---

price of corn, if it happened [1] at all. A variation in the value of money is of consequence to individuals, but is insignificant in its effects on the interests of a nation.

(193) p. 334. *It must be allowed then &c. &c.*[2]

[1] Replaces 'if it could happen'.
[2] A blank space was left for the comment in the MS, but it was not filled.

but even this principle acts according to the laws of supply and demand.

335   The reason why profits must fall as the land becomes more exhausted is, that the effective demand for necessaries cannot possibly increase in proportion to the increased expense of producing them.

The further demand for corn must cease when the last land taken into cultivation will but just replace the capital and support the population engaged in cultivating it.

336   But what would be the effect on profits of any particular amount of accumulation could not be predicted beforehand, as it must always depend upon the principles of demand and supply.]

CHAPTER VI

OF THE DISTINCTION BETWEEN
WEALTH AND VALUE

[A country possessing the greatest abundance of commodities 337
without labour might be rich without exchangeable value.

But in the real state in which man is placed on earth, wealth
and exchangeable value are more nearly connected than they have
sometimes been supposed to be.

When more commodities of the same quality are obtained by 338
improved machinery at the same cost, the distinction between
wealth and value is obvious; yet even here the possessor of the
increased quantity is only richer with a view to consumption, not
to exchange.

In comparing objects of different kinds, there is no other way
of estimating the degree of wealth which they confer, than by
the relative estimation in which they are held, evinced by their
relative exchangeable values.]

Wealth, however, it will be allowed, does not always increase 339
in proportion to the increase of value; because an increase of value
may sometimes take place under an actual diminution of the
necessaries, conveniences and luxuries of life; (194) but neither

---

(194)[1] p. 339. *Wealth, however, it will be allowed, does not
always increase in proportion to the increase of value;
because an increase of value may sometimes take place
under an actual diminution of the necessaries, conveniences,
and luxuries of life.*

This is my opinion but it is absolutely inconsistent with
Mr. Malthus's theory. In page 60 he says "What we want
further is some estimate of a kind which may be denominated
real value in exchange implying the quantity of the necessaries and conveniences of life which those wages, incomes

[1] The whole Note is ins.

does it increase in proportion to the mere quantity of what comes under the denomination of wealth, because the various articles of
340 which this quantity is composed may not be so propor-|tioned to the wants and powers of the society as to give them their proper value.

[Wealth depends partly upon the quantity of produce, and partly upon such adaptation of it to the wants and powers of the society as to give it the greatest value.

But where wealth and value are the most nearly connected, is, in the necessity of the latter to the production of the former.
341 It is the value of commodities, or the sacrifice which people are willing to make in order to obtain them, that, in the actual state of things, may be said to be the sole cause of the existence of wealth in any quantity.]
342 In short, the market prices of commodities are the immediate causes of all the great movements of society in the production of wealth, and these market prices always express clearly and unequivocally the exchangeable value of commodities at the time and place in which they are exchanged, and differ only from natural and necessary prices as the actual state of the demand and supply, with regard to any particular article, may differ from the ordinary and average state.
343 The reader of course will observe that in using | the term value, or value in exchange, I always mean it to be understood in that enlarged and, as I conceive, accustomed and correct sense, according to which I endeavoured to explain and define it in the Second Chapter of this work, and never in the confined sense in which it has been lately applied by Mr. Ricardo, as depending exclusively upon the actual quantity of labour employed in pro-

---

or commodities will enable the possessor of them to command.["]

In the one passage we are told that value is in proportion to the abundance of[1] necessaries and conveniences in the other we are assured that an increase of value may take place under an actual diminution of necessaries and conveniences.

[1] 'commodities' is del. here.

duction.* Understood in this latter sense, value, certainly, has not so intimate a connection with wealth. In comparing two countries together of different degrees of fertility, or in comparing an agricultural with a manufacturing and commercial country, their relative wealth would be very different from the proportion of labour employed by each in production; and certainly the increasing quantity of labour necessary to produce any commodity would be very far indeed from being a stimulus to its increase. In this sense therefore wealth and value are very different,

But if value be understood in the sense in which it is most generally used, and according to which | I have defined it, wealth and value, though certainly not always the same, will appear to be very nearly connected; and in making an estimate of wealth, it must be allowed to be as grave an error to consider quantity without reference to value, as to consider value without reference to quantity. |

344

* Mr. Ricardo says, (ch. xx. p. [275].) "That commodity is alone invariable, which at all times requires the same sacrifice of toil and labour to produce it." What does the term "invariable" mean here? It cannot mean *invariable* in its exchangeable value; because Mr. Ricardo has himself allowed that commodities which have cost the same sacrifice of toil and labour will very frequently not exchange for each other. (195) As a measure of value in exchange this standard is much more variable than those which he has rejected; and in what other sense it is to be understood, it is not easy to say.

---

(195) p. 343. *Mr. Ricardo says*

I have allowed that their market prices may differ, but I say commodities so situated will have the same natural price, and will therefore have a constant tendency to agree in market value also; for natural price is the great regulator of market price.

CHAPTER VII

ON THE IMMEDIATE CAUSES OF THE PROGRESS OF WEALTH

SECTION I

Statement of the particular Object of Inquiry

345   [The particular object of inquiry is to trace the causes which are most effective in calling forth the powers of production in different countries.

Moral and political causes are, in this respect, of primary importance; but it is intended chiefly to consider those which are more directly within the province of political economy.

346   Many countries, with great powers of production, are poor, and many, with scanty powers of production, are comparatively rich, without any very essential difference in the security of property.

347   If the actual wealth of a country be not, after a certain period, in some degree proportioned to its powers of production, there must have been a want of stimulus to produce; and the practical question for consideration is, what is the most immediate and effective stimulus to the progress of wealth.]

SECTION II

Of an Increase of Population considered as a Stimulus to the continued Increase of Wealth

[If want alone, or the desire of the necessaries of life among the labouring classes, were a sufficient stimulus to production, the earth would have been comparatively full of inhabitants.

348   A man whose only possession is his labour can make no effectual demand for produce if his labour be not wanted.

349   To justify the employment of capital, there must be a demand

for the produce of it, beyond that which may be created by the demand of the workmen employed.

The effect of the increase of population to raise profits by lowering wages must be very limited, and must soon be checked by want of demand.

By a reference to experience, it will be found that those states 350 often make the slowest progress in wealth where the stimulus arising from population alone is the greatest.

The practical question is, whether the pressure of the popula- 351 tion hard against the limits of subsistence is an adequate stimulus to the increase of wealth? And the state of most countries of the world determines the question in the negative.]

SECTION III

Of Accumulation, or the Saving from Revenue to add to Capital, considered as a Stimulus to the Increase of Wealth.

Those who reject mere population as an adequate stimulus to the increase of wealth, are generally disposed to make every thing depend upon accumulation. It is certainly true that no permanent and continued increase of wealth can take place without a continued increase of capital; and I cannot agree with Lord Lauderdale in thinking that this increase can be effected in any other way than by | saving from the stock which might have been destined 352 for immediate consumption, and adding it to that which is to yield a profit; or in other words, by the conversion of revenue into capital.*

But we have yet to inquire what is the state of things which generally disposes a nation to accumulate; and further, what is the state of things which tends to make that accumulation the most effective, and lead to a further and continued increase of capital and wealth.

It is undoubtedly possible by parsimony to devote at once a much larger share than usual of the produce of any country to

* See Lord Lauderdale's Chapter on Parsimony, in his Inquiry into the Nature and Origin of Public Wealth, ch. iv. p. 198. 2d. edit. Lord Lauderdale appears to have gone as much too far in deprecating accumulation, as some other writers in recommending it. This tendency to extremes is exactly what I consider as the great source of error in political economy.

the maintenance of productive labour; and it is quite true that the labourers so employed are consumers as well as unproductive labourers; and as far as the labourers are concerned, there would be no diminution of consumption or demand. But it has already been shewn that the consumption and demand occasioned by the persons employed in productive labour can never alone furnish a motive to the accumulation and employment of capital; and with regard to the capitalists themselves, together with the land-lords and other rich persons, they have, by the supposition, agreed

---

(196) p. 352. *But it has already been shewn &c.*

The consumption and demand, occasioned by the persons employed in producing any particular quantity of wealth, can never be a sufficient motive for producing it, if they are to have the whole of the commodities produced, and are to give for it only the labour which produced it; but suppose they take seven eighths of it, and their employer retains one eighth, with which he can again employ 5 or 10 additional men, who again take seven eighths of the commodities they produce, leaving the employer the power to employ additional labour the following year; cannot such accumulations go on while the land last cultivated[1] will yield more food than is consumed by the cultivators?—when it will not do that, there is an end on every system to all accumulation. But if a society consisted of nothing but landowners, farmers,[2] manufacturers of necessaries, and labourers, accumulation could go on to this point, provided only that population increased fast enough. If capital increased too rapidly for the population, instead of commanding seven eighths of the produce, they might command ninety nine hundredths,[3] and thus there would be no motive for further accumulation. If every man were disposed to accumulate every portion of his

[1] 'last cultivated' is ins.
[2] 'and' is del. here.
[3] 'or indeed the whole' is del. here.

to be parsimonious, and by depriving themselves of their usual |
conveniences and luxuries to save from their revenue and add to   353
their capital. Under these circumstances, I would ask, how it is
possible to suppose that the increased quantity of commodities,
obtained by the increased number of productive labourers, should
find purchasers, without such a fall of price as would probably
sink their value below the costs of production, or, at least, very
greatly diminish both the power and the will to save. (196)

It has been thought by some very able writers, that although

---

revenue but what was necessary to his urgent wants such
a state of things would be produced; for the principle of
population is not strong enough to supply a demand for
labourers so great as would then exist. But the condition
of the labourer would then be most happy, for what can be
more prosperous than the condition of him who has a commodity to sell for which there is an almost unlimited demand,
while the supply is limited, and increases at a comparatively
slow rate. All this is conformable to the general principle
which has been often mentioned. Profits would be low
because wages would be high, and would only continue so
till population increased and labour again fell.

Mr. Malthus asks "how is it possible to suppose that the
increased quantity of commodities, obtained by the increased number of productive labourers should find purchasers, without such a fall of price as would probably sink
their value below the cost of production, or, at least, very
greatly diminish both the power and the will to save?["]
To which I answer that the power and the will to save will
be very greatly diminished, for that must depend upon the
share of the produce allotted to the farmer or manufacturer.
But with respect to the other question where would the commodities find purchasers? If they were suited to the wants
of those who would have the power to purchase them, they

there may easily be a glut of particular commodities, there cannot
possibly be a glut of commodities in general; because, according
to their view of the subject, commodities being always exchanged

could not fail to find purchasers, and that without any fall
of price.

If a thousand hats, a thousand pairs of shoes, a thousand
coats, a thousand ounces of gold, were produced, they would
all have a relative value to each other, and that relative value
would be preserved, if they were suited to the wants of the
society, whether the greatest portion went to the labourers
or to their employers.

If wages are low, only one half may[1] perhaps be given
to the labourers. If high three fourths—but whether in the
hands of the masters or of the men they would not have
a different value.

If £500 in money were in the hands of the masters, and
500 hats, 500 qrs. of corn &c. &c. and the remaining quantity
in the hands of the workmen, they would have the same
relative value, as if £600 money were in the hands of the
masters and 600 of every other commodity, and the remaining quantity in the hands of the workmen. Which of
these distributions shall take place depends on the proportions between capital and labour, but whichever it may be,
no effect can be produced on price, if the commodities be
suited to the wants of those who can command them. If
they are not it is the interest of the producers to make them
so. It follows then, from what I have here said, that if the
commodities produced be suited to the wants of the purchasers, they cannot exist in such abundance as not to find
a market.

[1] Replaces 'will'.

for commodities, one half will furnish a market for the other half, and production being thus the sole source of demand, an excess in the supply of one article merely proves a deficiency in the

---

Mistakes may be made, and commodities not suited to the demand may be produced—of these there may be a glut; they may not sell at their usual price; but then this is owing to the mistake, and not to the want of demand for productions. For every thing produced there must be a proprietor. Either it is the master, the landlord, or the labourer. Whoever is possessed of a commodity is necessarily a demander, either he wishes to consume the commodity himself, and then no purchaser is wanted; or he wishes to sell it, and purchase some other thing with the money, which shall either be consumed by him, or be made instrumental to future production. The commodity he possesses will obtain him this or it will not. If it will, the object is accomplished, and his commodity has found a market. If it will not what does it prove? that he has not adapted his means well to his end, he has miscalculated. He wants for example cotton goods, and he has produced cloth with a view to obtain them. Either there are cotton goods in the market or there are not—if there are, the proprietor wishes to sell them only with a view to purchase some other commodity—he does not want cloth, but he does want silks, linen, or wine—this at once indicates that the proprietor of cloth has mistaken the means by which to possess himself of cotton goods, he ought to have produced silks, linen or wine; if he had, there would not have been a glut of any commodity, as it is there is certainly a glut of one, namely cloth; and perhaps of two, because the cotton goods may not be required by any other person. But there may be no cotton goods in the

supply of some other, and a general excess is impossible. M. Say, in his distinguished work on political economy, has indeed gone so far as to state that the consumption of a commodity by taking it out of the market diminishes demand, and the production of a commodity proportionably increases it.

This doctrine, however, to the extent in which it has been applied, appears to me to be utterly unfounded, and completely

---

market, what then should the person wanting them have produced to obtain them. Why, if there be no commodity with which he can purchase them, which is the most extravagant supposition[1], he can instead of producing cloth which he does not want, produce himself cotton goods which he does want. What I wish to impress on the readers mind is that it is at all times the bad adaptation of the commodities produced to the wants of mankind which is the specific evil, and not the abundance of commodities. Demand is only limited by the will and power to purchase.

Whoever has commodities has the power to consume, and as it suits mankind to divide their employments, individuals[2] will produce one commodity with a view to purchase another; —these exchanges are mutually beneficial, but they are not absolutely necessary, for every man might employ his funds, and the labour at his command, in producing the very commodities he and his workmen intended to consume; in which case, there would be no market, and consequently there could be no glut. The division of the produce between master and men, is one thing;—the exchanges made between those to whom they are finally awarded, is another.

I have been thus particular in examining this question as it forms by far the most important topic of discussion in

[1] Replaces 'proposition'.   [2] 'individuals' replaces 'they'.

to contradict the great principles which regulate supply and demand.

It is by no means true, as a matter of fact, | that commodities 354 are always exchanged for commodities. The great mass of commodities is exchanged directly for labour, either productive or unproductive; and it is quite obvious that this mass of commodities, compared with the labour with which it is to be exchanged,

---

Mr. Malthus' work[3]. If his views on this question be correct—if commodities can be so multiplied that there is no disposition to purchase and consume them, then undoubtedly the cure which he hesitatingly recommends is a very proper one. If the people entitled to consume will not consume the commodities produced, themselves, nor cause them to be consumed by others, with a view to reproduction[4]: if, of the two things necessary to demand, the will and the power to purchase[5] the will be wanting, and consequently a general stagnation of trade has ensued, we cannot do better than follow the advice of Mr. Malthus, and oblige the Government to supply the deficiency of the people. We ought in that case to petition[6] the King to dismiss his present economical ministers, and to replace them by others, who would more effectually promote the best interests of the country by promoting public extravagance and expenditure. We are it seems a nation of producers and have few consumers amongst us, and the evil has at last become of that magnitude that we shall be irretrievably miserable if the parliament or the ministers do not immediately adopt an efficient plan of expenditure.

[3] 'and what I think erroneous opinions are advanced with much perseverance in every part of his' is del. here.
[4] Replaces 'will not consume, nor cause to be consumed by others, with a view to reproduction, the things which they have power to command'.
[5] 'purchase' replaces 'consume'.
[6] 'parliament to' is del. here.

may fall in value from a glut just as any one commodity falls in
value from an excess of supply, compared either with labour or
money. (197)

In the case supposed there would evidently be an unusual
quantity of commodities of all kinds in the market, owing to the
unproductive labourers of the country having been converted, by
the accumulation of capital, into productive labourers; while the
number of labourers altogether being the same, and the power and
will to purchase for consumption among landlords and capitalists
being by supposition diminished, commodities would necessarily
fall in value, compared with labour, so as to lower profits almost
to nothing, and to check for a time further production. (198) But
this is precisely what is meant by the term glut, which, in this
case, is evidently general not partial.

355   M. Say, Mr. Mill,* and Mr. Ricardo, the prin-|cipal authors of

* Mr. Mill, in a reply to Mr. Spence, published in 1808, has laid down
very broadly the doctrine that commodities are only purchased by commodities, and that one half of them must always furnish a market for the
other half. The same doctrine appears to be adopted in its fullest extent by
the author of an able and useful article on the Corn Laws, in the Supplement
to the Encyclopædia Britannica, which has been referred to in a previous
chapter.

---

(197) p. 354. *The great mass of commodities*

It is quite true that commodities may exist in such abundance, compared with labour, as to make their value so to fall,
estimated in labour,[1] as not to afford any inducement to their
further production. In that case labour will command a great
quantity of commodities. It is this that Mr. Malthus subsequently denies. If Mr. Malthus means that there may be
such a glut of commodities as to make them ruinously cheap
in labour[2] I agree with him, but this is only saying that labour
is so high that it absorbs all that fund which ought to belong
to profits, and therefore the capitalist will have no interest
in continuing to accumulate.[3] But what will be the situation
of the labourer? will that be miserable?

[1] Replaces 'so fall, in labour,'.   commodities estimated in labour'.
[2] Replaces 'there may be a glut of   [3] The remainder is ins.

the new doctrines on profits, appear to me to have fallen into some fundamental errors in the view which they have taken of this subject.

In the first place, they have considered commodities as if they were so many mathematical figures, or arithmetical characters, the relations of which were to be compared, instead of articles of consumption, which must of course be referred to the numbers and wants of the consumers.

If commodities were only to be compared and exchanged with each other, then indeed it would be true that, if they were all increased in their proper proportions to any extent, they would continue to bear among themselves the same relative value; but, if we compare them, as we certainly ought to do, with the numbers and wants of the consumers, then a great increase of produce with comparatively stationary numbers and with wants diminished by parsimony, must necessarily occasion a great fall of value estimated in labour, so that the same produce, though it might have *cost* the same quantity of labour as before, would no longer *command* the same quantity; and both the power of accumulation and the motive to accumulate would be strongly checked. (199)

---

(198) p. 354. *In the case*

No one denies this. They would fall in labour value, but not in money value.

(199) p. 355. *If commodities were only*

I deny that the wants of the consumers generally[4] are diminished by parsimony—they are transferred with the power to consume[5] to another set of consumers. I acknowledge that the power and motive of the capitalist to accumulate would be checked.

Note. I deny and admit as above on the supposition that population does not increase with the same rapidity as the funds which are to employ it.

---

[4] 'generally' is ins.   [5] 'to consume' is ins.

It is asserted that effectual demand is nothing more than the offering of one commodity in exchange for another. But is this all that is necessary to effectual demand? Though each commodity may have cost the same quantity of labour and capital in its pro-356 duction, and they may be | exactly equivalent to each other in exchange, yet why may not both be so plentiful as not to command more labour, or but very little more than they have cost; and in this case, would the demand for them be effectual? Would it be such as to encourage their continued production? Unquestionably not. Their relation to each other may not have changed; but their relation to the wants of the society, their relation to bullion, and their relation to domestic and foreign labour, may have experienced a most important change. (200)

---

(200) p. 355. *It is asserted that effectual demand*

If I give an ounce of gold for a quarter of corn these commodities Mr. Malthus allows are equivalent to each other in exchange.

But he asks "may they not both be so plentiful as not to command more labour, or but very little more than they have cost? Would the demand for them be effectual? Would it be such as to encourage their continued production?["] I answer with Mr. Malthus, Unquestionably not. But is this the subject in dispute? This is merely saying that when labour is exceedingly dear as compared with commodities, profits will be so low as to afford no inducement to accumulate. Who denies this proposition? Mr. Malthus original question was this, If capital is accumulated and a great quantity of commodities produced they will not exchange freely for each other in the market; there will be no demand for them.[1] Can any two propositions be more different than these two. Because commodities are so plentiful as not to command much labour, would taxing the people and in-

[1] The last two lines, beginning 'they will not', replace 'will they   exchange freely for each other in the market?'

It will be readily allowed that a new commodity thrown into the market, which, in proportion to the labour employed upon it, is of higher exchangeable value than usual, is precisely calculated to increase demand; because it implies, not a mere increase of quantity, but a better adaptation of the produce to the tastes, wants and consumption of the society. But to fabricate or procure commodities of this kind is the grand difficulty; and they certainly do not naturally and necessarily follow an accumulation of capital and increase of commodities, most particularly when such accumulation and increase have been occasioned by economy of consumption, or a discouragement to the indulgence of those tastes and wants, which are the very elements of demand. (201)

Mr. Ricardo, though he maintains as a general position that

---

creasing the expenditure of Government raise profits, the only thing wanted to ensure the continued production of commodities?

(201) p. 356. *But to fabricate &c.*

Mr. Malthus talks of "an economy of consumption, and a discouragement to the indulgence of those tastes and wants which are the very elements of demand." The whole matter in dispute is centered in these few words. Mr. Say, Mr. Mill, and I say that there will be no economy of consumption no cessation of demand. What is Mr. Malthus's own representation of the state of the case? "Commodities are so plentiful as not to command more labour or but very little more than they cost." But if a great quantity of commodities will command little labour, every labourer will have the power to consume a great quantity of commodities. The will to consume exists wherever the power to consume is. Mr. Malthus proves that this power is not annihilated but is transferred to the labourer. We agree with him and say wherever the power and will to consume exists there will necessarily be demand.

capital cannot be redundant, is obliged to make the following concession. He says, "There is only one case, and that will be 357 temporary, in which the accumulation of capital with a | low price of food may be attended with a fall of profits; and that is, when the funds for the maintenance of labour increase much more rapidly than population;—wages will then be high and profits low. If every man were to forego the use of luxuries and be intent only on accumulation, a quantity of necessaries might be produced for which there could not be any immediate consumption. Of commodities so limited in number, there might undoubtedly be an universal glut; and consequently there might neither be demand for an additional quantity of such commodities, nor profits on the employment of more capital. If men ceased to consume, they would cease to produce." Mr. Ricardo then adds, "This admission does not impugn the general principle."* In this remark I cannot quite agree with him. (202) As, from the nature of population, an increase of labourers cannot be brought into the market, in consequence of a particular demand, till after the lapse of sixteen or eighteen years, and the conversion of revenue into capital may take place much more rapidly; a country is always liable to an increase of the funds for the maintenance of labour faster than the increase of population. But if, whenever this occurs, there may be a universal glut of commodities, how can it be maintained, as a general position, that capital is never redundant; and that because commodities may retain the same relative values, a glut can only be partial, not general? |

* Princ. of Polit. Econ. ch. xxi. p. [292–3]. 2d edit.

---

(202) p. 357. *In this remark I cannot quite agree with him*

I indeed say "that of commodities so limited in number there would be an universal glut." But could such a state of things exist? Would only[1] such a limited number of commodities be produced? Impossible, because the labourers would be glad to consume conveniences and luxuries if they could get them, and in the case supposed to promote the very object of the masters it would be their interest to produce

[1] 'only' is ins.

Another fundamental error into which the writers above- 358
mentioned and their followers appear to have fallen is, the not
taking into consideration the influence of so general and important
a principle in human nature, as indolence or the love of ease.

It has been supposed† that, if a certain number of farmers and
a certain number of manufacturers had been exchanging their
surplus food and clothing with each other, and their powers of
production were suddenly so increased that both parties could,
with the same labour, produce luxuries in addition to what they
had before obtained, there could be no sort of difficulty with
regard to demand, as part of the luxuries which the farmer produced would be exchanged against part of the luxuries produced
by the manufacturer; and the only result would be, the happy
one of both parties being better supplied and having more enjoyments.

But in this intercourse of mutual gratifications, two things are
taken for granted, which are the very points in dispute. It is
taken for granted that luxuries are always preferred to indolence,
and that the profits of each party are consumed as revenue. What
would be the effect of a desire to save under such circumstances,
shall be considered presently. The effect of a preference of indolence to luxuries would evidently be to occasion a want of
demand for the returns of the increased powers of production
supposed, and to throw labourers out | of employment. (203) 359
The cultivator, being now enabled to obtain the necessaries and
conveniences to which he had been accustomed, with less toil and

† Edinburgh Review, No. LXIV. p. 471.

---

the commodities for which their labourers had the will and
power to pay.

(203) p. 358. *But in this intercourse &c.*

Here again Mr. Malthus changes the proposition. We do
not say that indolence may not be preferred to luxuries.
I think it[2] may and therefore if the question was respecting
the motives to produce, there would be no difference between
us. But Mr. Malthus supposes the motive strong enough to

² 'it' replaces 'they'.

trouble, and his tastes for ribands, lace and velvet not being fully formed, might be very likely to indulge himself in indolence, and employ less labour on the land; while the manufacturer, finding his velvets rather heavy of sale, would be led to discontinue their manufacture, and to fall almost necessarily into the same indolent system as the farmer. That an efficient taste for luxuries, that is, such a taste as will properly stimulate industry, instead of being ready to appear at the moment it is required, is a plant of slow growth, the history of human society sufficiently shews; and that it is a most important error to take for granted, that mankind will produce and consume all that they have the power to produce and consume, and will never prefer indolence to the rewards of industry, will sufficiently appear from a slight review of some of the nations with which we are acquainted. But I shall have occasion for a review of this kind in the next section; and to this I refer the reader.

A third very serious error of the writers above referred to, and practically the most important of the three, consists in supposing that accumulation ensures demand; or that the consumption of the labourers employed by those whose object is to save, will create such an effectual demand for commodities as to encourage a continued increase of produce.

360   Mr. Ricardo observes, that "If 10,000 l. were | given to a man having 100,000 l. per annum, he would not lock it up in a chest, but would either increase his expenses by 10,000 l., employ it

---

produce the commodities, and then contends there would be no market for them after they were produced, as there would be no demand for them.

It is this proposition we deny. We do not say the commodities will under all circumstances be produced, but if they are produced we contend that there will always be some who will have the will and power to consume them, or in other words there will be a demand for them. Mr. Malthus brings forward a case of a society[1] not accumulating, preferring indolence to luxuries, not demanding labour, not

[1] 'society' replaces 'man'; and below 'their' replaces 'his'.

himself productively, or lend it to some other person for that purpose; in either case demand would be increased, although it would be for different objects. If he increased his expenses, his effectual demand might probably be for buildings, furniture, or some such enjoyment. If he employed his 10,000 *l*. productively, his effectual demand would be for food, clothing, and raw materials, which might set new labourers to work. But still it would be *demand*."*

Upon this principle it is supposed that if the richer portion of society were to forego their accustomed conveniences and luxuries with a view to accumulation, the only effect would be a direction of nearly the whole capital of the country to the production of necessaries, which would lead to a great increase of cultivation and population. But, without supposing an entire change in the usual motives to accumulation, this could not possibly happen. The usual motives for accumulation are, I conceive, either the future wealth and enjoyment of the individual who accumulates, or of those to whom he means to leave his property. And with these motives it could never answer to the possessor of land to employ nearly all the labour which the soil could support in cultivation; as by so doing he would necessarily destroy his neat rent, and render it impossible for him, without subsequently dismissing the greatest part of his workmen and | occasioning the   361
most dreadful distress, either to give himself the means of greater

* Princ. of Polit. Econ. chap. xxi. p. [291]. 2d edit.

---

cultivating their land as a proof of the evil effects which would result from the very opposite course; where capital would be accumulated, where activity would take place of indolence, where there would be the greatest demand for labour,—and where lands would be made the most productive; for all these are included in the meaning of the word accumulation. Men will prefer indolence to luxuries! luxuries will not then be produced, because they cannot be produced without labour, the opposite of indolence. If not produced they cannot want a market, there can be no glut of them.

enjoyment at a future distant period, or to transmit such means to his posterity. (204)

The very definition of fertile land is, land that will support a much greater number of persons than are necessary to cultivate it; and if the landlord, instead of spending this surplus in conveniences, luxuries and unproductive consumers, were to employ it in setting to work on the land as many labourers as his savings could support, it is quite obvious that, instead of being enriched, he would be impoverished by such a proceeding, both at first and in future. Nothing could justify such a conduct but a different motive for accumulation; that is, a desire to increase the population—not the love of wealth and enjoyment; and till such a change takes place in the passions and propensities of mankind, we may be quite sure that the landlords and cultivators will not go on employing labourers in this way. (205)

What then would happen? As soon as the landlords and cultivators found that they could not realize their increasing produce in some way which would give them a command of wealth in future, they would cease to employ more labour upon 362 the land;* and if the business of that part of the so-|ciety which was not engaged in raising raw produce, consisted merely in

* Theoretical writers in Political Economy, from the fear of appearing to attach too much importance to money, have perhaps been too apt to throw it out of their consideration in their reasonings. It is an abstract truth that we want commodities, not money. But, in reality, no commodity for which it is possible to | sell our goods at once, can be an adequate substitute for a circulating medium, and enable us in the same manner to provide for children, to purchase an estate, or to command labour and provisions a year or two hence. A circulating medium is absolutely necessary to any considerable saving; and even the manufacturer would get on

---

(204) p. 360. *Upon this principle it is supposed*

The question discussed here is as to the motives for accumulation—that is not the question in dispute, we have spoken only of the effects of accumulation. There is a very marked distinction between these two questions.

(205) p. 361. *The very definition*

In all this I agree but it is foreign to[1] the question.

[1] 'foreign to' replaces 'beside'.

preparing the other simple necessaries of life, the number required for this purpose being inconsiderable, the rest of those whom the soil could support would be thrown out of work. Having no means of legally demanding a portion of the raw produce, however plentiful it might be at first, they would gradually decrease in numbers; and the failure of effective demand for the produce of the soil would necessarily diminish cultivation, and throw a still greater number of persons out of employment. This action and reaction would thus go on till the balance of produce and consumption was restored in reference to the new tastes and habits which were established; and it is obvious that without an expenditure which will encourage commerce, manufactures, and unproductive consumers, or an Agrarian law calculated to change the usual motives for accumulation, the possessors of land would have no sufficient | stimulus to cultivate well; and a country such   363
as our own, which had been rich and populous, would, with such parsimonious habits, infallibly become poor, and comparatively unpeopled. (206)

The same kind of reasoning will obviously apply to the case noticed before. While the farmers were disposed to consume the luxuries produced by the manufacturers, and the manufacturers those produced by the farmers, all would go on smoothly; but

but slowly, if he were obliged to accumulate in kind all the wages of his workmen. We cannot therefore be surprized at his wanting money rather than other goods; and, in civilized countries, we may be quite sure that if the farmer or manufacturer cannot sell his products so as to give him a profit estimated in money, his industry will immediately slacken. The circulating medium bears so important a part in the distribution of wealth, and the encouragement of industry, that to set it aside in our reasonings may often lead us wrong.

---

(206) p. 363. *And a country such as our own which had been rich and populous*

That is to say there being no motive to parsimony and accumulation, with such limited wants, there would be no parsimony and accumulation, and therefore a country with such parsimonious habits, would become poor and comparatively unpeopled.

if either one or both of the parties were disposed to save with a
view of bettering their condition, and providing for their families
in future, the state of things would be very different. The farmer,
instead of indulging himself in ribands, lace, and velvets,* would
be disposed to be satisfied with more simple clothing, but by this
economy he would disable the manufacturer from purchasing the
same amount of his produce; (207) and for the returns of so much
labour employed upon the land, and all greatly increased in
productive power, there would evidently be no market. The
manufacturer, in like manner, instead of indulging himself in
sugar, grapes and tobacco, might be disposed to save with a view
to the future, but would be totally unable to do so, owing to the
parsimony of the farmers and the want of demand for manu-
factures.† |

364   An accumulation, to a certain extent, of common food and
common clothing might take place on both sides; but the amount
must necessarily be extremely confined. It would be of no sort
of use to the farmer to go on cultivating his land with a view

---

* Edinburgh Review, No. LXIV. p. 471.
† Of all the opinions advanced by able and ingenious men which I have
ever met with, the opinion of M. Say, which states that, *un produit consommé
ou détruit est un débouché fermé* (l. i. ch. | 15.) appears to me to be the most
directly opposed to just theory, and the most uniformly contradicted by
experience. Yet it directly follows from the new doctrine, that commodities
are to be considered only in their relation to each other,—not to the consumers. What, I would ask, would become of the demand for commodities,
if all consumption except bread and water were suspended for the next half
year? What an accumulation of commodities! Quels *débouchés!* What a
prodigious market would this event occasion!

---

(207) p. 363. *But by this economy he would disable the manu-
    facturer from purchasing the same amount of his produce*

True, but would not the manufacturer's labourers purchase it, or something that would be made instead of it?

(208) p. 365. *There would evidently therefore be a general want
    of demand, both for produce and population.*

The specific want would be for population. "It would be
of no sort of use," says Mr. Malthus, "to the farmer to go
on cultivating his land with a view merely to give food and

merely to give food and clothing to his labourers. He would be doing nothing either for himself or family, if he neither consumed the surplus of what they produced himself, nor could realize it in a shape that might be transmitted to his descendants. If he were a tenant, such additional care and labour would be entirely thrown away; and if he were a landlord, and were determined, without reference to markets, to cultivate his estate in such a way as to make it yield the greatest neat surplus with a view to the future, it is quite certain that the large portion of this surplus which was not required either for his own consumption, or to purchase clothing for himself and his labourers, would be absolutely wasted. If he did not choose to use it in the purchase of luxuries or the maintenance of unproductive labourers, it might as well be thrown into the sea. To save | it, that is to use it in   365
employing more labourers upon the land would, as I said before, be to impoverish both himself and his family.

It would be still more useless to the manufacturers to go on producing clothing beyond what was wanted by the agriculturists and themselves. Their numbers indeed would entirely depend upon the demands of the agriculturists, as they would have no means of purchasing subsistence, but in proportion as there was a reciprocal want of their manufactures. The population required to provide simple clothing for such a society with the assistance of good machinery would be inconsiderable, and would absorb but a small portion of the proper surplus of rich and well cultivated land. There would evidently therefore be a general want of demand, both for produce and population; (208) and while it is

---

clothing to his labourers, if he neither consumed the surplus of what they produced himself, *nor could realize it in a shape that might be transmitted to his descendants.*" What but a deficiency of population could prevent him from realizing it in a shape that might be transmitted to his descendants. I am a farmer possessed of a thousand quarters of corn, and my object is to accumulate a fortune for my family. With this corn I can employ a certain number of men on the land, which I rent, and after paying my rent the first year, realize

quite certain that an adequate passion for consumption may fully
keep up the proper proportion between supply and demand,
whatever may be the powers of production, it appears to be quite
as certain that a passion for accumulation must inevitably lead to
a supply of commodities beyond what the structure and habits of
such a society will permit to be consumed.†

But if this be so, surely it is a most important error to couple
366 the passion for expenditure and | the passion for accumulation
together, as if they were of the same nature; and to consider the
demand for the food and clothing of the labourer, who is to be
employed productively, as securing such a general demand for

† The reader must already know, that I do not share in the apprehensions
of Mr. Owen about the permanent effects of machinery. But I am decidedly
of opinion, that on this point he has the best of the argument with those
who think that accumulation ensures effective demand.

1300 qrs., or 300 qrs. profits. The next year if there be plenty
of labour in the market, I can employ a greater quantity
than before, and my 1300 quarters will become 1700, and
so from year to year I go on increasing the quantity till I have
made it ten thousand quarters, and if labour be at the same
price can command ten times the quantity of it that I could
when I commenced my operations.* Have I not then accumulated a fortune for my family? have I not given them
the power of employing labour in any way they please, and
of enjoying the fruits of it? And what is to prevent me

* Note. When I had the 1000 quarters the whole was
consumed within the year, and so at every subsequent period
—it is always consumed and reproduced. The word accumulation misleads many persons and sometimes I think it misleads Mr. Malthus. It is by many supposed that the corn is
accumulated, whereas to make such a capital productive and
to increase wealth it must be constantly consumed and reproduced.[1]

[1] This footnote is written on a loose slip of paper. Cp. above,
p. 231, n. 5.

commodities and such a rate of profits for the capital employed in producing them, as will adequately call forth the powers of the soil, and the ingenuity of man in procuring the greatest quantity both of raw and manufactured produce.

Perhaps it may be asked by those who have adopted Mr. Ricardo's view of profits,—what becomes of the division of that which is produced, when population is checked merely by want of demand? It is acknowledged that the powers of production have not begun to fail; yet, if labour produces largely and yet is ill paid, it will be said that profits must be high.

I have already stated in a former chapter, that the value of the materials of capital very frequently do not fall in proportion to the fall in the value of the produce of capital, and this alone will often account for low profits. But independently of this con-

---

doing so but an increase in the price of labour, or a diminution in the productive powers of the land? Of the latter we have already spoken; that necessarily limits all accumulation. Of the increase of the price of[1] labour I have also spoken; if population did not keep pace with capital, labour would rise, and the quantity of corn which I should annually obtain, instead of increasing in the proportions of 1000, 1300, 1700 and so on, might, by the sacrifices I should be obliged to make to obtain the labour required, increase my capital only in the proportions 1000, 1200, 1300 &c. &c. The precise reason then that my accumulation goes on at a slow pace, is that there is a scarcity of labour; how then can Mr. Malthus make it appear that "there will be a general want of demand both for produce, and population." Mr. Malthus may indeed say that my operations will increase the quantity of corn faster than it will be required to feed the actual population.

I grant it, but if my object be accumulation why should I produce corn particularly, why not any other commodity which may be in demand?

[1] 'the price of' is ins.

sideration, it is obvious that in the production of any other commodities than necessaries, the theory is perfectly simple. From
want of demand, such commodities may be very low in price,
and a large portion of the whole value produced may go to the
labourer, although in necessaries he may be ill paid, and his
wages, both with regard to the quantity of food which he receives
and the labour required to produce it, may be decidedly low. (209) |

367   If it be said, that on account of the large portion of the value
of manufactured produce which on this supposition is absorbed

---

(209) p. 366. *From want of demand such*

There is a great desire to accumulate capital. This is the
supposition. The consequences according to Mr. Malthus will
be, that the labourer "will be ill paid, and his wages both
with regard to the quantity of food, which he receives and
the labour required to produce it, may be decidedly low."

That is to say, I am desirous to accumulate capital from
my revenue—if I employ my revenue as capital I shall want
labour, the labourer can produce abundantly, and yet he will
be ill paid in the commodity which he produces, and to
crown the whole I shall not have large profits nor be able
to get rich.

(210) p. 367. *If it be said*

Under the circumstances supposed the labourer would
either get a large proportion of the corn produced on the
last land, or he would not get a large proportion of the goods
made by the manufacturer. The farmer on the last land is
a manufacturer of corn, he pays no rent. In whatever proportions between masters and workmen[1] the produce may
be divided in manufactures, in the same proportions will the
corn be divided, the produce of agriculture.[2]

Labour cannot be high in one and low in the other, nor
profits either. I think labour would be high in both—but

[1] Last four words are ins.   [2] Replaces 'will it be divided.'

by wages, it may be affirmed that the cause of the fall of profits is high wages, I should certainly protest against so manifest an abuse of words. The only justifiable ground for adopting a new term, or using an old one in a new sense, is, to convey more precise information to the reader; but to refer to high wages in this case, instead of to a fall of commodities, would be to proceed as if the specific intention of the writer were to keep his reader as much as possible in the dark as to the real state of things. (210)

In the production of necessaries however, it will be allowed,

---

Mr. Malthus protests against calling the labourers wages high because he is well remunerated in commodities. Now Mr. Malthus is the last man from whom this objection should come; from him we ought not to have heard that "this is using an old term in a new sense or adopting a new one, and would give the notion that it was the specific intention of the writer to keep his reader as much as possible in the dark as to the real state of things." I say Mr. Malthus should be the last man to do so because we are told by him that money wages are only nominal wages, that the real wages of labour consist in the abundance of necessaries and conveniences which those wages enable the labourer to command. In fact that it is these conveniences and necessaries which constitute real value, and every thing but them is nominal. I find then that in[3] the real value the labourer is well paid, and when I say that his wages are therefore high Mr. Malthus gravely tells me I use terms in a new sense which can have no other effect but to mislead and perplex.

Let it not be supposed that I adopt Mr. Malthus' measure on this occasion, wages are high both in his measure and in mine. The labourer will receive a large proportion of the produce, and therefore I say his wages are high. His wages will be high in money, unless money has varied in value, for

[3] 'in' replaces 'of'.

that the answer to the question is not quite so simple, yet still it may be made sufficiently clear. Mr. Ricardo acknowledges that there may be a limit to the employment of capital upon the land from the limited wants of society, independently of the exhaustion of the soil. In the case supposed, this limit must necessarily be very narrow, because there would be comparatively no population besides the agriculturists to make an effective demand for produce. Under such circumstances corn might be produced, which would lose the character and quality of wealth; (211) and, as I before observed in a note, all the parts of the same produce would not be of the same value. The actual labourers employed might be tolerably well fed, as is frequently the case, practically, in those

368 countries where the labourers are fed by the far-|mers,* but there would be little work or food for their grown up sons; and from varying markets and varying crops, the profits of the farmer might be the lowest at the very time when, according to the division of the produce, it ought to be the highest, that is, when there was the greatest proportionate excess of produce above what was paid

* In Norway and Sweden, particularly the former, where the agricultural labourer either lives in the farmer's family or has a portion of land assigned to him in lieu of wages, he is in general pretty well fed, although there is but little demand for labour, and considerable competition for such employment. In countries so circumstanced, (and there are many such all over the world,) it is perfectly futile to attempt to estimate profits by the excess of the produce above what is consumed in obtaining it, when for this excess there may be often little or no market. All evidently depends upon the exchangeable value of the disposable produce.

---

the same causes that operate to induce the farmer and manufacturer to give high wages in their commodities, must induce the holder of money to give high wages in his. No sufficient reason is advanced why money, corn, and manufactures shall alter in relative value.

(211) p. 367. *Under such circumstances*

Corn might be produced which would lose the character of wealth !—it would then be exceedingly cheap; cheap as compared with manufactures, cheap as compared with labour, and yet Mr. Malthus says that wages might be decidedly low. Low in what? not in corn his[1] real measure of value. See 357.[2]

[1] 'his' replaces 'the'.   [2] Note (202) above.

to the labourer. The wages of the labourer cannot sink below a certain point, but a part of the produce, from excess of supply, may for a time be absolutely useless, and permanently it may so fall from competition as to yield only the lowest profits.

I would observe further, that if in consequence of a diminished demand for corn, the cultivators were to withdraw their capitals so as better to proportion their supplies to the quantity that could be properly paid for; yet if they could not employ the capital they had withdrawn in any other way, which, according to the preceding supposition, they could not, it is certain that, though they might for a time make fair profits of the small | stock which they 369 still continued to employ in agriculture, the consequences to them as cultivators would be, to all intents and purposes, the same as if a general fall had taken place on all their capital. (212)

If, in the process of saving, all that was lost by the capitalist was gained by the labourer, the check to the progress of wealth would be but temporary, as stated by Mr. Ricardo; and the consequences need not be apprehended. But if the conversion of revenue into capital pushed beyond a certain point must, by diminishing the effectual demand for produce, throw the labouring classes out of employment, it is obvious that the adoption of parsimonious habits in too great a degree may be accompanied by the most distressing effects at first, and by a marked depression of wealth and population permanently. (213)

It is not, of course, meant to be stated that parsimony, or even

---

(212) p. 368. *I would observe further*

The farmers Mr. Malthus says could not employ their capitals in any other way than on the land—I contend that they would employ them another way[3] for in that way they would not be productive of profit. Either capitalists or labourers would have the right to demand the produce of labour. What they demanded would be produced.

(213) p. 369. *If in the process of saving*

Here the difference between Mr. Malthus and me is fairly stated. The reader must judge on which side truth lies.

[3] The remainder of the sentence is ins.

a temporary diminution of consumption,* is not often in the highest degree useful, and sometimes absolutely necessary to the progress of wealth. A state may certainly be ruined by extravagance; and a diminution of the actual expenditure may not only be necessary on this account, but when the capital of a country is deficient, compared with the demand for its products, a temporary economy of consumption is required, in order to provide that

370 supply of capital | which can alone furnish the means of an increased consumption in future. All that I mean to say is, that no nation can *possibly* grow rich by an accumulation of capital, arising from a permanent diminution of consumption; (215) because, such accumulation being greatly beyond what is wanted, in order to supply the effective demand for produce, a part of it would very soon lose both its use and its value, and cease to possess the character of wealth.

On the supposition indeed of a *given* consumption, the accumulation of capital beyond a certain point must appear at once to be perfectly futile. But, even taking into consideration the increased consumption likely to arise among the labouring classes from the abundance and cheapness of commodities, yet as this cheapness must be at the expense of profits, it is obvious that the limits to such an increase of capital from parsimony, as shall not

* Parsimony, or the conversion of revenue into capital, may take place without any diminution of consumption, if the revenue increases first. (214)

---

(214) p. 369 note. *Parsimony, or the conversion of revenue into capital may take place without any diminution of consumption*

I say it always take place without any diminution of consumption. Mr. Malthus clogs the proposition with a condition "if the revenue increases first." I do not understand what Mr. M. means:—if the revenue increases first. Before what?[1]

(215) p. 370. *All that I mean to say is*

By accumulation of capital from revenue is meant an in-

[1] Last three sentences, beginning 'Mr. Malthus clogs', are ins.

be attended by a very rapid diminution of the motive to accumulate, are very narrow, and may very easily be passed.

The laws which regulate the rate of profits and the progress of capital, bear a very striking and singular resemblance to the laws which regulate the rate of wages and the progress of population.

Mr. Ricardo has very clearly shewn that the rate of profits must diminish, and the progress of accumulation be finally stopped, under the most favourable circumstances, by the increasing difficulty of procuring the food of the labourer. I, in like manner, endeavoured to shew in my | Essay on the Principle 371 of Population that, under circumstances the most favourable to cultivation which could possibly be supposed to operate in the actual state of the earth, the wages of the labourer would become more scanty, and the progress of population be finally stopped by the increasing difficulty of procuring the means of subsistence.

But Mr. Ricardo has not been satisfied with proving the position just stated. He has not been satisfied with shewing that the difficulty of procuring the food of the labourer is the only *absolutely necessary* cause of the fall of profits, in which I am ready fully and entirely to agree with him: but he has gone on to say, that there is *no other cause* of the fall of profits in the actual state of things that has any degree of permanence. (216) In this latter statement he appears to me to have fallen into precisely the same kind of error as I should have fallen into, if, after having shewn

---

crease of consumption by productive labourers instead of by unproductive labourers. Consumption is as certain in one case as in the other, the difference is only[2] in the quantity of productions returned.

(216) p. 371. *But Mr. Ricardo has not been*

Have I not said that profits depend in all cases on wages, and I refer to my chapter on wages with confidence to shew that I have admitted other causes besides the difficulty of producing food, for high wages and for periods too of considerable duration.

[2] 'only' is ins.

that the unrestricted power of population was beyond comparison greater than the power of the earth to produce food under the most favourable circumstances possible, I had allowed that population could not be redundant unless the powers of the earth to keep up with the progress of population had been tried to the uttermost. But I all along said, that population might be redundant, and greatly redundant, compared with the demand for it and the actual means of supporting it, although it might most properly be considered as deficient, and greatly deficient, compared with the extent of territory, and the powers of such territory 372 to produce | additional means of subsistence; that, in such cases, notwithstanding the acknowledged deficiency of population, and the obvious desirableness of having it greatly increased, it was useless and foolish directly to encourage the birth of more children, as the effect of such encouragement, without a demand for labour and the means of paying it properly, could only be increased misery and mortality with little or no final increase of population.

Though Mr. Ricardo has taken a very different course, I think that the same kind of reasoning ought to be applied to the rate of profits and the progress of capital. Fully acknowledging that there is hardly a country in the four quarters of the globe where

---

(217) p. 372. *Though Mr. Ricardo*

Here again it is said that capital may be deficient, population abundant, and consequently wages low, and yet that the employment of capital will not be attended with[1] fair profits to the producer of commodities.

I should be glad if Mr. Malthus would tell us what he means by low wages in this case. I call wages in many cases[2] high, though nominally low, if they be paid to a man who will do little or no work.

If I had said that it was desirable to go on accumulating capital when it yielded no profits to the producer, there might have been some foundation for this charge. It is not

[1] Replaces 'and yet that capital will not afford'.   [2] 'in many cases' is ins

capital is not deficient, and in most of them very greatly deficient, compared with the territory and even the number of people; and fully allowing at the same time the extreme desirableness of an increase of capital, I should say that, where the demand for commodities was not such as to afford fair profits to the producer, and the capitalists were at a loss where and how to employ their capitals to advantage, the saving from revenue to add still more to these capitals would only tend prematurely to diminish the motive to accumulation, and still further to distress the capitalists, with little increase of a wholesome and effective capital. (217)

The first thing wanted in both these cases of deficient capital (218) and deficient population, is an effective demand for commodities, that is, a demand by those who are able and willing to pay an | adequate price for them; and though high profits are not followed   373 by an increase of capital, so certainly as high wages are by an increase of population, yet I believe that they are so followed more generally than they appear to be, because, in many countries, as I have before intimated, profits are often thought to be high, owing to the high interest of money, when they are really low; and because, universally, risk in employing capital has precisely the same effect in diminishing the motive to accumulate and the reward of accumulation, as low profits. At the same time it will

---

desirable to the capitalist, but it is never injurious to the country—it would be as reasonable to complain of too much production as of too much air, or water.[3] I say under such circumstances capital will not be accumulated.

(218) p. 372. *The first thing wanted*

What is here meant by deficient capital? If capital is deficient can any evil arise from accumulating capital by saving[4] from revenue;—from increasing the thing that is deficient?

Does not Mr. Malthus mean deficient profits on capital? With a deficient capital profits would be high.

[3] This sentence, beginning 'It is not', is ins.   [4] 'by saving' is ins.

be allowed that determined extravagance, and a determined indisposition to save, may keep profits permanently high. The most
powerful stimulants may, under peculiar circumstances, be re-
sisted; yet still it will not cease to be true that the natural and
legitimate encouragement to the increase of capital is that increase
of the power and will to save which is held out by high profits;
and under circumstances in any degree similar, such increase of
power and will to save must almost always be accompanied by
a proportionate increase of capital.

One of the most striking instances of the truth of this remark,
and a further proof of a singular resemblance in the laws that
regulate the increase of capital and of population, is to be found
in the rapidity with which the loss of capital is recovered during
a war which does not interrupt commerce. The loans to government convert capital into revenue, and increase demand at the
374 same time | that they at first diminish the means of supply.* The
necessary consequence must be an increase of profits. This
naturally increases both the power and the reward of accumulation; and if only the same habits of saving prevail among the
capitalists as before, the recovery of the lost stock must be rapid,
just for the same kind of reason that the recovery of population
is so rapid when, by some cause or other, it has been suddenly
destroyed.

It is now fully acknowledged that it would be a gross error in
the latter case, to imagine that, without the previous diminution
of the population, the same rate of increase would still have taken
place; because it is precisely the high wages occasioned by the
demand for labour, which produce the effect of so rapid an increase of population. On the same principle it appears to me as
gross an error to suppose that, without the previous loss of
capital occasioned by the expenditure in question, capital should
be as rapidly accumulated; because it is precisely the high profits

* Capital is withdrawn only from those employments where it can best
be spared. It is hardly ever withdrawn from agriculture. Nothing is more
common, as I have stated in the Chapter on Rent, than increased profits,
not only without any capital being withdrawn from the land, but under
a continual addition to it. Mr. Ricardo's assumption of constant prices
would make it absolutely impossible to account theoretically for things as
they are. If capital were considered as not within the pale of demand and
supply, the very familiar event of the rapid recovery of capital during a war
would be quite inexplicable.

of stock occasioned by the demand for commodities, and the consequent demand for | the means of producing them, which at 375 once give the power and the will to accumulate.

Though it may be allowed therefore that the laws which regulate the increase of capital are not quite so distinct as those which regulate the increase of population, yet they are certainly just of the same kind; and it is equally vain, with a view to the permanent increase of wealth, to continue converting revenue into capital, when there is no adequate demand for the products of such capital, as to continue encouraging marriage and the birth of children without a demand for labour and an increase of the funds for its maintenance. (219)

SECTION IV

Of the Fertility of the Soil considered as a Stimulus to the continued Increase of Wealth

[A fertile soil gives at once the greatest natural capability of wealth that a country can possess; and in speaking of the deficient wealth of a fertile country, it is meant to speak comparatively rather than positively.

---

(219) p. 375. *Though it may be allowed*

The[1] temptation to increase capital does not arise from the demand for its products, for that never fails; but from the profits arising from the sale of the products.—High wages may totally destroy those profits.

What Mr. Malthus calls a demand for capital I call high profits—capital is not bought and sold, it is borrowed at interest, and a great interest is given when profits are high. Mr. Malthus' language appears to me in this instance[2] "*new and unusual.*"[3]

[1] 'We all agree' is del. at the opening of the Note.
[2] 'in this instance' is ins.
[3] Cp. Malthus's p. 214–15, note; above, p. 194.

376   The settlers upon a very rich soil, with a vicious division of property at first, and unfavourably situated with regard to markets, might increase very slowly in wealth and population, and would be very likely to acquire indolent habits.]

377   It has been said, that those who have food and necessaries at their disposal will not be long in want of workmen, who will put them in possession of some of the objects most useful and desirable to them.* But this appears to be directly contradicted by experience. If the establishment, extension, and refinement of domestic manufactures were so easy a matter, our ancestors would not have remained for many hundred years so ill supplied with them; and been obliged to expend the main part of their raw produce in the support of idle retainers. They might be very

378   ready, when | they had the opportunity, to exchange their surplus raw produce for the foreign commodities with which they were acquainted, and which they had learnt to estimate. But it would be a very difficult thing, and very ill suited to their habits and degree of information, to employ their power of commanding labour in setting up manufactures on their own estates. Though the land might be rich, it might not suit the production of the materials most wanted; and the necessary machinery, the necessary skill in using it, and the necessary intelligence and activity of superintendence, would all unavoidably be deficient at first, and under the circumstances supposed, must be of very slow growth; so that after those ruder and more indispensable articles were supplied, which are always wanted and produced in an early stage of society, it is natural enough that a great lord should prefer distinguishing himself by a few splendid foreign com-

* Ricardo's Princ. of Polit. Econ. ch. xxi. p. [292]. 2d. edit.

---

(220) p. 377. *It has been said*

The observation was applied to this country and not to countries only half civilized.

(221) p. 378–9. *It is certainly true however*

If the labourers wages were high he might do as he pleased —he might prefer indolence or luxuries—but if his wages

modities, if he could get them, and a great number of retainers, than by a large quantity of clumsy manufactures, which involved great trouble of superintendance. (220)

It is certainly true, however, taking as an instance an individual workman, and supposing him to possess a given degree of industry and skill, that the less time he is employed in procuring food, the more time will he be able to devote to the procuring of conveniences and luxuries; but to apply this truth to whole nations, and to infer that the greater is the facility of procuring food, the more abundantly will the people be supplied with con-|veniences 379 and luxuries would be one among the many rash and false conclusions which are often made from the want of due attention to the change which the application of a proposition may make in the premises on which it rests. In the present case, all depends upon the supposition of a given degree of industry and skill, and the means of employing them. But if, after the necessaries of life were obtained, the workman should consider indolence as a greater luxury than those which he was likely to procure by further labour, the proposition would at once cease to be true. And as a matter of fact, confirmed by all the accounts we have of nations, in the different stages of their progress, it must be allowed that this choice seems to be very general in the early periods of society, and by no means uncommon in the most improved states. (221)

Few indeed and scanty would be the portion of conveniences and luxuries found in society, if those who are the main instruments of their production had no stronger motives for their exertions than the desire of enjoying them. It is the want of *necessaries* which mainly stimulates the labouring classes to produce luxuries;

---

were low, and profits high,[1] he has not a choice, he must produce conveniences and luxuries for his master or starve; and their amount and quality would depend on the facility, and time, which might be required to produce them.

[1] The remainder of the Note replaces: 'he must produce conveniences and luxuries for his master; if he can with great facility, and in a little time, produce the necessaries which he may require.'

and were this stimulus removed or greatly weakened, so that the necessaries of life could be obtained with very little labour, instead of more time being devoted to the production of conveniences, there is every reason to think that less time would be so devoted. (222)

380 At an early period of cultivation, when only rich soils are worked, as the quantity of corn is the | greatest, compared with the quantity of labour required to produce it, we ought always to find a small portion of the population engaged in agriculture, and a large portion engaged in administering to the other wants of the society. And there can be little doubt that this is the state of things which we really should see, were it true, that if the means of maintaining labour be found, there can be no difficulty in making it produce objects of adequate value; or that when food can be obtained with facility, more time will be devoted to the production of conveniences and luxuries. But in examining the state of unimproved countries, what do we really see?—almost invariably, a much larger proportion of the whole people employed on the land than in those countries where the increase of population has occasioned the necessity of resorting to poor soils; and less time instead of more time devoted to the production of conveniences and luxuries. (223)

---

(222) p. 379. *Few indeed and scanty*

Under the present circumstances of England, would not Mr. Malthus think that the situation of the labourer would be improved, if he could produce more necessaries in the same time, and with the same labour. Would he be alarmed at the love of indolence which would be the consequence?

(223) p. 380. *But in examining the state of unimproved countries*

An argument concerning the skill, state and power of the most improved country is answered by a reference to the state of unimproved countries, where they are without skill, and without even a knowledge of the comforts of the commonest conveniences. Is it true that *all* these countries ob-

Of the great landed nations of Europe, and indeed of the world, England, with only one or two exceptions, is supposed to have pushed its cultivation the farthest; and though the natural qualities of its whole soil by no means stand very high in the scale of comparative richness, there is a smaller proportion of the people employed in agriculture, and a greater proportion employed in the production of conveniences and luxuries, or living on monied incomes, than in any other agricultural country of the world. According to a calculation of Susmilch, in which he enumerates the different proportions | of people in different states, who live 381 in towns, and are not employed in agriculture, the highest is that of seven to three, or seven people living in the country to three living in the towns:* whereas in England, the proportion of those engaged in agriculture, compared with the rest of the population, is less than as two to three.†

This is a very extraordinary fact, and affords a striking proof how very dangerous it is, in political economy, to draw conclusions from the physical quality of the materials which are acted

---

* Susmilch, vol. iii. p. 60. Essay on Population, vol. i. p. 459. edit. 5th. In foreign states very few persons live in the country who are not engaged in agriculture; but it is not so in England.
† Population Abstracts, 1811.

---

tain food with great facility? If they have not our improvements, they are without some of our means of producing, with a small quantity of labour. Mr. Malthus says there is [1] a smaller proportion of the people employed in Agriculture in England than elsewhere. This is very possible, and very satisfactory if true, but we must not leave out of consideration the greater number of horses and cattle employed on the land in England; they come under the denomination of labourers, for they are substituted for them, and are supported by provisions like them.*

[*] To this must be added the superior [2] machinery employed in England in Agriculture.

[1] probably' is del. here.   [2] 'the superior' is ins.

upon, without reference to the moral as well as physical qualities of the agents. (224)

It is undoubtedly a physical quality of very rich land, if worked by people possessing a given degree of industry and skill, to yield a large quantity of produce, compared with the number of hands employed; but, if the facility of production which rich land gives has the effect, under certain circumstances, of preventing the growth of industry and skill, the land may become practically less productive, compared with the number of persons employed upon it, than if it were not distinguished for its richness.

Upon the same principle, the man who can procure the necessary food for his family, by two days labour in the week, has the physical power of working much longer to procure conveniences |

---

(224) p. 381. *This is a very extraordinary fact*

Whoever did draw any conclusions from the physical quality of the soil[1], without any consideration of its productiveness, in proportion to the labour employed upon it? Mr. Malthus bestows a great deal of time in endeavoring to refute what has never been advanced. He supposes me to have said that profits in all countries depend upon the fertility of the land last taken into cultivation, and he has been at great pains to shew this opinion unfounded.—I never entertained any such opinion, nor do not know who does.

Profits in every country are in proportion[2] to the productiveness of labour on the last land cultivated,—provided[3] always that the labourers in each are contented with the same quantity of necessaries; but as this is not the case, as from various cause the recompence for labour varies, profits depend upon the proportion of the whole produce, on the land last cultivated, which must be given to obtain it.

(225) p. 382. *Among the crowd of countries*

Here again Mr. Malthus gives an elaborate proof of what

---

[1] Replaces 'the state of the soil'.   [3] Replaces 'allowing'.
[2] 'to wages' ins. here, then del.

and luxuries, than the man who must employ four days in pro-   382
curing food; but if the facility of getting food creates habits of
indolence, this indolence may make him prefer the luxury of doing
little or nothing, to the luxury of possessing conveniences and
comforts; and in this case, he may devote less time to the working
for conveniences and comforts, and be more scantily provided
with them than if he had been obliged to employ more industry
in procuring food.

Among the crowd of countries which tend more or less to
illustrate and confirm by their present state the truth of these
positions, none perhaps will do it more strikingly than the Spanish
dominions in America, of which M. Humboldt has lately given
so valuable an account. (225)

---

is not disputed. Countries do now always[4] produce in proportion to their means of producing! Granted. But what
inference will Mr. Malthus draw from this?—will he say he
is[5] an enemy to giving new facilities to the production of
corn in England, because it will make the people indolent
—they will make them[6] lose their taste for luxuries, and will
induce them to be contented with the commonest fare? He
must mean this or his argument points at nothing. See the
effects of cheap means of production in South America, look
at the indolent race of inhabitants in that country. Why are
we to look to them, but as an example and a warning, if we
listen to the dangerous projects of those who would make
corn cheap in this country? My great complaint against
Mr. Malthus is that he is constantly departing from the
question in dispute. He first begins by disputing the position
whether certain measures will make corn cheap, but before
the end of the argument, he is endeavoring to prove that
it would not be expedient that it should be cheap, on account

4 'always' is ins.
5 Replaces 'I am'.

6 'make them' here, and 'induce
them to' in the following line,
are ins.

Speaking of the different plants which are cultivated in New Spain, he says of the banana, "Je doute qu'il existe une autre plante sur le globe qui, sur un si petit espace de terrain, puisse produire une masse de substance nourrissante aussi considérable."*

He calculates in another place more particularly, that "dans un pays éminemment fertile un demi hectare, ou un arpent légal cultivé en bananes de la grande espèce, peut nourrir plus de cinquantes individus, tandis qu'en Europe le même arpent ne donneroit par an, en supposant le huitième grain, que 576 kilogrammes de farine de froment, quantité qui n'est pas suffisante pour la subsistance de deux individus: aussi rien ne frappe plus 383 l'Européen | récemment arrivé dans la zone torride que l'extrême petitisse des terrains cultivés autour d'une cabane qui renferme une famille nombreuse d'indigènes."†

[The produce of the banana, compared with the labour employed upon it, is so prodigious, that the inhabitants of the districts where it prevails will never, it is said, be roused from their excessive indolence till the cultivation of it has been prohibited.

384   Though the labouring classes have such ample time to work for conveniences and comforts, they are almost destitute of them; and from improvident habits, suffer at times even for want of food.

385   This poverty is not confined to the lower regions of New Spain. In ascending the Cordilleras to the finest climates in the world, the state of things is not very different.

Maize, which is the chief food of the people on the Cordilleras, very greatly exceeds in productiveness the grains of Europe.

* Essai Politique sur la Nouvelle Espagne, tom. iii. l. iv. c. ix. p. 28.
† Nouvelle Espagne, tom. iii. l. iv. c. ix. p. 36.

---

of the moral effects which it would have on the people. These are two very distinct propositions.

It has been well said by M. Say that it is not the province of the Political Economist to advise:[1]—he is to tell you how you may become rich, but he is not to advise you to prefer riches to indolence, or indolence to riches.

[1] 'Hé, monsieur, une bonne conseille peu'; *Lettres à M. Malthus*, 1820, p. 85 and cp. p. 72. économie politique, je le répète,

Even in the town of Mexico subsistence may be obtained by 386
one or two days' labour in the week, yet the people are wretchedly
poor.

The same poverty prevails in the country districts; and famines, 387
from the failure of the crops of maize, combined with the indolence and improvidence of the people, are frequent, and are
mentioned by Humboldt as the most destructive check to population.

Such habits of indolence and improvidence necessarily act as 388
formidable obstacles in the way of a rapid increase of wealth and
population.]

That the indolence of the natives is greatly aggravated by their
political situation, cannot for a moment be doubted; but that,
in spite of this situation, it yields in a great measure to the usual
excitements is sufficiently proved by the rapid cultivation which
takes place in the neighbourhood of a new mine, where an
animated and effective demand is created for labour and produce.
"Bientôt le besoin réveille l'industrie; on commence à labourer
le sol dans les ravins, et sur les pentes des montagnes voisines, par
tout où le roc est couvert de terreau: des fermes s'établissent dans
le voisi-|nage de la mine: la cherté des vivres, le prix considérable 389
auquel la concurrence des acheteurs maintient tous les produits
de l'agriculture, dédommagent le cultivateur des privations aux-
quelles l'expose la vie pénible des montagnes."‡ (226)

When these are the effects of a really brisk demand for produce
and labour, we cannot be at a loss for the main cause of the slow
cultivation which has taken place over the greatest part of the
country. Except in the neighbourhood of the mines and near the

‡ Nouvelle Espagne, tom. iii. liv. iv. c. ix. p. 12.

---

(226) p. 388. *That the indolence of the natives*

This fact respecting the mine shews how little the whole
argument about South America is applicable to England.
Indeed it appears to me surprising that it should be brought
forward in justification of the opinion that both capital and
people, may be at the same time redundant in England.

Because I said, in reference to this country, and countries
resembling it, "If *I* had food and necessaries at *my* dis-

great towns, the effective demand for produce is not such as to induce the great proprietors to bring their immense tracts of land properly into cultivation: and the population, which, as we have seen, presses hard against the limits of subsistence, evidently exceeds in general the demand for labour, or the number of persons which the country can employ with regularity and constancy in the actual state of its agriculture and manufactures. (227)

In the midst of an abundance of fertile land, it appears that the natives are often very scantily supplied with it. They would gladly cultivate portions of the extensive districts held by the great proprietors, and could not fail of thus deriving an ample subsistence for themselves and families; but in the actual state of the demand for produce in many parts of the country, and in the

---

posal *I* should not be long in want of workmen who would put me in possession of some of the objects most useful or most desirable to me," Mr. Malthus has put the proposition in the most general form and says "it has been said that those who have food and necessaries at their disposal will not be long in want of men &c. &c."[1] He then refers to South America—endeavors to shew that there are persons there who have food and necessaries at their command but who do not employ workmen 1st because they do not want conveniences and luxuries, 2dly because the workmen have no skill in making them if the want existed, and besides are an indolent race, stimulated to work with great difficulty and 3dly because the commodity which can be most easily produced has so very confined a market, that there is a perpetual glut of it. Much of this statement respecting South America might be answered—the whole might be shewn to be perfectly consistent with the principles which it is brought forward to overturn, but it is so little applicable to countries with a dense population[2] abounding in capital, skill, com-

[1] Malthus's p. 377; above, p. 332.   [2] Last four words are ins.

actual state of the ignorance and indolence of the natives, such tenants might not be able to pay a rent equal to | what the land 390 would yield in its uncultivated state, and in this case they would seldom be allowed to intrude upon such domains; and thus lands which might be made capable of supporting thousands of people, may be left to support a few hundreds of cattle.

Speaking of a part of the Intendency of Vera Cruz, Humboldt says, "Aujourd'hui des espaces de plusieurs lieues carrées sont occupés par deux ou trois cabanes, autour desquelles errent des bœufs à demi-sauvages. Un petit nombre de familles puissantes, et qui vivent sur le plateau central, possèdent la plus grande partie du littoral des Intendances de Vera Cruz, et de San Luis Potosi. Aucune loi agraire ne force ces riches propriétaires de vendre

---

merce, and manufacturing industry, and with tastes for every enjoyment that nature, art or science will procure, that it does not require a serious examination.

(227) p. 389. *Except in the neighbourhood*

To me there appears a direct contradiction in this passage. "The effective demand for produce is not such as to induce the great proprietors to bring their immense tracts of land properly into cultivation." Can nothing be obtained for produce? Cannot labour be had in exchange for it? and may not all riches be obtained by means of labour? Mr. Malthus shall answer these questions. "The population presses hard against the limits of subsistence, and evidently exceeds in general the demand for labour, or the number of persons which the country can employ with regularity and constancy in the actual state of its agriculture." Here is a country the amount of the fertility of which is almost fabulous and incredible, with a numerous people pressing hard against the means of subsistence—willing to exchange their labour for produce, and yet there is so little demand for produce as not to afford a motive for the cultivation of their lands.

leurs majorats, s'ils persistent à ne pas vouloir défricher eux-
mêmes des terres immenses qui en dépendent."*

Among proprietors of this description, caprice and indolence
might often prevent them from cultivating their lands. (228)
Generally, however, it might be expected, that these tendencies
would yield, at least in a considerable degree, to the more steady
influence of self-interest. But a vicious division of territory
prevents the motive of interest from operating so strongly as it
ought to do in the extension of cultivation. Without sufficient
foreign commerce to give value to the raw produce of the land;
and before the general introduction of manufactures had opened
391 channels | for domestic industry, the demand of the great pro-
prietors for labour would be very soon supplied; and beyond
this, the labouring classes would have nothing to give them for
the use of their lands. Though the landholders might have ample
power to support an extended population on their estates, the
very slender increase of enjoyments, if any, which they might
derive from it, would rarely be sufficient to overcome their
natural indolence, or overbalance the possible inconveniences or
trouble that might attend the proceeding. Of that encouragement
to the increase of population, which arises from the division and
sub-division of land as new families are brought into being, the
country is deprived by the original state of property, and the
feudal customs and habits which it necessarily tends to generate.
And under these circumstances, if a comparative deficiency of

* Tom. ii. l. iii. c. viii. p. 342.

---

(228) p. 390. *Among proprietors of this description, caprice
and indolence might often prevent them from cultivating
their lands*

If so it is not to a want of demand for produce that we
must attribute their not being cultivated. "A vicious division
of territory prevents the motive of interest from operating so
strongly as it ought to do in the extension of cultivation."
This I can understand,—but this is not the case in Europe.
Mr. Malthus said before that the motive of interest did not
exist because there was no demand for produce.

commerce and manufactures, which great inequality of property tends rather to perpetuate than to correct, prevents the growth of that demand for labour and produce, which can alone remedy the discouragement to population occasioned by this inequality, it is obvious that Spanish America may remain for ages thinly peopled and poor, compared with her natural resources.

And so, in fact, she has remained. For though the increase of population and wealth has been considerable, particularly of late years, since the trade with the mother-country has been more open, yet altogether it has been far short of what it would have been, even under a Spanish govern-|ment, if the riches of the soil 392 had been called forth by a better division of landed property, or a greater and more constant demand for raw produce.

Humboldt observes that "Les personnes qui ont réfléchi sérieusement sur la richesse du sol Mexicain savent que, par le moyen d'une culture plus soignée, et sans supposer des travaux extraordinaires pour l'irrigation des champs, la portion de terrain déjà défriché pourroit fournir de la subsistance pour une population huit à dix fois plus nombreuse." He then adds, very justly, "Si les plaines fertiles d'Atalisco, de Cholula et de Puebla ne produisent pas des récoltes plus abondantes, la cause principale doit être cherchée dans le manque des consommateurs, et dans les entraves que les inégalités du sol opposent au commerce intérieur des grains, surtout à leur transport vers les côtes qui sont baignées par la mer des Antilles."† (229) In the actual state of these dis-

† Tom. iii. l. iv. c. ix. p. 89.

---

(229) p. 392. *Humboldt observes*

Mr. Malthus says "He then adds very justly 'Si les plaines fertiles d'Atalisco, de Cholula et de Puebla ne produisent pas des récoltes plus abondantes, la cause principale doit être cherchée dans le manque des consommateurs.'" Can it be true that in such a country there is a scanty demand for labour, and a people pressing against the limits of subsistence? See page 389.[1]

[1] Note (227) above.

tricts, the main and immediate cause which retards their cultivation is indeed the want of consumers, that is, the want of power to sell the produce at such a price as will at once encourage good cultivation, and enable the farmers to give the landlords something that they want, for the use of their land. And nothing is so likely to prevent this price from being obtained, as any obstacles natural or artificial to internal and external commerce.

[That it is the want of demand rather than the want of capital which retards the progress of wealth in New Spain, may be inferred from the abundance of capital noticed by Humboldt.

393   Altogether, the state of New Spain strongly illustrates the position, that fertility of soil alone is not an adequate stimulus to the increase of wealth.

394   A similar conclusion may be drawn from the state of Ireland.]

The cultivation of the potatoe, and its adoption as the general food of the lower classes of the people in Ireland, has rendered the

---

(230) p. 394. *The prominent feature of Ireland is, the power which it possesses and actually exercises, of supporting a much greater population than it can employ, and the natural and necessary effect of this state of things, is the very general prevalence of habits of indolence.*

That Ireland supports a greater population than she employs may be true, but she does not support a greater than she has the means of employing. Whoever eats, and is in health, may be made to work if he has no other means of obtaining food. From Mr. Malthus' statement it appears that very little work is done in Ireland, although a great population is supported,—in that country then for the quantity of labour performed a great price is paid—the capitalist has only a moderate[1] proportion of the produce, and therefore according to my theory profits are not very high,—they are not high[2] in proportion to the cheapness of food. Mr. Malthus denies this deduction. He contends that landlords

[1] Replaces 'small'.   [2] 'high' is ins.

land and labour necessary to maintain a family, unusually small, compared with most of the countries of Europe. The consequence of this facility of production, unaccompanied by such a train of fortunate circumstances as would give it full effect in the increase of wealth, is a state of things resembling, in many respects, countries less advanced in civilization and improvement.

The prominent feature of Ireland is, the power which it possesses and actually exercises, of supporting a much greater population than it can employ, and the natural and necessary effect of this state of things, is the very general prevalence of habits of indolence. The landed proprietors and principal tenants being possessed of food and necessaries, or at least of the ready means of procuring them, have found workmen in abundance at their command; but these workmen not finding sufficient employment in the farms on which they had settled, have rarely been able to put their landlords in possession of the objects "most useful and most desirable" to them. (230)

---

and capitalists are the possessors of a great quantity of food and necessaries, and yet have not been able to obtain the objects most useful and desirable to them in return. Profits do not depend upon quantity, but upon proportions. Why have not capitalists been able to obtain the objects most useful and desirable to them with the quantity of food and necessaries they possess? because in the actual state of skill and industry in Ireland a great quantity of this food, or what is the same thing the value of a great quantity must be paid for the result of a very moderate degree of skill and industry; and secondly, because the peculiar food and necessaries of Ireland are not of great [3] value in other countries, and therefore in those countries they will not exchange for any great quantity of the skill and industry of other countries. I have not [4] said that food and clothing which will support 100 men will procure the means of obtaining the same quantity of things useful and desirable in England, Ireland or South

[3] 'great' is ins.   [4] 'not' is ins.

Sometimes, indeed, from the competition for land occasioned bv an overflowing population, very high rents have been given for small portions of ground fit for the growth of potatoes; but as the power of paying such rents must depend, in a considerable 395 degree, upon the | power of getting work, the number of families upon an estate, who can pay high money rents, must have an obvious limit. This limit, there is reason to believe, has been often found in the inability of the Irish coʰar to pay the rent which he had contracted for; and it is generally understood that the most intelligent Irish landlords, influenced both by motives of humanitv and interest, are now endeavouring to check the progress of that redundant population upon their estates, which, while it generates an excessive degree of poverty and misery as well as indolence, seldom makes up to the employer, in the lowness of wages, for the additional number of hands which he is obliged to hire, or call upon for their appointed service in labour. He is now generally aware that a smaller number of more industrious labourers would enable him to raise a larger produce for the consumption of towns and manufacturers, and at the same time that they would thus contribute more largely to the general wealth of the country, would be in a more happy condition themselves, and enable him to derive a larger and more certain rent from his estates. It may fairly be said therefore, that the possessors

---

America, but I have said that they will procure things useful and desirable according to the state of skill and industry in the respective countries. If there be no skill in the country, and the commodities produced have no value in other countries, there will be little motive to accumulate capital or if there be skill in the country, and it be very rare and costly, that also may be a[1] reason why capital will not be rapidly accumulated. But what have all these suppositions to do with England, the country of which I was particularly speaking?

Is there any want of skill and industry here? Are there no objects useful and desirable to be procured by those who

[1] 'motive' is del. here.

of food and necessaries in Ireland have not been able to obtain the objects most useful and desirable to them in return.

The indolence of the country-labourers in Ireland has been universally remarked.

[The time which the Irish labourer has to spare does not, as appears from experience, put him in possession of an ample quantity of conveniences and luxuries.

The Irish peasant has not been exposed to the usual excitements 396 which create industry, owing to the abundance of people compared with the work to be done.

If the labour of the Irish peasant, whether in the house 397 or in the field, were always in demand, his habits might soon change.]

It may be said, perhaps, that it is capital alone which is wanted 398 in Ireland, and that if this want were supplied, all her people might be easily employed. That one of the great wants of Ireland is capital will be readily allowed; but I conceive it would be a very great mistake to suppose that the importation of a large quantity of capital, if it could be effected, would at once accomplish the object required, and create a quantity of wealth proportioned to the labour which seems ready to be employed in its production. The amount of capital which could be laid out in Ireland in preparing goods for foreign sale, must evidently depend

---

have the means of commanding labour? What limits the ability of those possessed of the means of commanding labour of obtaining these useful and desirable objects, but the price of labour? If it be high, the labourers will have the means of getting a part of these luxuries, if it be low, almost the whole will go to those who have the means of employing them.

In the case of Ireland Mr. Malthus does not estimate its wealth by its power of commanding labour, his standard measure of value, but by the things useful and desirable which this power will enable it to obtain.

What is the use of a measure of value if we never estimate value by it?

upon the state of foreign markets; and the amount that could be employed in domestic manufactures, must as evidently depend upon the domestic demand. (231) An attempt to force a foreign market by means of capital, must necessarily occasion a premature fall of profits, and might, after great losses, be quite ineffectual; and with regard to the domestic demand, while the habits of the great mass of the people are such as they are at present, it must be quite inadequate to take off the products of any considerable mass of new capital. In a country, where the necessary food is obtained with so little labour, and the population is still equal or nearly equal to the produce, it is perhaps impossible that the time not devoted to the produc-|tion of food should create a proportionate quantity of wealth, without a very decided taste for conveniences and luxuries among the lower classes of society, and such a power of purchasing as would occasion an effective demand for them. But it is well known, that the taste of the Irish peasant for articles of this description is yet to be formed. His wants are few, and these wants he is in the habit of supplying principally at home. Owing to the cheapness of the potatoe, which forms the principal food of the lower classes of the people, his money wages are low; and the portion which remains, after providing absolute necessaries, will go but a very little way in the purchase of conveniences. All these circumstances are most unfavourable to the increase of wealth derived from manufactures destined for home consumption. But the tastes and habits of a

---

(231) p. 398. *The amount of capital which could be laid out in Ireland &c. &c.*

If Ireland had equal skill in working up commodities with other countries, and her labour was really, and not nominally low; if a great deal of work could be procured for a very little money, what limit could there be to sales in foreign markets. If she sold would she not also purchase. Might she not successfully compete with all other countries in the goodness and cheapness of her goods? If the mass of the people would but work there would not be any deficiency of home demand. The want of demand only arises from a want of means. As soon as the results of labour were ob-

large body of people are extremely slow in changing; and in the mean time the application of capital in larger quantities than was suited to the progress of the change, would certainly fail to yield such profits as would encourage its continued accumulation and application in the same way. In general it may be said that demand is quite as necessary to the increase of capital as the increase of capital is to demand. They mutually act upon and encourage each other, and neither of them can proceed with vigour if the other be left far behind.

[In general, the checks which Irish manufactures and productions have received, have been more owing to want of demand than want of capital. Demand has generally produced capital, though capital has sometimes failed to produce demand.

Ireland might be much richer than England if her redundant 400 population were employed in commerce and manufactures; but to accomplish this object, a change of habits would be more effectual than a premature supply of capital.]

The state of Ireland then may be said to lead to nearly the same 401 conclusions as that of New Spain, and to shew—

That the power of supporting labour may often exist to a much greater extent than the will; (232)

That the necessity of employing only a small portion of time in producing food does not always occasion the employment of a greater portion of time in procuring conveniences and luxuries; (233)

---

tained, there would be not only the desire[1] but the means also of consuming them.

(232) p. 401. *That the power of supporting labour may often exist to a much greater extent than the will*

This must refer to the capitalist and not to the labourer, and is not I think applicable to Ireland. Is there any capital there unemployed?

(233) p. 401. *That the necessity &c. &c.*

Certainly not, if the choice be in the power of the labourers, in which case their wages must be high, or rather they must

[1] Replaces 'there would be a corresponding desire to'.

That the deficiency of wealth in a fertile country may be more owing to want of demand than to want of capital; (234)

And, in general, that the fertility of the soil alone is not an adequate stimulus to the permanent increase of wealth. (235)

SECTION V

Of Inventions to abridge Labour, considered as a Stimulus to the continued Increase of Wealth

[Inventions to save manual labour are generally called forth by the wants of mankind in the progress of improvement; and therefore seldom much exceed those wants.

402   But the same laws apply to machinery as to fertile land: a full use cannot be made of either without an adequate market.

The natural tendency of machinery is, by cheapening the commodity produced, so to extend the market for it, as to increase its whole value. This has been strikingly the case in the cotton trade; and when machinery has this effect, its enriching power is prodigious.]

403   When however the commodity to which machinery is applied is not of such a nature, that its consumption can extend with its cheapness, the increase of wealth derived from it is neither so great nor so certain. Still however it may be highly beneficial; but the extent of this benefit depends upon a contingency. Let us

---

be paid well for their work. As certainly yes, if labour be low, and the choice be in the power of the capitalists. To suppose otherwise is to suppose that much of the[1] capital will be unemployed.

(234) p. 401. *That the deficiency of wealth &c. &c.*

True if wages be really high, not true if they be low.

(235) p. 401. *And, in general, &c. &c.*

True if the people be indolent, be well paid, and be easily satisfied.

[1] 'much of the' is ins.

suppose a number of capitalists in the habit of employing 20,000*l.*
each in a manufacture of limited consumption, and that machines
were introduced which, by the saving of labour, would enable
them to supply the actual demand for the commodity with capitals
of ten thousand pounds each, instead of twenty. There would, in
this case, be a certain number of ten thousand pounds, and the
men employed by these capitals, thrown out of employment. On
the other hand, there would be a portion of revenue set free for
the purchase of fresh commodities; and this demand would
undoubtedly be of the greatest advantage in encouraging the |
employment of the vacant capitals in other directions. At the   404
same time it must be recollected that this demand is not a new
one, and, even when fully supplied. could only replace the
diminution of capital and profits in one department, occasioned
by the employment of so many ten thousands, instead of twenty
thousands. But in withdrawing capital from one employment
and placing it in another, there is almost always a considerable
loss. Even if the whole of the remainder were directly employed,
it would be less in amount. Though it might yield a greater produce, it would not command the same quantity of labour as
before; and, unless more menial servants were used, many persons
would be thrown out of work; and thus the power of the whole
capital to command the same quantity of labour would evidently
depend upon the contingency of the vacant capitals being withdrawn undiminished from their old occupations, and finding
immediately equivalent employment in others. (236)

---

(236) p. 404. *But in withdrawing capital &c.*

It is true that in withdrawing capital from one employment to place it [in][2] another, there is generally a considerable loss; but in the case supposed, it can never be equal to
the advantage resulting from the discovery of the machine.
The individual may suffer but the community benefits.[3]

It is true that if the whole capital of the country were

[2] 'place it' is ins.; 'in' is omitted
by an oversight.
[3] An unfinished passage is del.
here: 'Suppose that I employed
a hundred horses with 10 heavy
waggons to convey goods from
London to Birmingham, and that
each waggon was worth £100,
and the 10 £1000. Suppose now
that an improvement'.

If, in order to try the principle, we were to push it farther, and
to suppose that, without any extension of the foreign market for
our goods, we could by means of machinery obtain all the commodities at present in use, with one third of the labour now

valued either in money or in labour it would be worth less
after the improvement than before, but because the capital[1]
estimated at the current price of labour, is of less value, we
must not therefore infer, with Mr. Malthus, that it will really
employ less labour. The power of employing labour does
not depend upon the value of the capital, but depends
specifically upon the annual quantity of produce which it
will yield. I cannot therefore agree with Mr. Malthus that
"Though it might yield a greater produce, it would not
command the same quantity of labour as before; and unless
more menial servants were used many persons would be
thrown out of work; and thus the power of the whole
capital to command the same quantity of labour would
evidently depend upon the contingency of the vacant capitals
being withdrawn undiminished from their old occupations,
and finding immediately equivalent employment in others."
I understand Mr. Malthus to say this, suppose I had £20000
in a cotton manufactory and that cotton goods were furnished
so cheap by improved machinery that I should think it
expedient to quit the trade, there would not be so much
labour as before employed, unless I could sell all my property
in the cotton mill, and realize my £20000 in money, and
then find an equivalent employment for it in some other
concern.

Of this £20000—£10000 might consist of machinery, and
which it is possible might be utterly useless in any other
occupation. It would therefore not be practicable to with-

[1] 'can command less labour, or rather' is del. here.

applied, is it in any degree probable that the mass of vacant capitals could be advantageously employed, or that the mass of labourers thrown out of work could find the means of commanding an adequate share of the national produce? If there were other

---

draw more than £10,000. The question it must be remembered is not whether as great a value can be withdrawn, but whether as great a quantity of labour can be employed with the diminished capital. Now it is evident that in that particular trade, the whole quantity of labour employed, was not in proportion to the £20000, but to the £10000. No more labour could be employed than the £10000 could pay for, there is no occasion that any less shall [2] be employed after the discovery of the improved machinery. I admit indeed that a profit will be obtained only on £10000, instead of on £20000, by the individual who is obliged to remove his capital, but the question is whether any less quantity of labour will be employed, and whether the community will not be benefited in a greater degree than this individual loses, and on this point I have no need to use any further arguments to satisfy Mr. Malthus for he admits it,—he acknowledges that the whole capital would yield a greater produce. Now this is the point in which society is chiefly interested, it is desirable that the actual means of enjoyment should be increased, and that in the distribution of those enjoyments a smaller quantity should not fall to the share of the most numerous class of the people. We have seen that the same money capital will be employed in the support of labour, and as the people are not supposed to have increased or diminished, they will have the same money wages.

But commodities will altogether be in greater abundance

[2] Corrected in pencil, by another (apparently McCulloch's) hand, to read: 'and there is no reason why any less should'.

405 foreign trades which, by means of the | capital and labour thrown
out of employment, might be greatly extended, the case would be
at once quite altered, and the returns of such trades might furnish
stimulants sufficient to keep up the value of the national income.

---

and cheaper, consequently each man's wages will procure him
greater enjoyments. I have purposely made my case appear
as unfavorable to myself as possible, by supposing that the
£10000 in fixed capital, and which under the new circumstances was no longer applicable to the cotton trade, would
have no value whatever. If, as it is probable, it could be
made useful in any other manufacture, it would still further
tend to increase the quantity of produce which would be still
more favorable to consumers.

Unless with labour of the value[1] of £10000 as much
cotton goods could be made as were before made with labour
of the value of £10000 and fixed capital of the value of
£10000, cotton goods could not so fall as to make it expedient to abandon the £10000 fixed capital as totally worth-
less, for if the price of the cotton goods was enhanced on
account of the use of the former machinery £1500—the
goods must fall £1500 before it can be the manufacturers
interest to abandon it. When that happens he will only get
15 p.c. profit on one of his capitals, which by the supposition
he can get by the employment of his £10,000 in any other
trade.

Mr. Malthus says "If in order to try the principle we
were to push it farther, and to suppose that without any
extension of the foreign market for our goods, we could by
means of machinery obtain all the commodities at present in
use, with one third of the labour now applied, is it in any
degree probable that the mass of vacant capitals could be

[1] Replaces 'Unless a capital'.

But, if only an increase of domestic commodities could be obtained, there is every reason to fear that the exertions of industry would slacken. The peasant, who might be induced to labour an additional number of hours for tea or tobacco, might prefer

---

advantageously employed, or that the mass of labourers thrown out of work could find the means of commanding an adequate share of the national produce?"[2] I answer, yes: Suppose[3] three men employed 10 men each, one in the production of shoes, another in the manufacture of stockings, and the other in the manufacture of cloth, all which commodities were required and consumed in the society. Suppose now that each discovers an improved process, by which they can each produce the same quantity of their respective commodities with the labour of five men, will they not, having each the means of employing the labour of ten men, continue to employ the other five; not indeed in the production of cloth, shoes, and stockings, but in the production of some out of the numerous commodities which are useful and desirable to man. Would they not obtain, having it in their power so to do, hats, wine, beer, furniture or any other commodities for which they might have a greater inclination?—Mr. Malthus error appears to me to be in thinking that nothing could be done without the extension of foreign trade. Are we all satiated with our own productions? Would none of us like more and better clothes, an increase of furniture, more carriages and horses, and better and more commodious houses? While we have not too much of these things no facility of production can ever be indifferent to us. "The peasant who might be induced to labour an additional

---

[2] This quotation and the others that follow in this Note are from Malthus's pp. 404–6.   [3] Replaces 'If'.

indolence to a new coat. The tenant or small owner of land, who
could obtain the common conveniences and luxuries of life at one
third of their former price, might not labour so hard to procure
the same amount of surplus produce from the land. And the

---

number of hours for tea or tobacco might prefer indolence
to a new coat." In the case supposed no one would be called
on to labour an additional number of hours; he might have
the tobacco or tea, and his new coat without it and if he
had nothing more his master would have. To secure him
employment it is only necessary that his master should have
the wants, which Mr. Malthus thinks it so difficult to create
in the labourer[1].

"The trader or merchant, who would continue in his business in order to be able to drink and give his guests claret
and champagne, might think an addition of homely commodities by no means worth the trouble of so much constant
attention"! He would quit it then, and live on the interest
of his funds, which would, nevertheless, be as productively
employed, and with as much ardor by his successor, who had
not yet obtained a sufficient portion of homely commodities.

"Where the amount of the incomes of a country depend
in a considerable degree, upon the exertion of labour, activity
and attention, there must be something in the commodities
to be obtained sufficiently desirable to balance this exertion,
or the exertion will cease." This is no doubt true, but there
are hundreds, and thousands, in such a country as this, who
under any degree of improvement that can be contemplated
as probable[2] would be happy to furnish the activity and
attention necessary to obtain commodities, which to them

[1] Replaces 'master'.
[2] The last eleven words, beginning 'under any', were originally
placed at the end of the sentence,
after 'themselves'.

trader or merchant, who would continue in his business in order to be able to drink and give his guests claret and champagne, might think an addition of homely commodities by no means worth the trouble of so much constant attention. (237)

---

must be sufficiently desirable, with the funds of others, if entrusted to them for that purpose; even if it should be supposed, which I am far from believing, that the objects are not sufficiently desirable to stimulate the exertions of the proprietors themselves. "Very few indeed would attend a counting house six or eight hours a day, in order to purchase commodities which have no other merit than the quantity of labour which have been employed upon them."

I should not particularly admire the wisdom of such persons, but nothing is more common. From what circumstance is it that gold plate, jewellery, and lace derive their great value but from the quantity of labour that has been employed on them? and yet there are those who think no toil too great to obtain them.

(237) p. 405.

Mr. Malthus argument is a little contradictory here. You could not find employment for your labourers he says with the capitals disengaged in consequence of the employment of machinery. I expected then that he would have expatiated on the miserable condition of this class and would have opposed the unlimited use of[3] machinery on that ground; quite the contrary. The condition of the labourer which we are called upon to commiserate is of a different description; he will be balancing in his mind whether in addition to tea and tobacco he shall prefer[4] a new coat to indolence. The small tenant will not know on what to spend his surplus produce,—and

---

[3] 'the unlimited use of' is ins.   [4] Replaces 'whether he shall prefer tea, tobacco, or'.

It has been said that, when there is an income ready for the demand, it is impossible that there should be any difficulty in the employment of labour and capital to supply it, as the owner of such an income, rather than not spend it, would purchase a table or chair that had cost the labour of a hundred men for a year. This may be true, in cases of fixed monied revenues, obtained by inheritance, or with little or no trouble. We well know that some of the Roman nobles, who obtained their immense wealth chiefly 406 by the | easy mode of plunder, sometimes gave the most enormous prices for fancied luxuries. A feather will weigh down a scale when there is nothing in the opposite one. But where the amount of the incomes of a country depend, in a considerable degree, upon the exertion of labour, activity and attention, there must be something in the commodities to be obtained sufficiently desirable to balance this exertion, or the exertion will cease. And experience amply shews, by the number of persons who daily leave off business, when they might certainly have continued to improve their fortunes, that most men place some limits, however variable, to the quantity of conveniences and luxuries which they will labour for; and that very few indeed would attend a counting-house six or eight hours a day, in order to purchase commodities which have no other merit than the quantity of labour which has been employed upon them.

Still however it is true that, when a great income has once been created in a country, in the shape of a large mass of rents, profits and wages, a considerable resistance will be made to any essential fall in its value. (238) It is a very just remark of Hume,* that when the affairs of a society are brought to this situation; that is, when, by means of foreign trade, it has acquired the tastes necessary to give value to a great quantity of labour not employed upon actual necessaries, it may lose most of this trade, and yet 407 continue great and | powerful, on account of the extraordinary

* Essays, vol. i. p. 293.

the care of the merchant or trader will be whether he can find any market abroad in which he can exchange our home commodities for claret and champagne, for his situation will be so prosperous that nothing less than those refined beverages can stimulate him to continue his usual exertions.

efforts which would be made by the spare capital and ingenuity of the country to refine home manufactures, in order to supply the tastes already formed, and the incomes already created. But if we were to allow that the income of such a nation might, in this way, by possibility be maintained, there is little chance of its increasing; and it is almost certain that it would not have reached the same amount, without the market occasioned by foreign commerce.

Of this I think we shall be convinced, if, in our own country, we look at the quantity of goods which we export chiefly in consequence of our machinery, and consider the nature of the returns obtained for them. In the accounts of the year ended the 5th of January 1818, it appears that the exports of three articles alone in which machinery is used—cottons, woollen and hardware, including steel goods, &c. are valued at above 29 millions. And among the most prominent articles of the imports of the same year, we find coffee, indigo, sugar, tea, silks, tobacco, wines, and cotton-wool, amounting in value all together to above 18 millions out of thirty! Now I would ask how we should have obtained these valuable imports, if the foreign markets for our cottons, woollens, and hardware had not been extended with the use of machinery? And further, where we could have found substitutes at home for such imports, which would have been likely to have produced the same effects, in stimulating the cultivation of the land, the accumulation | of capital, and the increase of population? And when to these considerations we add the fortunes which have been made in these manufactures, the market for which has been continually extending, and continually requiring more capital and more people to be employed in them; and contrast with this state of things the constant necessity of looking out for new modes of employing the same capital and the same people, a portion of which would be thrown out of their old occupations by every new invention;—we must be convinced

408

If these are all the sufferings that will be entailed upon us from a want of demand for home commodities, I am prepared to meet them, and care not how soon they begin.

(238) p. 406. *Still however it is true*

In what sense is the word value used here?

that the state of this country would have been totally different from what it is, and that it would not certainly have acquired the same income in rents, profits and wages, if the same ingenuity had been exercised in the invention of machinery, without the same extension of the market for the commodities produced. (239)

[If, from the time of Edward I. we had had no foreign commerce, our revenue from the land alone would not have approached to what it is at present, and still less our revenue from trade and manufactures.

---

(239) p. 408. *And when to these considerations &c.*

This is merely asserting that considerable advantages have been obtained by the extension of the market for the commodities which we have been enabled to produce with considerable facility by the invention and use of machinery, and by the great ingenuity of our people. No remark can be more just, and excepting by Mr. Spence, and a few of his way of thinking, I have never known these advantages to be denied.[1] I at any rate shall not be suspected of undervaluing the benefits of a free trade. Commerce is an interchange of conveniences and luxuries. In proportion as the market is extended, the people of every country are enabled to make the best division of their labour, and the most advantageous use of their exertions. Not only does it enable them to procure better and cheaper commodities, which, if there be no other means of getting, they can make themselves, but it furnishes them with the means of getting other commodities, which but for foreign commerce they would never get at all; their climate being unfitted to their production.

The advantages which we have derived from foreign trade then are fully admitted. Improvements in Machinery, with

[1] Cp. the sub-title of Mill's *Commerce Defended* (1808) 'An Answer to the Arguments by which Mr. Spence, Mr. Cobbett, and Others, have attempted to prove that Commerce is not a Source of National Wealth.'

Most of the states of Europe, with their actual divisions of
landed property, would have been comparatively unpeopled,
without the excitements arising from manufactures and extended
markets.]

In carrying on the late war, we were powerfully assisted by our   409
steam-engines, which enabled us to command a prodigious quantity of foreign produce and foreign labour. But how would their
efficacy have been weakened if we could not have exported our
cottons, cloths and hardware? (240) |

---

an extensive market abroad, will be much more beneficial to
us than improvements without these advantages, for it enables us to devote our time and attention[2] exclusively to
the manufacture of a commodity in the making of which
we possess superior skill. This is however not the subject
in dispute. What we want to know is whether improvements
can[3] be otherwise than beneficial to us under any circumstances? Mr. Malthus's argument is that they can.

(240) p. 409. *In carrying on the late war &c. &c.*

The advantages from steam engines &c. are in this instance I think exaggerated by Mr. Malthus. The introduction of these cheaper means of manufacturing commodities
lowered their price, and consequently we were obliged to
give more of them to foreign countries in exchange for a
given quantity of their commodities. The advantages then
to foreign countries, from our improvements, are, after a
very short interval, as great, as those which we derive from
them ourselves. They are a common benefit to all the consumers of the commodities who are admitted to buy them.

Supposing that a country discovered very improved
machinery by the means of which she manufactured a

[2] 'more' was ins. here, and then
del.

[3] The first part of the sentence
replaces 'Can improvements'.

410   If the mines of America could be successfully worked by machinery, and the King of Spain's tax could be increased at will, so as to make the most of this advantage, what a vast revenue might they not be made to afford him! But it is obvious that the effects of such machinery would sink into insignificance, if the market for the precious metals were confined to the adjacent countries, and the principal effect of it was to throw capital and labour out of employment.

In the actual state of things in this country, the population and wealth of Manchester, Glasgow, Leeds, &c. have been greatly increasing; because, on account of the extending demand for their goods, more people have been continually required to work them up; but if a much smaller number of people had been required, on account of a saving of labour from machinery, without an adequate extension of the market, it is obvious that these towns would have been comparatively poor, and thinly peopled. To what extent the spare capital and labour thrown out of employment in one district would have enriched others, it is impossible

---

commodity which was made wholly for the foreign market, and none was consumed at home,—in that case the whole advantage of the improvement would be obtained by the foreign country, and none whatever by the country which used and invented the improved machinery—excepting indeed this advantage, that in the distribution of employments, none perhaps enabled her to employ her industry with better effect, as a means of obtaining the foreign commodities which she was desirous of purchasing.

This conclusion cannot I think be denied by those who agree with me that the prices of commodities sink at home, and consequently abroad, in proportion to the facility of producing them.

It is singular that Mr. Malthus who estimates so justly at its value the benefit resulting from the extension of the market, should so much underrate the advantages which would be derived from a free trade in corn. Extension of

to say; and on this subject any assertion may be made, as we cannot be set right by an appeal to facts. But I would ask, whether there are any grounds in the slightest degree plausible for saying, that not only the capital spared at any time from these manufactures would be preserved and employed elsewhere; but that it would be employed as profitably, and create as much exchangeable value in other places as it would have done in | Manchester and Glasgow, 411 with an extending market? In short, are there any plausible grounds whatever for stating that, if the twenty millions worth of cottons which we now export, were entirely stopped, either by successful foreign competition or positive prohibitions, we should have no difficulty in finding employment for our capital and labour equally advantageous to individuals in point of profit, and equally enriching to the country with respect to the exchangeable value of its revenue? (241)

Unquestionably any country has the power of consuming all that it produces, however great in quantity; and every man in health has the *power* of applying his mind and body to productive

---

the market, and free trade, are two names for the same thing, for what can give a greater extension to the market for our cotton goods, cloth, and hardware, than the admitting freely the commodity with which foreign countries can most conveniently purchase them?

(241) p. 410. *But I would ask, whether there are*

I am one who think that the capital would have been employed elsewhere, and employed at the same rate of profits too, and yet I have no doubt that if the export of cotton goods was stopped, and we were obliged to employ the capital absorbed by that trade elsewhere, we should be great sufferers by such an arrangement.

The rate of profits does not depend on foreign trade, but on the returns for labour on the land last cultivated at home, and the distribution of the produce. Suppose these to continue unaltered, and nothing in the change from foreign to home trade can alter them, profits would continue at the

labour for ten or twelve hours of the day. But these are dry assertions respecting the powers of a country, which do not necessarily involve any practical consequences relating to the increase of wealth. If we could not export our cottons, it is quite certain that, though we might have the power, we should not have the will, to consume them all in kind at home; and the maintenance of our national wealth and revenue would depend entirely upon the circumstance whether the capital thrown out of

---

same rate. If before with a capital of £20000 I obtained £2000 p^r. Ann. profit I should continue to obtain the same, but with my £2000 I should not be able to command the same quantity of foreign and home made commodities. The whole revenue of the country would be of the same money value, and I should say of the same real value, but as that value would be represented by fewer commodities many of them being enhanced in price there would be fewer enjoyments to be purchased with the same real revenue.

Mr. Malthus and I do not substantially differ on this subject. He thinks that less money profits would be made, commodities remaining at the same price—I think the same money gain would be made but commodities would be enhanced in price.

Our seeming[1] difference proceeds from the different medium in which we estimate value.

(242) p. 411. *Unquestionably*

It requires an exertion of some magnitude to apply one's body and mind to productive labour for ten or twelve hours of the day, but no exertion at all to consume what one has before been at the pains of producing. The one gives pain, the other pleasure. How can things so dissimilar be considered as alike?

We should not[2] perhaps have the wish to consume all our

---

[1] 'seeming' is ins.　　　[2] 'it is true' is del. here.

the cotton trade could be so applied as to produce commodities which would be estimated as highly and consumed as eagerly as the foreign goods before imported. (242) There is no magic in foreign markets. The final demand and consumption must always be at home; and if goods could be produced at home, which would excite people to work as many | hours in the day, would   412 communicate the same enjoyments, and create a consumption of the same *value*, (243) foreign markets would be useless. We know

---

cotton goods in the case supposed, but the labour which produces them might produce other things which we might be disposed to consume.

(243) p. 412. *And create a consumption of the same "value."*

The happiness of a country depends on the quantity of the things which it has to enjoy and not on the "value" of those commodities.

After all it is difficult to understand what Mr. Malthus would wish respecting the use of machinery. The world may be considered as a large country—So considered Mr. Malthus has no objection to the most extensive use of machinery, and in this I agree with him. Where we appear to differ is in this—I am persuaded that a people living in the most limited district, which by some accident might never have had nor should ever in future have, any commerce with foreign countries, would nevertheless derive unmixed advantages from "accumulation of capital, improved fertility of soil, and inventions to save labour["][3]—Mr. Malthus thinks that in many cases these would be disastrous presents to them, they must be accompanied, according to him by demand to make them beneficial. Now as I think that demand depends only on supply, the means of obtaining abundance of commodities can never I think[4] be otherwise than beneficial.

[3] See Malthus's p. 413.
[4] Last eleven words, beginning 'the means', replace 'they can never'.

however from experience, that very few countries are capable of producing commodities of the same efficacy, in this respect, as those which may be obtained by a trade to various climates and soils. Without such a trade, and with a great increase in the power of production, there is no inconsiderable danger that industry, consumption, and exchangeable value would diminish; and this danger would most unquestionably be realized if the cheapness of domestic commodities occasioned by machinery, were to lead to increased saving rather than to increased expenditure.

But it is known that facilities of production have the strongest tendency to open markets, both at home and abroad. In the actual state therefore of most countries, there is little reason to apprehend any permanent evil from the introduction of machinery. The presumption always is, that it will lead to a great extension of wealth and value. But still we must allow that the pre-eminent advantages derived from the substitution of machinery for manual labour, depend upon the extension of the market for the commodities produced, and the increased stimulus given to consumption; and that, without this extension of market and increase of consumption, they must be in a great degree lost. Like the fertility of land, the invention of good machinery confers a prodigious power of production. But neither of these great powers |
413   can be called fully into action, if the situation and circumstances, or the habits and tastes of the society prevent the opening of a sufficient market, and an adequate increase of consumption.

The three great causes most favourable to production are, accumulation of capital, fertility of soil, and inventions to save labour. They all act in the same direction; and as they all tend to

---

(244) p. 413. *We have seen that the powers of*

True; a faulty distribution would have these effects, but what security can you have against it better than that of allowing every[1] man to produce what he pleases, and to consume the commodity he produces himself, or to exchange it for the produce of other men's labour. His power of demanding commodities must depend on the ability with which he selects the objects he produces.

    [1] Written above 'each', which however is not del.

facilitate supply, without reference to demand, it is not probable that they should either separately or conjointly afford an adequate stimulus to the continued increase of wealth, which can only be kept up by a continued increase of the demand for commodities.

SECTION VI

Of the Necessity of a Union of the Powers of Production with the Means of Distribution, in order to ensure a continued Increase of Wealth

We have seen that the powers of production, to whatever extent they may exist, are not alone sufficient to secure the creation of a proportionate degree of wealth. Something else seems to be necessary in order to call these powers fully into action; and this is, such a distribution of produce, and such an adaptation of this produce to the wants of those who are to consume it, as constantly to increase the exchangeable value of the whole mass. (244) |

In individual cases, the power of producing particular com- 414
modities is called into action, in proportion to the effective demand for them; and the greatest stimulus to their production is a high market price, or an increase of their exchangeable value, before more capital and labour have been employed upon them.

In the same manner, the greatest stimulus to the continued production of commodities, taken all together, is an increase in the exchangeable value of the whole mass, before more labour and capital have been employed upon them. (245) And this increase

---

(245) p. 414. *In the same manner*

What is meant by "an increase in the exchangeable value of the whole mass of commodities, before more labour and capital have been employed upon them"? If it be meant that they are more valuable as compared with labour it is a round-about way of saying, that labour has fallen in value[2]. As

---

[2] 'that labour has fallen in value' replaces 'either that commodities have risen in value without a corresponding rise of labour, or that labour has positively fallen'.

of value is effected by such a distribution of the actual produce as is best adapted to gratify the existing wants of society, and to inspire new ones.

It has been stated in a preceding section, that if all the roads and canals of the country were broken up, and the means of distributing its produce were essentially impeded, the whole value of the produce would greatly fall; indeed, it is obvious that if it were so distributed as not to be suited to the wants, tastes, and powers of the actual population in different situations, its value might sink to such a degree as to be comparatively quite inconsiderable. Upon the same principle, if the means of distributing the produce of the country were still further facilitated, and if the adaptation of it to the wants, tastes and powers of the consumers were more complete than at present, there can be no doubt that a great increase in the value of the whole produce would follow.

415   But to illustrate the power of distribution in in-|creasing the mass of exchangeable value, we need only refer to experience. Before the introduction of good roads and canals in England, the prices of produce in many country districts were extremely low compared with the same kind of produce in the London markets. After the means of distribution were facilitated, the price of

---

Mr. Malthus measures the value of labour by the quantity of commodities earned by the labourer,[1] whenever from any cause more commodities are given for labour, labour may be said to rise, and whenever fewer commodities are given labour may be said to fall.

(246) p. 415. *After the means of distribution*

In the case supposed of a free intercourse between London and the Country—I should say it would be followed by a fall in the value of labour. If corn could be with greater facility conveyed from the country to London its value would fall in London, and as corn is a regulator of the price of labour,

[1] Last nine words replace 'by commodities and not by their value'.

country produce, and of some sorts of London produce which were sent into the country in exchange for it, rose; and rose in a greater degree than the country produce fell in the London markets, or the London produce fell in the country markets; and consequently the value of the whole produce, or the supplies of London and the country together, was greatly increased; and while encouragement was thus given to the employment of a greater quantity of capital by the extension of demand, the temporary rise of profits, occasioned by this extension, would greatly contribute to furnish the additional capital required. (246)

It will be asked, perhaps, how an increase in the exchangeable value of the whole produce of a country is to be estimated? It has before been stated that real value in exchange, from its very nature, admits of no accurate and standard measure; and consequently, in the present case, no measure can be mentioned which is perfectly satisfactory. Yet even bullion, our most common measure of value, might, in general, and for short periods, be referred to; and though abstractedly considered, wealth is nearly independent of money; yet in the actual state of the relations of the dif-|ferent countries of the world with each other, it rarely **416** happens that any great increase or decrease in the bullion value of all the commodities of a country takes place, without an increase

---

labour would probably fall also, and profits would rise. But why does corn fall in London? because a less quantity of labour is necessary from first to last to grow it and take it there.

The facility of intercourse would lower country produce in London, and London produce in the country, but country produce would neither rise nor fall[2] in the country, neither would London produce in London. Their prices in the places in which they were produced and indeed in all other places would be regulated by their cost of production.*

[*] In cost of production I always include profits at their current rate.

[2] Last four words replace 'not rise'.

or decrease of demand for commodities, compared with the
supply of them.

It happens however, undoubtedly, sometimes, that the value
of bullion alters, not only generally, but in particular countries;
and it is not meant to be said that a country cannot possibly be
stimulated to an increase of wealth after a fall has taken place in
the money-price of all its commodities. As the best approximation to a measure of real value in exchange, in application to the
commodities of different countries and different times, I before
proposed a mean between corn and labour;* and to this measure
I should be disposed always to refer, when any commodities are
to be estimated, with the exception of corn and labour themselves.
But as, in speaking of national wealth, it is necessary to include
the exchangeable value of food; and as food cannot well be the
measure of food, I shall refer generally to the labour, domestic and
foreign, which the bullion-price of the produce will command,

* Chap. ii. sect. vii.

---

(247) p. 417. *Whenever there is a great demand for com-*
modities, that is, whenever the exchangeable value of the
whole mass will command more labour than usual at the
same price, there is the same kind of reason for expecting
a general increase of commodities, as there is for expecting
an increase of particular commodities when their market-
prices rise.

Mr. Malthus, it will be observed, loses no occasion of in-
sisting on the importance of demand, in stimulating countries
to exertions, and is always fearful of a deficiency of this
invigorating force. It is desirable then to ascertain correctly
what meaning he attaches to the word "demand." Here we
are told that a great demand for commodities means that the
exchangeable value of the mass shall command more labour
than usual at the same price.

Suppose I have hats, shoes, stockings &c. of the value of
£1000, and labour to be worth 2/ a day, the mass of my
commodities will be worth ten thousand days labour. If

or the sacrifices which people are willing and able to make of their own or other persons exertions in order to obtain it, as the best practical measure of value that can be applied; and though undoubtedly not accurate, yet sufficiently so for the present purpose. |

General wealth, like particular portions of it, will always follow effective demand. Whenever there is a great demand for commodities, that is, whenever the exchangeable value of the whole mass will command more labour than usual at the same price, there is the same kind of reason for expecting a general increase of commodities, as there is for expecting an increase of particular commodities when their market-prices rise. And on the other hand, whenever the produce of a country estimated in the labour which it will command falls in value, it is evident that with it the power and will to purchase the same quantity of labour must be diminished, and the effective demand for an increase of produce must, for a time, be checked. (247)

417

---

labour fell to 1/8 a day my commodities would still sell for £1000, but they would command twelve thousand days labour.—According to Mr. Malthus then the demand for my commodities would have increased, and this increased demand would as surely lead to an increased production, as an increased market price of a particular commodity would lead to the increased production of that commodity. Instead of calling this an increased demand, and instead of saying that commodities had increased in value, because they would command more labour, merely perhaps because there was a redundant population, for nothing else can make a low commodity price of labour [1] if I may be allowed the expression, I should say that commodities remained at the same value and labour had fallen in value, and that in consequence of the fall of labour profits had risen. The demand for commodities would neither be greater nor less, but the masters would have the right to consume more, and the men less. These

[1] 'of labour' is ins.

24-2

Mr. Ricardo, in his chapter on Value and Riches, has stated that "a certain quantity of clothes and provisions will maintain and employ the same number of men, and will therefore procure the same quantity of work to be done, whether they be produced by the labour of a hundred or of two hundred men; but they will be of twice the value, if two hundred have been employed in their production." * But, even taking his own peculiar estimate of value, this statement would very rarely indeed be true.

* Princ. of Polit. Econ. ch. xx. p. [279].

---

high profits, might, or might not, lead to further productions, accordingly as the masters accumulated, or spent their increased incomes. When profits are universally high, the temptation to produce an increased quantity of commodities is very different from that which a high market price of a particular commodity affords, for the production of that particular commodity.

In the latter case, the high profits can only be obtained by producing that one commodity, in the other high profits are enjoyed by all. It would be a mistake too to suppose that because the commodities estimated in labour were now worth 12,000 days labour instead of 10,000, that therefore men who could execute 12,000 days labour would [1] be employed —this would be true if all that the masters had and all they [2] saved, was employed productively, but that by no means follows. If a friend in Portugal were to give me a pipe of port worth one thousand days labour, the commodities of the country would be worth 1000 days labour more than before but if I drank the wine with my family not one additional man would be employed. [3] I never wish to see

[1] Last nine words replace 'therefore 12000 would'.
[2] 'had and all they' is ins.
[3] In MS this sentence is written on a slip stuck with wafers upon the sheet. It covers a continuation of the preceding sentence, which read: 'follows, no more than ten thousand may be in constant employment and in full

The clothes and provisions which had cost only one hundred days' labour would never, but in the most unnatural state of things, be able to procure the same quantity of work to | be done as if **418** they had cost two hundred days' labour. (248) To suppose it, is to suppose that the price of labour, estimated in necessaries, is the same at all times and in all countries, and does not depend upon the plenty or scarcity of necessaries compared with labour, a supposition contradicted by universal experience. Nine quarters of wheat will perhaps command a year's labour in England; but

---

"the exchangeable value of the mass of commodities command more labour than usual *at the same price*," for great as I estimate the benefits resulting from high profits I never wish to see those profits increased at the expence of the labouring class. I am sure that Mr. Malthus has the same feeling as myself on this subject, and does not perceive that this is the condition annexed to the increased value of the mass of commodities without an increase of their quantity.[4] What we should desire is to increase the quantity of commodities without increasing their value.[5] The mass of commodities may then be of the same money value as before, and if labour falls from 2/-, to 1/8, p[r]. day, the labourer may be better off, as with 1/8 he may get more than he got with 2/- before. The rate of profits will be increased in the same way as before, but it will not be at the expence of the labouring class,—it will follow only from the increased productiveness of labour.

(248) p. 417. *The clothes and provisions which had cost*

I know it, and am rejoiced at it. If they could, all the advantage would go to profits. It is highly desirable that a part should go to increase the enjoyments of the labourer.

work one sixth of the...'; this was altered to 'follows, any more than that those who now can earn ten thousand days work are in constant employment and in full work.'; this was replaced as above.

[4] Last six words are ins.

[5] Last four words are ins.

sixteen quarters will hardly procure the same quantity of work to be done in America. And in the case either of a sudden increase of productive labour, by a rapid conversion of revenue into capital, or a sudden increase of the productiveness of the same quantity of labour, there is not the slightest doubt that a given portion of necessaries would be quite unable to set in motion the same quantity of labour; and, if the exchangeable value of the produce should fall in a greater ratio than its quantity increases, (which may very easily happen,) then the same quantity of labour would not be set in motion by the increased quantity of necessaries, and the progress of wealth would receive a decided check. (249)

Such a check would still more obviously be the consequence

---

(249) p. 418. *And in the case either of a sudden*

I am a farmer and produce 100 qrs. of corn of which I give 50 to my labourers. I improve the productiveness of my land without employing more labour, and get 120 qrs., and I now give 55 to my labourers. The hatter, the clothier, the shoemaker make the same improvements in their trades, and divide the produce they obtain in the same proportions, between themselves and their labourers. Is not the society enriched? Is it not better off than before? Call value what you please, talk of the rising or falling of commodities, must not the state of the society be improved?

Mr. Malthus says[1] that "By a sudden increase of the productiveness of the same quantity of labour, there is not the slightest doubt that a given portion of necessaries would be quite unable to set in motion the same quantity of labour." To whom will the produce belong? To the masters, or to the workmen. If to the former, they have the power of commanding more labour. If to the latter, although the same quantity of labour should not be employed, the labourers would be in affluence, and with the diminished quantity of labour the masters would be as well off as before. In this case

[1] Replaces 'Can Mr. Malthus be right when he says'.

of a diminished demand for produce, owing to the decline of foreign commerce, or any other cause. Under these circumstances, both the quantity and value of produce would soon be diminished; and though labour, from the want of demand, would be very cheap, the capitalists would soon lose both the will and the power to employ it in the same quantity as before. (250) |

In every case, a continued increase in the value of produce 419 estimated in labour seems to be absolutely necessary to a continued and unchecked increase of wealth; because without such an increase of value it is obvious that no fresh labour can be set in motion. (251) And in order to support this value it is necessary that an effective distribution of the produce should take place,

---

does Mr. Malthus speak of it as an evil that[2] a given portion of necessaries would be quite unable to set in motion the same quantity of labour? It is most desirable that it should not.

(250) p. 418. *Such a decided*

How erroneous this conclusion appears to me!

(251) p. 419. *In every case*

I fear I am wearying the reader by so long dwelling on this subject, but Mr. Malthus' assertion here must mean this. If a country doubles its productions of all kinds it will not be more wealthy unless it can command more labour. I should say its profits might be no higher in value[3] but they would command double the quantity of enjoyments, it would be doubly rich.

Mr. Malthus agrees that wealth and value are not the same thing, and yet he here asserts "that a continued increase in the *value* of produce seems to be absolutely necessary to a continued and unchecked increase of wealth." Will not the wealth of a country increase if without any more labour you contrive to double the quantity of commodities?[4]

[2] 'the same quantity of necessaries' is del. here.

[3] Replaces 'its profits would be no higher'.

[4] This paragraph is ins.

and a due proportion be maintained between the objects to be consumed and the number, wants, and powers of the consumers, or, in other words, between the supply of commodities and the demand for them.

It has already been shewn that this value cannot be maintained in the case of a rapid accumulation of capital occasioned by an actual and continued diminution in the expenditure and consumption of the higher classes of society.* Yet it will be most readily allowed that the saving from revenue to add to capital is an absolutely necessary step in the progress of wealth. How then is this saving to take place without producing the diminution of value apprehended?

It may take place, and practically almost always does take place, in consequence of a previous increase of value, or of revenue, in which case a saving may be effected, not only without any diminution of demand and consumption, but under an actual increase of demand, consumption and value during every part of the process. (252) And it is in fact this previous increase of value
420 and revenue | which both gives the great stimulus to accumulation, and makes that accumulation effective in the continued production of wealth.

[M. Sismondi limits the value of the produce of any year to the value of the revenue of the preceding year; but this would preclude increase of value. A great increase of exchangeable value and demand may take place in any one year by a better distribution of produce, and a better adaptation of it to the wants of the society.]

* Sect. III. of this chapter.

---

(252) p. 419. *It may take place*

This is one way undoubtedly.

(253) p. 421. *The fortune of a country*

It will however be allowed that an individual may improve his fortune by a diminished expenditure on objects of luxury and enjoyment. Why may not a country do the same?

(254) p. 421. *Many a merchant has made a*

True, but a brother merchant who avoided an increased

The fortune of a country, though necessarily made more 421
slowly, is made in the same way as the fortunes of individuals in
trade are generally made,—by *savings*, certainly; but by savings
which are furnished from increased gains, and by no means
involve a diminished expenditure on objects of luxury and
enjoyment. (253)

Many a merchant has made a large fortune although, during
the acquisition of this fortune, there was perhaps hardly a single
year in which he did not rather increase than diminish his expenditure in objects of luxury, enjoyment, and liberality. (254)
The amount of capital in this country is immense, and it certainly
received very great additions during the last twenty-five years;
but on looking back, few traces are to be found of a diminished
expenditure in the maintenance of | unproductive labour. If some 422
such traces however are to be found, they will be found in exact
conformity to the theory here laid down; they will be found
during a period, when, from particular circumstances, the value of
the national produce was not maintained, and there was in consequence a great diminution of the power of expenditure, and a
great check to the production of wealth.

Perhaps it will be said, that to lay so much stress on distribution, and to measure demand by the exchangeable value of the
whole produce, is to exalt the gross revenue at the expense of the
neat revenue of a country, and to favour that system of cultivation
and manufacturing which employs on each object the greatest
number of hands. (255) But I have already shewn that the saving
of labour, and the increase of skill, both in agriculture and manufacturing industry, by enabling a country to push its cultivation

---

expenditure on objects of luxury, enjoyment and liberality
with the same profits, would get rich faster than him.

(255) p. 422. *Perhaps, it will be said*

Here again demand is measured by the exchangeable value
of commodities. Exchangeable value in what? In labour?
Suppose you were to add 20 p.c. in quantity [1] to all the goods
of the country and were by better wages to enable the
labouring class to command all these additional commodities,

[1] 'in quantity' is ins.

over poorer lands, without diminution of profits, and to extend far
and wide the markets for its manufactures, must tend to increase
the exchangeable value of the whole; and there cannot be a doubt
that in this country they must have been the main sources of that
rapid and astonishing increase in the value of the national wealth,
which has taken place during the last thirty or forty years.

To dwell therefore mainly on the gross revenue of a country
rather than on its neat revenue is in no respect to under-rate the
prodigious advantage derived from skill and machinery, but
merely to give that importance to the value of the whole pro-
423 duce | to which it is so justly entitled. No description of national
wealth, which refers only to neat revenue, can ever be in any
degree satisfactory. The Economists destroyed the practical
utility of their works by referring exclusively to the neat produce of the land. And the writers who make wealth consist of
rents and profits, to the exclusion of wages, commit an error
exactly of the same kind though less in degree. Those who live
upon the wages of labour, unproductive as well as productive,
receive and expend much the greatest part of the annual produce,
pay a very considerable sum in taxes for the maintenance of the
government, and form by far the largest portion of its physical
force. Under the prevalence of habits of prudence, the whole of
this vast mass might be nearly as happy as the individuals of the
other two classes, and probably a greater number of them, though
not a greater proportion of them, happier. In every point of
view therefore, both in reference to the part of the annual pro-

---

would you not have increased the value of commodities
because the greater quantity will only command the same
labour as before? Will there be no increased demand because they can command no more labour, altho' every
labourer will have the power and will to demand and consume an additional quantity of commodities. "It is not the
interest of the producer to furnish commodities on such
terms", that is no answer, they are furnished. We do not
deny that there is no motive in the capitalist to produce
commodities which will not command more labour than

duce which falls to their share, and the means of health and happiness which it may be presumed to communicate, those who live on the wages of labour must be considered as the most important portion of the society; and any definition of wealth which should involve such a diminution of their numbers, as to require for the supply of the whole population a smaller annual produce, must necessarily be erroneous.

In the First Chapter of this Work, having defined wealth to be "the material objects which are ne-|cessary, useful, and agree- 424 able to mankind," I stated as a consequence that a country was rich or poor according to the abundance or scantiness in which these objects were supplied, compared with the extent of territory. It will be readily allowed that this definition does not include the question of what may be called the amount of disposable produce, or the fund for taxation; but still I must consider it as a much more correct definition of the wealth of a country than any that should refer to this disposable part alone. What should we say of the wealth of this country, if it were possible that its rents and profits could remain the same, while its population and produce were reduced two-thirds? Certainly it would be much poorer according to the above definition; and there are not many that would dissent from such a conclusion.

That it would be desirable, in a definition of national wealth, to include the consideration of disposable produce, as well as of actual quantity and value, cannot be doubted; but such a definition seems to be in its nature impossible, because in each individual

---

has been bestowed on their production, but if he acts contrary to this interest, how does he injure his country? Why doubt the demand and consumption of the commodities produced? Why is it necessary to recommend to this individual not to go on producing? Will not his own interest tell him that he is producing for another to consume? And above all how is taxation to relieve him? Because he has no profits on a part of his capital, something is to be taken from him, or from the labourer he employs. What relief that should afford him I cannot divine.

case it must depend upon opinion, what increase of disposable produce should be accounted equivalent to a given diminution of gross produce.

We must content ourselves therefore with referring generally to the amount and value of national produce; and it may be subsequently stated as a separate, though very important consideration, that particular countries, with the same amount and |

425   value of produce, have a larger or smaller proportion of that produce disposable. In this respect, no doubt, a country with a fertile territory will have a prodigious advantage over those whose wealth depends almost entirely on manufactures. With the same population, the same rate of profits, and the same amount and value of produce, the landed nation would have much the largest portion of its wealth disposable. (256)

Fortunately, it happens but seldom that we have to determine the amount of advantage or disadvantage occasioned by the increase of the neat, at the expense of the gross revenue. The interest of individual capitalists uniformly prompts them to the

---

(256) p. 425. *In this respect no doubt a country*

Mr. Malthus says that an agricultural country "with the same population, the same rate of profits, and the same amount and value of produce as a manufacturing country, would have much the largest proportion of its wealth disposable." I ask how they could have the same population, the same rate of profits, and the same amount and value of produce? The amount of the value and produce in the manufacturing country is to be divided between wages and profits—in the agricultural between rent, wages, and profits. If out of an equal value you give the same value to wages and profits in each, what remains for rent in the Agricultural country?

(257) p. 425. *From what has been here said*

Mr. Malthus says "the additional two millions of men would some of them unquestionably have a part of their wages disposable." Then they would have a part of the

saving of labour, in whatever business they are engaged; and both theory and experience combine to shew that their successful efforts in this direction, by increasing the powers of production, afford the means of increasing, in the greatest practicable degree, the amount and value of the gross produce,* provided always

* From what has been here said, the reader will see that I can by no means agree with Mr. Ricardo, in his chapter *On Gross and Net Revenue.* I should not hesitate a moment in saying, that a country with a neat revenue from rents and profits, consisting of food and clothing for five millions of men, would be decidedly richer and more powerful, if such neat revenue were obtained from seven millions of men, rather than five, supposing them to be equally well supported. The whole produce would be greater; and the additional two millions of labourers would some of them unquestionably have a part of their wages disposable. (257) But I would further ask what is to become of the capital as well as the people in the case of such a change? It is obvious that a con-|siderable portion of it must become redundant and useless. I quite agree with Mr. Ricardo, however, in approving all saving of labour and inventions in machinery; but it is because I think that their tendency is to increase the gross produce and to make room for a larger population and a larger capital. If the saving of labour were to be accompanied by the effects stated in Mr. Ricardo's instance, I should agree with M. Sismondi and Mr. Owen in deprecating it as a great misfortune.

---

neat revenue. I do not deny that wages may be such as to give to the labourers a part of the neat revenue—I limited my proposition to the case when wages were too low to afford him any surplus beyond absolute [1] necessaries. Mr. Malthus has not quoted me correctly. I said,[2] "If five millions of men could produce as much food and clothing as was necessary for ten millions, food and clothing for five millions would be the net revenue. Would it be of any advantage to the country, that to produce this same net revenue seven millions of men should be *required*, that is to say that seven millions should be employed to produce food and clothing for twelve millions? The food and clothing for five millions would be still the net revenue. The employing a greater number of men would enable us neither to add a man to our army and navy, nor to contribute one guinea more in taxes."

"It is not on the grounds of any supposed advantage from

[1] 'absolute' is ins.   [2] Above, I, 348.

426 that such a dis-|tribution and consumption of the increased supply
of commodities takes place as constantly to increase their exchangeable value.

In general, an increase of produce and an increase of value go
on together; (258) and this is that natural and healthy state of
things, which is most favourable to the progress of wealth. An
increase in the quantity of produce depends chiefly upon the
power of production, and an increase in the value of produce upon
its distribution. Production and distribution are the two grand
elements of wealth, which, combined in their due proportions,
are capable of carrying the riches and population of the earth in
no great length of time to the utmost limits of its possible resources; but which taken separately, or combined in undue proportions, produce only, after the lapse of many thousand years,
the scanty riches and scanty population, which are at present
scattered over the face of the globe.

---

a large population or of the happiness that may be enjoyed
by a greater number of human beings that Adam Smith supports the preference of that employment of capital, which
gives motion to the greatest quantity of industry; but expressly on the ground of its increasing the power of the
country" &c. &c.

Mr. Malthus supposes 7 millions not to be required—that
is changing my proposition not refuting it.[1] M. Say has also
remarked on this passage,[2] and although I had carefully
guarded myself, by the observation, that I was only answering
Adam Smith's argument respecting the power of paying taxes
&c., and was not considering what was undoubtedly on any
other occasion most worthy of consideration[3] the happiness
of so many human beings, yet[4] he speaks as if this consideration was wholly unimportant in my estimation. I as-
sure him that he has done me injustice—it was not one

[1] Last four words replace 'argument.'
[2] In a note to the French transla-
tion of Ricardo's *Principles*, 1819,
vol. 2, pp. 222–4; cp. above, I,
349, n. 3.
[3] Last four words are ins.
[4] 'M. Say' is del. here.

SECTION VII

Of the Distribution occasioned by the Division of Landed Property considered as the means of increasing the Exchangeable Value of the whole Produce

[The three causes most favourable to distribution are, the division of landed property; internal and external commerce; and the maintenance of unproductive consumers.

In the first settlement of new colonies, an easy subdivision of the land is necessary to give effect to the principle of population.]

The rapid increase of the United States of America, taken as a whole, has undoubtedly been aided very greatly by foreign commerce, and particularly by the power of selling raw produce, obtained with little labour, for European commodities which have cost much labour. (259)

---

moment absent from my mind, nor did I fail to regard it with its due weight.

(258) p. 426. *In general, an increase of produce &c.*

It very seldom happens otherwise, all savings made from expenditure and added to capital increase the amount of commodities and at the same time add to the power of commanding labour Mr. Malthus criterion of increased value.⁵

It is barely possible that accumulation might be made so rapidly that the supply of labour should not keep pace with it. In that case the mass of commodities might not command more labour.

(259) p. 428. *The rapid increase of the United States*

It can be of no consequence to America, whether the commodities she obtains in return for her own, cost Europeans much, or little labour, all she is interested in, is that they shall cost her less labour by purchasing than by manufacturing them herself.

¹ 'All improvements in machinery have the same effect.' is del. here.

[The rapid increase of the establishments in North America depended greatly upon the facility of settling new families on the land as they branched off from their parent stocks.

429   The vicious distribution of landed property almost all over Europe, derived from the feudal times, was the main cause which impeded the progress of cultivators and wealth in the middle ages.]

Adam Smith has well described the slack kind of cultivation which was likely to take place, and did in fact take place, among the great proprietors of the middle ages. But not only were they bad cultivators and improvers; and for a time perhaps deficient in a proper taste for manufactured products; yet, even if they had possessed these tastes in the degree found to prevail at present, their inconsiderable numbers would have prevented their demand from producing any important mass of such wealth. We hear of great splendour among princes and nobles in every period of history. The difficulty was not so much to inspire the rich with a love of finery, as to break down their immense properties, and to create a greater number of demanders who were able and willing to purchase the results of productive labour. (260) This, 430 it is obvious, could only be effected very gradually. | That the increasing love of finery might have assisted considerably in accomplishing this object is highly probable; but these tastes alone, unaccompanied by a better distribution of property, would have been quite inefficient. The possessor of numerous estates, after he had furnished his mansion or castle splendidly, and provided himself with handsome clothes and handsome carriages, would not change them all every two months, merely because he had the power of doing it. Instead of indulging in such useless and troublesome changes, he would be more likely to keep a number of servants and idle dependants, to take lower rents with a view of having a greater command over his tenants, and perhaps to sacrifice the produce of a considerable portion of his land in order to encourage more game, and to indulge, with more effect and less interruption, in the pleasures of the chase. Thirty or forty

---

(260) p. 429. *The Difficulty was not so much*

[What difference could it make whether there was one great demander or a great many small ones? It was not demanders,

proprietors, with incomes answering to between one thousand and five thousand a year, would create a much more effective demand for wheaten bread, good meat, and manufactured products, than a single proprietor possessing a hundred thousand a year.

[It is physically possible for a small number of very rich proprietors and capitalists to create a very large demand; but practically, it has always been found that the excessive wealth of the few is never equivalent, in effective demand, to the more moderate wealth of the many.

But though it be true that the division of landed property to 431 a certain extent is favourable to the increase of wealth, it is equally true that beyond a certain extent it is unfavourable.

It will be found that all the great results in political economy 432 respecting wealth, depend upon proportions; and this important truth is particularly obvious in the division of landed property.]

On the effects of a great sub-division of property, a fearful 433 experiment is now making in France. The law of succession in that country divides property of all kinds among all the children equally, without right of primogeniture or distinction of sex, and allows but a small portion of it to be disposed of by will.

This law has not yet prevailed long enough to shew what its effects are likely to be on the national wealth and prosperity. If the state of property in France appears at present to be favourable to industry and demand, no inference can thence be drawn that it will be favourable in future. It is universally allowed that a division of property to a certain extent is extremely desirable; and so many traces yet remain almost all over Europe of the vast landed possessions which have descended from the feudal times, that there are not many states in which such a law as that of France might not be of use, with a view to wealth, for a certain number of years. But if such a law were to continue per-|manently to 434 regulate the descent of property in France; if no modes of evading it should be invented, and if its effects should not be weakened by the operation of an extraordinary degree of prudence in marriage,

---

but producers and accumulators of capital that were wanted. Objects too on which to expend revenue were required.][1]

[1] The whole Note is del.

which prudence such a law would certainly tend to discourage, there is every reason to believe that the country, at the end of a century, will be quite as remarkable for its extraordinary poverty and distress, as for its unusual equality of property. The owners of the minute divisions of landed property will be, as they always are, peculiarly without resource, and must perish in great numbers in every scarcity. Scarcely any will be rich but those who receive salaries from the government. (261)

In this state of things, with little or none of the natural influence of property to check at once the power of the crown and the violence of the people, it is not possible to conceive that such a mixed government as France has now established can be maintained. Nor can I think that a state of things, in which there would be so much poverty, could be favourable to the existence and duration of a republic. And when, in addition to this, we consider how extremely difficult it is, under any circumstances, to establish a well-constituted republic, and how dreadfully the chances are against its continuance, as the experience of all history shews; it is not too much to say, that no well-grounded hope

---

(261) p. 433. *This law has not yet prevailed*

Why should this law occasion so great a subdivision of property? Not only prudence in marriage will counteract it, but the acquisition of wealth, made by each member of the family. These acquisitions will probably enable him to leave to his children as large a patrimony as he received from his father. His children in their turn will be again inclined and probably[1] enabled to follow their father's example. Is not this practice actually prevailing in England in all families excepting the Aristocratical. Do not all the merchants, Bankers, manufacturers, farmers, shopkeepers, &c. &c.[2] divide their property equally amongst their children, and are any of the ill effects, expected by Mr. Malthus, in the case of France, found to proceed from it?

[1] 'inclined and probably' is ins.   [2] 'farmers, shopkeepers, &c. &c.' is ins.

could be entertained of the permanent prevalence of such a form of government. (262)

But the state of property above described would be the very soil for a military despotism. If the | government did not adopt 435 the Eastern mode of considering itself as sole territorial proprietor, it might at least take a hint from the Economists, and declare itself co-proprietor with the landlords, and from this source, (which might still be a fertile one, though the landlords, on account of their numbers, might be poor,) together with a few other taxes, the army might easily be made the richest part of the society; and it would then possess an overwhelming influence, which, in such a state of things, nothing could oppose. The despot might now and then be changed, as under the Roman emperors, by the Prætorian guards; but the despotism would certainly rest upon very solid foundations.

[In the British empire, the immense landed possessions which formerly prevailed have been divided by the prosperity of commerce and manufactures.

A large body of middle classes has been formed from com- 436

Because the land may be very much subdivided in consequence of the apportioning it amongst children, it does not follow, either, that it should be separately cultivated by those children, or that each should continue to be the proprietor of his original share of[3] it. Sales would be made, and leases would be granted, and as well as a great proprietor now divides his land into separate farms for the convenience, and advantage of better cultivation, so would various small contiguous[4] proprietors accumulate their small lots of land into one good farm for the same purpose.

(262) p. 434. *In this state of things*

I cannot participate with Mr. Malthus in his fears for the duration[5] of a free Government, under such a system.

---

3 'his original share of' is ins.   5 Replaces 'preservation'.
4 'contiguous' is ins.

merce, manufactures, professions, &c. who are likely to be more effective demanders than small proprietors of land.

437   Under these circumstances, it might be rash to conclude that the abolition of the right of primogeniture would increase the wealth of the country; but if we could come to this conclusion, it would not determine the policy of a change.

There is reason to think that the British constitution could not be maintained without an aristocracy; and an effective aristocracy could not be maintained without the right of primogeniture.

438   It is not easy to say to what extent the abolition of the law of primogeniture would divide the landed property of the country; but the division would probably be unfavourable to good government.

439   Although therefore a *more* equal distribution of landed property might be better than that which actually prevails, it might not be wise to abolish the law of primogeniture.

But whatever laws may prevail, the principle will remain true, that the division of landed property is one of the great means of distribution which tends to keep up and increase the exchangeable value of the whole produce.]

440   SECTION VIII

Of the Distribution occasioned by Commerce, internal and external, considered as the Means of increasing the exchangeable Value of Produce

The second main cause favourable to that increase of exchangeable value, which depends upon distribution, is internal and external commerce.

[Every exchange which takes place in a country effects a distribution of its commodities better adapted to the wants of the society, and calculated to give a greater market value to the whole produce.]

441   The Economists, in their endeavours to prove the unproductive nature of trade, always insisted that the effect of it was merely to equalize prices, which were in some places too high and in others

too low, but in their amount the same as they would be after the exchange had taken place. This position must be considered as unfounded, and capable of being contradicted by incontrovertible facts. The increase of price at first, from the extension of the market, is unquestionable. And when to this we add the effect occasioned by the demand for further produce, and the means thus afforded of rapid accumulation for the supply of this demand, it is impossible to doubt for a moment the direct tendency of all internal trade to increase the value of the national produce.

If indeed it did not tend to increase the value of the national produce, it would not be carried | on. It is out of this increase 442 that the merchants concerned are paid; and if some London goods are not more valued in Glasgow than in London, and some Glasgow goods more valued in London than in Glasgow, the merchants who exchange the articles in which these towns trade, would neither be doing themselves any good, nor any one else. It is a mere futile process to exchange one set of commodities for another, if the parties, after this new distribution of goods has taken place, are not better off than they were before. The giving one article for another has nothing to do with effectual demand, unless the commodity received so far exceeds in value the labour employed on the commodity parted with, as to yield adequate profits to the capitalists concerned, and to give them both the power and the will to set fresh labour to work in the same trade. (263)

---

(263) p. 442. *It is out of this increase that*

Here as well as in many other places Mr. Malthus appears to think that commerce and the exchange of commodities adds greatly to the value of commodities and enables merchants to add to the amount and value of their profits, and further that it is from this source that all the great savings and accumulations are made.

It is undoubtedly true that if "some of the London goods were not more valued in Glasgow than in London, and some Glasgow goods more valued in London than in Glasgow,

It has been said that the industry of a country is measured by the extent of its capital, and that the manner in which this capital is employed, though it may make some difference to the enjoyment of the inhabitants, makes very little in the *value* of the

---

the merchants who exchange the articles in which these towns trade, would be neither doing themselves any good nor any one else," by exchanging them.

But how does this prove that these goods attain any higher value by this exchange or afford any additional profits for capital to the merchants who are concerned in sending them from one place to another?

Will the mass of goods in the country, in consequence of these exchanges, command more labour, or will they exchange for more of any medium of a known value?

The price of hardware in London depends on its cost of production, that is to say it will only be produced on the condition that its price repays all the expences bestowed upon it, together with the ordinary and general rate of profits. Whether the common and usual demand be for a given quantity, or for ten times that quantity, after an inconsiderable interval, that will be its price. Mr. Malthus might say that that interval was one of great importance, and if there be a demand for the commodity, the manufacturer will in that interval obtain great profits, and be able to make valuable savings.—I grant it, but at whose expence will these greater profits[1] be made, and will they add to the value of the mass of commodities? If the ordinary price of a certain quantity of hardware be £100, and in consequence of demand, I am obliged to give £110 for it, the dealer will get larger profits, but who pays them?

---

[1] 'greater profits' replaces 'savings'.

national revenue. This would be true on one supposition, and on one supposition only; namely, that the inhabitants could be persuaded to estimate their confined productions just as highly, to be as eager to obtain and consume them, and as willing to work

---

Mr. Malthus looks only at the manufacturer and would have us believe that he gets larger profits, and no one is the worse for them, and therefore that they are clear gains to the country. But I say the consumer pays them for one of three things he must do, he must content himself with a less quantity of hardware—he must deny himself the expenditure of £10 on some other commodity which he usually consumed, or if he enjoys the same quantity of commodities as before he is not[2] enabled to add to his capital from savings by £10 to the amount he used to do. If he saves the £10 from his expenditure he indeed enables the manufacturer of hardware to add £10—to his capital from his increased profits, but the same result would have taken place if by any other means he could have been prevailed upon to save £10—out of his expenditure, with this difference indeed that in the one case it would be added to his own capital in the other to the capital of the Hardware manufacturer.—In both cases the national capital will be increased in value £10.—and more labour can be employed, if it has not risen in value. And here I would just remark that this saving out of increased gains, which is the means by which all great fortunes are made according to Mr. Malthus, is a saving really effected by diminished expenditure, a source of saving very much undervalued by Mr. Malthus as will be seen in Page 421 of his work. But to revert to the subject immediately before us. If the purchaser of hardware pur-

---

[2] 'not' is ins.

hard for them, and to make great sacrifices for them, as for the commodities which they obtain from a distance. But are we at 443 liberty to make such a supposition? It is specifi-|cally to overcome the want of eagerness to purchase domestic commodities that the merchant exchanges them for others more in request. Could we but so alter the wants and tastes of the people of Glas-

---

chases the usual quantity of goods he is not enabled to save so much by £10 as before and in this case the saving *may* indeed be made by the hardware manufacturer, but at the expence of the saving of another member of the community, and nothing whatever will be added to the national capital. If now you suppose that the demand of the merchant for the Glasgow market does not raise the price of hardware in London, but that he can nevertheless charge a high profit to the Glasgow[1] consumer for it, I have a similar remark to make. Either he makes only the usual and ordinary profits on his stock, or he makes greater profits. If he makes only the usual profits there can be no pretence for saying that he has added any thing by this particular transaction to the Natl. capital. If his profits are[2] high and above the usual level they can only remain so till other capitalists[3] can be brought to compete with him, and then his profits, and the price of his goods will sink to their natural level. I may be again told that it is during this interval of high profits, that savings are made, and capitals increased—but my answer is the same as before. When the price of hardware sinks in Glasgow to its level price, will the saving made by the purchasers of this article be expended on other things or will it be added to capital. If I am told they will be expended

---

[1] 'merchant' is del. here.   [3] Replaces 'capitals'.
[2] 'are' replaces 'have only been as'.

gow as to make them estimate as highly the profusion of cotton goods which they produce, as any articles which they could receive in return for them under a prosperous trade, we should hear no more of their distresses. It may be allowed that the quantity of productive industry maintained in a country is nearly proportioned to the quantity of capital employed; but the value

---

on other things then I acknowledge that the transfer of £10 from the pocket of the consumer to the pocket of the merchant during the season of high profit might be favorable to the accumulation of capital, for I know one to be extravagant and the other may possibly be saving, but here again it must be allowed that effects quite as good would have resulted, if by lowering the price of goods the consumer had saved £10 from his expenditure, and added it to his capital.

The general profits of a country depend as I have frequently said on the state of wages, when wages are low profits must be high—but the particular profits of a particular set of manufacturers, or a particular set of merchants, must depend, whatever may be the state of wages, on the[4] price which they can charge for their commodities to the consumers.

The natural price of a certain quantity of cloth a certain quantity of shoes, a certain quantity of hats &c., we will suppose to be £100. If the owner of the cloth can get £110 for his cloth, it must be at the expence of the consumer, and as[5] these consumers can only purchase this particular commodity with the commodity of which they are possessed, its rise is the same thing to them as the fall of their commodity. If before the rise, the shoemaker gave half the quantity of his shoes for half the quantity of the cloth, he must now when

4 'relative' is del. here.   5 Replaces 'if'.

of the revenue will be greater or less, according to the market prices of the commodities produced. These market prices must obviously depend upon the interchange of goods; and consequently the value of the revenue, and the power and will to increase it, must depend upon that distribution of commodities which best adapts them to the wants and tastes of the society.

The whole produce of a nation may be said to have a market price in money and labour. When this market price is high, that is, when the prices of commodities rise so as to command a greater excess of labour above what they had cost in production than before, while the same capital and number of people had been

---

the price of cloth has risen to £110—give one tenth more or 55 p.c. of his shoes for the same quantity. In all cases then the excess of profits of a particular trade[1] are made at the expence of the consumer, and in proportion as it adds to the power of one of increasing his capital, it diminishes the power of another to add to his. When a merchant makes large profits by selling[2] his goods at a high price, to foreign countries, his profits are profits to the country[3] of which he is an inhabitant, but they are not less obtained at the expence of the consumer, but in this case the consumer is a foreigner, and the transfer is made from one country to another.

From any thing which I have said it must not be inferred that I undervalue the benefits which would result both to Glasgow and London from the interchange of their commodities, I only deny that these benefits would shew themselves in the form of high profits, and increased value. Inasmuch as the labour both of London and Glasgow will be more productively directed, they will both derive advantages from this trade. If Glasgow made the hardware for

---

[1] Last eight words replace 'the particular profits of a trade'.

[2] Replaces 'When a merchant sells'.

[3] Replaces 'nation'.

employed upon them, it is evident that more fresh labour will be set in motion every year, and the increase of wealth will be certain and rapid. On the other hand, when the market prices of commodities are such as to be able to command very little more | labour than the production of them has cost, it is as evident that   444 the national wealth will proceed very slowly, or perhaps be quite stationary.

In the distribution of commodities, the circulating medium of every country bears a most important part; and, as I intimated before in a note, we are much more likely to obscure our reasonings than to render them clearer, by throwing it out of our

---

herself, or London the cotton goods, they would each obtain less hardware, and cotton goods, together, with a given capital.—By the better division of labour, cotton goods will be more cheap in London, and hardware more cheap in Glasgow—the advantage then to both places is not they have any increase of value, but with the same amount of value they are both able to consume and enjoy an increased[4] quantity of commodities, and if they should have no inclination to indulge themselves in the purchase of an additional quantity, they will have increased means of making savings from their expenditure. It cannot be true then "that the value of the revenue will be greater or less, according to the market prices of the commodities produced"[5] for supposing the cost of production of commodities not to alter, the high market value of one really means the low market value of another, for commodities are purchased with commodities, and if the value of cloth is high estimated in silk, silk must be low estimated in cloth. If the profits of the clothier are high estimated in silk and all other commodities, it is only because a contribution is made to those profits out of the funds of all the consumers of cloth.

[4] Replaces 'a given'.

[5] See Malthus's p. 443; above, p. 394.

consideration. It is not easy indeed, without reference to a circulating medium, to ascertain whether the commodities of a country are so distributed as to give them their proper value. (264)

It may be said, perhaps, that if the funds for the maintenance of labour are at any time in unusual abundance, it may fairly be presumed that they will be able to command a more than usual quantity of labour. But they certainly will not be able to command more labour, nor even so much, if the distribution of them be defective; and in a country which has a circulating medium, the specific proof of the distribution being defective is, that the whole produce does not exchange for so large an amount of circulating medium as before, and that consequently the producers have been obliged to sell at a great diminution of money profits, or a positive money loss.

From the harvest of 1815 to the harvest of 1816, there cannot be a doubt that the funds for the maintenance of labour in this country were unusually abundant. Corn was particularly plenti-

---

(264) p. 444. *In the distribution of commodities*

It is of no importance in elucidating correct principles in what medium value is estimated, provided only that the medium itself is invariable. Money—corn, labour are all equally good. Mr. Malthus in using money appears to me frequently to mistake the variations of money itself, for the variations in the commodities of which he is speaking. An alteration in the [1] value of money has no effect on the relative value of commodities, for it raises or sinks their price in the same proportion; but it is the alteration in the relative value of commodities, particularly of necessaries, and luxuries, which produce the most important consequences in the view of the Political Economist.

(265) p. 445. *But if the farmer sold his produce*

Whether he would command the same quantity of labour next year, would depend on the price of labour. It is prob-

---

[1] 'relative' is del. here.

ful, and no other necessaries were deficient; yet it is an acknow-
ledged fact, that great numbers were | thrown out of employment, 445
partly from the want of power, and partly from the want of will
to employ the same quantity of labour as before. How is this fact
to be accounted for? As I have said before, it would not be easy
to account for it without referring to a circulating medium;
because, without such reference, the proof of a defective distribution would be extremely difficult. But the moment we refer to
a circulating medium, the theory of the fact observed becomes
perfectly clear. It is acknowledged that there was a fall in the
money value of the raw produce, to the amount of nearly one
third. But if the farmer sold his produce for only two thirds of
the price at which he had before sold it, it is evident that he would
be quite unable to command the same quantity of labour, and to
employ the same quantity of capital on his farm as he did the year
before. (265) And when afterwards a great fall of money price
took place in all manufactured products, occasioned in a con-

---

able that the farmer would be much distressed even if labour
fell in some proportion to corn, because his contract with his
landlord is to pay him a money rent; this rent remains the
same whatever may be the price of produce. If however
the farmer can employ less labour, the landlord, if he receive
his rent, can employ more. Mr. Malthus thinks that there
will be a diminished power to employ labour, and consequently a diminished demand for it—he allows[2] that the
price of corn, the chief article consumed by the labourer,
will fall, and yet in his argument he assumes that labour
will be at the same price as before. Mr. Malthus adds "And
when afterwards a great fall of money price took place in all
manufactured products." But why should manufactured
products fall? their cost of production is the same as before,
and corn falls relatively to them only because corn is abundant,—is cheaply produced, and they are not so.

What has happened? an addition to the quantity of corn,

[2] Replaces 'he thinks too'.

siderable degree by this previous fall of raw produce, it is as evident that the manufacturers would be unable to command the labour of the same number of workmen as before. In the midst of the plenty of necessaries, these two important classes of society would really have their power of employing labour diminished, while all those who possessed fixed incomes would have their power of employing labour increased, with very little chance of an increase of will to extend their demand in proportion; and the general result would resemble the effects of that partial distribution
446 of products which | would arise from the interruption of accustomed communications. The same, or a greater quantity of commodities might be produced for a short time; but the distribution not being such as to proportion the supply in each quarter to the demand, the whole would fall in exchangeable value, and a very decided check to production would be experienced in reference to the whole country. It follows, that the labouring classes of society may be thrown out of work in the midst of an abundance

---

—an increased quantity of commodities in fact compared with the whole population, and what is to be the result, according to Mr. Malthus? Universal distress to all classes. I can understand why the farmer should be distressed as I have already explained. But every man is not a producer of corn, and under engagements to pay money rents. Suppose wages to fall in proportion to the saving made by the labourer in the purchase of his corn, *he* would still be able to purchase as many manufactured commodities as before— if his wages did not fall, he could purchase more. Every manufacturer himself could purchase more manufactured commodities from other manufacturers. Having less to expend on bread, he would have more to expend on other things—the landlord would be in the same situation, and although the demand for manufactures would undoubtedly be diminished on the part of the agricultural class, it cannot I think be disputed that it would be increased in respect of

of necessaries, if these necessaries are not in the hands of those who are at the same time both able and willing to employ an adequate quantity of labour. (266)

It is of no use therefore to make suppositions about a great increase of produce, and, rejecting all reference to a circulating medium, to conclude that this great increase will be properly distributed and effectively consumed. It is a conclusion which we have no right whatever to make. We know, both from theory and experience, that if the whole produce falls in money value, the distribution must be such as to discourage production. As long as this fall in the money price of produce continues to diminish the power of commanding domestic and foreign labour, a great discouragement to production must obviously continue; and if, after labour has adjusted itself to the new level of prices, the permanent distribution of the produce and the permanent tastes and habits of the people should not be favourable to an adequate degree of consumption, the clearest principles of political

---

the other classes—manufactures would not then fall in money price, nor would the manufacturers be unable to command the labour of the same number of workmen as before. If the price of labour fell, they would be able to command more.

(266) p. 446. *The same, or a greater quantity*

Mr. Malthus says "the whole would fall in exchangeable *value*" what does this mean? would they fall in money value? Mr. Malthus would answer in the affirmative. I ask then whether this money value would command a greater quantity of labour. Mr. Malthus says the labouring classes would be thrown out of work—if so, the money value would command more labour than before. Have not the commodities[1] then risen in real value according to Mr. Malthus's definition of real value?

[1] Replaces 'Have they not'.

447 eco-|nomy shew that the profits of stock might be lower for any length of time than the state of the land rendered necessary; (267) and that the check to production might be as permanent as the faulty distribution of the produce and the unfavourable tastes and habits which had occasioned it.

[Referring to the command over labour as the final measure of the value of the whole produce, its bullion value should be previously referred to, in order to ascertain whether its distribution be such as to enable it to command labour in some proportion to its quantity.

448 The distribution of commodities, occasioned by internal trade, is the first step towards any considerable increase of wealth and capital.]

449 The motives which urge individuals to engage | in foreign commerce are precisely the same as those which lead to the interchange of goods between the more distant parts of the same country, namely, an increase in the market price of the local products; and the increase of profits thus made by the individual, or the prevention of that fall of profits which would have taken place if the capital had been employed at home, must be consi-

---

(267) p. 447. *The clearest principles of Political Economy shew that the profits of stock might be lower for any length of time than the state of the land rendered necessary.*

On the land last cultivated, and paying no rent, profits could not be lower for any length of time, than the state of the land and the reward to the workman [1] rendered necessary. There must then be two rates of profit for capital, one for capital employed in Agriculture, another for capital employed in Manufactures, and yet the one capitalist may freely remove his capital to the employment of the other. Can this be?

(268) p. 448. *The motives which urge individuals*
   See remark 442.[2]

   [1] Last six words are ins.   [2] Note (263) above.

dered as a proportionate increase in the value of the national produce. (268)

Mr. Ricardo begins his Chapter on Foreign Trade by stating that "No extension of foreign trade will immediately increase the amount of value in a country although it will very powerfully contribute to increase the mass of commodities and therefore the sum of enjoyments." This statement is quite consistent with his peculiar view of value, as depending solely upon the labour which a commodity has cost. However abundant may be the returns of the merchant, or however greatly they may exceed his exports in value according to the common acceptation of the term, it is certain that the labour employed in procuring these exports will at first remain the same. But, as it is so glaring and undeniable a fact that the returns from an unusually favourable trade will exchange for an unusual quantity of money, labour and domestic commodities; as this increased power of commanding money, labour and commodities is in reality what is meant by the merchant when he talks of the extension of the foreign market and a favourable trade, (269) it appears to me that such | a state of 450 things which may, and often does last a sufficient time to produce

---

(269) p. 449. *But as it is so glaring &c.*

I quite agree with Mr. Malthus that this is the fair criterion by which to judge of the merchants profits, but I contend that they are not clear gain—they are often made at the expence of the savings of some of his fellow citizens.

"If a foreign power says Mr. Malthus[3] were to send to a particular merchant commodities of a new description which would sell in the London market for fifty thousand pounds, the wealth of that merchant would be increased to that extent; and who I would ask would be the poorer?"[4] That would depend on the nature of the commodities, and on the fund from which these goods were purchased, by the consumers, from the merchants. If they were purchased

[3] Replaces 'as Mr. Malthus sup-   [4] Malthus's p. 450; below, p. 403.
poses'.

the most important results, is alone, and at once, a decisive proof
that the view of exchangeable value, which makes it depend
exclusively upon the cost of production, is essentially incorrect,
and utterly useless in solving the great phenomena which attend
the progress of wealth.

Mr. Ricardo seems to think that value cannot increase in one
department of produce without diminishing it in some other.*
This again may be true according to his view of value, but is
utterly unfounded according to that more enlarged view of ex-

* It appears to me that if the two first sentences in Mr. Ricardo's Chapter
on Foreign Trade were well founded, there would be no such intercourse
between nations. (270)

---

from that fund which would otherwise have been saved,
and the commodities so bought were[1] immediately consumed the capital of the country would not be increased by
the present—[2] the only consequence would be an increased
quantity of enjoyments for that particular year. If they were
purchased instead of some other commodity,—that other
commodity was given to the merchant in exchange for the
foreign commodity,[3] and employed by him as capital, there
would be, on the whole, an increased saving of £50000 in
consequence of this present. This case differs in nothing
from the case of Glasgow and London. The accumulation
is made in consequence of[4] greater savings made out of the
annual revenue of the country. You have had £50000 given
you which you resolve to save, and add to your capital.

(270) p. 450. *It appears to me that if the two*

Mr. Malthus misunderstands me. I do not mean literally
that the commodity imported will be of no more value than
the commodity exported it must at least be so much greater
value as to compensate for the labour employed in bringing

[1] Last five words are ins.
[2] 'as before' is del. here.
[3] Last six words are ins.

[4] 'diminished expenditure' is del.
here.

changeable value which is established and confirmed by experience. If any foreign power were to send to a particular merchant commodities of a new description which would sell in the London market for fifty thousand pounds, the wealth of such merchant would be increased to that extent; and who, I would ask, would be the poorer for it? It is no doubt true that the purchasers of these commodities may be obliged to forego the use of some of the articles which they had before been in the habit of buying,†

† This, however, will not necessarily happen. The greater temptation offered to consumption may induce some persons to spend what they otherwise would have saved, and in many cases the wealth of the country, instead of suffering by this change, will gain by it. The increased consumption, as far as it goes, will occasion an increase of market prices and

---

it in, together with the profits of the merchant for the time his capital was employed, that constitutes in fact the cost of production of that commodity. But the commodity sent out has for the same reasons the same value added to it, and therefore if you have increased the cost of production and the value of one commodity, so also have you increased the cost of production and value of the other. If I send £100 worth of hats which sell for £105 in France, and receive £100 worth of claret which sells for £105 here, it appears as if I gave £100 for £105 and to the French merchant it will appear as if he received £105 for £100, but in fact they both give and receive the same value, the £5 is added to compensate for expences and profits of capital. Any £100 employed at home for the same time, and attended with the same expences of carriage, or expences of any other kind, would equally yield £105. By the foreign trade then we have got a more desirable commodity, but not a more valuable commodity. Am I not then justified in saying that "No extension of foreign trade will immediately increase the amount of value in a country although it will very powerfully contribute to increase the mass of commodities and therefore the sum of enjoyments."

451 and so | far in some quarters may diminish demand; but, to
counterbalance this diminution, the enriched merchant will become a purchaser of additional goods to the amount perhaps of
the whole fifty thousand pounds, and thus prevent any general
fall in the value of the native produce consumed in the country,
while the value of the foreign produce so consumed has increased
to the amount of the whole of the new produce imported. I see
no difference between a present from abroad, and the unusual
profits of a new foreign trade, in their effects upon the wealth of
a state. They are equally calculated to increase the wealth of the
community, by an increase both of the quantity and *value* of the
produce obtained.

It will be said perhaps that, neither the people nor the money
of the country having been by supposition increased, the value of
the whole produce estimated in labour or money cannot be
increased.

With regard to labour I would observe that, when I speak of
the value of the whole produce of a country being able to command more labour than before, I do not mean to refer specifically
to a greater *number* of labourers, but to say that it could either
purchase more at the old price, or pay the actual labourers
higher; (271) and such a state of things, with a population which
452 cannot imme-|diately be increased, always occasions that demand

profits. The increase of | profits will soon restore the capital which for a short
time had been diverted from its destined office; and the country will be left
with habits of greater consumption, and at the same time with proportionate
means of supplying them.

---

(271) p. 451. *With regard to labour I would observe*

Here is a new explanation of Mr. Malthus' measure of
real value in exchange. If I wanted to know whether I had
a greater value this year than last—I cannot ascertain this
fact by a comparison of the number of labourers I could
employ last year and the number I can employ[1] this—[2] for
I should equally have a greater value if I could command

[1] Replaces 'I could command'.   [2] 'but either by determining
                                      whether' is del. here.

for labour, which so powerfully encourages the exertions of those
who were before perhaps only half paid and half employed; and
is at once the surest sign and most effective stimulus of increasing
wealth. It is the natural consequence of the value of the produce
estimated in labour increasing faster than the population, and
forms the true and healthy encouragement to the further increase
of numbers.

With regard to money, this most useful measure of value would
perform its functions very indifferently, if it could in no respect
accommodate itself to cases of this kind; and if the importation
of a valuable commodity always proportionably reduced the
price of the other parts of the national produce. But this is far
from being the case, even if we do not suppose any fresh importation of the precious metals. The occurrence of such an event is
precisely the period, when a greater velocity is given to the circulation of the money actually in use, and when fresh paper may
be issued without a fall in the rate of foreign exchanges, or a rise
in the price of bullion and of goods. One or other, or both of
these resources will be applied, except in the most barbarous
countries; and though undoubtedly, in the case of the importation
of foreign commodities which come directly into competition
with domestic goods, such goods will fall in price, and the producers of them be for a time rendered poorer, yet it will very
rarely indeed happen that | other goods not affected by such   453
competition will fall in money value; and altogether no fall will
take place in particular commodities sufficient to prevent a rise
in the money price of the whole produce. (272)

---

no more labour but paid the actual labourers higher. If
I understand this it means, I shall have a greater value if
I can exchange my commodities for more of this measure
of value—and I shall equally have a greater value if I cannot.

(272) p. 453. *And altogether no fall will take place in particular
commodities, sufficient to prevent a rise in the money price
of the whole produce.*

Suppose we allow this, the question whether the gain of the
merchant is a new value, or a value obtained at the expence

It may naturally be expected however that more money will be imported; and, in fact, a successful extension of foreign trade is exactly that state of things which most directly leads to the importation of bullion. For what is it that the merchant exporter specifically considers as a successful extension of foreign commerce in dealing with civilized nations? Undoubtedly the power of selling his exports abroad for a greater value than usual, estimated in bullion; and of course, if the goods which he would import in return will not sell at home so much higher as to warrant their importation, a part or the whole of the returns will be imported in money. But if only such an amount be imported as shall bear the same proportion to the returns in goods as the whole of the currency of the country does to the whole of its produce, it is obvious that no difficulty whatever can occur in the circulation of the commodities of the country at their former prices, with the single exception of those articles with which the foreign goods might directly enter into competition, which in this case would never be sufficient to prevent a general increase of value in the whole produce.

I distinctly therefore differ from Mr. Ricardo in the conclusion implied in the following passage. "In all cases the demand
454 for foreign and home | commodities together, as far as regards

---

of the consumers is not thereby determined. Mr. Malthus and I both allow that an advantage is gained by the introduction of cheap or desirable [1] foreign commodities, but I say that the whole of it should belong to the consumer and if at any time the merchant enjoys it, it is at the expence of the consumer and by depriving him of it. With the consumer it must finally rest.

(273) p. 454. *It appears to me that in almost every case*

If four men have a thousand a year each they cannot spend more than £4000 a year.

The more value they expend on foreign commodities, the less they will have to expend on home commodities. [2]

---

[1] 'or desirable' is ins.
[2] Replaces 'The more foreign
commodities they buy, the ['less' was omitted here by a mistake]

value, is limited by the revenue and capital of the country. If one increases, the other must diminish."* It appears to me that in almost every case of successful foreign trade, it is a matter of unquestionable fact that the demand for foreign and home commodities taken together decidedly increases; and that the increase in the value of foreign produce does not occasion a proportionate diminution in the value of home produce.

I would still however allow that the demand for foreign and home commodities together, as far as regards value, is limited by the revenue and capital of the country; but, according to my view of the subject, the national revenue, which consists of the sum of rents, profits, and wages, is at once decidedly increased by the increased profits of the foreign merchant, without a proportionate diminution of revenue in any other quarter; whereas Mr. Ricardo is evidently of opinion that, though the abundance of commodities is increased, the revenue of the country, as far as regards value, remains the same; and it is because I object rather to the conclusion *intended* to be conveyed, than to the actual terms of the passage quoted, that I have used the word *implied* rather than *expressed*. (273)

* Princ. of Polit. Econ. c. vii. p. [130]. 2d edit.

It will be of immense importance to buy cheap, that is to say to obtain plenty of commodities for a little value; and inasmuch as foreign trade, and an extensive market, enables them to do this, it is beneficial to the country. Mr. Malthus says "But according to my view of the subject, the national revenue, which consists of the sum of rents, profits, and wages is at once decidedly increased by the increased profits of the foreign merchant." The national revenue is increased ! in what? in the greater quantity or better quality of consumable commodities; but not in their greater value.[3] But

quantity [replaced by 'value'] of home commodities they can purchase.'—'Observe I say "value they expend" not quantity bought' is del. here.

[3] Replaces an unfinished version: 'Increased ! in what? in the quantity of consumable commodities; in this we agree, the question is whether'.

It will readily be allowed that an increase in the *quantity* of commodities is one of the most desirable effects of foreign commerce; but I wish particularly to press on the attention of the 455 reader | that in almost all cases, another most important effect

---

how does this benefit shew itself? perhaps for a short time in the increased profits of the merchant, but always finally in the cheap value of the foreign commodity. It is precisely the same as in the case of a manufacturer who discovers an improved[1] machine with which to manufacture his goods. While competition does not fully act upon him, and oblige him to sink the price of his goods to the cost of production, he gets great profits, but finally the advantage of the improvement rests wholly with the consumer.[2]

The argument in my chapter on foreign trade is grounded on the supposition which is I believe not disputed that excepting for short intervals of time profits in foreign trade cannot be elevated above the general rate of profit, and whenever they are I am of opinion, and have given my reasons for that opinion, that the equalization of profits will be brought about by a fall in the profits of foreign trade, and not by the general rise of profits in other trades.

During the interval that profits in foreign trade are elevated above general profits, those who are engaged in it will get more and nobody else less, and so far the national revenue will be increased; but as soon as the competition of other capitalists have sunk the profits of foreign trade, to the general level of profits, although the national revenue, when estimated in money, will be of less value than before, nothing will be lost to the country, the advantage which was before

---

[1] Replaces 'a useful'.
[2] The two paragraphs that follow were ins. later in the MS; a fresh sheet being used, they were attached by mistake at the end of Note (275) below, where they are obviously out of place.

accompanies it, expressly rejected by Mr. Ricardo, namely, an increase in the amount of exchangeable value. And that this latter effect is so necessary, in order to create a continued stimulus to productive industry, and keep up an abundant supply of com-

---

reaped by the merchant will be now enjoyed by the consumer. The merchant sells at a lower price and gets less profit—the consumer buys at a cheaper price and the saving which he makes is precisely equal in amount to the profit[3] which was before enjoyed and is now relinquished[4] by the merchant. But in this interval the whole produce of the country was of greater value! Of a greater market value certainly, but was this attended with any real advantage to the country, seeing that immediately when it is relinquished it is equally enjoyed by another part of the community? The case is precisely similar to a man who discovers a new machine, and for some time can keep his secret—he will enjoy during that interval, large profits, and the annual revenue of the country will be increased while he sells his goods above their natural price, but will one particle of this advantage be lost when his cheaper mode of producing the commodity is universally known, and the consumer is enabled to gain an advantage precisely equal indeed more than equal[5] to that which the particular manufacturer relinquishes? If the larger gains of the foreign merchant, or of the individual manufacturer be desirable, then is it an argument for a general system of monopolies—a system which considers only the profits of capitalists, and is little solicitous about the comforts and advantages of consumers.

[3] 'in amount to the profit' replaces 'to that'.
[4] 'and is now relinquished' is ins.

[5] Last eight words replace 'a value precisely equal'.

modities, that in the few cases in which it does not take place, a stagnation in the demand for labour is immediately perceptible, and the progress of wealth is checked. An extension of foreign commerce, according to the view which Mr. Ricardo takes of it, would, in my opinion, place us frequently in the situation in which this country was in the early part of 1816, when a sudden abundance and cheapness of corn and other commodities, from a great supply meeting a deficient demand, so diminished the value of the income of the country, that it could no longer command the same quantity of labour at the same price; the consequence of which was that, in the midst of plenty, thousands upon thousands were thrown out of employment—a most painful but almost unavoidable preliminary to a fall in the money wages of labour,

---

(274) p. 454. *It will readily be allowed*

"An increase in the amount of exchangeable value"! in what medium?

Are not the common and usual profits of stock a sufficient stimulus to productive industry?

"So diminished the value of the income of the country [1] that it could no longer command the same quantity of labour at the same price; the consequence of which was &c. &c." But if commodities fell in price, and would command the same quantity of labour at a lower price, who would suffer by it? Not the employers of labour for with the same quantity of commodities they could command the same labour,—not the labourers for they could command in exchange for their labour the same quantity of commodities. And if either did suffer, a corresponding benefit would be obtained by the other. This is merely a variation in money.[2]

(275) p. 455. *Mr. Ricardo always seems to*

What are we to say to a system of political economy which at one moment insists that value is measured by the quantity

---

[1] 'In what medium?' is del. here.   [2] Last sentence is ins.

which it is obvious could alone enable the general income of the country to employ the same number of labourers as before, and, after a period of severe check to the increase of wealth, to recommence a progressive movement. (274)

Mr. Ricardo always seems to think that it is quite the same to the labourer, whether he is able to command more of the necessaries of life by a rise in the money price of labour, or by a fall in | the money price of provisions; but these two events, though 456 apparently similar in their effects, may be, and in general are, most essentially different. (275) An increase in the wages of labour, both nominal and real, invariably implies such a distribution of the actual wealth as to give it an increasing value, to ensure full employment to all the labouring classes, and to create

---

of labour it can command, and at the next moment rejects that measure, and shews its insufficiency. If money wages remain the same, and every commodity on which the labourers wages are expended fall in [3] money price, the labourers wages are really increased,[4] in Mr. Malthus measure of value and, if the amount of commodities be not increased, they must have fallen in his measure of real value, because under these circumstances the same quantity of commodities cannot command the same quantity of labour. If money wages increase, and the price of commodities do not rise, real wages will also increase and in this case too if commodities be not increased in quantity their real value will have fallen. Are not these two cases precisely the same? I know Mr. Malthus will say that the rise in the money price of wages will be an indication of an increased quantity of commodities and an increased demand for labour, but the falling price of com-

---

[3] 'value' is del. here.
[4] The remainder of the sentence replaces: 'and, if the amount of commodities be not increased, they must have fallen in real value, if labour be the measure of value; because the same quantity of commodities cannot command the same quantity of value.'

a demand for further produce, and for the capital which is to obtain it. In short, it is the infallible sign of health and prosperity. Whereas a general fall in the money price of necessaries often arises from so defective a distribution of the produce of the country, that the general amount of its value cannot be kept up; in which case, under the most favourable circumstances, a temporary period of want of employment and distress is unavoidable; and in many cases, as may be too frequently observed in surveying the different countries of the globe, this fall in the money price

---

modities with stationary money wages will afford no such indication.

But he has given no proof of this.

May not money become more valuable, and in that case would not a falling price of commodities with stationary money wages indicate an increasing demand for labour.

Why should commodities fall in price generally from any other cause but that of an increased value of money? I know of no other cause which could produce such an effect except new facilities in the production of them all save only money.[1]

(276) p. 455. *Mr. Ricardo always seems to think*

Mr. Malthus mistakes me. I fully agree with him that an increase in the wages of labour implies full employment to all the labouring classes, but so does a fall in the money price of provisions without a fall in money wages[2] provided the fall in the price of provisions is not caused by an accidental glut, but by a cheaper mode of producing provisions.

Mr. Malthus' error is in supposing that cheap corn, and cheap commodities, necessarily imply a glut of corn and

[1] In the MS two further paragraphs were attached at the end of this Note by mistake: they are now printed as part of Note (273), to which they properly belong (see above, p. 408, foot-note 2). The interposition of this extraneous matter explains the anomaly of two Notes, (275) and (276), under the same heading.

[2] 'without a fall [replacing 'an increase'] in money wages' is ins.

of necessaries is the accompaniment of a permanent want of employment, and the most abject poverty, in consequence of retrograde and permanently diminished wealth. (276)

The reader will be fully aware that a great fall in the price of particular commodities, either from improved machinery or foreign commerce, is perfectly compatible with a continued and great increase, not only in the exchangeable value of the whole produce of the country, but even in the exchangeable value of the whole produce of these particular articles themselves. (277)

---

commodities. We agree that a glut is an evil. It generally implies production without profit, and sometimes without even the return of the capital employed. It arises always I think from a bad selection in the object produced, but cheapness from facility of production, which I think is the only legitimate cheapness, never fails of being attended with the happiest effects, and is as different from a glut, as light is from darkness.

(277) p. 456. *The reader will be aware*

These are compatible, but not essential to each other and in general do not happen at the same time.[3] The advantage from a cheap price of corn, in consequence of facilities, either of production or importation, would be great, although it may be clearly demonstrated that from the loss of rents the money value of the mass of commodities would fall, and for a time at least, they would not command any great additional quantity of labour.*

* Insert this. And why not? because the demand for labour would be greatly increased without a corresponding supply—wages would be high and the condition of the labourer most happy.

[3] Replaces 'It is compatible, but not essential to it, and in general does not accompany it.'

It has been repeatedly stated that the whole value of the cottons |
457 produced in this country has been prodigiously increased, notwithstanding the great fall in their price. The same may be said
of the teas, although when they were first imported, the price per
pound was greatly higher than at present; and there can be little
doubt, that if we were to attempt to make our own wines by
means of hot-houses, they would altogether be worth much less
money, and would give encouragement to much less industry
than at present.

Even when the commodity is of such a nature as not to admit
of an extension of the market for it from reduced price, which
very rarely happens, yet the capital and labour, which in this case
will be thrown out of employment, will generally, in enterprising
and commercial countries, find other channels into which they
may be directed, with such profit as to keep up, and often more
than keep up, the value of the national income. At the same time
it should be observed, and it is a point of great importance, that
it is precisely among cases of this description, where the few
exceptions occur to the general and powerful tendency of foreign
commerce, to raise the value of the national income; and whenever these exceptions do take place, that is, whenever the value
of the national income is diminished, estimated even in money,
a temporary distress from a defective distribution of the produce

---

(278) p. 458. *If it could be proved*

If it could be proved![1] which I believe it cannot in any
case. But may not the national produce have less power in
the command of labour, and yet both wealth and population
increase?[2] If with the same produce wages were to rise,
population would probably increase, and though profits
would be diminished, might they not yet be sufficiently
high to allow further savings to be made? and further wealth
to be acquired?[3]

If from £1000 my profits were reduced to £500, I should
nevertheless increase my wealth if I saved £100.

[1] Replaces 'Certainly, if it could
be proved,'.
[2] 'Suppose with' is del. here.

[3] Last two lines, beginning 'might
they', replace 'might not further
savings be made?'

cannot fail to take place. If this diminished value be estimated in labour, the distress among the labouring classes, and check to the progress of wealth, will continue as long as the | diminished value 458 so estimated lasts: and if it could be proved that, under particular circumstances, any species of foreign trade tended permanently to diminish the power of the national produce in the command of domestic and foreign labour, such trade would certainly have the effect of checking permanently the progress of wealth and population. (278)

The causes of an increase in the effective demand for particular commodities are of very easy explanation; but it has been considered, and with reason, as not very easy to explain the cause of that general briskness of demand which is sometimes so very sensibly felt throughout a whole country, and is so strikingly contrasted with the feeling which gives rise to the expression of trade being universally very dead. As the specific and immediate cause of this general increase of effective demand, I should decidedly point to such a distribution of the produce, and such an adaptation of it to the wants and tastes of the society as will give the money price for which it sells an increased command of domestic and foreign labour; and I am inclined to think that, if this test be applied to all the striking cases that have occurred, it will rarely or never be found to fail. (279)

---

(279) p. 458. *As the specific and immediate cause*

In[4] all cases a good distribution of the produce, and an adaptation of it to the wants and tastes of society are of the utmost importance to the briskness of trade and the accumulation of capital. The want of this is in my opinion the only cause of the stagnation which commerce at different times experiences. It may be all traced to miscalculation, and to the production of a commodity which is not wanted instead of one which is wanted.

But in allowing this must we deny the beneficial effects

---

[4] A paragraph is del. at the beginning of the Note: 'No one can doubt the importance of the commodities produced being well adapted to the general wants as a cause of briskness of trade and the increase of wealth.'

It cannot for a moment be doubted, for instance, that the annual increase of the produce of the United States of America, estimated either in bullion or in domestic and foreign labour, has been greater than that of any country we are acquainted with, and that this has been greatly owing to their | foreign commerce, which, notwithstanding their facility of production, has given a value to their corn and raw produce equal to what they bear in many of the countries of Europe, and has consequently given to them a power in commanding the produce and labour of other countries quite extraordinary, when compared with the quantity of labour which they have employed. It can as little be doubted that in this country, from 1793 to 1814, the whole exchangeable value of the produce, estimated either in domestic and foreign labour, or in bullion, was greatly augmented every year. In this increase of value, as well as riches, the extension of our foreign commerce has been considered, almost without a dissentient opinion, as a most powerful agent; and certainly till 1815, no appearances seemed to indicate, that the increasing value of our imports had the slightest tendency to diminish the value of our

---

which arise from the fall in the price of commodities, on account of the increased facility of their production? Increase that facility ten fold, yet if the commodities you do produce are well adapted to the wants of the society, they will all be in demand, and if they are not, it only proves that the producers have been mistaken on that point and have not fulfilled the conditions necessary to ensure that briskness of demand, which could not fail to have followed from a more judicious selection of objects.

(280) p. 459. *In this increase of value &c. &c.*

If a nation saves, and employs more labour in production, it will increase the quantity and [1] value of its products. In such case it is certain that it may increase the value of foreign imports, without any diminution in the value of home com-

[1] 'quantity and' is ins.

domestic produce. They both increased, and increased greatly, together, estimated either in bullion or labour. (280)

But while in every country to which it seems possible to refer, an increase of value will be found to accompany increasing prosperity and riches, I am inclined to think that no single instance can be produced of a country engaged in a successful commerce, and exhibiting an increasing plenty of commodities, where the value of the whole produce estimated in domestic and foreign labour was retrograde or even stationary. And of the two ways in which capital may be accumulated, as stated by Mr. Ricardo in his chapter on Fo-|reign Commerce, namely an increase of revenue from increased profits, or a diminished expenditure, arising from cheap commodities,* I believe the latter never has been, nor ever will be, experienced as an effective stimulus to the permanent and continued production of increasing wealth. (281)

460

Mr. Ricardo will perhaps say, and say truly, that according to his own view of value, foreign commerce will increase it, as soon as more labour has been employed in the production of all the

* Princ. of Pol. Econ. ch. vii. p. [131]. 2d edit.

---

modities. Mr. Malthus could not suppose that I meant to say that the value and amount[2] of foreign and home commodities might not increase at the same time.

(281) p. 460. *I believe the latter never*

I believe, quite the contrary—I believe it is a more powerful stimulus even than that to which Mr. Malthus exclusively refers. Is not this opinion of Mr. Malthus inconsistent with that which he gives in another part of his work[3] on the beneficial effects to the national wealth[4] which have resulted from improvements on the land. How did these operate but by enabling us to make greater savings from expenditure. I know no other way of saving, but saving from unproductive expenditure to add to productive expenditure.

[2] 'and amount' is ins.   [4] 'to the national wealth' is ins.
[3] Malthus's p. 165; above, p. 142.

commodities taken together, which the country obtains; and that the plenty produced by foreign trade will naturally encourage this employment. But what I wish specifically to state is, that the natural tendency of foreign trade, as of all sorts of exchanges by which a distribution is effected better suited to the wants of society, is *immediately* to increase the value of that part of the national revenue which consists of profits, without any proportionate diminution elsewhere, and that it is precisely this *immediate* increase of national income arising from the exchange of what is of less value in the country, for what is of more value, that furnishes both the power and will to employ more labour, and occasions the animated demand for labour, produce and capital, which is a striking and almost universal accompaniment of successful foreign commerce; whereas, a mere abundance of commodities 461 falling very greatly in value compared with labour, | would obviously at first diminish the power of employing the same number of workmen, and a temporary glut and general deficiency of demand could not fail to ensue in labour, in produce, and in capital, attended with the usual distress which a glut must occasion. (282)

Mr. Ricardo always views foreign trade in the light of means

---

(282) p. 460. *But what I wish specifically &c. &c.*

A merchant is possessed of a bale of cotton goods, which he exports, and gets in exchange a pipe and a quarter of wine, he sells the pipe in England for a bale of cotton goods, and retains the quarter pipe for his own profit, and disposes of it as he may think best.

He discovers a new market, and recommences his operation, and for his bale of cotton goods he gets not only a pipe and a quarter of wine, but also[1] 100 lbs. of indigo. If he can still exchange a pipe of wine for a bale of cotton goods at home[2], his profits will have increased;—instead of a quarter of a pipe of wine, as before, he will get that and the indigo besides. But suppose, that as well as four fifths of

[1] 'a barrel of' is del. here.   [2] 'at home' is ins.

of obtaining *cheaper* commodities. But this is only looking to one half of its advantages, and I am strongly disposed to think, not the larger half. In our own commerce at least, this part of the trade is comparatively inconsiderable. The great mass of our imports consists of articles as to which there can be no kind of question about their comparative cheapness, as raised abroad or at home. If we could not import from foreign countries our silk, cotton and indigo, our tea, sugar, coffee and tobacco, our port, sherry, claret and champagne, our almonds, raisins, oranges and lemons, our various spices and our various drugs, with many other articles peculiar to foreign climates, it is quite certain that we should not have them at all. To estimate the advantage derived from their importation by their cheapness, compared with the quantity of labour and capital which they would have cost, if we had attempted to raise them at home, would be perfectly preposterous. In reality, no such attempt would have been thought of. If we could by possibility have made fine claret at ten pounds a bottle, few or none would have drunk it; and the actual quantity of labour and capital employed in obtaining these | foreign commodities is at 462 present beyond comparison greater than it would have been if we had not imported them.

---

his wine, he must also give four fifths of the indigo for[3] the bale of cotton goods, his profits indeed will have fallen to the general level of profits, at which I suppose they were in the first instance,—but will not every man who has a bale of cotton goods or goods of an equivalent value, gain what he gives up, and have they not precisely the same power of saving which he before had. The question seems to me too clear to be for one moment doubted. Here is the same quantity in both cases of English and foreign commodities, and why should there be a glut more in one case than in the other? Mr. Malthus never states a specific simple case for the purpose of following it in all its bearings, if he did, we could not differ as we appear to do.

[3] 'his' is del. here.

We must evidently therefore estimate the advantage which we derive from such a trade upon a very different principle. This is the simple and obvious one often adverted to as the foundation of every act of barter, whether foreign or domestic, namely, the increased value which results from exchanging what is wanted less for what is wanted more. After we had, by our exports of home commodities, obtained in return all the foreign articles above-mentioned, we might be very much puzzled to say whether we had increased or decreased the *quantity* of our commodities, but we should feel quite certain that the new distribution of produce which had taken place, by giving us commodities much better suited to our wants and tastes than those which had been sent away, had decidedly increased the exchangeable value of our possessions, our means of enjoyment, and our wealth.

Taking therefore a very different view of the effects of foreign commerce on exchangeable value from Mr. Ricardo, I should bring forwards the extension of markets as being, in its general tendency, pre-eminently favourable to that increase of value and wealth which arises from distribution. (283)

---

(283) p. 462. *Taking therefore a very different view*

From what Mr. Malthus has himself said in respect to my opinions he must know that I as well as himself "should bring forward the extension of markets as being, in its general tendency, pre-eminently favorable to that increase of wealth which arises from distribution." Yet his language here would lead his reader to suppose otherwise. I should not say it would increase the value of such[1] wealth because

[1] 'such' is ins.

SECTION IX

*Of the Distribution occasioned by unproductive Consumers,
considered as the Means of increasing the exchangeable
Value of the whole Produce*

The third main cause which tends to keep up and increase the
value of produce by favouring its distribution is the employment
of unproductive labour, or the maintenance of an adequate proportion of unproductive consumers.

It has been already shewn that, under a rapid accumulation of
capital, or, more properly speaking, a rapid conversion of unproductive into productive labour, the demand, compared with
the supply of material products, would prematurely fail, and the
motive to further accumulation be checked, before it was checked
by the exhaustion of the land. It follows that, without supposing
the productive classes to consume much more than they are
found to do by experience, particularly when they are rapidly
saving from revenue to add to their capitals, it is absolutely
necessary that a country with great powers of production should
possess a body of unproductive consumers. (284)

In the fertility of the soil, in the powers of man to apply
machinery as a substitute for labour, and in the motives to exertion
under a system of privāte property, the great laws of nature have

---

as the reader knows I measure value by a different medium
from Mr. Malthus.

(284) p. 463. *It has been already shewn*

A body of unproductive labourers [2] are just as necessary
and as useful with a view to future production,[3] as a fire,
which should consume in the manufacturers warehouse the
goods which those unproductive labourers would otherwise [4]
consume.

[2] 'labourers' replaces 'necessaries'.

[3] Last six words are ins.

[4] 'otherwise' is ins.

464 provided for the leisure of a certain portion of society; and | if this beneficent offer be not accepted by an adequate number of individuals, not only will a positive good, which might have been so attained, be lost, but the rest of the society, so far from being benefited by such self-denial, will be decidedly injured by it.

What the proportion is between the productive and unproductive classes of a society, which affords the greatest encouragement to the continued increase of wealth, it has before been said that the resources of political economy are unequal to determine. (285) It must depend upon a great variety of circumstances, particularly upon fertility of soil and the progress of invention in machinery. A fertile soil and an ingenious people can not only support a considerable proportion of unproductive consumers without injury, but may absolutely require such a body of demanders, in order to give effect to their powers of production. While, with a poor soil and a people of little ingenuity, an attempt to support such a body would throw land out of cultivation, and lead infallibly to impoverishment and ruin.

Another cause, which makes it impossible to say what proportion of the unproductive to the productive classes is most favourable to the increase of wealth, is the difference in the degrees of consumption which may prevail among the producers themselves.

Perhaps it will be said that there can be no occasion for un-

---

(285) p. 464. *What the proportion is*

I should find no difficulty to determine. They may be useful for other purposes but not in any degree for the production of wealth.

(286) p. 465. *With regard to unproductive &c.*

In what way can a man's consuming my produce, without making me any return whatever, enable me to make a fortune? I should think my fortune would be more likely to be made, if the consumer of my produce returned me an equivalent value.

productive consumers, if a consumption sufficient to keep up the value of the produce | takes place among those who are engaged 465 in production.

With regard to the capitalists who are so engaged, they have certainly the power of consuming their profits, or the revenue which they make by the employment of their capitals; and if they were to consume it, with the exception of what could be beneficially added to their capitals, so as to provide in the best way both for an increased production and increased consumption, there might be little occasion for unproductive consumers. But such consumption is not consistent with the actual habits of the generality of capitalists. The great object of their lives is to save a fortune, both because it is their duty to make a provision for their families, and because they cannot spend an income with so much comfort to themselves, while they are obliged perhaps to attend a counting-house for seven or eight hours a day. (286)

It has been laid down as a sort of axiom among some writers that the wants of mankind may be considered as at all times commensurate with their powers; (287) but this position is not always true, even in those cases where a fortune comes without trouble; and in reference to the great mass of capitalists, it is completely contradicted by experience. Almost all merchants and manufacturers save, in prosperous times, much more rapidly than it would be possible for the national capital to increase, so as to keep

---

(287) p. 465. *It has been laid down &c.*

I believe this to be absolutely true, but supposing it false of what advantage can it be to me that another man who returns nothing to me shall consume my goods? How does such a consumption enable me to realize profits?

I cannot express in language so strong as I feel it my astonishment at the various propositions advanced in this section.

To enable the capitalists to continue their habits of saving says Mr. Malthus "they must either consume more or produce less."

up the value of the produce. But if this be true of them as a body, taken one with another, it is quite obvious that, with their actual |
466 habits, they could not afford an adequate market to each other by exchanging their several products.

There must therefore be a considerable class of other consumers, or the mercantile classes could not continue extending their concerns, and realizing their profits. In this class the landlords no doubt stand pre-eminent; but if the powers of production among capitalists are considerable, the consumption of the landlords, in addition to that of the capitalists themselves and of their workmen, may still be insufficient to keep up and increase the exchangeable value of the whole produce, that is, to make the increase of quantity more than counterbalance the fall of price. And if this be so, the capitalists cannot continue the same habits of saving. They must either consume more, or produce less; and when the mere pleasure of present expenditure, without the accompaniments of an improved local situation and an advance in rank, is put in opposition to the continued labour of attending to business during the greatest part of the day, the probability is that a considerable body of them will be induced to prefer the latter alternative, and produce less. But if, in order to balance the demand and supply, a permanent diminution of production takes place, rather than an increase of consumption, the whole of the national wealth, which consists of what is produced and consumed, and not of the excess of produce above consumption, will be decidedly diminished.

Mr. Ricardo frequently speaks, as if saving were an end instead
467 of a means. (288) Yet even with | regard to individuals, where this view of the subject is nearest the truth, it must be allowed that

---

(288) p. 466. *Mr. Ricardo frequently speaks, as if saving were an end instead of a means*

Where? I have no recollection of having done so in any one instance.

(289) p. 467. *If however commodities &c.*

How can unproductive consumption increase profits? Commodities consumed by unproductive consumers are

the final object in saving is expenditure and enjoyment. But, in reference to national wealth, it can never be considered either immediately or permanently in any other light than as a means. It may be true that, by the cheapness of commodities, and the consequent saving of expenditure in consumption, the same surplus of produce above consumption may be obtained as by a great rise of profits with an undiminished consumption; and, if saving were an end, the same end would be accomplished. But saving is the means of furnishing an increasing supply for the increasing national wants. If however commodities are already so plentiful that an adequate portion of them is not consumed, the capital so saved, the office of which is still further to increase the plenty of commodities, and still further to lower already low profits, can be comparatively of little use. On the other hand, if profits are high, it is a sure sign that commodities are scarce, compared with the demand for them, that the wants of the society are clamorous for a supply, and that an increase in the means of production, by saving a considerable part of the new revenue created by the high profits, and adding it to capital, will be specifically and permanently beneficial. (289)

National saving, therefore, considered as the means of increased production, is confined within much narrower limits' than individual saving. While some individuals continue to spend, other | individuals may continue to save to a very great extent; but the national saving, or the balance of produce above consumption, in reference to the whole mass of producers and consumers, must necessarily be limited by the amount which can be advantageously employed in supplying the demand for produce; and to create this demand, there must be an adequate consumption

468

---

given to them, not sold for an equivalent. They have no price—how can they increase profits?

Mr. Malthus has defined demand to be the will and power to consume. What power has an unproductive consumer? Will the taking 100 pieces of cloth from a clothiers manufactory, and clothing soldiers and sailors with it, add to his profits? Will it stimulate him to produce?—yes, in the same way as a fire would.

either among the producers themselves, or other classes of consumers.

Adam Smith has observed "that the desire of food is limited in every man by the narrow capacity of the human stomach; but the desire of the conveniences and ornaments of building, dress, equipage, and household furniture, seems to have no limit or certain boundary." That it has no *certain* boundary is unquestionably true; that it has no limit must be allowed to be too strong an expression, when we consider how it will be practically limited by the countervailing luxury of indolence, or by the general desire of mankind to better their condition, and make a provision for a family; a principle which, as Adam Smith himself states, is on the whole stronger than the principle which prompts to expense.* But surely it is a glaring misapplication of this statement in any sense in which it can be reasonably understood, to say, that there is no limit to the saving and employment of capital except the difficulty of procuring food. (290) It is to found a doctrine upon the unlimited desire of man-|kind to consume; then to suppose this desire limited in order to save capital, and thus completely alter the premises; and yet still to maintain that the doctrine is true. Let a sufficient consumption always take place, whether by the producers or others, to keep up and increase

469

* Wealth of Nations, Vol. ii. B. ii. ch. ii. p. 19. 6th edit.

---

(290) p. 468. *But surely it is a glaring*

The limit is not exactly the difficulty of procuring food, but the difficulty of procuring labour in which the difficulty of procuring food is included—for if you came to an end of your power of procuring food you would not long be able to increase your supply of[1] labour.

(291) p. 469. *Let a sufficient consumption*

This is all that I contend for. But how capital and population should be both redundant while you can increase the supply of necessaries I am at a loss to conceive. It is a contradiction in terms, it is saying there is a capital un-

[1] 'increase your supply of' replaces 'maintain more'.

most effectually the exchangeable value of the whole produce; and I am perfectly ready to allow that, to the employment of a national capital, increasing only at such a rate, there is no other limit than that which bounds the power of maintaining population. (291) But it appears to me perfectly clear in theory, and universally confirmed by experience, that the employment of a capital, too rapidly increased by parsimonious habits, may find a limit, and does, in fact, often find a limit, long before there is any real difficulty in procuring the means of subsistence; and that both capital and population may be at the same time, and for a period of great length, redundant, compared with the effective demand for produce.

Of the wants of mankind in general, it may be further observed, that it is a partial and narrow view of the subject, to consider only the propensity to spend what is actually possessed. It forms but a very small part of the question to determine that if a man has a hundred thousand a year, he will not decline the offer of ten thousand more; or to lay down generally that mankind are never disposed to refuse the means of increased power and enjoyment. The main part of the question respecting the wants of mankind, relates to their | power of calling forth the exertions necessary to   470 acquire the means of expenditure. (292) It is unquestionably true that wealth produces wants; but it is a still more important truth,

---

employed because its owner [2] cannot find labourers, and there are people unemployed because there is no one having a capital to employ them.

We might just as well say, bread cannot be sold because there are no purchasers, and at the same time there are men who are starving and who have the means and the will of purchasing bread but there is none to be had—both propositions cannot be true.

(292) p. 469. *The main part of the question*

This [3] is true. I agree with Mr. Malthus "that the difficulty relates to the power of calling forth the exertions

[2] 'its owner' replaces 'it'.   [3] 'would be true if the' is del. here.

that wants produce wealth. Each cause acts and re-acts upon the other, but the order, both of precedence and of importance, is with the wants which stimulate to industry; and with regard to these, it appears that, instead of being always ready to second the physical powers of man, they require for their developement, "all appliances and means to boot." The greatest of all difficulties in converting uncivilized and thinly peopled countries into civilized and populous ones, is to inspire them with the wants best calculated to excite their exertions in the production of wealth. One of the greatest benefits which foreign commerce confers, and the reason why it has always appeared an almost necessary ingredient in the progress of wealth, is, its tendency to inspire new wants, to form new tastes, and to furnish fresh motives for industry. Even civilized and improved countries cannot afford to lose any of these motives. It is not the most pleasant employment to spend eight hours a day in a counting-house. Nor will it be submitted to after the common necessaries and conveniences of life are attained, unless adequate motives are presented to the mind of the man of business. Among these motives is undoubtedly the desire of advancing his rank, and contending with the landlords in the enjoyment of leisure, as well as of foreign and domestic luxuries. |

471   But the desire to realize a fortune as a permanent provision for a family is perhaps the most general motive for the continued exertions of those whose incomes depend upon their own personal skill and efforts. Whatever may be said of the virtue of parsimony or saving, as a *public* duty, there cannot be a doubt that it is, in

---

necessary to acquire the means of expenditure." But what is this but saying that a man must produce before he can be entitled to consume, and the difficulty is to induce him to produce—there will be none in inducing him to consume after he has produced.

(293) p. 471. *But if, from the want &c.*

Here Mr. Malthus's anxiety is not about securing consumption, he is afraid only that without it, there will not be sufficient motive for future production. No mischief can

numberless cases, a most sacred and binding *private* duty; and were this legitimate and praiseworthy motive to persevering industry in any degree weakened, it is impossible that the wealth and prosperity of the country should not most materially suffer. But if, from the want of other consumers, the capitalists were obliged to consume all that could not be advantageously added to the national capital, the motives which support them in their daily tasks must essentially be weakened, and the same powers of production would not be called forth. (293)

It has appeared then that, in the ordinary state of society, the master producers and capitalists, though they may have the power, have not the will, to consume to the necessary extent. And with regard to their workmen, it must be allowed that, if they possessed the will, they have not the power. It is indeed most important to observe that no power of consumption on the part of the labouring classes can ever, according to the common motives which influence mankind, alone furnish an encouragement to the employment of capital. As I have before said, nobody will ever employ capital merely for the sake of the demand occasioned by those who work for him. (294) Unless | they produce an excess of value   472
above what they consume, which he either wants himself in kind, or which he can advantageously exchange for something which he desires, either for present or future use, it is quite obvious that his capital will not be employed in maintaining them. When indeed this further value is created and affords a sufficient excitement to the saving and employment of stock, then certainly the power of consumption possessed by the workmen will greatly

---

arise then immediately from non-consumption but only remotely as weakening the motive to exertion.

(294) p. 471. *As I have before said*

Why not? I may employ 20 workmen to furnish me food and necessaries for 25, and then these 25 to furnish me food and necessaries for 30—these 30 again to provide for a greater number. Should I not get rich although I employed capital "merely for the sake of the demand occasioned by those who work for me["]?

add to the whole national demand, and make room for the employment of a much greater capital.

It is most desirable that the labouring classes should be well paid, for a much more important reason than any that can relate to wealth; namely, the happiness of the great mass of society. But to those who are inclined to say that unproductive consumers cannot be necessary as a stimulus to the increase of wealth, if the productive classes do but consume a fair proportion of what they produce, I would observe that as a great increase of consumption among the working classes must greatly increase the cost of production, it must lower profits, and diminish or destroy the motive to accumulate, before agriculture, manufactures, and commerce have reached any considerable degree of prosperity. If each labourer were actually to consume double the quantity of corn which he does at present, such a demand, instead of giving a stimulus to wealth, would probably throw a great quantity of
473 land out of cultivation, | and greatly diminish both internal and external commerce. (295)

There is certainly however very little danger of a diminution of wealth from this cause. Owing to the principle of population, all the tendencies are the other way; and there is much more reason to fear that the working classes will consume too little for their own happiness, than that they will consume too much to

---

(295) p. 472. *It is most desirable &c.*

Nothing can be more just than the observation "that a great increase of consumption among the working classes must greatly increase the cost of production, it must lower profits, and diminish or destroy the motive to accumulate, before agriculture, manufactures and commerce have reached any considerable degree of prosperity." But would the consumption of the unproductive class remedy this. What is the consumption of the productive class over and above what is a reasonable reward for their labour, but unproductive consumption,—consumption without an adequate return?

"If each labourer were actually to consume double the

allow of an adequate increase of wealth. (296) I only adverted to
the circumstance to shew that, supposing so impossible a case as
a very great consumption among the working producers, such
consumption would not be of the kind to push the wealth of a
country to its greatest extent.

[It might be desirable, on other accounts than with a view to 474
wealth, that the labouring classes should not work so hard; but
as this could only be accomplished by a simultaneous resolution
among workmen, it cannot take place.

With the single exception of the effects to be expected from 475
prudential habits, there is no chance of an increased consumption
among the working classes; and if there were, it is not the kind
of consumption best calculated to encourage the employment of
capital.

When the demands of the landlords have been added to those
of the productive classes, it appears from experience that profits
have often prematurely fallen.

But if the master producers have not the will to consume 476
sufficiently, and the working producers have not the power, then,
if the aid of the landlords be not found sufficient, the consumption
required must take place among the unproductive labourers of
Adam Smith.

Every country must necessarily have a body of unproductive 477

---

quantity of corn which he does at present, such a demand,
instead of giving a stimulus to wealth, would probably
throw a great quantity of land out of cultivation, and greatly
diminish both internal and external commerce." If it had
that effect would it be for any other reason than because
one half of this consumption would be unproductive consumption? And yet this is the very consumption that
Mr. Malthus thinks so essential to the progress of wealth.

(296) p. 473. *There is certainly however*

That the labourers will have too little and not too much
is indeed the great danger to be apprehended and if possible [1]
guarded against.

[1] 'if possible' is ins.

labourers; but it is a most important practical question to determine, whether they detract from the wealth of a country, or
encourage it.

478   The solution of this question depends upon the solution of the
greater questions, 1st. whether the motive to accumulate may be
checked from the want of demand, before it is checked by the
difficulty of procuring food; and 2dly, whether such check is
probable.

An attempt has been made to determine these two questions
in different parts of the present work, and if the determination
be just, we may conclude that a body of unproductive labourers
is necessary as a stimulus to wealth.

479   Of the persons constituting the unproductive classes, those
which are paid voluntarily will be considered in general as the
most useful in exciting industry, and the least likely to be prejudicial by interfering with the costs of production.

Those which are supported by taxes are equally useful with
480   regard] to distribution and de-|mand; they frequently occasion
a division of property more favourable to the progress of
wealth than would otherwise have taken place; they ensure that
consumption which is necessary to give the proper stimulus to
production; and the desire to pay a tax, and yet enjoy the
same means of gratification, must often operate to excite the
exertions of industry quite as effectually as the desire to pay a
lawyer or physician. Yet to counterbalance these advantages,
which so far are unquestionable, it must be acknowledged that
injudicious taxation might stop the increase of wealth at almost
any period of its progress, early or late;* and that the most
judicious taxation might ultimately be so heavy as to clog all the
channels of foreign and domestic trade, and almost prevent the
possibility of accumulation.

The effect therefore on national wealth of those classes of

---

* The effect of obliging a cultivator of a certain portion of rich land to
maintain two men and two horses for the state, might in some cases only
induce him to cultivate more, and create more wealth than he otherwise
would have done, while it might leave him personally as rich as before, and
the nation richer; but if the same obligation were to be imposed on the
cultivator of an equal quantity of poor land, the property might be rendered at once not worth working, and the desertion of it would be the
natural consequence. An indiscriminate and heavy tax on gross produce
might immediately scatter desolation over a country, capable, under a
better system, of producing considerable wealth.

unproductive labourers which are supported by taxation, must be very various in different countries, and must depend entirely upon the powers of production, and upon the manner in | which 481 the taxes are raised in each country. As great powers of production are neither likely to be called into action, or, when once in action, kept in activity without great consumption, I feel very little doubt that instances have practically occurred of national wealth being greatly stimulated by the consumption of those who have been supported by taxes. Yet taxation is a stimulus so liable in every way to abuse, and it is so absolutely necessary for the general interests of society to consider private property as sacred, that one should be extremely cautious of trusting to any government the means of making a different distribution of wealth, with a view to the general good. But when, either from necessity or error, a different distribution has taken place, and the evil, as far as it regards private property, has actually been committed, it would surely be most unwise to attempt, at the expense of a great temporary sacrifice, a return to the former distribution, without very fully considering whether, if it were effected, it would be really advantageous; that is, whether, in the actual circumstances of the country, with reference to its powers of production, more would not be lost by the want of consumption than gained by the diminution of taxation. (297)

[If distribution be a necessary element of wealth, it would be rash to affirm, that the abolition of a national debt must certainly increase wealth and employ the people.

If the powers of production in a well peopled country were 482 tripled, the greatest difficulty would be the means of distribution; and it would depend upon the circumstance of proper means of

---

(297) p. 480. *The effect therefore on national wealth*

This argument in favour of taxation is quite consistent with Mr. Malthus opinion of the advantages resulting from unproductive consumption.

Mr. Malthus is a most powerful ally of the Chancellor of the Exchequer.[1]

[1] 'the Chancellor of the Exchequer' replaces 'Mr. Vansittart'.

distribution being found, whether the increased powers were a great good, or a great evil.

483   It may be a question, whether, with the great powers of production possessed by this country, and with its actual division of property in land, the same stimulus could be given to the increase of wealth, without the distribution occasioned by a national debt.

484   Still there are serious evils belonging to a national debt. It is both a cumbersome and a dangerous instrument of distribution.]

A third objection to such a debt is, that it greatly aggravates the evils arising from changes in the value of money. When the 485 currency falls in value, the an-|nuitants, as owners of fixed incomes, are most unjustly deprived of their proper share of the national produce; when the currency rises in value, the pressure of the taxation necessary to pay the interest of the debt, may become suddenly so heavy as greatly to distress the productive classes;* and this kind of sudden pressure must very much enhance the insecurity of property vested in public funds.

[On these accounts it might be desirable to diminish the debt, and discourage its growth in future; but after being accustomed to a great consumption, we cannot recede without passing through a period of great distress.]

486   It is, I know, generally thought that all would be well, if we could but be relieved from the heavy burden of our debt. And yet I feel perfectly convinced that, if a spunge could be applied to it to-morrow, and we could put out of our consideration the poverty and misery of the public creditors, by supposing them to be supported comfortably in some other country, the rest of the society, as a nation, instead of being enriched, would be impoverished. It is the greatest mistake to suppose that the landlords and capitalists would either at once, or in a short time, be prepared for so great an additional consumption as such a change

* In a country with a large public debt, there is no duty which ought to be held more sacred on the part of the administrators of the government than to prevent any variations of the currency beyond those which necessarily belong to the varying value of the precious metals. I am fully aware of the temporary advantages which may be derived from a fall in the value of money; and perhaps it may be true that a part of the distress during the last year, though I believe but a small part, was occasioned by the measure lately adopted, for the restoration of the currency to its just value. But some such measure was indispensably necessary; and Mr. Ricardo deserves the thanks of his country for having suggested one which has rendered the transition more easy than could reasonably have been expected.

would require; and if they adopted the alternative suggested by Mr. Ricardo in a former instance, of saving, and lending their increased incomes, the evil would be aggravated tenfold. The new distribution of produce would diminish the demand for the results of productive labour; and if, in addition to this, more revenue were converted into capital, profits would fall to nothing, and a much greater quantity of capital would emigrate, or be destroyed at home, and a much greater number of persons would be starving for want of employment, than before the extinction of the debt.

[The landlords would probably employ more menial servants, 487 and this would be the best remedy that in the actual circumstances could be applied; but the structure of society would be greatly deteriorated by the change.]

With regard to the capitalists, though they would be relieved from a great portion of their taxes, yet there is every probability that their habits of saving, combined with the diminution in the number of effective demanders, would occasion such a fall in the prices of commodities as greatly to diminish that part of the national income which depends | upon profits; and I feel very 488 little doubt that, in five years from the date of such an event, not only would the exchangeable value of the whole produce, estimated in domestic and foreign labour, be decidedly diminished, but a smaller absolute quantity of corn would be grown, and fewer manufactured and foreign commodities would be brought to market than before. (298)

[A country with land, labour, and capital, has certainly the power of recovering from this state of things; but it would have passed through a period of great stagnation; and finally a considerable body of unproductive labourers may be absolutely necessary to call forth its resources.]

It has been repeatedly conceded, that the pro-|ductive classes 489 have the power of consuming all that they produce; and, if this power were adequately exercised, there might be no occasion, with a view to wealth, for unproductive consumers. But it is

---

(298) p. 488. *And I feel very little doubt*

I should think Mr. Malthus must be the only man in England who would expect such effects from such a cause.

found by experience that, though there may be the power, there is not the will; and it is to supply this will that a body of unproductive consumers is necessary. Their specific use in encouraging wealth is, to maintain such a balance between produce and consumption as to give the greatest exchangeable value to the results of the national industry. (299) If unproductive labour were to predominate, the comparatively small quantity of material products brought to market would keep down the value of the whole produce, from the deficiency of quantity. If the productive classes were in excess, the value of the whole produce would fall from excess of supply. It is obviously a certain proportion between the two which will yield the greatest value, and command the greatest quantity of domestic and foreign labour; (300) and we may safely conclude that, among the causes necessary to that distribution, which will keep up and increase the exchangeable value of the whole produce, we must place the maintenance of a certain body of unproductive consumers. This body, to make it effectual as a stimulus to wealth, and to prevent it from being prejudicial, as a clog to it, should vary in different countries, and at different times, according to the powers of production; and the most 490 favourable result evidently depends upon | the proportion between productive and unproductive consumers, being best suited to the natural resources of the soil, and the acquired tastes and habits of the people.

---

(299) p. 489. *Their specific use in encouraging*

How can they by their consumption give value to the results of the national industry? It might as justly be contended that an earthquake which overthrows my house and buries my property, gives value to the national industry.

(300) p. 489. *It is obviously*

Mr. Malthus often estimates value by the command which it gives us over foreign as well as domestic labour. What have we to do with the quantity or the value of foreign labour. Every foreign commodity is bought with a quantity of our domestic labour, and by that only must we value both home and foreign commodities.

SECTION X

*Application of some of the preceding Principles to the Distresses
of the Labouring Classes, since 1815, with general Observations*

[The distresses of the labouring classes have been attributed
to deficient capital. The capital may be deficient compared with
the population, and yet not deficient compared with the effective
demand for it.

If one fourth of the capital of a country were suddenly de-   491
stroyed, or transported to a different part of the world, profits
would be high and saving would be the remedy required.]

On the other hand, if the capital of the country were diminished
by the failure of some branches | of trade, which had before been   492
very prosperous, and absorbed a great quantity of stock; or even
if capital were suddenly destroyed, and from peculiar circumstances a period were to succeed of diminished consumption and
slack demand, the state of things, with the exception of the
distresses of the poor, would be almost exactly reversed. The
remaining capitalists would be in no respect benefited by events
which had diminished demand in a still greater proportion than
they had diminished capital. Commodities would be every
where cheap. Capital would be seeking employment, but would
not easily find it; and the profits of stock would be low.
There would be no pressing and immediate demand for capital,
because there would be no pressing and immediate demand for
commodities; and, under these circumstances, the saving from
revenue to add to capital, instead of affording the remedy required,
would only aggravate the distresses of the capitalists, and fill the
stream of capital which was flowing out of the country. The
distresses of the capitalists would be aggravated, just upon the
same principle as the distresses of the labouring classes would be
aggravated, if they were encouraged to marry and increase, after
a considerable destruction of people, although accompanied by
a still greater destruction of capital which had kept the wages of
labour very low. There might certainly be a great deficiency of

population, compared with the territory and powers of the
country, and it might be very desirable that it should be greater;
493 but if the wages of labour | were still low, notwithstanding the
diminution of people, to encourage the birth of more children
would be to encourage misery and mortality rather than population. (301)

Now I would ask, to which of these two suppositions does the
present state of this country bear the nearest resemblance? Surely
to the latter. That a great loss of capital has lately been sustained,
is unquestionable. During nearly the whole of the war, owing
to the union of great powers of production with great consumption and demand, the prodigious destruction of capital by the
government was much more than recovered. To doubt this would
be to shut our eyes to the comparative state of the country in
1792 and 1813. The two last years of the war were, however,
years of extraordinary expense, and being followed immediately
by a period marked by a very unusual stagnation of demand, the
destruction of capital which took place in those years was not
probably recovered. But this stagnation itself was much more
disastrous in its effects upon the national capital, and still more
upon the national revenue, than any previous destruction of
stock. It commenced certainly with the extraordinary fall in the
value of the raw produce of the land, to the amount, it is supposed,
of nearly one third. When this fall had diminished the capitals of
the farmers, and still more the revenues both of landlords and
farmers, and of all those who were otherwise connected with the
land, their power of purchasing manufactures and foreign pro-
494 ducts was of necessity greatly diminished. The | failure of home

---

(301) p. 492. *There might certainly be*

The evils of a redundant population are fully admitted,
but no mistake can be greater than to suppose any evils whatever can result from an [1] accumulation of capital. The sole
consequences might be an indisposition to accumulate further
from the fall of profits, which would arise from the liberal
wages which a deficient population could command.

[1] Replaces 'any'.

demand filled the warehouses of the manufacturers with unsold goods, which urged them to export more largely at all risks. But this excessive exportation glutted all the foreign markets, and prevented the merchants from receiving adequate returns; while, from the diminution of the home revenues, aggravated by a sudden and extraordinary contraction of the currency, even the comparatively scanty returns obtained from abroad found a very insufficient domestic demand, and the profits and consequent expenditure of merchants and manufacturers were proportionably lowered. While these unfavourable changes were taking place in rents and profits, the powerful stimulus which had been given to population during the war continued to pour in fresh supplies of labour, and, aided by the disbanded soldiers and sailors and the failure of demand arising from the losses of the farmers and merchants, reduced generally the wages of labour, and left the country with a generally diminished capital and revenue;—not merely in proportion to the alteration of the value of the currency, but in reference to the bullion value of its produce, and the command of this bullion value over domestic and foreign labour. (302) For the four or five years since the war, on account of the change in the distribution of the national produce, and the want of consumption and demand occasioned by it, a decided check has been given to production, and the population, under its former impulse, has increased, not only faster than the demand for labour, but faster than the actual pro-|duce; yet this produce, though decidedly deficient, compared with the population, and compared with past times, is redundant, compared with the effectual demand for it and the revenue which is to purchase it. Though 495

---

(302) p. 494. *While these unfavourable changes* [2]

If the termination of the war, has left the country with a diminished capital and revenue, must not the goods which capital produces have also diminished in quantity? Is not produce now in the same proportion to capital as it was during the war? How does this account for the low price and glut of commodities? [3]

[2] In MS, 'exchanges'.   [3] Last sentence is ins.

labour is cheap, there is neither the power nor the will to employ it all; because not only has the capital of the country diminished, compared with the number of labourers, but, owing to the diminished revenues of the country, the commodities which those labourers would produce are not in such request as ensure tolerable profits to the reduced capital. (303)

[But when profits are low, and capital is on that account flowing out of the country; to encourage saving, is like the policy of encouraging marriage when the population is starving and emigrating.

Our present low profits have been attributed to the cultivation of poor land, heavy taxation, and restrictions on commerce; but it is difficult to admit a theory of our distresses inconsistent with the theory of our prosperity.

496   Whatever may be the final tendency of these causes; yet as the country was more than usually prosperous when they prevailed in a greater degree than at present, we must look elsewhere for the immediate sources of the existing distress.]

How far our artificial system, and particularly the changes in the value of our currency operating upon a large national debt, 497 may have aggravated | the evils we have experienced, it would be extremely difficult to say. But I feel perfectly convinced that a very considerable portion of these evils might be experienced by a nation without poor land in cultivation, without taxes, and without any fresh restrictions on trade. (304)

---

(303) p. 495. *Yet this produce though decidedly deficient compared with the population, and compared with past times,
is redundant compared with the effectual demand for it
and the revenue which is to purchase it.*

Labour is paid by commodities. Commodities are much too abundant for the effectual demand, and yet with these commodities you cannot employ more labour, because they are[1] deficient compared with the population. Is not this saying that commodities are abundant and deficient at the same time?

[1] Replaces 'it is'.

If a large country, of considerable fertility, and sufficient inland communications, were surrounded by an impassable wall, we all agree that it might be tolerably rich, though not so rich as if it enjoyed the benefit of foreign commerce. Now, supposing such a country gradually to indulge in a considerable consumption, to call forth and employ a great quantity of ingenuity in production, and to save only yearly that portion of its revenue which it could most advantageously add to its capital, expending the rest in consumable commodities and unproductive labour, it might evidently, under such a balance of produce and consumption, be increasing in wealth and population with considerable rapidity. But if, upon the principle laid down by M. Say, that the consumption of a commodity is a diminution of demand, the society were greatly and generally to slacken their consumption, and add to their capitals, there cannot be the least doubt, on the great principles of demand and supply, that the profits of capitalists would soon be reduced to nothing, though there were no poor land in cultivation; and the population would be thrown out of work and would be starving, although without a single tax, or any restrictions on trade. (305) |

The state of Europe and America may perhaps be said, in some 498 points, to resemble the case here supposed; and the stagnation which has been so generally felt and complained of since the war, appears to me inexplicable upon the principles of those who think that the power of production is the only element of wealth, and

---

(304) p. 497. *But I feel perfectly convinced*

So do I, because I feel perfectly convinced, that without those evils, stagnation in trade, after such a war, and with great temptation to capital to leave a country where profits are comparatively low will produce much distress.

(305) p. 497. *But if upon the principle laid down by M. Say &c.*

How could the society generally slacken their consumption, and add to their capitals? Does adding to capital in any case slacken consumption? Without slackening consumption how could the population be thrown out of work, and be starving?

who consequently infer that if the powers of production be
increased, wealth will certainly increase in proportion. Now it is
unquestionable that the powers of production were increased by
the cessation of war, and that more people and more capital were
ready to be employed in productive labour; but notwithstanding
this obvious increase in the powers of production, we hear every
where of difficulties and distresses, instead of ease and plenty. In
the United States of America in particular, a country of extraordinary physical resources, the difficulties which have been
experienced are very striking, and such certainly as could hardly
have been expected. These difficulties, at least, cannot be attributed to the cultivation of poor land, restrictions upon commerce,
and excess of taxation. (306) Altogether the state of the commercial world, since the war, clearly shews that something else
is necessary to the continued increase of wealth besides an increase
in the power of producing.

That the transition from war to peace, of which so much has
been said, is a main cause of the effects observed, will be readily
allowed, but not as the operation is usually explained. It is gene-
499 rally said that there has not been time to transfer | capital from the
employments where it is redundant to those where it is deficient,
and thus to restore the proper equilibrium. But I cannot bring
myself to believe that this transfer can require so much time as
has now elapsed since the war; and I would again ask, where are
the under-stocked employments, which, according to this theory,
ought to be numerous, and fully capable of absorbing all the
redundant capital, which is confessedly glutting the markets of
Europe in so many different branches of trade? It is well known
by the owners of floating capital, that none such are now to be
found; and if the transition in question is to account for what has
happened, it must have produced some other effects besides that
which arises from the difficulty of moving capital. This I conceive
to be a great diminution of the whole amount of consumption and
demand. The necessary changes in the channels of trade would be

---

(306) p. 498. *These difficulties, at least*

A country may suffer by restrictions on trade, although it
does not impose the restrictions itself.

(307) p. 500. *This saving is quite natural and proper and*

effected in a year or two; but the general diminution of consumption and demand, occasioned by the transition from such a war to a peace, may last for a very considerable time. The returned taxes, and the excess of individual gains above expenditure, which were so largely used as revenue during the war, are now in part, and probably in no inconsiderable part, saved. I cannot doubt, for instance, that in our own country very many persons have taken the opportunity of saving a part of their returned property-tax, particularly those who have only life-incomes, and who, contrary to the principles of just taxation, | had been assessed at 500 the same rate with those whose incomes were derived from realized property. This saving is quite natural and proper, and forms no just argument against the removal of the tax; (307) but still it contributes to explain the cause of the diminished demand for commodities, compared with their supply since the war. If some of the principal governments concerned spent the taxes which they raised in a manner to create a greater and more certain demand for labour and commodities, particularly the former, than the present owners of them, and if this difference of expenditure be of a nature to last for some time, we cannot be surprised at the duration of the effects arising from the transition from war to peace.

[This diminished consumption must have operated very differently in different countries. Some it must have relieved, others it has distressed. Those which suffered the least by the war have suffered the most by the peace.

The distress which has attended the peace is an unfortunate 501 association; but it should be recollected that it has arisen from peculiar circumstances, which in the same degree are not necessarily connected with the termination of a war.

On account of the evils likely to be felt from a sudden diminu- 502 tion of consumption, the policy which has often been recommended of raising the supplies for a war within each year may fairly be doubted.]

---

forms no just argument against the removal of the tax.

If Mr. Malthus's reasoning be correct it forms an irresistible argument against the removal of the tax. Can any conclusion be more at variance with the premises?

If the country were poor, such a system of taxation might completely keep down its efforts. It might every year positively diminish its capital, and render it every year more ruinous to furnish the same supplies; (308) till the country would be obliged to submit to its enemies from the absolute inability of continuing to oppose them with effect. On the other hand, if the country were rich, and had great powers of production, which were likely |

503 to be still further called forth by the stimulus of a great consumption, it might be able to pay the heavy taxes imposed upon it, out of its revenue, and yet find the means of adequate accumulation; but if this process were to last for any time, and the habits of the people were accommodated to this scale of public and private expenditure, it is scarcely possible to doubt that, at the end of the war, when so large a mass of taxes would at once be restored to the payers of them, the just balance of produce and consumption would be completely destroyed, and a period would ensue, longer or shorter, according to circumstances, in which a very great stagnation would be felt in every branch of productive industry, attended by its usual concomitant general distress.

504 [Although it is necessary to save, in order to recover the capital which the country has lost; yet if profits are low and uncertain, saving is not the first step wanted.

505 What the country wants is an increased national revenue, or an increase of the exchangeable value of the whole produce. When this has been attained we may save with effect.

The question, how this increase of revenue is to be attained, has been attempted to be answered in the latter sections of this chapter.

---

(308) p. 502. *It might every year positively diminish its capital; and render it every year more ruinous to furnish the same supplies.*

Do not loans every year positively diminish the capital of the country?

(309) p. 507. *But if the distribution of wealth*

How does the national debt *create* the middle classes of society? Must not every holder of stock have been possessed

An increased revenue is not so easily attained as an increased 506 proportion of capital to revenue.]

Still, however, it is of the utmost importance to know the immediate object which ought to be aimed at; that if we can do but little actually to forward it, we may not, from ignorance, do much to retard it. With regard to the first main cause | which 507 I have mentioned, as tending to increase the exchangeable value of the national produce, namely the division of landed property, I have given my reasons for thinking that, in the actual and peculiar state of this country, the abolition of the law of primogeniture would produce more evil than good; and there is no other way in which a different division of land could be effected, consistently with an adequate respect for the great fundamental law of property, on which all progress in civilization, improvement, and wealth, must ever depend. But if the *distribution* of wealth to a certain extent be one of the main causes of its increase, while it is unadvisable directly to interfere with the present division of land in this country, it may justly become a question, whether the evils attendant on the national debt are not more than counterbalanced by the distribution of property and increase of the middle classes of society, which it must necessarily create; and whether by saving, in order to pay it off, we are not submitting to a painful sacrifice, which, if it attains its object, whatever other good it may effect, will leave us with a much less favourable distribution of wealth? (309) By greatly reducing the national debt, if we are able to accomplish it, we may place ourselves perhaps in a more safe position, and this no doubt is an important consideration; but grievously will those be disappointed who

---

of the same amount of property before he became a stockholder? Would he not then have been in the middle class of society if there had been no national debt? I cannot conceive how the Natl debt can have *created* any of this class. If again we pay it off, do we annihilate this middle class as Mr. Malthus appears to fear we should do? Will not every stockholder be in possession of a capital after payment of the debt.[1]

[1] Last sentence is ins.

think that, either by greatly reducing or at once destroying it, we can enrich ourselves, and employ all our labouring classes. |

508   [A greater freedom might be given to commerce without diminishing the revenue of the customs. The permanent effects of opening the trade with France would certainly be beneficial.

509   But in looking forward to changes of this kind, we should attend to the caution given by Adam Smith, which would be particularly applicable to the silk trade.

510   When the opening of any trade would produce temporary distress, it is because it would diminish for a time the exchangeable value of the whole produce; but, in general, the extension of trade increases it.

511   A knowledge of the effects of unproductive consumers on national wealth will make us proceed with more caution in our efforts to diminish them.

Public works, the making and repairing of roads, and a tendency among persons of fortune to improve their grounds, and keep more servants, are the most direct means within our power of restoring the demand for labour.]

512   If by the operation of these three causes, either separately or conjointly, we can make the supply and consumption bear a more advantageous proportion to each other, so as to increase the exchangeable value of the whole produce, the rate of profits may then permanently rise as high as the quality of the soil in cultivation combined with the actual skill of the cultivators will allow,* which is far from being the case at present. And as soon as the

* The profits of stock cannot be higher than the state of the land will allow, but they may be lower in any degree. (see p. 300.) The great difference between Mr. Ricardo and me on this point is, that Mr. Ricardo thinks profits are *regulated* by the state of the land; I think they are only *limited* by it one way, and that if capital be abundant, compared with the demand for commodities, profits may be low in any degree, in spite of the fertility of the land. (310)

---

(310) p. 512. *The profits of Stock &c.*

Mr. Malthus is greatly mistaken if he supposes that I contend profits must *always* be high while we have fertile land still in reserve. Profits will be low as I have said a hundred times if wages are high, and wages

capitalist can begin to save from steady and improving profits, instead of from diminished expenditure, that is, as soon as the national revenue, | estimated in bullion, and in the command of 513 this bullion over domestic and foreign labour, begins yearly and steadily to increase, we may then begin safely and effectively to recover our lost capital by the usual process of saving a portion of our increased revenue to add to it.

[It is thought by many that the revenue of the country would be most effectually increased, and the balance of consumption restored, by an abundant issue of paper; but this opinion is founded on a mistaken view of the effects of a depreciated currency.

A great issue of paper now would have a very different effect 514 from that which it had during the war.]

Perhaps a sudden increase of currency and a new facility of borrowing might, under any circumstances, give a temporary stimulus to trade, but it would only be temporary. Without a large expenditure on the part of the government, and a frequent conversion of capital into revenue, the great powers of production acquired by the capitalists, operating upon the diminished power of purchasing possessed by the owners of fixed incomes, could not fail to occasion a still greater glut of commodities than is felt at present; and experience has sufficiently shewn us, that paper cannot support prices under such circumstances. (311) In the history of our paper transactions, it will be found that the abundance or scantiness of currency has followed and aggravated high or low prices, but seldom or never led them; and it is of the utmost importance to recollect that, at the end of the war, the prices failed before the contraction of the currency began. It was, in fact, the failure of prices, which destroyed the country banks, and shewed us the frail foundations on which the excess of our paper-currency rested. This sudden contraction no doubt aggravated

---

may be very high, with very abundant resources in land.

(311) p. 514. *Without a large expenditure on the part of Government &c. &c.*

Here are Mr. Malthus's peculiar opinions fairly avowed.

very greatly the distresses of the merchants and of the country; and for this very reason we should use our utmost endeavours to avoid such an event in future; not, how-|ever, by vain efforts to keep up prices by forcible issues of paper, in defiance at once of the laws of justice and the great principles of supply and demand, but by the only effectual way, that of steadily maintaining our paper of the same value with the coin which it professes to represent, and subjecting it to no other fluctuations than those which belong to the precious metals.

In reference to the main doctrine inculcated in the latter part of this work, namely, that the progress of wealth depends upon proportions; it will be objected, perhaps, that it necessarily opens the way to differences of opinion relating to these propositions, and thus throws a kind of uncertainty over the science of political economy which was not supposed to belong to it. If, however, the doctrine should be found, upon sufficient examination, to be true; if it adequately accounts for things as they are, and explains consistently why frequent mistakes have been made respecting the future, it will be allowed that such objectors are answered. We cannot make a science more certain by our wishes or opinions; but we may obviously make it much more uncertain in its application, by believing it to be what it is not.

Though we cannot, however, lay down a certain rule for growing rich, and say that a nation will increase in wealth just in the degree in which it saves from its revenue, and adds to its capital: yet even in the most uncertain parts of the science, even in those parts which relate to the proportions of production and consumption, we are not left | without guides; and if we attend to the great laws of demand and supply, they will generally direct us into the right course. It is justly observed by Mr. Ricardo that "the farmer and manufacturer can no more live without profit than the labourer without wages. Their motive for accumulation will diminish with every diminution of profit, and will cease altogether when their profits are so low as not to afford them

---

(312) p. 516. *Mr. Ricardo applies this passage*

Here again Mr. Malthus has mistaken me and I refer to his own account of my opinions in Page ¹ to shew that

¹ Blank in MS. Probably Malthus's p. 326; above, p. 285.

an adequate compensation for their trouble, and the risk which they must necessarily encounter in employing their capital productively."* Mr. Ricardo applies this passage to the final and necessary fall of profits occasioned by the state of the land. I would apply it at all times, throughout all the variable periods which intervene between the first stage of cultivation and the last. Whenever capital increases too fast, the motive to accumulation diminishes, and there will be a natural tendency to spend more and save less. When profits rise, the motive to accumulation will increase, and there will be a tendency to spend a smaller proportion of the gains, and to save a greater. These tendencies, operating on individuals, direct them towards the just mean, which they would more frequently attain if they were not interrupted by bad laws or unwise exhortations. If every man who saves from his income is necessarily a friend to his country, it follows that all those who spend their incomes, though they may | not be absolute enemies, 517 like the spendthrift, must be considered as failing in the duty of benefiting their country, and employing the labouring classes, when it is in their power; and this cannot be an agreeable reflection to those whose scale of expenditure in their houses, furniture, carriages and table, would certainly admit of great retrenchment, with but little sacrifice of real comfort. But if, in reality, saving is a national benefit, or a national disadvantage, according to the circumstances of the period; and, if these circumstances are best declared by the rate of profits, surely it is a case in which individual interest needs no extraneous assistance. (312)

Saving, as I have before said, is, in numerous instances, a most sacred private duty. How far a just sense of this duty, together with the desire of bettering our condition so strongly implanted in the human breast, may sometimes, and in some states of society, occasion a greater tendency to parsimony than is consistent with the most effective encouragement to the growth of public wealth, it is difficult to say; but whether this tendency, if let alone, be ever

* Princ. of Polit. Econ. ch. vi. p. [122].

---

this is not my doctrine, but the one which he supposes me without any just ground to hold.

Mr. Malthus never appears to remember that to save is to spend, as surely, as what he exclusively calls spending.

too great or not, no one could think of interfering with it, even in its caprices. There is no reason, however, for giving an additional sanction to it, by calling it a public duty. The market for national capital will be supplied, like other markets, without the aid of patriotism. And in leaving the whole question of saving to the uninfluenced operation of individual interest and individual feelings, (313) we shall best conform to | that great principle of political economy laid down by Adam Smith, which teaches us a general maxim, liable to very few exceptions, that the wealth of nations is best secured by allowing every person, as long as he adheres to the rules of justice, to pursue his own interest in his own way.

[Though the science of Political Economy must, from its nature, resemble more the science of morals or of politics than that of mathematics, yet if its principles be founded on a sufficiently extended experience, they will rarely in their application disappoint our just expectations.]

There is another objection which will probably be made to the doctrines of the latter part of this work, which I am more anxious to guard against. If the principles which I have laid down be true, it will certainly follow that the sudden removal of taxes will often be attended with very different effects, particularly to the labouring classes of society, from those which have been generally ex-| pected. And an inference may perhaps be drawn from this conclusion in favour of taxation. But the just inference from it is,

---

(313) p. 517. *And in leaving the whole question of saving &c. &c.*

Who has ever proposed to leave it to any other?

(314) p. 519. *But the just inference from it is*

But another just inference is that if once laid, they must not be taken off; and it also follows that it would often be wise to impose them. If the people will not expend enough themselves, what can be more expedient than to call upon the state to spend for them? What could be more wise if Mr. Malthus doctrine be true than to increase the army, and double the salaries of all the officers of Government?

that taxes should never be imposed, nor to a greater amount, than the necessity of the case justifies, and particularly that every effort should be made, consistently with national honour and security, to prevent a scale of expenditure so great that it cannot proceed without ruin, and cannot be stopped without distress. (314)

Even if it be allowed that the excitement of a prodigious public expenditure, and of the taxation necessary to support it, operating upon extraordinary powers of production, might, under peculiar circumstances, increase the wealth of a country in a greater degree than it otherwise would have increased; yet, as the greatest powers of production must finally be overcome by excessive borrowing, and as increased misery among the labouring classes must be the consequence, whether we go on or attempt to return, it would surely have been much better for the society if such wealth had never existed. It is like the unnatural strength occasioned by some violent stimulant, which, if not absolutely necessary, should be by all means avoided, on account of the exhaustion which is sure to follow it. (315)

[It is the duty of governments to avoid war if possible; but if 520 it be unavoidable, so to regulate the expenditure as to produce the least fluctuation of demand.

Other classes are often relieved by the taking off of taxes; but 521 nothing can compensate to the labouring classes the want of demand for labour.

To state these facts is not to favour taxes, but to bring forward

---

(315) p. 519. *It is like the unnatural*

But we are under the influence of the stimulant, and are suffering from the folly of discontinuing it. My principles lead to quite opposite conclusions. The annihilation of the national debt either by paying it from the capital of the country, or by refusing to pay the stockholder either principal or interest, would not have the effects generally attributed to them.

After the annihilation of the debt we should have no more capital or revenue than before, it would only be differently distributed.. Inasmuch as the payment of the debt would

additional reasons against imposing them without a strong necessity.

522   The labouring classes suffer more from low wages in adversity than they are benefited by high wages in prosperity. To them fluctuations are most unfavourable. The interests of the great mass of society require peace and equable expenditure.]

---

relieve us from a great load of taxation, it would diminish the temptation to remove capital from this country, to others, not so burthened. It would relieve us from the army of tax gatherers, revenue officers, and smugglers who are now supported out of the industry of the country, and which aggravates the evil of the taxes. Many other collateral benefits would result, which it would not be expedient now to enumerate.[1]

[1] Corrected in pencil, by another (perhaps McCulloch's) hand, to read 'which we shall not here stop to enumerate.'

INDEX

TO MALTHUS'S PRINCIPLES OF POLITICAL ECONOMY

whole produce, 383–388—the distribution occasioned by commerce considered as a means of increasing such exchangeable value, 388–420—an increase in the exchangeable value of the whole produce, necessary to remove the existing distresses of this country, 444, 446–451

Exceptions. See *Limitations*

Exports (British), amount of, in consequence of machinery, 359

F

Fertility of land, the only source of permanently high returns for capital, 217–219—other advantages resulting from a fertile soil, 219–223—fertility of soil, considered as a stimulus to the continued increase of wealth, 331–350

Fortune, the desire of realizing one, a sacred duty in private life, 428, 429

France, rates of wages of labour in, for the last two centuries, 247—succession to property there, how regulated, 385—considerations on its probable results, 385–386

G

Garnier (M.), refutation of the opinions of, that performers on musical instruments are unproductive labourers, while the instruments themselves are considered riches, and that the servants of Government are unproductive labourers, 23

Gold. See *Metals (precious)*

H

Habits, influence of, on the condition of the labouring classes, 228–229

I

Importation of Corn, how it affects the price of that commodity, 181—its influence on the connexion of the interests of the landlord and of the state importing corn, 198–208

Improvements in agriculture, influence of, on rent, 139–143—a main source of the increase of rents, 187, 188—the United States of America, almost the only country where rents may be increased without agricultural improvements, 188—agricultural improvements, why effected chiefly by the tenants, and not by the land owners, 200, 201

Interest, rate of, in China, 131—cause of the high rate of, there and in India, 131, 132—rate of in England, during the reign of George II, 275—reduction of it, accounted for, 431—and also the reduction of interest in Italy, in 1685, *ib.*

Interference. See *Non-interference*

Ireland, state of wages of labour, and of profits of stock in, cannot be reduced, and why, 188—cause of the increase of its population, 215, 229—the power of supporting labour exists there, to a greater extent than the will, 344–346—the character of the Irish peasantry vindicated, 347—the deficiency of wealth in this country, owing more to a want of demand than of capital, 347–349—prodigious capabilities of Ireland for manufacturing and commercial wealth, 349

L

Labour, divided into productive and unproductive, 15—Adam Smith's definition of productive labour considered, 15—a classification of the different kinds of labour necessary, and why, 15–17—the distinction of the Economists considered, 17—real nature of productive labour stated, 17–20, 23—examination of Adam Smith's definition of unproductive labour, 20–22—the labour realized upon material products is the only labour susceptible of accumulation and definite valuation, 23—the labour, which a commodity has cost, considered as a measure of exchangeable value, 55–79—the labour, which a commodity

tive cost of production is a cause of the high comparative price of corn, 181, 182—the value of the whole produce of a country how to be estimated, 241–245—facilities of production promote the opening of markets, 366—an union of the powers of production with the means of distribution, necessary, in order to ensure a continued increase of wealth, 367–382—and to remove the present distresses of the labouring classes, 444–446

Productive labour, defined, 17–19 —examination of Adam Smith's definition of it, 15–17

Profits of the cultivator, on the necessary separation of, from the rent of land, 120–133—refutation of the error, that when land is successively thrown out of cultivation, the rate of profits will be high in proportion to the superior natural fertility of the land, which will then be least fertile in cultivation, 172–179

Profits of capital, defined, 251—in what manner they are affected by the increasing difficulty of procuring the means of subsistence, 251–258—also by the proportion which capital bears to labour, 258–270—and by the causes practically in operation, 271–285 —remarks on Mr. Ricardo's theory of profits, 285–296

Property, succession to, how regulated in France. See *Land, Wealth*

Proportions, importance of considering in forming great results on political economy, 385

Q

Quality of land, how far a primary cause of the high price of raw produce, 107–109

R

Rent of land, defined, 103—its nature and causes, 103–119—the circumstance of the cost of the main food of a country being almost entirely resolvable into wages and profits, does not prevent rent from forming a component part of the price of the great mass of commodities, 67, 68—on the necessary separation of rent from the profits of the cultivator, and the wages of the labourer, 120–133—rent is paid by cattle, and in what manner and proportions, 69, 70—what causes tend to raise rents in the ordinary progress of society, 133–161—what causes tend to lower the rents, 161–166—on the dependence of the actual quantity of produce obtained from the land, upon the existing rents and the existing prices, 166–179—prospect of exorbitant rent, from a competition of farmers, in what respect a cause of injury to landlords and to the country, 182, 183—cautions to them in raising their rents, 183, 184—improvements in agriculture, a main source of the rise of rents, 187, 188

Resources of a country cannot be altered by humanity, 226, 227

Restrictions on the importation of corn, effect of, 203–206

Revenue, saving from, to add to the capital, considered as a stimulus to the increase of wealth, 301–331 —an increased national revenue wanted to extricate this country from its present distresses, 444— an union of the means of distribution with the powers of production is absolutely necessary for this purpose, 367–382, 444, 445

Ricardo (Mr.), character of his principles of political economy, 11, 12, 194, *note* †—observations on his opinion on the influence of demand and supply on prices, 42, 43—his proposition, that a rise in the price of labour lowers the price of a large class of commodities, proved to be true, 59–66— his opinion considered on the influence of fertility of land on the increase of rents, 112, 113, 121— his theory of rent controverted,